The Argumentative

Turn in Policy Analysis

and Planning

The Argumentative

Turn in Policy Analysis

and Planning

Edited by

Frank Fischer and John Forester

Duke University Press

Durham and London

1993

Designed by Cherie Holma Westmoreland
Typeset in Melior and Frutiger by Yankee Typeset-
ters, Inc.

Library of Congress Cataloging-in-Publication Data

The Argumentative turn in policy analysis and planning / edited by Frank Fischer and John Forester.
p.   cm. Includes bibliographical references and
index.
ISBN 0–8223–1354–5. — ISBN 0–8223–1372–3 (pbk.)
1. Policy sciences.   2. Debates and debating.   3. Persuasion (Rhetoric)   I. Fischer, Frank, 1942–
II. Forester, John, 1948–
H97.A65 1993   320'.6—dc20   93–16710 CIP

Patsy Healey's chapter was published in an earlier
version as "Planning Through Debate: The Communicative Turn in Planning Theory," *Town Planning
Review* 63, no. 2 (1992): 143–162, and appears in this
volume by permission of Liverpool University Press.

Duncan MacRae's chapter was published in an earlier version as "Professional Knowledge for Policy
Discourse," *Knowledge in Society* 1, no. 3 (1988): 6–
24, and appears in this volume by permission of
Transaction Publishers.

James Throgmorton's chapter was published in an
earlier version as "Planning as a Rhetorical Activity:
Survey Research as a Trope in Arguments about Electric Power Planning in Chicago," *Journal of the
American Planning Association* 59, no.3 (Summer
1993), and appears in this volume by permission of
the journal.

To Mary Ellen and

Frank Fischer

and

To Kate and Daniel

Falcão Forester

Contents

Editors'

Introduction

Frank Fischer and

John Forester

What if our language does not simply mirror or picture the world but instead profoundly shapes our view of it in the first place? This question lies at the heart of controversies in contemporary social science between phenomenologists and behaviorists, objectivists and relativists, and symbolic interactionists and institutionalists.[1] This question also animates major debates in epistemology and social philosophy; witness such major figures as Wittgenstein, Austin, Gadamer, Habermas, Foucault, and Derrida, and a new, if hardly illuminating, vocabulary of labels: postmodern, postempiricist, poststructuralist, postpositivist, and so on.[2]

The controversy of relevance to policy analysis and planning here involves central questions of truth and power. If analysts' ways of representing reality are necessarily selective, they seem as necessarily bound up with relations of power, agenda setting, inclusion and exclusion, selective attention, and neglect. If analysts' ways of representing policy and planning issues must make assumptions about causality and responsibility, about legitimacy and authority, and about interests, needs, values, preferences, and obligations, then the language of policy and planning analyses not only depicts but also constructs the issues at hand.

Thus Giandomenico Majone begins his recent *Evidence, Argument, and Persuasion in the Policy Process* with the words, "As politicians know only too well but social scientists too often forget, public policy is made of language. Whether in written or oral form, argument is central in all stages of the policy process."[3]

So, too, following Deborah Stone's recent *Policy Paradox and Political Reason*, can we see that policy-making is a constant discursive

struggle over the criteria of social classification, the boundaries of problem categories, the intersubjective interpretation of common experiences, the conceptual framing of problems, and the definitions of ideas
that guide the ways people create the shared meanings which motivate
them to act.[4] These discursive struggles involve far more than manipulative rhetoric. The institutionally disciplined rhetorics of policy and
planning influence problem selection as well as problem analysis, organizational identity as well as administrative strategy, and public access
as well as public understanding.

The growing concern with the place of argumentation in policy and
planning practice draws upon diverse theoretical perspectives: from
British ordinary language analysis to French poststructuralism, from the
Frankfurt school of critical social theory to a renewed appropriation of
American pragmatism. From these rich sources we come to important
research questions. We need to understand just what policy analysts and
planners do, how language and modes of representation both enable and
constrain their work, how their practical rhetoric depicts and selects,
describes and characterizes, includes and excludes, and more.

Bringing together the work of authors drawing upon such diverse
traditions, the essays that follow examine and refine the turn to argumentation to reconstruct our understanding and practice of policy analysis
and planning. This book, accordingly, explores practically and politically a simple but profound insight: Policy analysis and planning are
practical processes of argumentation.[5]

In actual practice, policy analysts and planners do a great deal
more than they have been given credit for doing.[6] They scan a political
environment as much as they locate facts, and they are involved with
constructing senses of value even as they identify costs and benefits.
When meeting with representatives of other agencies and affected parties, analysts protect working relationships as well as press on to gather
data. As they attempt to foresee streams of consequences, analysts try not
only to predict those consequences, but to understand why they are
consequential, how they will matter ethically and politically.[7]

To see policy analysis and planning as argumentative practices is
to attend closely to the day-to-day work analysts do as they construct
working accounts of problems and possibilities. Recognizing these accounts as politically constrained, organizational accomplishments in the
face of little time and poor data, we can evaluate the analysts' arguments
not only for their truth or falsity but also for their partiality, their selective framing of the issues at hand, their elegance or crudeness of presentation, their political timeliness, their symbolic significance, and more.

Policy and planning arguments are practical productions. They can play many roles at once, including description, prediction, evaluation, agenda setting, symbolic reassurance, and proposal testing. But always these arguments make claims that can be criticized by others or can subtly shape their attention to issues at hand. Thus, the argumentative turn in policy analysis and planning leads us to study critically the production of analysts' claims—not to take them as "truth," and not to take every claim to be as valid as any other. So the focus on argumentation in practice gives no ground to relativists. We should be more suspicious than ever of policy arguments that cannot meet public tests of evidence. If we cannot distinguish policy argument from sales talk, we should consider it propaganda undeserving of the name "analysis." So, too, we should recognize that policy arguments with little relation to decision processes may only be rhetorical justifications for the exercise of power; they are expressions of practical ideology at work, but hardly arguments that have contributed to the deliberative work of decision making or informed public opinion.

To understand what policy analysts and planners actually do, we need to assess the political conditions in which analysts work. We need also to probe the daily politics of problem definition and framing, of rigor tension with engagement, of rationality in constant tension with sources of bias.

No one knows better than practicing planners and policy analysts how intricately related are the issues of analytical content and institutional setting. A director of a metropolitan city planning department once stated the problem beautifully. Asked about the difficulties of presenting project analyses at contentious commission meetings, he remarked, "The most difficult part of that is knowing what *not* to say." He knew that his words mattered, and what he could or couldn't say practically depended on his reading of the particular political setting in which he found himself.

But, like many planners, policy analysts know that if they attend only to political, organizational, and institutional conditions, they will quickly sacrifice the substantive integrity of their studies. They know too that if they care only about the internal coherence and quality of their analysis, they can produce reports that are careful but too late, rigorous but perhaps irrelevant to decision makers' needs, formally elegant but dangerously oblivious to crucial political concerns. In practice, clearly, analysts must attend to the demands of both substantive analysis and cogent articulation.[8] We can think of this necessary duality of practice— these moments of analysis and articulation—as reflecting the challenge of doing politically astute and rationally sound policy analysis and planning.[9]

Yet, unless we understand the argumentative character of policy and planning analysis, the requirements of being politically astute *and* rationally sound will appear to be wholly contradictory. As long as students and practitioners of policy analysis and planning think of the political and the rational as antithetical and mutually threatening, planners and policy analysts will seem to have impossible jobs. For these analysts are political animals whether they wish to be or not. Vulnerable to external political events and influences, they work in complex organizations structured by complex political processes. They tackle messy issues involving diverse populations with multiple and conflicting interests.

Despite such an apparently crazy environment, these analysts are asked, and often mandated by law, to produce rationally considered, systematic assessments of policy choices. They are asked not just to present data as window dressing for decisions already made (though, of course, that happens too), but also to apply their expertise and judgment in a rational and professional, and not whimsical or arbitrary, manner.

Yet as policy analysis and planning are generally understood today, analysts cannot fill both roles without constantly apologizing for one or the other. Seeking to anticipate and respond to political pressures and influences, analysts can feel sheepish in public in seeming to compromise the abstract rationality of their analyses. Alternatively, in seeking to abstract their analyses from the actual review and implementation processes at hand, analysts may feel vulnerable to charges that they have neglected the political realities that will determine whether anyone will really listen to their analyses.

In assessing policy analysis and planning as argumentative, we wish to exploit the systematic ambiguity of the term *argument*, for it refers both to an analytic content ("the logic of the argument") and to a practical performance ("the argument fell on deaf ears"). We argue that all policy analysis and planning is systematically ambiguous in this way, requiring attention to content and performance, to technical analysis and political articulation.

In the essays that follow, the focus on the argumentative character of analysts' work integrates institutional and political concerns with substantive and methodological questions. This is the practical challenge the argumentative turn illuminates: to do their work well, in real time, planners and policy analysts must make practical arguments that are internally coherent *and* externally compelling, persuasively gauged to real and thus diverse political audiences.

As editors of this volume, we have distinct but complementary research interests. Intrigued by what planners do in everyday practice, Forester continues to be astonished by the richness of that work and the poverty of analytic models that claim to represent what planning and policy analysts actually do. Struck by the continuing strength of claims to expertise in highly political contexts, Fischer investigates how complex institutional forces shape the public's understanding of policy processes and policy substance. In this volume we have assembled a series of probing accounts of policy analysis and planning that seek to do justice to the actual complexities of that practice. We have sought essays that speak at once to issues of truth and power while denying the province of neither, essays that clarify how the most benign claims of analysts can work in subtle symbolic and political ways, essays that honor the challenges of practice while locating that practice both politically and institutionally.

Our focus on argumentation in policy analysis and planning echoes the oft-cited "linguistic turn" in twentieth-century philosophy. By focusing on the work of argumentation we can avoid radically separating epistemological concerns (the claims made "within" the argument) from institutional and performative concerns (how in *deed* the argument is made).

Our concern with argumentation stops far short of turning all policy issues into textual matters, unless that simply means that interpretation is an essential element of knowing. We are concerned with embodied and articulated interpretations—planners' and policy analysts' claims actually made, spoken or written—as offers seeking to shape a listener's or an audience's understanding of a practical problem. The controversies surrounding poststructuralism are not the focus of this book. Instead, we pay close attention to the actual performances of argumentation and the practical rhetorical work of framing analyses, articulating them, constructing senses of value and significance, and so we illuminate the discretion involved in such institutionally staged, organizational performances.[10]

What do we stand to gain by understanding policy analysis and planning as argumentative processes? What can we say to the skeptic's query, "So what?"

First, we can appreciate the many ways practitioners formulate and construct what "the problem" shall be taken practically to be—before they can delineate plausible alternatives or recommendations. In a few words, problem solution depends on the prior work of problem construction and reconstruction, and this work is deeply rhetorical and interpretive, if little understood.[11]

Second, the argumentative view is a deeply practical one. We ask not only *what* an analysis claims but when it does, to whom, in what language and style, invoking what loyalties, and appealing to what threat and dangers.[12] We study, for example, not only the economic policy analyst's findings but the rhetoric of the economic analysis as well.[13]

Third, when we recognize policy analysis and planning as argumentative, we can understand immediately how they can be complex exercises of agenda-setting power. In some cases, what analyes do not say matters more than what they do say. Analysis focuses attention selectively and deliberately, enabling a more focused consideration of some alternatives and excluding others from practical consideration altogether. So we can study the micropolitics of analytical practice by assessing the political constitution and influence of analysts' practical arguments.

Fourth, a focus on argumentation enables us to assess the organizational networking, "boundary spanning," relationship building, and ritualized bargining that analysts must do to work in policy and planning processes at all.[14] If we are too focused on the work of technical analysis, we may look too much to the content of presumably ultimate documents; in doing so we will be likely to miss the rich work that precedes and follows document production: the scanning of the political environment for support for and opposition to potential recommendations, the anticipation of threats and dangers that policy and planning measures might counteract, and the subtle negotiating that transpires between agency staff who are always seeking to learn, to protect working relationships, and to maintain their own strategic position as well.

Fifth, we can see more clearly that "problems" can be represented in many languages, discourses, and frames. We can explore the link between the language of the analysts' arguments and the language of the political setting in which they work. We can be more sensitive to the ways that shifts in political power—from election to election, elite to elite, or coalition to coalition—are reflected not only in policy decisions but in the very language in which policy issues and choices are presented to the public in the first place.

Sixth, recognizing the argumentative character of policy analysis and planning practice, we can more readily appreciate its potentially pedagogic functions. In urban planning, for example, we can appreciate planning analyses less as engineering exercises to calculate results and more as potentially democratic efforts to educate public opinion about urban issues and options.[15] The argumentative view does much more than simply announce the underwhelming news that policy analysis is an interpretive enterprise. Instead, this view suggests far more provocatively and productively that careful analysis of policy and planning problems can develop better technical information *and* cultivate the moral imagination of all those involved in the policy and planning process.[16] Perhaps the point is better made in reverse: when planners and policy analysts forget that decision makers and affected publics alike can be baffled and mystified by the languages of expertise, the analysts' efforts are likely to create more heat than light, more neglect than serious consideration, an impoverishment rather than a refinement of public understanding and ethical imagination.[17]

By focusing on the argumentative character of policy analysis and planning, this book takes a practical turn from abstracted epistemological problems of analytical practice to the political and sociological staging and significance of that practice. In sociological terms, these essays teach us about the context-specific rhetoric character of analytical practices—the ways the symbolism of their language matters, the ways the consideration of their audiences matters, the ways they construct problems before solving them.[18] In political terms, these essays teach us about the ways policy and planning arguments are intimately involved with relations of power and the exercise of power, including the concerns of some and excluding others, distributing responsibility as well as causality, imputing praise and blame as well as efficacy, and employing particular political strategies of problem framing and not others.[19]

These essays are concerned with the contingencies of democratic deliberation.[20] Planning and policy arguments cannot be presumed to be optimally clear, true, cogent, and free from institutional biases. Democratic deliberation is always precarious and always vulnerable, if inevitably argumentative as well. Through thoughtful, passionate, and informed argumentative processes, what Benjamin Barber calls "democratic talk," citizens can learn, and policy and planning analysts can promote that learning. Yet, planning and policy arguments can be skewed by inequalities or resources, by outstanding and entrenched relations of power and production, and by the deliberate play of power, and in such cases we find not what Robert Reich calls "civic discovery" but civic manipulation instead.[21]

In sum, a focus on the argumentative practices of planners and policy analysts can provide both ordinary realism and theoretical insight. This view can enhance our sense of realism simply because interpreting, marshaling, and presenting arguments is what analysts do all the time. This view can produce theoretical insight, too, because it can help us learn from current theories of rhetoric and discourse, interpretation, and practical judgment to reveal not only the daily challenges faced by practicing planners and policy analysts but the skills those analysts already employ—skills whose qualities students of planning and policy analysis may barely recognize today.

The essays that follow are presented in three complementary sections, beginning with cases and ending with more general theoretical implications.

Part 1 introduces the ways policy argumentation can shape decision-making and deliberative processes. In "Policy Discourse and the Politics of Washington Think Tanks," Frank Fischer shows that the argumentative turn emerges as much from political conflict as from epistemological debates. Examining the uses of public policy analysis in the Johnson and Reagan eras, Fischer identifies an emerging policymaking strategy based on the use of technocratic policy expertise and think tanks. Elite policy discourse coalitions not only involve experts from liberal and conservative think tanks in national policy agenda setting, they also align the articulated advice of leading experts with the interests of economic and political elites.

The result, Fischer argues, is a politicization of policy expertise, a process of argumentation and counterargumentation that substantially changes the actual practice of policy analysis. Having demystified the technocratic conception of policy analysis as *science*, this politicization of the analytical process opens the door to a postpositivistic, interpretive, and dialogical conception of policy analysis—a topic explored further in the following essays.

Pursuing many of these same themes, Maarten Hajer's "Discourse Coalitions and the Institutionalization of Practice" illustrates how two competing coalitions, which he dubs the "ad hoc technocratic" and the "ecological modernization" coalitions, have struggled to control the discussion, formulation, and implementation of acid rain policy in Great Britian. For Hajer, the challenge to "argumentative analysis is to find ways of combining the analysis of the discursive production of reality with the analysis of the (extradiscursive) social practices from which social constructs emerge and in which the actors that make these statements engage." Toward this end, Hajer introduces the concept of a discourse coalition, "a group of actors who share . . . an ensemble of ideas, concepts, and categories" through which a given phenomenon is politically framed and given social meaning. When the narrative or story line of a discourse comes to dominate a society's conventional ways of reasoning and the practices of its dominant social and political institutions, the process is called discourse institutionalization.

The idea of discourse institutionalization allows Hajer to explain how the discursive practices of the ecological modernization coalition triumphed over those of the technocratic coalition without resulting in a new policy direction. The ecological coalition failed to supplant the technocrats' hold on the institutional practices of the environmental ministries. The key to success, Hajer argues, ultimately lodges in a discourse coalition's ability to imbed its own linguistic categories in the very structure of the methodologies and practices that shape and guide everyday policy deliberations. As his analysis demonstrates, even though the technocratic discourse has begun to lose its force—if not its credibility—its influence continues through bureaucratically institutionalized policy procedures.

Robert Hoppe and Bruce Jennings take up the challenge of specifying an interpretively oriented professional practice based on argumentation. They focus on the troublesome questions of decision criteria and judgments that inevitably lie at the heart of political argumentation: How should planners and analysts make judgments about competing policy claims in a world of clashing ideologies?

In "Political Judgment and the Policy Cycle: The Case of Ethnicity Policy Arguments in the Netherlands," Robert Hoppe uses the evolution of ethnicity policy belief systems to clarify both the uses of arguments and the task of assessing them. Building on Fischer's logic of policy evaluation, Ronald Beiner's concept of political judgment, and Paul Sabatier's model of policy belief systems, Hoppe links policy argumentation to a four-phase logic of political judgment, with each phase related to the deliberative processes of the policy-making cycle more generally; for example, political agenda setting, policy formulation, implementation, and evaluation. Applying his criteria of judgment to the evolution of ethnicity policy belief systems in the Netherlands, Hoppe illustrates his scheme to chart policy belief systems and assess the structure of specific policy arguments.

To conclude part 1, Bruce Jennings, in "Counsel and Consensus: Norms of Argumentation in Health Policy," examines far-reaching attempts at Medicaid reform in Oregon and proposes that we understand policy analysis as a discourse of counsel and civic consensus. The aim of policy counsel, as Jennings conceives it, is threefold: first, to grasp the significance of problems as they are experienced, adapted to, and resisted by purposive members of the political community; second, to clarify the meaning of those problems so that public officials and policy-makers can devise efficacious and just solutions to those problems; and, third, to guide the selection of one preferred policy from the possible set of solutions in light of both a general vision of the good of the community and the more discrete interests of the policymakers themselves.

Jennings also proposes a solution to the nagging question of epistemological relativism that has long plagued advocates of argumentative approaches to policy analysis and planning. One might worry, for example, that argumentation in policy contexts would only lead, even in principle, to an endless cycle of debate, with no way of distinguishing the quality of one claim from another. Jennings argues that such a cycle will be broken to the extent that we can achieve a radicalization of the process of policy argumentation ensuring preconditions for relatively dialogic democratic practices. This idealized solution to the threat of relativism, we should recall, is hardly more idealized than the quite traditional notions of scientific criticism in the community of inquirers whose collective and mutually responsive efforts contribute to what we claim to know at any given time.

The essays in part 2 show how analysts' arguments construct and frame policy problems in quite subtle ways. Jim Throgmorton's "Survey Research as Rhetorical Trope: Electric Power Planning Arguments in Chicago" focuses on the rhetorical aspects of argumentation. Extending the important work of the Iowa Project on the Rhetoric of Inquiry, the essay illustrates the ways planning is as much a rhetorical activity as it is the technical endeavor it is more popularly presented and construed to be.

While *rhetoric* is often viewed by planners and other professionals as "the use of seductive language to sway or manipulate others into embracing a speaker's preferred values, beliefs, and behaviors," Throgmorton shows how much more there is to rhetoric than "gloss and seduction." Rhetorical persuasion, he argues, is fundamental to, and in deed constructive of, central features of our social life, in particular character, culture, and community.

At the heart of such ubiquitous rhetorical persuasion, Throgmorton suggests, lies the use of various rhetorical devices, or "tropes," such as metaphor, metonymy, and irony that permit us to use words to suggest more than their literal meaning. A rhetorical perspective enables us to understand a policy or planning document as an interweaving of such tropes in narrative form. So a rhetorical approach to planning and policy analysis can assess the roles these devices play in proposing explanations, inspiring public visions, and recommending actions. Treating survey research as a rhetorical enterprise, Throgmorton shows how research methodology gains its contingent, specific meaning—and thus its power—from a particular audience, time, place, and articulation.

Martin Rein and Donald Schön's "Reframing Policy Discourse" looks systematically at the process of framing in policy analysis and assesses how frame-reflective discourse functions within communities of inquirers—scientific and political.

Framing, as Rein and Schön describe it, "is a way of selecting, organizing, interpreting, and making sense of a complex reality to provide guideposts for knowing, analyzing, persuading, and acting." A frame is a "perspective from which an amorphous, ill-defined, problematic situation can be made sense of and acted upon." Basic to policy frames are the stories, or narratives, participants are disposed to tell about policy situations. Frequently constructed around "generative metaphors," problem-setting stories "link causal accounts of policy problems to particular proposals for action" and so link accounts of "is" and "ought."

Thomas Kaplan's "Reading Policy Narratives: Beginnings, Middles, and Ends" explores narrative forms of interpreting and explaining policy issues. For example, because its narrative structure emphasizes an organized beginning, middle, and end, a story can be a policy analyst's device for pulling together scattered multiple events into a coherent, readable plot. The analyst or planner who can recognize an "ordering plot" that weaves through differing—even contradictory—values and events of a complex issue can reach insights and conclusions that might not otherwise be attained. To illustrate his claims Kaplan contrasts the narrative strategies of policy documents with the more common chronicle approach in which terse analyses present pros and cons without an integrating plot knitting together qualitative and quantitative elements. The narrative approach allows the analyst or planner to "weave together a variety of factors and come to a conclusion that flows naturally out of these factors." But not all stories are equally good ones, of course, and Kaplan devotes a substantial discussion to differentiating better from worse stories in policy and planning contexts.

In "Learning from Practice Stories: The Priority of Practical Judgment" John Forester explores the descriptive, moral, political, and deliberative work of practitioners' stories in the daily conduct of planning and policy analysis. Planners and analysts tell practical stories not typically to entertain but to teach. These stories present not all the facts of a situation, but the facts that matter, the facts that are taken to be relevant and important for the purposes at hand. Practice stories not only describe behavior, they also characterize others, constructing selves and identities in the process. These stories also do more, Forester argues; they help shape what others are to take as important in the cases at hand.

But how, given the messiness and complexity of actual practice stories, do planners and policy analysts learn from them? Forester provides two answers. First, planners and analysts learn from story telling in practice because problem constructing must always precede problem solving. Stories can help planners and analysts pay attention to the details that matter and help analysts get a better fix on "what the problem really is."

Second, Forester explores a more novel line of response: we learn from practice stories, he suggests, not through virtual experimentation but in the same ways that we learn from friends. Stories remind us of what matters and what is at stake; they help us to deliberate; they show us a world of passion and engagement that many forms of data presentation do not, and perhaps could not, show us. Forester's account of story telling in practice settings seeks not only to do justice to the complexity of analysts' and planners' stories but also to clarify the practical rationality practitioners may employ as storytellers and as listeners to the planning and policy stories of others.

Part 3 presents four essays that explore the theoretical arguments holding that the argumentative approach is a viable epistemological alternative to the troubled scientistic approaches that still dominate the policy sciences. The section begins with John Dryzek's "Policy Analysis and Planning: From Science to Argument," a review of the epistemological orientations that have traditionally defined policy analysis and planning. Too often, Dryzek explains, the epistemological orientations of positivism and critical rationalism have led us to normative judgments and policy alternatives that are "highly constrained and insensitive to the aspirations of ordinary policy actors." These methods could "never be more than gross oversimplifications of a complex reality, rooted as they are in a single analytical framework chosen from the many that could be employed." This multiplicity of incommensurable analytical frames has undermined the authoritative claims of the more scientistic approaches that have long defined the policy sciences.

Rather than seeing incommensurable frames as methodological barriers to analytical progress, the turn to argumentation in policy analysis and planning appreciates competing frames as the foundation of the analytical process itself. Indeed, the interplay of competing frames is a source of new knowledge rather than an impediment to it, for no single analytical approach will do for all purposes, for all problems, for all time. Dryzek argues that a forensic model of policy argumentation allows us to tease out the essential and problematic features that define, interpret, and explain any particular policy problem. Still, the forensic model, developed by such writers as Churchman, Mitroff, and Mason, can too easily become relativistic.[22] Thus Dryzek suggests that the forensic approach must be grounded in a radicalized conception of communicative ethics, for only a communicative ethics can supply standards and norms capable of "exposing and counteracting manipulation of agendas, illegitimate exercises of power, skewed distribution of information, and attempts to distract attention" that otherwise govern forensic practice and leave it vulnerable to charges of relativism. Dryzek's discussion of discursive ethics, like Patsy Healey's essay, particularly echoes and extends Bruce Jennings's analysis in part 1.

Healey's "Planning Through Debate: The Communicative Turn in Planning Theory," addresses not only postmodernist suspicions of planning and policy rationality but the challenges of respecting political, cultural, and aesthetic differences as well. She explores planning as a communicative enterprise in which engagement, debate, and deliberation are central. When planning and policy options involve diverse ethnic, racial, territorial, or ideological groups, how can a "plural socialist project" recognize such political differences and assess systematic political economic forces too? Healey suggests that a broadly Habermasian account of communicative rationality can bring systematic analysis and respect for difference together, practically and politically.

As massive environmental problems loom before us, political talk will become more and not less important. These problems are technically complex, and they are politically ambiguous too. Recognizing that participants in plural political processes not only bargain, given their interests, but also refine and learn about those interests, Healey develops a notion of planning through debate that radicalizes earlier pluralists models. She wants to move us beyond "Lindblomian marginal adjustments to the present," toward a vision of political and communicative rationality that is future seeking, future defining.

William Dunn's seminal "Policy Reforms as Arguments" assesses the problem of moving from theory to practice. In this influential essay Dunn explores the failure of the social sciences, as sciences, to provide valid and useful information for practice, and he traces this failure to the conflict between two competing modes of reason: the scientific and that of ordinary language.

Traditionally, the policy sciences have regarded policy reforms as "experiments," particularly following the theoretical contributions of Donald Campbell and Sir Karl Popper.[23] Dunn proposes that we view policy reforms as ordinary language arguments, rooting policy analysis more congenially "in the everyday social interaction of policymakers, scientists, and citizens at large." Toward this end, Dunn develops a transactional model of argumentation, based on Stephen Toulmin's jurisprudential account of argumentation and its informal logic of the structure of arguments. This account of policy arguments enlarges the number of "frames of reference, standards, and norms employed for challenging and evaluating knowledge claims." By examining policy arguments in this way, a critically oriented social science can uncover the hidden standards and unexamined assumptions that shape, and often distort, the production and application of knowledge.

Complementing Dunn's argument, Duncan MacRae, Jr.'s "Guidelines for Policy Discourse: Consensual verse Adversarial" distinguishes two types of policy-relevant discourse: a deliberative discussion of relatively like-minded participants, and an adversarial discourse of winners and losers. MacRae seeks to provide guidelines not only for strategic argumentation but also for deliberative discourse in which both ends and means are explored, in which claims are examined and refined before being pressed more strategically. In his wide-ranging contribution MacRae argues persuasively that analysts will find themselves engaged sometimes with "reasoned proposal selection" and at yet other times with the "requirements of persuasion"—processes calling, of course, for distinct abilities and sensitivities.

In sum, the argumentative turn in policy analysis and planning represents practical, theoretical, and political advances in the field. Practically, the focus on argumentation allows us to examine closely the communicative and rhetorical strategies that planners and analysts use to direct attention to the problems and options they are assessing. Theoretically, the focus on argumentation allows us to recognize the complex ways analysts not only solve but formulate problems, the ways their arguments express or resist broader relations of power and belief, and the ways their practical arguments are inescapably both normative and descriptive. Finally, our focus on argumentation reveals both the micropolitics of planners' and analysts' agenda setting, selective representations, and claims, and the macropolitics of analysts' participation in larger discourses, whether those are articulated in relatively organized discourse coalitions or through more diffuse, if perhaps more subtly influential, ideologies and systems of political belief.

Notes

1. See, for example, R. Bernstein, *The Restructuring of Social and Political Theory* (Philadelphia: University of Pennsylvania Press, 1978), and his *Beyond Objectivism and Relativism* (Philadelphia: University of Pennsylvania Press, 1983).

2. See J. McGowan, *Postmodernism and Its Critics* (Ithaca: Cornell University Press, 1990). Cf. note 7 below.

3. G. Majone, *Evidence, Argument, and Persuasion in the Policy Process* (New Haven: Yale University Press, 1989), 1.

4. D. Stone, *Policy Paradox and Political Reason* (Glenview, Ill.: Scott Foresman, 1988).

5. Argumentation involves, at a minimum, two challenges: analysis (what is argued) and articulation (how the speaker or writer engages the attention of the practical audience). Analysis without articulation may never make a difference. Articulation without analysis may be empty at best, deceptive flimflam at worst. For related work on argumentation and rhetoric in the social sciences, see, e.g., J. Nelson, A. Megill, and D. McCloskey, eds., *The Rhetoric of Human Sciences: Language and Argument in Scholarship and Public Affairs* (Madison: University of Wisconsin Press, 1987); for a more systematic analysis of argumentation see D. Walton, *Informal Logic: A Handbook for Critical Argumentation* (Cambridge: Cambridge University Press, 1989).

6. John Austin wrote of the limits of ordinary expressions, "Fact is richer than diction," and the same continues to be true for the adequacy of accounts of planning and policy analysis practice. See, e.g., M. Feldman, *Order Without Design* (Stanford: Stanford University Press, 1988); L. Peattie, *Planning: Rethinking Cuidad Guayana* (Ann Arbor: University of Michigan Press, 1987); and P. Marris, *Meaning and Action* (London: RKP, 1987).

7. To trace the roots of the turn to argumentation as a research strategy in policy analysis and planning, see F. Fischer, *Politics, Values, and Public Policy* (Boulder: Westview Press, 1980); D. McCloskey, *The Rhetoric of Economics* (Madison: University of Wisconsin Press, 1985); J. Forester, *Critical Theory and Public Life* (Cambridge: MIT Press, 1985); and W. Dunn, *Public Policy Analysis: An Introduction* (Englewood Cliffs, N.J.: Prentice-Hall, 1981). A highly influential precursor in this field was C. W. Churchman; see, e.g., *The Design of Inquiring Systems* (New York: Basic Books, 1971) and *The Systems Approach and Its Enemies* (New York: Basic Books, 1979). In social theory and the humanities, of course, concern with argumentation, discourse, and language is widespread and can be found in the massive literature discussing the work of Stephen Toulmin, Jürgen Habermas, Michel Foucault, and Jacques Derrida. For just one of many assessments here see P. Dews, *Logics of Disintegration* (London: Verso, 1987).

8. See Harold Wilensky's *Organizational Intelligence* (New York: Basic Books, 1967); G. Benveniste, *Politics of Expertise*, 2d ed. (San Francisco: Boyd and Fraser, 1977); A. Meltsner, *Policy Analysts in the Bureaucracy* (Berkeley: University of California Press, 1976); F. Fischer, *Technocracy and the Politics of Expertise* (Beverly Hills: Sage, 1990); and the work of Feldman, Marris, and Peattie, cited above (n. 6).

9. For an extensive discussion see J. Forester, *Planning in the Face of Power* (Berkeley: University of California Press, 1989); and N. Krumolz and J. Forester, *Making Equity Planning Work: Leadership in the Public Sector* (Philadelphia: Temple University Press, 1990).

10. For a closer look at the practical communicative work of planning analysts, see Forester, *Planning in the Face of Power.*

11. See the work of J. Seeley, "Social Science? Some Probative Problems," in M. Stein and A. Vidich, eds., *Sociology on Trial* (Englewood Cliffs, N.J.: Prentice-Hall, 1963); G. Vickers, *The Art of Judgment* (New York: Harper and Row, 1965); and Rein and Schön's and Forester's essays in this volume.

12. See J. Gusfield, *The Culture of Public Problems* (Chicago: University of Chicago Press, 1981); cf. the remarks of an associate director of a city planning office: "Our staff are sending memos to the mayor all the time, and if they can't write and write well, we look like idiots. If someone can't write, we can't use them."

13. See, e.g., D. McCloskey, *The Rhetoric of Economics* (Madison: University of Wisconsin Press, 1985).

14. Some accounts of policy analysis focus on the "interactive" dimension; see, e.g., A. Wildavsky, *Speaking Truth to Power* (New York: Little, Brown, 1979).

15. Compare Norman Krumholz's efforts in Cleveland, where as planning director he used zoning reports as occasions to brief the press and other news media about the issues confronting Cleveland's neighborhoods; see Krumholz and J. Forester, *Making Equity Planning Work.*

16. We might call this a critical Aristotelian approach, adapting the arguments relating literature, moral imagination, and moral learning, sketched by Marsha Nussbaum in her *Love's Knowledge* (Oxford: Oxford University Press, 1990); see especially in that volume "Finely Aware and the Richly Responsible: Literature and the Moral Imagination." On neo-Aristotelian and critical theories of practical judgment, see S. Ben Habib, "In the Shadow of Aristotle and Hegel: Communicative Ethics and Current Controversies in Practical Philosophy," in M. Kelly, ed., *Hermeneutics and Critical Theory in Ethics and Politics* (Cambridge: MIT Press, 1990); cf. the earlier research of Carol Weiss on the "enlightenment function" of applied research.

17. The point holds whether one is speaking of an EPA official presenting an analysis of waste disposal methods, a Department of Labor analyst assessing a job-training proposal, or a local city planner presenting an analysis of a site-

specific zoning dispute. In each case the narrative qualities of the analysis may either educate others about the issues at hand or baffle them, reveal particular values at stake or fail to identify them, disclose responsibilities or remain silent about them. Cf. Nussbaum, *Love's Knowledge*.

18. Compare the work of J. B. White; e.g., "Law as Rhetoric, Rhetoric as Law: The Arts of Cultural and Communal Life," *University of Chicago Law Review* 52, no. 3 (1985): 684–702.

19. Cf. M. Edelman, *Constructing the Political Spectacle* (Chicago: University of Chicago Press, 1988). The argumentative turn allows one to focus on the discursive production and implementation of policies and programs—including the discursive suppression of issues, voices, and interests. See M. Foucault, *Power/ Knowledge: Selected Interviews and Other Writings, 1972–1977*, ed. Colin Gordon (New York: Pantheon, 1980).

20. On deliberation, see the closely resonant opening chapters in Majone, *Evidence, Argument, and Persuasion in the Policy Process*.

21. The systematic analysis of unnecessary (contingent) distortions of planning and policy processes of argumentation is a neglected area of research in political theory; see the analysis in "The Politics of Muddling Through," in Forester, *Planning in the Face of Power*.

22. See, e.g., Churchman, *The Design of Inquiring Systems*; R. Mason, "A Dialectical Approach to Strategic Planning," *Management Science* 15, no. 8 (April 1969): B-403–B-414; and I. Mitroff, "A Communications Model of Dialectical Inquiring Systems—A Strategy for Strategic Planning," *Management Science* 17, no. 10 (June 1971): B-634–B-648.

23. See, e.g., D. Campbell, "Reforms as Experiments," in E. Struening and M. Guttentag, eds., *Handbook of Evaluation Research* (Beverly Hills: Sage, 1965), 1:71–100; cf. K. Popper, *The Logic of Scientific Discovery* (London: Hutchinson, 1968).

The Argumentative Turn:

Policy Institutions and

Practices

I

Policy Discourse and

the Politics of Washington

Think Tanks

Frank Fischer

Much of the discussion about arguments in public policy analysis derives from epistemological and methodological considerations, particularly those raised by criticism of the discipline's technocratic tendencies. By contrast, far too little attention has focused on the political regime shifts that have contributed to the argumentative turn. Indeed, as I have argued elsewhere, methodological shifts in policy analysis have often been influenced by basic shifts in the control of government (Fischer 1987). The failure to recognize the relationship between basic political changes and the practices of policy analysis has led to overly narrow interpretations of the discipline and its development. Too often understood within the confines of scientific terminology, policy analysis has frequently failed to perceive the deeper political forces that in many ways have given shape to the disciplinary project. The purpose of this essay is to illustrate how the argumentative turn emerges as much from larger political and institutional conflicts in the society as from methodological issues.

The first three sections focus on the critiques, both radical and conservative, of the Great Society of the Johnson administration, seen to be the paradigm case of the liberal technocratic strategy.[1] My purpose is to illustrate the liberal strategy's reliance on policy experts and their technical discourses and to identify specific ways in which these discourses functioned to shape the Democratic party's reform agenda. Focusing in particular on the uses of policy analysis, the critics argued that it represented far more than a value-neutral scientific methodology designed to supply better information to liberal policymakers. More fundamentally, critics saw policy analysis as a key element of a technocratic strategy that served—both wittingly and unwittingly—to supplant the everyday, less sophisticated opinions of the common citizen with liberal "new class" arguments disguised and legitimated in the languages of technical discourses. According to the harshest critics, a growing emphasis on technocratic methodologies increasingly undercuts ordinary political discourse with the specialized languages of the social sciences (Banfield 1980:1).

The essay then examines the conservative political response to a liberal-technocratic reform strategy. As a direct challenge to the liberals' strategy, the conservative politics of the middle 1970s and the 1980s instituted an alternative policy approach that—rhetoric aside—can be interpreted as a conservative version of the liberal reform strategy. Contrary to the stated objectives of the conservative challenge—namely, to sever the political link between liberal politicians and leading policy experts—the primary result has been to *politicize* rather than *eliminate* the uses of policy analysis. I conclude with an assessment of the implications of this politicization of policy argumentation for the discipline of policy analysis.

Technocratic Discourse and the New Class

The theory of technocracy, a variant of elite theory, refers to a governance process dominated by technically trained knowledge elites. The function of the technocratic elite is to replace or control democratic deliberation and decision-making processes (based on conflicting interests) with a more technocratically informed discourse (based on scientific decision-making techniques). The result is the transformation of political issues into technically defined ends than can be pursued through administrative means.

The technocratic approach to policy-making emerged most visibly in the United States during the years of the Democratic party's Great Society and the Vietnam War. Critiques of this period, especially those of the radical Left, singled out the corporate welfare/warfare state and its managerial ideologies of expertise as fundamental political problems. During these years, the Left elevated concerns about the role of experts and intellectuals to a central position in its critique of society. Managerial and policy experts were seen as a "technical intelligentsia" who provided much more than a purely technical service to politicians, as suggested by mainstream interpretations. Indeed, writers such as Alvin Gouldner (1970), Noam Chomsky (1971), and Bertram Gross (1980) portrayed experts as a *driving* force behind the political process itself.

According to the radical version of the technocracy thesis, managerial and policy experts constituted nothing less than a new technocratic class or cadre striving for political power. Moreover, the ascent of this technocratic class was analyzed as a central governance strategy of the liberal corporate welfare state. Technocratic experts were portrayed, in fact, as the social engineers of a liberal political-economic formation fundamentally aligned with the political organization that ruled in its name, the Democratic party. Consider Gouldner's (1970, 500) words: "In the context of the burgeoning Welfare-Warfare State . . . liberal ideologues serve . . . to increase the centralized control of an ever-growing Federal Administrative Class and of the master institutions on behalf of which it operates." As technical cadres of a central governing strategy, these liberal technocrats produced "information and theories that serve to bind the poor and the working classes to the state apparatus and the political machinery of the Democratic party."

Every bit as interesting was the fact that somewhat later in the decade (and continuing well into the 1980s), remarkably similar refrains could be heard from the political Right, particularly from the so-called neoconservatives, who were largely disheartened Great Society liberals. Especially important here were such writers as Irving Kristol, Edward Banfield, Jeanne Kirkpatrick, Nathan Glazer, and Samuel Beer (Steinfels 1979).

Neoconservatives were deeply disturbed by the uses (or misuses) of the social sciences in the Great Society era. Adhering largely to the tenets of traditional democratic theory, they singled out policy experts as a fundamental threat to the future of representative government. Although they distanced themselves from their radical counterparts, neoconservatives also spoke of an emerging technocratic system of government dominated by a new class: the technical intelligentsia. Banfield (1980:5) put it this way: Policy science developed during "a long series of efforts by the Progressive Movement and its heirs to change the character of the American political system—to transfer power from the corrupt, the ignorant, and the self-serving to the virtuous, the educated, and the public spirited." Such motives "inspired proposals to replace politicians with experts in the legislatures and to do away with political parties." Samuel Beer (1978:44) went so far as to describe the phenomenon as a "technocratic takeover." While on its surface the idea of a new class takeover of the policy process is difficult to take seriously, the argument had substantial clout. Indeed, it helped to carry Ronald Reagan into the White House.

What can be made of such arguments? In and of itself, the technocracy–new class thesis tells us very little about the actual role of expertise in policy-making or the struggles that have shaped its role. In significant part, the problem is due to ideological excesses. Too often the intent has been limited to scapegoating a "technocratic class" as the impediment to either free-market capitalism (the argument of the political Right) or democratic socialism (that of the Left). Stripped of its polemical baggage, however, the thesis does correctly point to a new and more powerful role of experts and expert discourses in the policy-making processes of U.S. government. In fact, the increasing importance of the expert discourses of policy professionals are beginning to reflect a new policy-making style—a kind of politics of expertise—that is emerging as part of contemporary governance strategies. In an effort to move from the abstractions of these ideological critiques to a more concrete understanding of this phenomenon, let us first locate the contemporary origins of this new policy role for experts in the governance strategies of the Democratic administrations of the 1960s, particularly Lyndon Johnson's Great Society.

The Great Society as Technocratic Politics

The Great Society is widely seen as a primary political phenomenon that spurred the contemporary restructuring of policy processes. The technocratic discourse of the period has been widely discussed (Straussman 1978). It was a period that took seriously, in some form or another, the "end of ideology" thesis that Daniel Bell had put forward a few years earlier (Waxman 1968); and numerous technocratic, "apolitical" approaches were indeed introduced during these years.[2] Among the most important was the experimentation with Keynesian tax cuts, which were seen to signify real progress toward the technical—if not scientific —management of economic affairs. During these years, in fact, the economics profession was dubbed the "new priesthood" by *Time* magazine.

Another major technocratic thrust was the introduction in all federal agencies of the Planning-Programming-Budgeting-Systems decision-making technique (PPBS), based on the latest thinking in managerial science. This technique was designed to guide policy deliberation and program evaluation. Lyndon Johnson once described PPBS as the management technique that made possible the Great Society's programmatic assault on poverty (Fischer 1990:152).

Throughout this period the development and implementation of the liberal political agenda was shaped by the contributions of "policy intellectuals" and the tools of the social sciences. Theodore White (1967) captured this for *Life* magazine in three articles that portray the period as the "Golden Age of the action intellectuals." White described what he saw as nothing less than the appearance of a new system of power in U.S. politics. These new intellectuals, acting in concert with political leaders in both the White House and Congress, were the "driving wheels" of the Great Society. This new generation with special problem-solving skills sought "to shape our defenses, guide our foreign policy, redesign our cities, eliminate poverty, reorganize our schools, and more." Policy professionals represented a "bridge across the gulf between government and the primary producers of really good ideas." The White House served as "a transmission belt, packaging and processing scholars' ideas to be sold to Congress as programs."

Research foundations and academic journals celebrated the significance of this "professionalization of reform" (Moynihan 1965). In the process, policy research became a growth industry for think tanks, university research institutes, and management consulting firms (Dickson 1971). In turn, this promoted the development of the discipline of policy analysis, which emerged as a new and central research focus in the social sciences. Moreover, the strategy set into motion a revolving door that linked the major research universities, government agencies, and Washington think tanks, particularly the Brookings Institution (which is largely identified with the Democratic party administrations of this period).

But beyond the mass influx of economists and social scientists, how was the policy-making process in Washington actually changing? Extending the work of Barry Karl (1975) brings into view a specific political formula, a kind of "liberal reform strategy" somewhat similar to patterns found in earlier periods such as the Progressive era and the New Deal.

Basically, the liberal reform strategy can be delineated in five interrelated steps: (1) a group of experts, mainly social scientists, is assembled by a reform-minded president; (2) the experts devote their time to defining and articulating a social or economic problem and spelling out the need for specific political reforms; (3) a larger group of journalists, philanthropists, and business leaders is then gathered to discuss the problem and to develop a consensus capable of broadening the reform coalition; (4) following these exchanges, a report is produced containing all the assumptions, information, and arguments on which the reform program would be designed and implemented; and (5) finally, with considerable fanfare the report is communicated to the public as a re-form agenda from the "pulpit" of the presidency and through the mass media.

On its surface, this pattern seems to be consistent with the standard conceptualization of the policy expert's role (i.e., to provide information to political leaders). But closer observation reveals that the specific dynamics of this reform methodology play a much greater role in determining the political agenda than the conventional model would suggest. In fact, this central role in the reform strategy provides policy experts with very real opportunities to shape the course of political events.

The·Technical Framing of Political Reality

Both radicals and neoconservatives perceived a significant departure from accepted policy-making practices during the Great Society. According to the standard interpretation of representative government, policy-making is primarily geared to the demands and struggles of competing political parties and interest groups. In sharp contrast, these writers began to depict a process in which political leaders and their experts operated more and more independently of public pressures. They saw a much more technocratic, elitist policy discourse and decision process divorced in very significant ways from the public, interest groups, and political parties (Moynihan 1965:7; Fischer 1990:153–55). Two sources of technocratic influence were identified in the liberal reform strategy, one concerned with the elevation of experts to a much more powerful position in the decision-making hierarchy, the other emphasizing the nature of their modes of decision making. With regard to the first point, the degree to which this new elite actually had final decision-making authority is open to debate. However, one need not subscribe to the new class thesis to recognize the substantial role played by experts in both the development of the War on Poverty agenda and the planning of its implementation.

But just how did this power manifest itself? How did the experts' *technocratic* discourses play an influential role? In an effort to pin down the specific dynamic that gave liberal policy advice its less obvious and thus more troublesome influence, neoconservatives tended to focus on the expert's role in defining problems, which, they recognized, is more than an analytical activity. It is also the ability to bring to political consciousness problems—such as poverty—that would otherwise be accorded little attention by either politicians or the public (Lane 1966:662).

This analytical task, in and of itself, is an important political function, albeit indirect. But when explicitly incorporated into a policy strategy such as that employed by liberal administrations, the function can constitute a powerful and much more direct form of political influence. As the neoconservative analysis sought to make clear, the fact that experts tell people that a problem exists sets up a "social disequilibrium," which can be translated by politicians into a political demand for compensatory action. Indeed, this is just how the liberal reform methodology worked.

Through this particular political strategy, then, experts can emerge as an independent force for social change. At times, in fact, they have literally been a driving force behind public policy. Furthermore, for both radicals and neoconservatives, the technocratic modes of problem definition that policy-oriented social scientists brought to the task made the process especially invidious.

Policy analysts, by virtue of their scientifically oriented mode of discourse, are often seen as suffering from a technical view of society that distorts political reality. Committed to the ideals of scientific rationality and technical efficiency, they are prone to finding fault everywhere in the political system (Banfield 1980:18). Against the ideals of technical rationality, nothing in the political world seems to work. Policy problems appear to abound in every domain of a system that is described as slow, ineffective, and inefficient. But in the *real* world of politics, according to the criticism, it is inappropriate to define and deliberate about political problems using scientific criteria external to their societal contexts. Such problems must be discussed and defined in ordinary political language by the political actors themselves. A "political" problem exists only if political groups say it exists (Kristol 1979). According to the technocratic critique, liberal social scientists tend to uncover what are more appropriately defined as social "conditions" rather than political "problems" per se. The recognition of a social condition, such as poverty, is not in itself an argument for action.

Perversely, then, policy experts—technocrats in particular—busy themselves finding fault where none necessarily exists. As an opportunistic strategy for creating political rhetoric that can in turn be translated into electoral demands, the strategy has rather ingeniously served Democratic administrations. But, in the neoconservative view, as a method of policy-making it constitutes nothing less than a form of "metaphysical madness" (Banfield 1980:1).

Conservative Policy Discourse: The Politicization of Think Tanks

While the radical and neoconservative critiques of the relationship between social scientists and politicians are strikingly similar on many points, I focus on the neoconservative response. My reason is pragmatically related to the rise of the conservative party's political fortunes. In the course of the conservatives' ascent to political power in the 1980s, it was conservative political strategy that gave shape to a counterstrategy based on partisan think tanks and the institutionalization of a conservative policy "discourse coalition."

In turning from neoconservative *theory* to the conservative political *practices* that it helped to shape, one curiously finds something again quite at odds with the tenets of representative democracy. Indeed, one discovers the emergence of a practice that looks remarkably like a conservative version of the social reform strategy. With regard to policy-oriented social scientists, conservative political initiatives during the 1970s took a new direction. In earlier periods, the traditional conservative response to liberal policy experts, if not intellectuals generally, was direct and uncompromising: they were bid a speedy return to the disinterested life of academe. Typically, conservatives sought to discredit liberal social scientists and their ideas (usually said to be "socialistic"), portraying them as impractical, power-seeking elitists. More suitably trained for the job of advice giving were lawyers and businessmen grounded in the practical concerns of political and economic affairs. They were viewed as being more in touch with genuine public concerns.

But during the 1970s the conservative political response was different. Following the advice of neoconservative intellectuals, influential conservative politicians and business leaders began to confront the need to sever the strategic link between liberal reform politics and the use of expertise. Instead of merely dismissing experts and intellectuals as wrong-headed academics, neoconservative leaders began to counsel other conservatives to recognize and accept the importance of the "war of ideas" and to reach out to their own—often forgotten—conservative colleagues in the intellectual world, particularly those in the academic realm.

Conservative leaders increasingly came to understand that a modern conservative political movement had no choice but to get into the policy expertise business. Because of the complexities of modern technological society (and perhaps even the inevitability of a more technocratic form of discourse), conservatives were exhorted to no longer view the elevation of experts as an aberration in the patterns of U.S. politics. Social scientific policy expertise was now an integral part of the governance process, and the time had come for conservatives to train and hire their own experts, a process William Simon (1979) called the creation of a "conservative counterintelligentsia."

Seeking to counter liberal policy expertise on its own terms, the strategy was essentially to politicize the process of expert advice giving. No one was more important in launching this movement than Irving Kristol. For Kristol, the new technocratic class had become the "permanent brain trust" of American politics, mainly liberal politics. Having long sought their place in the sun, these "new class" technocrats were now "in the process of seizing and consolidating" their political position. The experts' critical role in modern government and industry made it imperative for conservatives to launch a struggle to win their political allegiance. Kristol (1978) put it this way: "If one cannot count on these people to provide political, social, and moral stability—if they do not have a good opinion of our society—how long . . . can . . . stability and good opinion survive?"

Basic to the task was the development of active involvement on the part of conservative business leaders, a role they had heretofore largely shunned. Specifically, steps had to be taken to establish a working political relationship between corporate business leaders and the conservative experts of the various "policy communities." Most important, top executives were asked to invest in conservative-oriented research and education projects (Simon 1979). And this they did. Throughout the 1970s and 1980s, corporate elites financed the development of a multimillion-dollar network of policy institutes, research centers, educational programs, and endowed chairs at major universities (Saloma 1984). The centerpiece of the effort was a dramatic expansion of conservative think tanks—the reinvigoration of old ones with massive amounts of money as well as the founding of new ones (Peschek 1987).

These think tanks sought to perform two primary functions: first, to organize more regularized discussions between conservative economic and political leaders and leading conservative academics, and, second, through these interactions to help shape the comservative policy agenda. Most important in this respect have been the American Enterprise Institute for Public Policy Research (AEI), the Heritage Foundation, the Center for Strategic and International Studies, the Cato Institute, the Hoover Institution, the Institute for Contemporary Studies, and the Institute for Education Affairs. Whereas the Brookings Institution supplied Democratic administrations with both advisers and advice (and was later dubbed "the Great Society in exile"), the newer conservative think tanks have become its Republican counterparts (Peschek 1987).

As the political basis of a counterstrategy, these organizations gave rise to an unprecedented politicization of expertise. The result looked much like the liberal reform strategy in conservative clothing. Indeed, with some important differences, conservatives virtually institution-alized the reform strategy. The very phenomenon neoconservatives pur-ported to deplore now reappeared in much more concerted and vigorous political form, this time in the conservative political-planning organiza-tions.

Consider the role of these organizations in terms of the five-step model presented above. First and foremost, conservative policy-planning organizations represent the formal gathering of policy experts who seek to define political problems, investigate policy alternatives, and devise conservative policy arguments. Second, they are institutions designed to bring together economic and political elites (from corpora-tions, philanthropic organizations, and the public sector) to facilitate consensus about issues for governmental decision making. And third, they are designed to promote conservative policy arguments in the pub-lic realm through public information offices and press officers; books, articles, and pamphlets; conferences and lectures; news services; brief-ings; radio segments; and speakers' bureaus.

These points include all the elements of the reform method em-ployed by liberal-progressive administrations, with one crucial differ-ence. Whereas the locus of this activity for Democrats was the White House (although often in the process engaging such institutions as Brookings for advice), the point of coordination and direction institu-tionally shifted to the ongoing and regularized activities of the conserva-tive policy-planning organizations themselves. The process of formulat-ing the "reform" agenda was now largely outside the formal govern-mental institutions.

The political result was both a new commitment on the part of corporate business to conservative policy-oriented social scientists and the development of a reform agenda more dramatic in its implications than that of the Great Society. With regard to corporate commitment, a member of the powerful Business Roundtable summed it up this way: "I can remember the early days when chief executive officers didn't want to have anything to do with these god-damned professors. Now we under-stand more about the impact of ideas" (Blumenthal 1986). The reform agenda forged in conservative planning organizations gave shape to nothing less than the "Reagan revolution," which restructured the course of U.S. domestic and foreign policy and reshaped the very language used to talk about and evaluate public policy.

In terms of intellectual respectability, the AEI clearly became the most prestigious of the conservative think tanks. Today, in fact, many contend that it is intellectually more impressive than the Brookings Institution, long the model of respectability. But in direct political terms, no institution was more influential in giving shape to the Reagan revolution than the Heritage Foundation. It has been estimated, for example, that some two-thirds of the policy ideas advanced by the staff at the Heritage Foundation were adopted by the Reagan administration in its first term (*Public Administration Times* 1985). The Heritage Foundation has boasted of its role in advancing such major administration initiatives as supply-side economics, deregulation of the marketplace, tax reform, the institution of cost-benefit analysis as the primary decision criterion for all governmental programs, the development of free enterprise zones, and the Strategic Defense Initiative, among many others (Peschek 1987).

With the emergence of the conservative strategy also came a very different orientation toward policy advice. In earlier decades, organizations such as the Brookings Institution, the Council on Foreign Affairs, and the Committee on Economic Development shunned any suggestion that they played a political role. Functioning largely under the carefully guarded guise of nonpartisanship, they presented themselves as part of a "good government movement" designed to bring factual, objective information and analysis to bear on public issues (Smith 1989). Such organizations explicitly avoided partisan identification and assiduously skirted anything that resembled a direct political function. But contemporary conservative think tanks have softened this claim of nonpartisanship and in some cases have dropped it altogether. In the process, many of their policy experts began to operate in an argumentatively contentious adversarial style that openly featured their political biases (Landers 1986; *Time* 1986). Some have even described them as "hired guns." Consider, for example, the remarks of Stuart Butler of the Heritage Foundation: "It is naive, in the public policy area, to assume that people don't have an ideological predisposition toward things. Every economist subscribes to a school of economics. . . . Unlike other institutions that pretend ideological neutrality, we're conservatives, no bones about it. We don't pretend to be anything different from what we are" (Tolchin 1985).

Although the basic impetus for this explicit argumentative style was the changing political climate of the 1970s and 1980s, conservative social scientists were able to facilitate this process by finding within their trade a number of technical considerations that imbued this politics of expertise with a measure of intellectual respectability. Most important were the recognition of the growing complexity of the kinds of economic and social problems that had to be dealt with, the limitations of the available data, and the inadequacies of the research techniques employed to measure and analyze these problems. To liberal policy analysts of the Great Society, solving social problems often seemed to be largely a matter of commitment and resources. By the 1970s, however, a more cautious breed of politicians and social scientists saw only complexity and unanticipated consequences. Henry J. Aaron (1978) captured the point in these words:

> Such puzzles as why earnings are distributed as they are and how policies of various kinds would affect the distribution, or what makes prices and wages increase and how to alter that rate of increase, are at least as complex as any addressed in the physical or biological sciences. Underlying these puzzles are all the variations in human personality and the mystery of its development . . . , the operations of labor markets involving the decisions of millions of businessmen and tens of millions of workers, and the myriad laws that guide and shape behavior, often indirectly and in surprising ways.

In the face of such complexity any particular set of facts could—at least arguably—be consistent with a variety of theories. Moreover, it was often impossible—or excessively costly—to acquire the data necessary to sort out and reject false claims. In the context of this highly interpretative character of policy arguments, the acceptability of a particular policy proposal turned increasingly on a combination of the political mood of the times, the prestige of the policy advocate, and the persuasiveness of the argument. Policy argumentation, in fact, began to sound much more like political debate than like the science-based discourse it has long endeavored to be. Instead of appealing to objectivity and proof, the formal standards of the policy analysis discipline, the practice now reflected a combination of ideological obfuscation and political persuasion.

Think Tanks as Policy Discourse Coalitions

The implications of this politicization of elite think tanks and their experts raise numerous issues for traditional democratic theory, some of which are quite profound. Of particular importance for the present dis-

cussion are the broader significance of elite think tanks for public deliberation in the political agenda-setting process and the political influence
of experts in the discourses of these policy-planning organizations.

First, consider the implications of elite policy-planning organizations for the theory of democratic practices, in particular the give-and-
take of competing arguments about interests and goals. Above I described a set of elite institutions that provide a small and select number
of business and political leaders with a centralized mechanism for coordinating a coherent policy agenda geared to their own interests and
activities and the ability to significantly shape the contours of the public
debate about it. By integrating private sector intelligence-gathering systems with public sector policy-making processes—White House decision processes in particular—these think tanks supply governmental
leaders with both broad political direction and specific policy arguments. Thus, as policy-planning organizations play a larger and larger
role in shaping the political agenda, formal governmental policymakers—the president, Congress, and the federal agencies—increasingly
constitute a later phase of a much more complex and subtle process of
agenda development. The governmental processes, featuring pluralistic
deliberation and compromise, appear to be only the visible tip of the
iceberg.[3]

Also important is the growing recognition that elite Washington
think tanks have begun to fill a vacuum created by the decline of political
parties (Blumenthal 1986). Whereas policy ideas traditionally made their
way onto the agenda through public opinion and party debate, today
they increasingly emerge in policy-planning organizations quite independently of public discussion. Thomas Ferguson and Joel Rogers (1981)
documented the degree to which the policy positions of conservative
policy-planning organizations during the Reagan years were advanced
independently of changes in public opinion and open political deliberation.

Missing from conventional explanations, then, is the critical fact
that the agenda for policy consideration is increasingly shaped and approved by the private deliberations of elites outside the government
before political parties and formal policymakers become actively involved in the process. To be sure, the actual influence of party leaders
and governmental decision makers on this process of agenda formation
is a sophisticated empirical question that requires more study. Even in
the absence of more detailed findings, however, the role of policy-
planning organizations and the reform strategy—conservative as well as

liberal—raises serious questions for democratic government and the traditional understanding of the public's role in it.

The underpinnings of a more convincing interpretation of the role of these think tanks can be found in the theories put forward by William Domhoff (1979, 1987) and Thomas Dye (1987), who see policy-planning organizations serving as central coordinating mechanisms of highly structured elite policy networks. The most prestigious policy-planning organizations, such as the AEI and Brookings, are described as "off the record" forums for the ruling establishment (top corporate executives, bankers, university trustees, philanthropists, heads of major law firms, media magnates, and selected political leaders). Such think tanks function as "consensus-seeking organizations" for the development and maintenance of an ongoing discourse on national policy issues, particularly a discourse capable of bridging the political tensions between liberal and conservative elites. Elites recognize the importance of discussing their political differences in private rather than in public. Policy-planning organizations are seen as mechanisms for doing that (Domhoff and Dye 1987).

Elsewhere I have argued that Domhoff and Dye overestimate the ability of elites to work out their differences, a point that requires more attention.[4] Here I want to discuss the role of experts and their discourses in these policy-planning organizations. While the foregoing discussion scarcely supports a "technocratic takeover," the institutionalization of the reform strategy offers a new theoretical avenue. Rather than interpreting the growth of expert influence as a direct challenge to traditional political elites, as generally has been the case in technocratic theory, it is possible to posit two different types of elites—political and technical—more and more working alongside one another. With the policy-planning organization serving as an institutional coordinating mechanism, selected elite experts are drawn into a working relationship with traditional economic and political elites, a kind of policy "discourse coalition" to use the term advanced by Peter Wagner (Wagner et al. 1991) and Maarten Hajer (in this volume). The forging of such a relationship, in fact, was the explicit intention of the conservative strategy of the 1970s and 1980s.

To be sure, traditional elites remain the dominant partners in such discourse coalitions. The fact that policy-planning organizations are privately funded by corporations and foundations provides traditional business elites (and business-oriented political elites) with significant influence over the premises that govern the research, policy deliberations, and public discourses in which these organizations engage (Domhoff 1987). Moreover, much of the discourse in these think tanks tends to focus on the selection of competing ways and means to carry out elite policy agendas rather than on the formation of the agendas per se (Dye 1987). But to leave the matter here seriously underestimates the substantial status and new power that these discourse coalitions afford to knowledge elites. Social scientists chosen to serve at the top levels of these policy organizations can, in fact, participate in the initiation of ideas and alternatives. A creative game ensues in which experts, often in the role of "policy entrepreneurs," invent and broker policy solutions among competing elites, which in turn can be viewed as the power to reshape policy discourses and discourse coalitions (Roberts and King 1991).

During the Reagan years, experts in the conservative coalition played major roles in the largely successful effort to restructure policy discourse in the United States. Not only did they help to discredit the liberal welfare state, they legitimized the political symbols and decision-making approaches of the new conservative agenda (Peschek 1985). Basic to their discourse was the ideology of the marketplace and such market-oriented decision techniques as cost-benefit analysis, which became the dominant approach to policy analysis. They also formulated many of the actual policies that gave content to this new conservative discourse, in particular supply-side economics, tax reform, and deregulation. These were the basic components of the "Right Turn" in American politics (Ferguson and Rogers 1986).

It is clear, then, that since the mid-1960s social scientists have been assuming a new importance in the policy process. Because of the complexity of the issues facing the contemporary state, as well as the use of experts in the development of reform agendas, social science has penetrated traditional political discourse. Regardless of a group's political strength, it is no longer enough for its leaders to rely on the strategic exercise of their political influence. For those seeking to extend their political influence, both the decentralized character of power in the political system and the technical complexity of modern policy issues necessitate attention to policy arguments. Normative arguments and empirical evidence have become unavoidable components of modern policy struggles, and the social science community has emerged as principal supplier of the necessary intellectual ammunition (Easterbook 1986). This is reflected everywhere today in the increasingly technical—and quasi-technical—nature of policy argumentation. Social science and the languages of expertise have become primary currencies of modern policy discourse. New policies today have to be advanced on rational—or purportedly rational—grounds.

The proliferation of policy think tanks is a central manifestation of this phenomenon.[5] The rapid growth of think tanks across the broader political spectrum—especially adversarial think tanks—signifies the growing importance of this new medium of policy discourse (Hoover 1989; Dror 1984). Without access to expertise (or counterexpertise), an interest group today cannot participate effectively in the policy process.

It is not surprising, then, that the late 1970s and the 1980s witnessed a conservative-initiated competition among elites for the allegiance of policy-oriented social scientists. Given the central importance of policy-oriented knowledge and technically oriented discourses, it has become more and more important for elites to control the processes through which data are collected, interpreted, and formulated into policy arguments. While decisions are seldom determined by technical experts alone (certainly not in the traditional sense of scientific decision making), the central importance of the expert's commodity must be carefully managed and controlled. Elite partisan think tanks are an effort—largely successful—to confront this need to organize and control the leading experts and their policy discourses.

Implications for Democratic Discourse

Finally, let us examine the implications of these practices for public deliberation. Most fundamentally, the need to bring citizens back into the policy-making process is widely recognized as one of the primary challenges to both democratic theory and practice. The role of the citizen in the United States has been increasingly weakened by the growth of big institutions, both economic and governmental. The growing importance of expertise and the technical framing of political arguments is a key factor contributing to this marginalization of citizen participation, the cornerstone of democratic governance (Dahl 1989; Fischer 1990).

To be sure, this impediment to citizen participation is in part a structural feature of the complexity of contemporary policy issues: complexity requires expertise. But it is also a function of the mystifying technical languages that serve—often intentionally—to intimidate those who attempt to deliberate with the experts (Forester 1989). In short, we confront here one of the critical issues facing the future of democracy in the high-tech "information society." Any credible theory of democratic practice must thus devote attention to the possibility of democratizing the mechanisms that integrate scientific expertise and political discourse. Prestigious Washington think tanks, as one set of such mechanisms, are today clearly working to serve an elitist rather than a democratic politics. While this is not the place to elaborate on such reforms, I can point to some necessary changes.

A first step would be to build on the demystification of technocratic expertise created, perhaps unwittingly, by politicization and the resultant processes of counterargumentation. Until quite recently, the policy analysis has remained enshrouded in a neopositivist conception of knowledge and the technocratic— "or decisionistic"—concept of policy-making long associated with it. As a step toward methodological reform, the contemporary emphasis on arguments and discourse potentially opens the door to a very different kind of epistemological orientation based on a social constructivistic conception of knowledge (Berger and Luckmann 1972), a dialectical mode of argumentation, and the interpretive methods common to both.

Such an approach is not, of course, altogether new to policy analysis. It can be identified as the emerging "postpositivist" orientation that increasingly gained recognition in disciplinary discussions during the 1980s (in particular the effort to integrate both normative and empirical inquiry into a more comprehensive methodological framework). What is new is the more immediate political and practical relevance of the epistemological issues postpositivism has sought to develop. In the future, such issues will doubtless move more and more from the margins of the profession toward center stage.

In and of itself, such an orientation constitutes an important epistemological advance. Integrally associated with this advance, however, are political and practical issues. Changes in the practice of policy analysis have generally depended as much on political developments as they have on methodological innovations. The same holds true for a postpositivist practice. The successful emergence of such an alternative methodological orientation will depend on a number of political and institutional reforms. Beyond the issues of epistemological reconstruction, a postpositivist policy analysis can have practical meaning only in a participatory setting. The future of such an approach will inevitably depend on the progress of a struggle to further democratize political decision making. There are, in short, no epistemological fixes.

The postpositivist orientation thus depends on the equally difficult political task of building new policy institutions that permit the public to engage in a much wider range of discourse. A significant step in this direction would be a return to the participatory experiments begun in the

1960s, when a number of important projects brought together experts and citizens. Especially important were the public interest science movement and the emergence of public interest science centers, many of which were supported by the National Science Foundation. Such efforts show that citizens can, in fact, intelligently grapple with complex policy arguments (Peterson 1984). Unfortunately, most such experiments were financially and politically squeezed out of existence during the Reagan years.

From where will the forces for such change come? Consider two interrelated possibilities. One possibility is the arrival of a more progressive reform administration on the national level. Typically, liberal-progressive agendas provide openings for experimental innovations and approaches. Although such an agenda would doubtless fall short of the goals of a truly participatory society, it would help to bring the kinds of ideas suggested here closer to the forefront of policy analysis. In this respect, perhaps the Clinton administration holds out some new prospects.

The other possibility concerns the discipline of policy analysis itself. The academic side of the discipline shows promising signs. Given the political as well as the epistemological crisis facing the standard technocratic methodologies, the prospects of the postpositivist theorists are comparatively bright. Indeed, when an editor of a leading policy analysis journal can muse about the future of the discipline in the "postpositivist era," something is surely afoot (Ascher 1987).

Notes

1. This discussion appeared previously in Frank Fischer, "American Think Tanks: Policy Elites and the Politicization of Expertise," *Governance: An International Journal of Policy and Administration* 4, no. 3 (July 1991): 332–53.

2. The end-of-ideology thesis is nowhere better reflected than in an oft-quoted speech delivered by President John F. Kennedy at Yale University:

> Most of us are conditioned for many years to have a political viewpoint. Republican or Democratic—liberal, conservative, moderate. The fact . . . is that most of the problems . . . we now face are technical problems, are administrative problems. They are very sophisticated judgments which do not lend themselves to the great sort of passionate movements which stirred this country so often in the past. Now they deal with questions which are beyond the comprehension of most men, most governmental administrators, over which experts may differ, and yet we operate through our traditional system. (Kennedy 1963)

3. Pluralism thus still has a role to play in the explanation of this phenomenon, although this pluralism is very elitist at best. While such think tanks pluralistically promote their political differences in public, they seldom openly display their private elitist decision-making processes. There is, in this respect, little justification for seeing the new role of think tanks as the basis of a genuine revitalization of pluralism and representative government. One thing, however, is certain: the development poses a new and fascinating issue for the longstanding debate between the two theoretical camps.

4. While the conceptualization of leading policy think tanks as central coordinating mechanisms for elite agenda setting is an advance over pluralist interpretations, the foregoing discussion suggests that the work of Domhoff and Dye tends to exaggerate the ability of liberal and conservative elites to resolve their political differences. Their accounts lack an explanation for the kind of politicization of think tanks witnessed in recent years. Perhaps because they have tended to focus on earlier periods in the development of policy-planning organizations, often stopping short of the more politically turbulent Reagan years, the work of Domhoff and Dye seems to best correspond to periods of "normal politics" in American government, especially the normal politics of big government and the welfare state long associated with the Democratic party and liberal Republicans.

During a period of fundamental political realignment, however, the conservatives apparently found the established think tanks politically unsuited for working out their differences with mainstream liberals. Indeed, the conservative political realignment was seen to require a realignment of the think tanks themselves, the result of which has been more an external institutionalization of dissensus than an internal consensus. Instead of shielding policy disputes from the public, think tanks today as often as not openly display and promote their political differences. Even though a significant effect of this conservative challenge has been the movement of traditional think tanks more toward the center-right of the political spectrum, thus reducing a number of important ideological tensions, the overall political impact has been an institutionalization of competition among conservative and liberal policy intellectuals and experts.

5. There are today an estimated one thousand private nonprofit policy organizations in the United States (Smith 1989:178, 1990), approximately one hundred of which are located in Washington, D.C.

References

Aaron, H. J. 1978. *Politics and the Professors: The Great Society in Perspective.* Washington, D.C.: Brookings Institution.

Ascher, C. 1987. Editorial Comment: Policy Science in the Postpositivist Era. *Policy Sciences* 19:1.

Banfield, E. 1980. Policy Science as Metaphysical Madness. In R. A. Goodwin, ed., *Bureaucrats, Policy Analysts, Statesmen: Who Leads?*, 1–12. Washington, D.C.: American Enterprise Institute for Public Policy Research.

Beer, S. H. 1978. In Search of a New Public Philosophy. In A. King, ed., *The New American Political System*, 40–55. Washington, D. C.: American Enterprise Institute for Public Policy Research.

Benveniste, G. 1972. *The Politics of Expertise.* San Francisco: Boyd and Fraser.

Berger, P., and T. Luckmann. 1972. *The Social Construction of Reality.* New York: Doubleday.

Blumenthal, S. 1986. *The Rise of the Counter-Establishment.* New York: New York Times Books.

Chomsky, N. 1971. *American Power and the New Mandarins.* New York: Vintage.

Dahl, R. A. 1989. *Democracy and Its Critics.* New Haven: Yale University Press.

Dickson, P. 1971. *Think Tanks.* New York: Atheneum.

Domhoff, W. G. 1979. *The Powers That Be.* New York: Vintage.

———. 1987. Where Do Government Experts Come From? In W. Domhoff and T. Dye, eds., *Power Elites and Organizations*, 189–203. Beverly Hills: Sage.

Dror, Y. 1984. Required Breakthroughs in Think Tanks. *Policy Sciences* 16:199–225.

Dye, T. 1976. *Who's Running America?* Englewood Cliffs, N.J.: Prentice-Hall.

———. 1978. Oligarchic Tendencies in National Policy-Making: The Role of the Private Policy-Planning Organizations. *Journal of Politics* 40:310–31.

———. 1987. Organizing for Policy Planning: The View from the Brookings Institution. In W. Domhoff and T. Dye, eds., *Power Elites and Organizations*, 169–88. Beverly Hills: Sage.

Easterbook, G. 1986. Ideas Move Nations. *Atlantic Monthly* (January): 66–80.

Ferguson, T., and J. Rogers, eds. 1981. *The Hidden Election: Politics and Economics in the 1980 Presidential Campaign.* New York: Random House.

———. 1986. *Right Turn.* New York: Hill and Wang.

Fischer, F. 1990. *Technocracy and the Politics of Expertise.* Newbury Park, Calif.: Sage.

Forester, J. 1989. *Planning in the Face of Power.* Berkeley: University of California Press.

Gellner, W. 1990. Political Think Tanks: Functions and Perspectives of a Strategic Elite. Paper presented at the annual meeting of the American Political Science Association, San Francisco, August 30–September 2.

Goodman, R. 1971. *After the Planners.* New York. Simon and Schuster.

Gouldner, A. W. 1970. *The Coming Crisis of Western Sociology.* New York: Avon Books.

Gross, B. 1980. *Friendly Fascism.* New York: Evans.

Hoover, K. 1989. The Changing World of Think Tanks. *PS: Political Science and Politics* 22 (September): 563–72.

Karl, B. 1975. Presidential Planning and Social Science Research: Mr. Hoover's Experts. In *Perspectives in American History*. Vol. 3. Cambridge, Mass.: Charles Warren Center for Studies in American History.

Kennedy, J. F. 1963. Commencement Address at Yale University. In *Public Papers of the President of the United States: John F. Kennedy, 1962*. Washington, D.C.: Government Printing Office.

Kristol, I. 1979. Where Have All the Answers Gone? *National Forum* 69:7.

Landers, R. K. 1986. Think Tanks: The New Partisans? *Editorial Research Reports* (20 June): 471.

Lane, R. E. 1966. The Decline of Politics and Ideology in a Knowledgeable Society. *American Sociological Review* 31 (October): 662–83.

Moynihan, D. P. 1965. The Professionalization of Reform. *Public Interest* (Fall): 6–16.

National Academy of Sciences. 1968. *Government's Need for Knowledge and Information*. Washington, D.C.: Government Printing Office.

Peschek, Joseph G. 1987. *Policy-Planning Organizations*. Philadelphia: Temple University Press.

Peterson, J. C., ed. 1984. *Citizen Participation in Science Policy*. Amherst: University of Massachusetts Press.

Public Administration Times. January 2, 1985. Bad Advice from Heritage.

Roberts, N. C., and P. J. King. 1991. Policy Entrepreneurs: Their Activity Structure and Functions in the Policy Process. *Journal of Public Administration* 1:147–75.

Saloma, J. S. 1984. *Ominous Politics. The New Conservative Labyrinth*. New York: Hill and Wang.

Simon, W. 1979. *A Time for Truth*. New York: Reader's Digest Books.

Smith, J. A. 1989. Think Tanks and the Politics of Ideas. In D. Colander and A. W. Coates, eds., *The Spread of Economic Ideas*. Cambridge: Cambridge University Press.

———. 1990. *The Idea Brokers: Think Tanks and the Rise of the New Policy Elite*. New York: Free Press.

Steinfels, P. 1979. *The Neoconservatives*. New York: Simon and Schuster.

Straussman, J. D. *The Limits of Technocratic Politics*. New Brunswick: Transaction, 1978.

Time Magazine. September 1, 1986, 23.

Tolchin, M. 1985. Working Profile: Stuart Butler. *New York Times*, July 22, 10.

Wagner, P., B. Wittrock, and H. Wollmann. 1991. Social Science and the Modern State: Policy Knowledge and Political Institutions in the United States. In P. Wagner, C. Weiss, B. Wittrock, and H. Wollmann, eds., *Social Science and*

Modern States: National Experiences and Theoretical Crossroads, 28–85. Cambridge: Cambridge University Press.

Waxman, C. I., ed. 1968. *The End of Ideology Debate.* New York: Funk and Wagnalls.

White, T. H. 1967. The Action Intellectuals. *Life,* June 9, 16, and 23.

Discourse Coalitions

and the Institutionalization of Practice:

The Case of Acid Rain in Britain

Maarten A. Hajer

The attitude of the British government in the acid rain controversy has earned Britain the label of "the dirty man of Europe."[1] In the face of an international moral outcry Britain has been notoriously stubborn in denying accusations that the sulfur dioxide and nitrogen oxide emissions of its coal-fired power stations have caused environmental damage abroad. Analysts trying to pinpoint the reasons for Britain's failure to deal with the problem point to inherent conflicts of interest. Britain's unwillingness to act is interpreted as governmental delaying tactics, while the government's reference to scientific uncertainty is described as using science as a "fig leaf" for policy. The inaction is explained in terms of the conscious exercise of power by key actors.[2]

It seems obvious that powerful vested interests such as the electricity industry have tried to delay preventive action, but the acid rain controversy signifies a more fundamental conflict. The acid rain issue is the first of a series of new environmental issues, followed by the depletion of ozone layer, global warming, and less discussed but equally significant issues such as the nitrification of water. These issues mark a new era in the politics of pollution. Before the early 1980s pollution problems were fairly localized and were approached on an ad hoc basis: if incidents occurred, a solution was found. The nonincidental nature of the new environmental issues has rendered this ad hoc policy-making strategy obsolete. What is called for is a structural policy of "sustainable development."[3] This was exactly what critics of Britain's policy in the 1980s argued. They interpreted acid rain within the context of what they perceived to be the crisis of industrial society. Hence the differences of opinion in the acid rain controversy transcended the debate over the interpretation of scientific facts and signified a far wider disagreement.

Did the acid rain problem prove that the old ad hoc strategy had faltered, and did it call for a new approach to environmental policy-making? This essay seeks to illuminate the importance of this deeper meaning of the acid rain controversy and aims to show how the various interests involved had to position themselves in the broader debate.

How can we analyze how the conflict over the future of environmental policy-making influenced the actual debate on acid rain? An analysis of the actual discourse—that is, the examination of argumentative structure in documents and other written or spoken statements—provides insight into this interplay. Two main approaches to pollution politics have competed for dominance in the realm of British pollution politics, and British pollution control has a long-standing historical disposition, or bias,[4] toward pragmatic remedial measures.

Discourse and Discourse Coalitions in Politics

It is almost a commonplace to state that political problems are socially constructed.[5] Whether or not a situation is perceived as a political problem depends on the narrative in which it is discussed. To be sure, large groups of dead trees as such are not a social construct; the point is how one makes sense of dead trees. In this respect there are many possible realities.[6] One may see dead trees as the product of natural stress caused by drought, cold, or wind, or one may see them as victims of pollution. The acid rain narrative labels the dead trees as victims of pollution, and thus dead trees become a political problem.

This example highlights the changing perception of the role of language in political life. In the positivist tradition in the social sciences, language was seen as a *means*, as a neutral system of signs that described the world. With the coming of the postpositivist social sciences, however, language lost this neutral status and itself became problematized. Language is recognized as a *medium*, a system of signification through which actors not simply describe but *create* the world.[7] For instance, in a narrative on acid rain, dead trees are given a specific meaning. They are no longer an incident; they signify a structural problem: the fact that rain is no longer natural, that it kills life instead of nourishing it. The concept of acid rain is part of a discourse that relates environmental change to something bigger, such as the crisis of industrial society. This immediately raises other questions. For example, what kind of society tolerates dying forests? The usage of language in political life or political discourse thus becomes an important object of political study.

The linguistic turn potentially provides the policy analyst with useful new tools to analyze how certain relations of dominance are structured and reproduced. After all, determining the way a phenomenon is linguistically represented has repercussions for politically essential questions such as Who is responsible? What can be done? What should be done? The study of discourse opens new possibilities to study the political process as *mobilization of bias*.[8] Here I argue that the analysis of discursive constructions such as narratives is especially powerful in the context of the study of the social-historical conditions in which the statements were produced and received.[9] In this case it is better to speak of an argumentative turn instead of a linguistic turn. Michael Billig writes that "to understand the meaning of a sentence or whole discourse in an argumentative context, one should not examine merely the words within that discourse or the images in the speaker's mind at the moment of utterance. One should also consider the positions which are being criticized, or against which a justification is being mounted. Without knowing these counter-positions, the argumentative meaning will be lost."[10] Hence the argumentative turn requires the analysis to go beyond the investigation of differences of opinion about technical facts alone. The real challenge for argumentative analysis is to find ways of combining the analysis of the discursive production of reality with the analysis of the (extradiscursive) social practices from which social constructs emerge and in which the actors that make these statements engage. This is the function of the concept of *discourse coalition*.[11]

A discourse coalition is basically a group of actors who share a social construct.[12] Social constructs such as acid rain can be seen as a way to give meaning to ambiguous social circumstances (e.g., unexplained dying of forests or lakes). Obviously, this process of constructing, or framing, political problems is a highly significant element of the political process. Actors try to impose their views of reality on others, sometimes through debate and persuasion, but also through manipulation and the exercise of power. Yet, social constructs do not arise in a historical vacuum. They emerge in the context of historical discourses which contain knowledge of how similar phenomena were dealt with in the past. *Discourse* is here defined as an ensemble of ideas, concepts, and categories through which meaning is given to phenomena. Discourses frame certain problems; that is to say, they distinguish some aspects of a situation rather than others. The ideas, concepts, and categories that constitute a discourse can vary in character: they can be normative or analytic convictions; they can be based on historical references; they can reflect myths about nature. As such, discourse provides the tools with which problems are constructed. Discourse at the same time forms the context in which phenomena are understood and thus predetermines the definition of the problem. *Discourse structuration* occurs when a discourse starts to dominate the way a society conceptualizes the world.

However, at a time when social constructivism and discourse analysis can rejoice in widespread attention, it is paramount to emphasize that social constructs do not "float" in the world; they can be tied to specific institutions and actors. If a discourse is successful—that is to say, if many people use it to conceptualize the world—it will solidify into an institution, sometimes as organizational practices, sometimes as traditional ways of reasoning. This process is called *discourse institutionalization.*[13] For instance, if air pollution is predominantly seen as a problem of urban smog, as it was during the 1950s and 1960s, the monitoring of air quality might be concentrated in cities; after all, why monitor the countryside if smog only occurs in cities? Of course, discourse institutionalization facilitates the reproduction of a given discourse. Actors who have been socialized to work within the frame of such an institutionalized discourse will use their positions to persuade or force others to interpret and approach reality according to their institutionalized insights and convictions.

In the everyday sense the word *discourse* is mostly used in the singular. However, it is more in accordance with reality to speak of plural discourses. After all, political discourse is not a uniform whole. Discourse formation takes place on many different levels and in many different localities.[14] In politics we characteristically deal with mixes of elements drawn from various discourses. For instance, even in the case of environmental politics, the natural sciences constitute a particularly powerful and legitimate form of discourse. This scientific set of concepts and categories dominates the way that meaning is given to the phenomenon of acid rain. The scientific assessment of how forest dieback or lake acidification is caused, dominates the political debate and sets limits to the range of solutions that are considered.

However, the case of environmental politics also illustrates that problems are often complex and comprise many different aspects. Consequently, the political arguments of actors typically rest on more than one discourse at a time. For instance, a persuasive argument or a viable solution for the acid rain problem must combine elements of scientific discourse (What is acid rain?), economical discourse (What are the costs to society?), engineering discourse (What can be done about it?), as well as political considerations (Do we want to commit ourselves to a specific solution?). Hence the political debate draws on many different discourses. Still, the remarkable fact that people from widely varying backgrounds seem to find ways to communicate receives little attention in policy analysis.

This apparent negligence is misleading. In the actual discussion of specific problems different discursive elements are presented as a narrative, or *story line,* in which elements of the various discourses are combined into a more or less coherent whole and the discursive complexity is concealed. Nevertheless only a few actors fully grasp complex problems like acid rain. Although many of the actors involved are experts of some sort, they still depend on other experts for a full understanding. Story lines thus have an important organizational potential. These discourse clusters are held together by *discursive affinity:* arguments may vary in origin but still have a similar way of conceptualizing the world. An important example from pollution politics is the discursive affinity among the moral argument that nature should be respected, the scientific argument that nature is to be seen as a complex ecosystem (which we will never fully understand), and the economic idea that pollution prevention is actually the most efficient mode of production (this is the core of the discourse of sustainable development).

The discourse coalition approach suggests that once a new discourse is formulated, it will produce story lines on specific problems, employing the conceptual machinery of the new discourse (e.g., sustainable development). A discourse coalition is thus the ensemble of a set of story lines, the actors that utter these story lines, and the practices that conform to these story lines, all organized around a discourse. The discourse coalition approach suggests that politics is a process in which different actors from various backgrounds form specific coalitions around specific story lines. Story lines are the medium through which actors try to impose their view of reality on others, suggest certain social positions and practices, and criticize alternative social arrangements. For instance, the reemergence of environmentalism in the late 1960s was not just a protest against the perceived risk implied in new large-scale technological projects. It was also a celebration of the virtues and morality of unspoiled nature and a call to change the conceptual framework and start thinking about nature in terms of beauty and as necessary to life instead of in terms of domination and as a system of cause-and-effect relationships.[15] This also implied a critique of the positions and practices that came with the prevailing scientific mode of thinking (expert decision making, quantification of damage, etc.).

New story lines can become a popular way of conceptualizing the world, but a discourse coalition can be said to dominate a given political realm only if it fulfills two conditions: (1) it dominates the discursive space; that is, central actors are persuaded by, or forced to accept, the rhetorical power of a new discourse (condition of discourse structuration); and (2) this is reflected in the institutional practices of that political domain; that is, the actual policy process is conducted according to the ideas of a given discourse (condition of discourse institutionalization).

To summarize, the politics of discourse is best seen as a continuous process of giving meaning to the vague and ambiguous social world by means of story lines and the subsequent structuration of experience through the various social practices that can be found in a given field. The discourse coalition approach thus has three advantages: (1) it analyzes strategic action in the context of specific sociohistorical discourses and institutional practices and provides the conceptual tools to analyze controversies over individual issues such as acid rain in their wider political context; (2) it takes the explanation beyond mere reference to interests, analyzing how interests are played out in the context of specific discourses and organizational practices; and (3) it illuminates how different actors and organizational practices help to reproduce or fight a given bias without necessarily orchestrating or coordinating their actions or without necessarily sharing deep values.

Two Discourse Coalitions in British Pollution Politics

Until the early 1980s pollution problems were predominantly conceptualized in terms of *traditional pragmatist discourse* with historical roots in the nineteenth century. In 1863 the British Alkali Inspectorate, the world's first air pollution inspectorate, was created. At that time pollution control was a marginal state interest. Pollution was perceived as a problem only if it posed a direct and acute threat to human health. The organization of pollution control was reactive in nature; it aimed at minimizing organizational disturbances and searched for pragmatic, piecemeal solutions; hence "ad hoc."[16] The discourse was widely shared; the critics of the government that initiated the Alkali Acts of 1863 drew on this discourse saw as their goal to ascertain "whether legislative measures could be introduced . . . not only without injury, but with profit to our manufacturers."[17]

The traditional pragmatist discourse also reflects the typical nineteenth-century scientification of politics. Traditionally, British pollution control has been strongly committed to the judgment of experts.

Since the Alkali Acts of 1863, pollution has been defined as an apolitical matter best left to the discretion of scientific and technical experts. Authority is given to experts who, being above the sphere of politics and competition, are supposed to be able to define the "practicable" course of action. Over the years both Conservative and Labor governments have reinforced this practice. In 1969, for instance, a time when the alleged "expertocracy" was under widespread popular protest, Prime Minister Harold Wilson (Labor) initiated both the Central Scientific Unit on Pollution and the Royal Commission on Environmental Pollution (finally sworn in 1971). This increased coordination between government and science de facto reinforced the existing traditional pragmatist discourse coalition.

Still, the wave of environmentalism that rolled over Britain during the 1970s put the traditional pragmatist style of policy-making on trial. Whereas the prevailing sentiment among the grass-roots movement was an ethical critique on the instrumentalist attitude to nature, the movement's leaders quickly added another line. In the much celebrated study *Small is Beautiful*, for instance, E. F. Schumacher emphasized that the negligence of nature is not only morally wrong but is in fact also grossly inefficient.[18]

This realist element in the environmentalist critique led to the formulation of an alternative to the traditional pragmatist policy discourse in the early 1980s. The document *World Conservation Strategy* (1980) became a key element in the newly formulated approach to pollution politics: *ecological modernization*. This approach was further disseminated in British documents such as the *U.K. Response to the World Conservation Strategy* and the *Tenth Report* of the Royal Commission on Environmental Pollution.[19] The principal point was that pollution could no longer be seen as incidental, and pollution control had to be integrated into the overall process of societal modernization, industrial production in particular. As the Royal Commission put it, "Control of environmental pollution is not an optional extra: it is a fundamental component of national economic and social policy."[20] Rather than *reacting* to pollution incidents and aiming at *remedial* strategies after the occurrence of pollution problems, this discourse turns toward *pollution prevention*. The rationale is simple: pollution prevention pays, or, as the Confederation of British Industry argued in 1983, "Environmental protection makes sense—as many companies have found to their gain."[21]

In the early 1980s actors within the government also became aware that the old a postiori and traditional pragmatist approach was rapidly losing its legitimacy. In 1984 the Department of the Environment (DOE) started to contemplate the introduction of a policy discourse based on eco-modernist principles. In November 1985 the Central Policy Planning Unit at the DOE produced the *Environmental Policy Review*, an internal review document. It came out strongly in favor of ecological modernization.

This rethinking of the basis of policy-making at the DOE had been strongly promoted by both the chief scientist at the DOE, Martin Holdgate, and the junior minister for the environment, William Waldegrave, who had joined the DOE in June 1983. Until that time the department had been primarily reactive in its approach to environmental problems. They argued pollution control had to be integrated into the economic system. One of the key features of the new approach would be that the government would encourage industry "to adopt a new positive philosophy— to build environmental impact, with its cleanliness, energy efficiency and public acceptability—into the first sketch of its new ideas."[22]

The discourse of ecological modernization can be captured in five points:

1. Nature should no longer be regarded as a "sink." In economic terms this calls for a recognition of nature as a resource. Damage is regarded as usage of natural resources which has to be paid for.
2. Pollution prevention is put forward as a more rational approach than piecemeal reactive response.
3. The discourse recognizes the intricate nature of environmental problems and the complexity of ecosystems. Rigorous and unambiguous scientific proof should therefore no longer be regarded as a *sine qua non*.
4. The discourse recognizes the importance of the social perception of risk. The public's perception of risk should no longer be simply refuted as irrational.
5. In light of points 2 and 3, the new discourse argues for the reversal of the burden of proof: a substance should no longer automatically be regarded as innocent until proven guilty, but more often as guilty until proven innocent.

In the face of the moral outcry over the state of the environment during the 1980s, the discourse of ecological modernization, with *sustainable development* as central story line, came to be the most legitimate way to speak about environmental problems.[23] However, if ecological modernization was indeed to be executed, a fundamental shift from remedial to preventive action was necessary in the actual institutional practices. The key word, implicit in all five points, in the ecomodernist vocabulary was *precaution*: on the basis of the awareness of the seriousness of the environmental crisis one anticipated the worst and aimed to prevent extra "stress." Between 1979 and 1988 this discourse of precaution had become well structured into the environmental domain. In 1979 the Environment Ministers of the European Community agreed on a declaration that recognized precaution as the cornerstone of future environmental policy; in 1988 the British government fully endorsed the UN report *Our Common Future* and announced that it would reconsider its policies in this light. Yet the translation of this discourse into institutional practices was quite a different matter.

Now, it is interesting to note that during the early 1980s the debate on the terms of environmental discourse heavily drew on concrete problems such as lead in the environment or acid rain. These issues functioned, as it were, as metaphor for the much larger problematic of environmental decline. Acid rain in particular was constantly put forward by the discourse coalition of ecological modernization as a case in point to show that the environmental problems were of a different nature and required an unconventional approach. But what was the impact of the new discourse coalition on the debate on acid rain?

The British Acid Rain Controversy

The acid rain controversy really started in 1972, but concern about acid rain has a much longer history.[24] Acid rain was first described by the French pharmicist M. Ducros in 1842,[25] but it was Robert Angus Smith who, in 1852, first related the phenomenon to pollution.[26] The current European concern originates from the 1968 publications of Svante Odén, a Swedish soil scientist who related the acidification of Swedish fresh waters to sulfur dioxide emissions from continental Europe and Britain. The Swedish government, concerned about the possibility of transboundary air pollution, raised the issue to the Organization for Economic Cooperation and Development (OECD) in 1969. Subsequently the Swedish government called for a large international meeting on environmental decline, which eventually became the 1972 United Nations Conference on the Human Environment, held at Stockholm. Here Sweden formally launched its international campaign against transboundary air pollution. The remainder of the 1970s was devoted to scientific scrutiny of the phenomenon. At that time the debate was almost entirely confined to a limited circle of scientific experts, and the issue appeared on the public or governmental agenda only when interim research findings were published or conferences devoted to discussing these findings were held.

In June 1982, the tenth anniversary of the 1972 UN conference, the Swedish government organized a conference to evaluate progress. This conference heralded a new period in the history of the acid rain controversy. First of all, prior to the conference the Swedes assembled an international forum of experts, who agreed that enough was known about the nature and impact of acid rain to warrant the definition and implemention of an effective abatement policy.[27] Perhaps more important was the fact that at the actual Ministerial Conference on Acidification of the Environment, the Swedish government got unexpected support in its push for international action from the West German government, which, in response to the discovery of the scale of forest dieback in the southern part of the Federal Republic, announced a comprehensive program to retrofit their coal-fired power plants with SO_2 scrubbers, so-called flue gas desulfurization equipment (FGD). With the exception of Scandinavia, the German FGD program was the first clear-cut policy commitment to combat acid rain in western Europe. It was, at the same time, a clear case of the poacher turning gamekeeper, since until then Germany had not only been a major pollution culprit but had also been a fierce opponent of international agreements on sulfur emission control. Britain's contribution at Stockholm was limited to the announcement that it was willing to reverse its earlier decision to cut research funding on acid rain.

The British government emphasized that there was no firm evidence that its SO_2 emissions were responsible for fish deaths and acidification in the Swedish lakes and therefore argued that it could not justify the high costs of SO_2 scrubbers. It also argued that since Britain was responsible for just 10 percent of the Swedish SO_2 imports, it was unlikely that emission reduction would result in substantial environmental improvements. Finally, the British government questioned whether emission reduction through the use of FGD equipment was the most cost-effective way of improving the environmental situation; it argued that tall stacks (to dilute and disperse pollution) and the liming of lakes (to counterbalance the acidification) were much cheaper and more effective means.

Yet, from the 1982 Stockholm conference onward, the British government found itself under increasing pressure to act. The FRG, eager to shake off the competitive disadvantage that resulted from having installed FGD equipment unilaterally, made sure that the European Community (EC) became active on the issue. In 1988, after five years of laborious negotiations, during which Britain refused many a compromise, the member countries agreed on the Large Combustion Plant Directive,[28] which required that new plants should be fitted with FGD equipment and low NOx burners. Furthermore, all EC countries agreed to reduce SO_2 emissions. Britain, however, managed to secure a lenient percentage in the negotiations.[29]

On the domestic front protests built up more slowly. To be sure, the acid rain issue never generated widespread popular protest in Britain: a high percentage of the population was concerned, but the political conflict always remained at the level of an elite group of experts, politicians, and journalists. Acid rain was an invisible, cumulative pollutant that damaged the (foreign) natural environment more than it harmed people and asked for expensive solutions that would have to be paid for by consumers. As such, acid rain was never likely to become as central a public issue as nuclear power had been in the 1970s. Moreover, in the early 1980s the environmental debate was preoccupied with the lead issue. It was not until the debate about lead was resolved in April 1983 that campaigners, politicians, and government officials really became sensitive to the issue of acid rain.

One of the high points in the controversy was the 1984 inquiry into acid rain undertaken by the House of Commons Select Committee for the Environment, whose hearings clearly indicated the polarized nature of the debate. A majority of the experts who gave evidence argued that enough was known about acid rain to warrant taking action. A small but influential group argued that "policy was in danger of running ahead of science," as Minister of the Environment Patrick Jenkin put it. The Select Committee report, however, argued that enough was known and urged the government to join the "30 percent club" (30 percent reduction of SO_2 emissions by 1993). In December 1984 the government responded with a proposal that aimed for a reduction in SO_2 emissions of 30 percent by the end of the 1990s but did not accept the necessity of installing expensive FGD scrubbers.[30] Then, in September 1986, on the basis of new scientific evidence, the government suddenly proposed to install FGD equipment in all new coal-fired power stations. The government also announced plans to retrofit three of its twelve large coal-fired power stations with FGD equipment at a total cost of about £600 million.

The Acid Rain Story Line of the Traditional Pragmatist Discourse Coalition

The acid rain controversy, although seemingly about technical facts, is best understood in the context of a struggle for hegemony between two competing discourse coalitions. The discursive space in which the acid rain controversy was played out was within a challenge of the traditional pragmatist discourse by the discourse of ecological modernization.[31] Each discourse coalition had its own story line on acid rain, yet, unlike the new discourse of ecological modernization, the traditional pragmatist discourse was institutionally well entrenched.

The most eloquent and outspoken protagonist within the traditional pragmatist story line was the Central Electricity Generating Board (CEGB). Even the government more or less echoed the detailed arguments presented by the CEGB, adding its own political dimension. The traditional pragmatist story line evolved around a scientific argument that doubted whether any genuine environmental damage was attributable to power plant sulfur emissions. If this could be proven, however, and if FGD equipment could be shown to be both environmentally effective as well as the most cost-effective solution, FGD scrubbers should be installed. However, the CEGB argued that the available evidence was anecdotal and intuitive and that "proper" research was needed.[32] It argued that there was no real scientific understanding, let alone a consensus, of the mechanisms involved in lake acidification. In 1984 the chairman of the CEGB, Lord Marshall (then Sir Walter), maintained: "I simply do not accept any of the scientific agruments I have yet seen."[33] This position implied that until SO_2 emissions were proved to be harmful to the environment, CEGB omissions should be allowed to continue.

The CEGB presented its own argument to the view of the Scandinavian and German governments. In the early 1980s these governments argued that no further research was needed and claimed that the state of knowledge at that time justified immediate action. The CEGB, on the other hand, pointed at the lack of scientific understanding. In so doing the CEGB portrayed the politicians of foreign governments as emotional and irresponsible and itself as level-headed, rational, and scientific.

A key element to substantiate this scientific commitment was the SWAP research project. The SWAP project (Surface Waters Acidification Program), launched by the CEGB in September 1983, is a major £5 million research study into the acidification of fresh waters funded by the CEGB and the British Coal Board. In the political process the actors within the traditional pragmatist discourse coalition frequently referred to SWAP and to the involvement of the Royal Society of London and the Swedish Royal Academy of Sciences, which were put forward by the CEGB as the "most prestigious scientific academies in the entire world."[34]

The politicians operating within the traditional pragmatist discourse never failed to emphasize the scientific core of their argument.

This is the natural basis of a strict utilitarian approach to the decision-making problem. The British government always insisted that it would be willing to act if action would be "environmentally effective and economically feasible,"[35] arguing that it did "not believe that the very substantial expenditure (running into hundreds of millions of pounds) which would be required to install flue-gas desulphurisation plant at existing power stations can be justified while scientific knowledge is developing and the environmental benefit remains uncertain."[36] Here the governmental emphasis on the need for a better chemical understanding was positioned against "giving in" and making "heroic efforts" because politicians rush (EC) or are in danger of rushing (Britain) to conclusions on the basis of fallacious data and argument. Like the CEGB the government thus positioned itself as more rational than its foreign counterparts. The target of the 30 percent club, for instance, was perceived to be an irrational and arbitrary basis for action which would place Britain at an unfair disadvantage.

The aura of the responsible bookkeeper, characterized by restraint and knowledgeability, was further reinforced by numerous references to the success of its approach to air pollution in the past: Britain's "proud record" in air pollution control. The fact that SO_2 emissions had fallen by about 40 percent since the early 1970s was used to prove this assertion.

Traditional Pragmatism as a Political Practice

The traditional pragmatist discourse coalition had been dominating the field of pollution politics for more than a century. It is hardly surprising, therefore, that this discourse was well institutionalized. In the context of the acid rain controversy three sets of institutional practices stand out: (1) the urban- and health-oriented definition of air pollution reflected in the system of air pollution monitoring; (2) the science-based policy approach; and (3) the politics of consultation and best practicable means. Each practice encompassed a bias that worked against swift action on the acid rain issue.

The Urban-Health Bias and the Urban Monitoring System

British air pollution control was originally a response to the notorious smogs that haunted the Victorian city. Even as late as 1952 a period of smog caused thousands of deaths. British air pollution was always primarily perceived as an urban problem, and policies were aimed at clearing up the urban skies and reducing health risks. What was important was reducing the concentrations of particles, smoke, and heavy metals such as lead. If SO_2 was perceived as a problem, it was always as ground-level concentration (where it was a direct threat to human health) and not its emission as such. For that reason the official SO_2 policy remained dilute and dispersed: until 1986 high stacks were seen as the appropriate strategy toward SO_2 emissions.

This urban- and health-oriented definition of the air pollution problem solidified in institutional arrangements and became a distinct bias: institutions of pollution control were not perceptive of other forms of air pollution. One particularly important practice in this respect was the monitoring system. Most monitoring stations set up under the 1956 Clean Air Act were confined to cities: only 150 out of 1,200 were located in rural areas. This urban bias in monitoring helps to explain the prevalence of the myth that acid rain did not affect the British countryside: for a long time there simply were no relevant data. However, SO_2 was at least recognized as a problem. This was certainly not true for two other acid rain–related pollutants: ozone and NOx. In 1984 the lack of monitoring stations prevented a clear picture of the effects and distribution of these pollutants in the United Kingdom.

This urban- and SO_2-related definition of air pollution proved to be a particularly persistent and powerful element in the ad hoc technocratic story line on acid rain. It kept reappearing, although as early as 1976 a government spokesman had already officially admitted that British acid rain fell on Scandinavia and thereby acknowledged that the air pollution problem was far from being confined to the urban realm.[37]

The urban definition was reinforced by new confirmations; for example, by Secretary of State for the Environment Michael Heseltine in 1979: "Sulphur dioxide emissions . . . fell [after 1970] by about 16% and recently seem to have been roughly stable at a new low level, while average urban concentrations have fallen about 50% since the early 1960s; the difference between the patterns in emissions and concentrations is the result of more effective means of dispersal, e.g., higher chimneys."[38] The paper fails to mention the then well-known fact that the unintended negative consequence of the tall stack policy was the aggravation of the acid rain problem. The CEGB also used the lack of data to reinforce its case. In evidence presented to the Select Committee the CEGB mentioned that "recently there were 104 occasions when a particular value (for ozone pollution) was exceeded in Germany and only once in the United Kingdom."[39] Considering the lack of measurement, this is hardly surprising.

An additional reason for the persistence of the urban-health bias is explained by the fact that rural conservation in Britain, as with so many issues, has always been defined in terms of land use planning. Countryside conservation in Britain is interpreted as protection against urban sprawl, not pollution. This is reflected in the institutional practices of the environmental movement, for instance in its expertise and in the direction of its lobbying activity.[40]

The Science-based Policy Approach

Decisions on pollution issues rely on a scientific assessment of the seriousness of the situation. This dominant role of science in British pollution control originally was meant to keep decision making insulated from pressure groups and to keep pollution control policy out of the sphere of corporatism and interest groups. It was meant to make sure that abatement measures will be introduced only when there is firm scientific understanding of the phenomenon. It is essential to appreciate the fundamental part played by this science-based policy approach in the acid rain controversy. As William Waldegrave, then minister at the DOE, said in 1984: "We see no point in making heroic efforts, at great cost, to control one out of many factors unless there is a reasonable expectation that such control will lead to real improvement in the environment."[41]

The science-based policy approach to environmental politics is clarified in *Pollution Paper* no. 11, in which the government describes British environmental policy. Here the technocratic tendency is clear:

> People are naturally very much concerned about the effects of pollution on health. . . . It is inherent in our society that such pressures should arise, but to accede to them unquestioningly could often involve a waste of resources as well as the possible loss of activities and benefits on which society places value. . . . It is important to ensure that the standards being imposed do not rest on an unsound scientific justification or require disproportionate economic costs, since this would make it difficult later to introduce further measures, however well founded. In explaining standards, however, the risk of gross misinterpretation of data and the need to avoid disclosure of truly confidential information need to be borne in mind.[42]

In other words, decision making cannot be based on social concern; it has to be legitimized through scientific discourse. Here the government seems to distinguish real, objective risks from perceived risks based on misinformation. Trust in the scientific system must be restored.[43] At the same time, the public cannot be told everything.

However, the definition of the science-based policy approach is not unproblematic: as I will show, *de facto* refers to a particular type of science. Moreover, it would be quite wrong to suggest that the government's reading of the scientific evidence reflected the opinion of the British scientific community at large. The 1984 House of Commons inquiry indicated that a majority of experts actually were of the opinion that enough *was* known. Yet this is not immediate evidence that the government acted contrary to its better knowledge. The explanation for this paradox is primarily sociological. The government legitimized its stubborn stand by referring to the opinion of the Royal Society of London, the institution that sets the standards of "good science" in Britain. Although primarily concerned with pure research, this prestigious scientific institution's influence on the mundane world of pollution politics can hardly be overestimated. The traditional pragmatist discourse coalition held that to be recognized as firm evidence in British pollution science, research should meet the strong positivistic epistemological requirements that are commonly found in disciplines such as physics and chemistry. Other scientists, however, argued that pollution-related research should be seen as something fundamentally different from experimental research and that knowledge was a product of gradually accumulating evidence from many different corners. So, in March 1984, Patrick Jenkin, secretary of state at the DOE, could argue that it was "necessary to establish a clear idea of the cause and effect before spending millions of pounds which might turn out to be useless,"[44] whereas scientists working in the field maintained that "the complexity of acidification processes is such that absolute proof of causality in terms of acid deposition affecting biota, is never likely to be obtained."[45]

Two moments were crucial for the impact of the reductionist epistemology on the acid rain controversy. First, in September 1983 the Royal Society organized a major conference on acid rain to discuss the state of knowledge on the effects of sulfur and nitrogen compounds on the environment. Although the initiators had hoped the conference could provide a basis for action, it ended up criticizing the partial and imprecise data available. This served the cause of the electricity industry. Lord Marshall (then Sir Walter), the chairman of the CEGB and himself a fellow of the Royal Society, announced the launch of the SWAP project, which was to be conducted jointly with the Royal Swedish Academy and the Norwegian Academy of Science and Letters.

Second, in June 1984 (i.e., during the Select Committee inquiry), the prime minister invited leading scientists from the major research institutions working on the topic to the prime minister's retreat at Chequers to get an update on the state of knowledge on acid rain. The CEGB representatives, having done by far the most research, dominated the debate. They emphasized the lack of knowledge and referred to the SWAP project, which would soon provide answers to the many questions. In so doing they not only postulated the supremacy of Royal Society science but also ridiculed those who argued for immediate action. Other specialists failed to convey to the prime minister, indeed failed to argue, that in environmental affairs conclusive evidence of biochemical mechanisms is rarely found and that less rigid epistemological requirements are usually applied to environmental phenomena.

As a result, the SWAP project came to be the linchpin in the acid rain controversy. The government's decision to retrofit three power stations with FGD scrubbers in September 1986 was clearly linked to developments in the SWAP project. In June that year two CEGB directors had accepted the results of certain SWAP experiments in Norway as being decisive: they accepted the evidence that sulfur emissions contributed to fish death, albeit in a more complicated way than environmentalists had maintained. The great political commitment to SWAP and the involvement of the Royal Society meant that these projects could not easily be dismissed; certainly the 1986 decision would not have occurred without SWAP.

However, although the SWAP results played a key role, they do not suffice for a full explanation of the 1986 decision. As a matter of fact, the emergence of this scientific evidence coincided with the internal publication of new forecasts of energy demand, which predicted an important increase. This implied that SO_2 emissions would increase rather dramatically. The new knowledge acquired through SWAP made it clear that this would cause a dramatic increase in acidification levels. What is more, it would go against all U.K. commitments to contain SO_2 emissions. Apart from this, the scientific basis fitted the managerial concerns nicely. The research indicated that the CEGB would not need to initiate a crash program like the Germans had done; it could wait until new plants came on line around the turn of the century, thus avoiding the costs of extra retrofits. It had, in other words, not seen the light and had reversed its stand on acid rain: it had found the critical limit.

To summarize, the symbolic order of the Royal Society, the cooperation of the Norwegian and Swedish academies, and commitment to a socially constructed practice of "good science" tied up the participants and precluded any discussion. The science-based policy approach was not just a rhetorical device but a complicated policy practice that structured the argumentative process through which power was exercised and interests were mediated.

The Politics of Consultation and the "Best Practicable Means"

British air pollution control has always relied on close consultation between the inspectorate and the polluting industries.[46] In Britain, pollution control is not a matter of setting uniform standards and forcing the industry to comply. The idea is more to help individual industries find practicable solutions to avoid pollution. In this respect the Alkali Inspectorate requires industries to use the *best practicable means* (BPM) to avoid pollution. BPM has been used in air pollution control since 1874 but was first properly defined by statute in the 1956 Clean Air Act: "'Practicable' means reasonably practicable having regard, amongst other things, to local conditions and circumstances, to the financial implications and to the current state of technical knowledge."[47] Like the science-based policy discourse, BPM allocates a central role to the expert. The inspectorate regularly publishes *Notes on BPM* to determine which pollution abatement strategy is considered the best practicable means. This practice thus eliminates both politics and the public: BPM works on the basis of a relationship of mutual trust and respect between experts from the inspectorate and industry.

BPM is a practice that can, in principle, work surprisingly well in initiating new abatement strategies, but in the acid rain controversy it did not speed up action. Both the government and the inspectorate kept up the image of the inspectorate as a strong and autonomous working institute. For instance, in 1984 the government argued that "flue gas desulphurisation is a proven technology for removing sulphur dioxide from power station plumes but the . . . Inspectorate have not required its installation, because at a capital cost of some 150 million pounds for each major power station, they have regarded it as too expensive an imposition to constitute 'best practicable means.'"[48] This suggests that the inspectorate will set the standards if necessary. If the inspectorate does not require FGD equipment, politicians can use this as an expert argument against popular pressure. But the price of electricity is, of course, primarily a political problem—something which clearly exceeds the discretion of the air pollution inspectorate.

Although the inspectorate could have argued that FGD equipment was the best practicable means, it never did. The 1986 decision to retrofit power stations did not originate with the inspectorate but was recommended to the government by the CEGB itself. As a matter of fact, the inspectorate did not consider FGD equipment to constitute the best practicable means until after both the government *and the industry* had agreed to install scrubbers. The inspectorate had made its own assessment that the benefits to nature did not outweigh the costs to industry. Here the reliance on expert authority to make decisions on environmental matters, characteristic for the ad hoc technocratic discourse coalition, clearly worked against the installation of FGD equipment.

Acid Rain According to the Ecomodernist Discourse Coalition

The ad hoc technocratic story line on acid rain has been fiercely attacked by actors both within Parliament and outside. The three key actors were the House of Commons Select Committee for the Environment, the Royal Commission on Environmental Pollution, and Friends of the Earth U.K. (FOE). All three drew on the ecomodernist discourse to challenge the existing policy practice.

The ecomodernist story line on acid rain inevitably started from the perception that acid rain was not just another unimportant issue: the Select Committee saw acid rain as "one of the major environmental hazards faced by the industrial world today"; the Royal Commission argued that "acid deposition is one of the most important pollution issues of the present time," while the FOE contended that "acid rain is already widespread in Britain."[49]

According to the ecomodernists, knowledge about acid rain is imperfect, but time is running out. Enough is now known, they have argued from 1982 onward, to justify the spending on curative measures. They also knew what had to be done: like the Swedish government they saw the CEGB power stations as the main culprit, and so retrofitting power stations with FGD scrubbers was put forward as the proven technology to cure the problem. In reply to the figure showing the overall decline in SO_2 emissions presented by the traditional pragmatists, the ecomodernists illustrated their argument with a graph that indicated the relative increase of the role of power stations therein. The ecomodernist story line also emphasized that Britain was still the largest producer of SO_2 in western Europe.[50]

The most influential statement of the ecomodernists on acid rain is undoubtedly the *Fourth Report of the House of Commons Environment Select Committee,* published in 1984, which is entirely devoted to the problem of acid rain. It pulls together various elements of knowledge and assesses the consequences of the strategies available.

Like the traditional pragmatist story line, the ecomodernist argument evolved around a scientific core, yet with the opposite outcome: it argued that enough *is* known. Expert bodies such as the National Environment Research Council and the Nature Conservancy Council were invoked to legitimize the claim that decisions could and should be taken. The Select Committee also argued for direct symbolic action: Britain should join the 30 percent club immediately.

The ecomodernists also attacked the denial of responsibility on the part of the CEGB and the government. The Select Committee drew attention to the fact that the CEGB spends £1.5 million on the environmental effects of acid rain but just £200,000 on FGD-related research.[51] The effect of this intervention was a symmetric positioning: the CEGB portrayed the politicians of the Select Committee as unconstructive and irresponsible because they rush to conclusions and want to spend public money without first properly assessing the need and effectivity of the investment; the Select Committee viewed the CEGB as unconstructive and irresponsible because it does not actively search for solutions that would result in a delay or would force the British government to buy foreign technologies, while in the meantime the natural environment is further degraded.

Interestingly, the ecomodernists presented only part of the acid rain problem. For strategic reasons the Select Committee especially emphasized the fact that acid rain is responsible for damage to historic buildings: acid rain is "slowly but surely dissolving away our architectural heritage and modern buildings," it argued.[52] Later, emphasis was put on the effects of acid rain on British broadleaf trees. This conscious bias in the presentation of the acid rain issue aimed to appeal to the British public.

The Select Committee also chose a certain emphasis in apportioning the blame. It argued that nonnuclear power stations are responsible for most of the SO_2 and NOx emissions, and that action should therefore focus on that single source.[53] In its recommendation to install FGD equipment the Select Committee thus carefully left small industrial plants and car owners out of the issue.[54]

More insight into the ecomodernist discourse coalition can be derived from the contributions of a second key actor within this discourse coalition: the Royal Commission on Environmental Pollution. Its *Tenth Report* (1984) is a *tour de horizon* evaluating the main environmental issues. The report argues that the government must exercise a responsible stewardship to the environment, and maintains that pollution prevention pays. However, the commission's recommendations on acid rain policy do not, in fact, really match the ecomodernist tone of the *Tenth Report*. Although the commission asserted that enough is known about the damage due to acid rain and argued that FGD retrofits are the only short-term solution available, it failed to make the recommendations that would match its analysis. Its recommendations boil down to the statement that "high priority should be given to research on acid deposition, in particular on the causes and effects, on the interaction with other pollutants, and on remedial action." In addition it recommended that the CEGB should introduce, *on a pilot basis*, certain abatement options. For strategic reasons it also refrained from recommending that Britain join the 30 percent club.[55]

The third key actor operating within the ecomodernist frame was the Friends of the Earth. The FOE emphasized the extent to which acid rain threatens the British flora and fauna. Twice the FOE has organized a survey of tree health in Britain to prove that acid rain is not just a problem for far-away Scandinavia. The FOE argued strongly for an electricity conservation program that would reduce demand by 5 percent as an additional measure to the FGD retrofits. This should be based on the usage of more efficient appliances of various sorts. Later, this sort of prevention should replace scrubbing as a policy strategy. The FOE promoted this preventive strategy on the basis of the conviction that "it is likely to be more expensive to act later rather than sooner."[56] Like the Royal Commission, the FOE referred to *The Conservation and Development Programme for the UK* as a useful way of looking at environmental problems. The FOE was strongly in favor of joining the international initiative of the 30 percent club.

Ecological Modernization in Action: The Challenge Examined

At first the features of the acid rain controversy seem well defined. Could there be a bigger difference than that between the ecomodernists' call for immediate action and the extreme reluctance characteristic of the traditional pragmatists? Yet, if one reflects on the ecomodernist challenge, one is struck by the common ground between the two discourse coalitions. Both approaches conceptualized acid rain as a problem of sulfur dioxide (far less attention was paid to other possible causes such as nitrogen oxides, ammonia, or ozone); coal-fired power stations were seen as the cause of the problem (far less or no attention was paid to the possible contribution of traffic, agriculture, or industry); FGD was seen as the solution to the problem (other possible solutions, such as reducing electricity demand, using low-sulfur coal, replacing private traffic with public transport, reducing speed limits, and installing catalytic converters, received far less or no attention). Furthermore, both discourse coalitions employed utilitarian arguments: even the ecomodernists were committed to scientific arguments and were reluctant to use moral arguments.

This apparent agreement was to a large extent the result of a strategic choice. In the context of the acid rain controversy the ecomodernists consciously opted for the reformist approach, respecting the parameters of normal policy practice, trading a radical stance for a more respectable one, hoping to gain influence. But the course of affairs cannot be explained by reference to the strategic considerations of the ecomodernists alone. On the contrary, the outcome of the acid rain controversy in Britain should be understood as the result of the interplay of actors, discourse, and institutional practices. Indeed, the interaction of the two approaches to environmental policy was decisively influenced by the existing institutional arrangements. Political entrepreneurs who tried to make a case for a preventive acid rain policy found themselves not only arguing an intricate technical case but challenging key institutional practices of British pollution politics at the same time.

First, the buildup of support for action was hampered by the lack of available data on the effects of acid rain on the British countryside (as opposed to effects on far-away Scandinavia). Breaking the urban bias in the air pollution monitoring network was essential. The first reliable evidence of rainfall acidity in Britain was established by the Institute for Terrestrial Ecology (ITE), which established its own monitoring network in 1977. The ITE was, perhaps not surprisingly, among the first scientific bodies to claim that the levels of acid deposition warranted action.[57] Another important activity in this respect was the tree health surveys the Friends of the Earth conducted in 1985. The significance of both initiatives was not restricted to the realization that acid rain might affect the beloved British countryside. It also brought to light the intimation that the picture of Britain's "proud record" in air pollution control might be false. Institutes such as the Forestry Commission were portrayed as irresponsible actors, and they reacted by portraying the Friends of the Earth as irrational scaremongers.

Second, actors operating within the coalition of ecological modernization had difficulty finding the right approach to the mobilization of bias contained in the science-based policy approach. In March 1984 the prestigious Royal Commission on Environmental Pollution published its *Tenth Report*. Although this was an ecological modernist critique of the traditional pragmatist discourse, it failed to argue for immediate action on acid rain because of the power of the science-based approach and the social status of the SWAP project in particular. The Royal Commission realized it was pointless to speak out on the acid rain issue before at least some results from SWAP were known.[58] The appraisal was not inaccurate: many other quasi-governmental agencies found that their recommendations were overruled because the Royal Society had not yet given its opinion. Furthermore, the science-based approach prevented the Royal Commission from arguing in favor of joining the 30 percent club. The 30 percent figure had been identified by many British institutions as purely arbitrary (which it was, of course), and the Royal Commission wanted to be seen as committed to the science-based approach. Speaking out in favor of something symbolic and political in nature might harm its reputation.

Third, the role of the inspectorate in operating the BPM practice also hampered the application of ecomodernist principles. In the first place, BPM was understood as the best practicable *available* means. The industry was under no obligation to develop new technologies. BPM thus failed to stimulate the invention and implementation of new pollution abatement equipment. "Economic incapacity" was a legitimate reason for inaction, which made BPM both dependent on the business cycle and vulnerable to biased presentations of costs and economic capacity of firms. Moreover, even though the inspectorate had to judge the economic capabilities of firms, it employed neither economists nor accountants.[59]

However, although best practicable means is often seen as an impediment to the process of ecological modernization, it can, in fact, be a contributor. What is more, there is evidence that quite early on, in 1982, the inspectorate itself thought that if new power stations were to be built, FGD equipment should probably be considered, even though the inspectorate did not admit to the existence of acid rain.[60] Here the inspectorate was swimming with the tide of ecological modernization. In the actual controversy, however, the inspectorate kept a low profile and did not take the initiative to prevent pollution, anticipating that it would be politically unacceptable. Again, in the concrete case of acid rain the anticipated reaction helped to sustain the ad hoc technocratic approach to pollution politics at a moment when most actors acknowledged that it should be reconsidered.

Conclusion: The Paradox of Ecological Modernization

The British acid rain controversy was the first major test case for the newly emerged ecomodernist discourse coalition. Could the new rhetoric be put to work? The intricate nature of the issue (only partly understood by experts), the possibility of extensive environmental decline, and the widespread concern among the public made acid rain an ideal issue to show that the old ad hoc technocratic discourse coalition was not qualified to cope with the new environmental problems and was therefore no longer a legitimate basis for policy-making. Acid rain appeared to be, to use the words of philosopher of science Jerome Ravetz, a typical case that called for hard decisions made by politicians having at their disposal merely "soft" or potentially controversial, scientific evidence.[61]

A discourse coalition becomes dominant if (1) the central actors are persuaded by, or are forced to accept, the rhetorical power of a new story line (discourse structuration); and (2) this is reflected in the organizational practices of a given domain (discourse institutionalization). In the British debate on the environmental question in the 1980s, the traditional pragmatist discourse coalition seemed to be making way for a new, ecomodernist discourse. Politicians at the highest level paid lip service to ecological modernization. However, the case study on the acid rain controversy illuminates the fact that the actual decision-making process was still conducted according to the format of the traditional pragmatist discourse coalition.

Earlier I distinguished five key elements of the challenge of ecological modernization in Britain: nature should no longer be regarded as a "sink," pollution prevention pays, unambiguous scientific proof should no longer be regarded as a *sine qua non*, public perceptions of risk should no longer be refuted as irrational, and substances should more often be regarded as guilty until proven innocent. Official government publications recognized the credibility of these claims. Good reasons might be given for this apparent success: the concepts formed a suitable reply to the spreading public concern over the environment; the ecomodernist concepts constituted a coherent and reasonable perspective which did not threaten the basic social order; and, last but not least, prevention of pollution appeared to make economic sense.

However, the analysis of the content of the controversy over acid rain illustrates that the controversy (1) focused on the *damage* caused by acid rain, which suggests that emissions as such were still regarded as legitimate; (2) emphasized the costs involved in avoiding pollution; (3) showed that only unambiguous scientific proof could persuade the British government to install FGD equipment; (4) showed that the public perceptions of the problem were not allowed to have an immediate impact; and (5) indicated that until SO_2 was proven guilty it was regarded as innocent. So, when put to the test, the ecomodernist discourse coalition failed both to impose its story line on the actual acid rain debate and to illuminate the anachronistic nature of the existing institutional arrangements. What is more, as the ecomodernists failed to convey the wider meaning of their discourse and exchanged the abstractness of the environmental problem at large for the concreteness of a solution for the acid rain problem, the wider meaning of their challenge was lost. In the end the ecomodernists and the ad hoc technocrats argued the same case: both were committed to FGD equipment as a solution. How is this paradox to be explained?

The first element of the explanation concerns the strategic action that was involved in the social construction of the acid rain problem. The acid rain controversy not only reflected the difference between the traditional pragmatist discourse and the challenging discourse of ecological modernization, it also showed a broad agreement among actors of both discourse coalitions to confine the acid rain problem within narrow boundaries. This was partly based on strategic deliberations. All the actors consciously tried to follow the prevailing definition of the problem. It was thus conceptualized as an SO_2-related problem, with the CEGB as the main culprit and FGD scrubbers the obvious solution. Albeit for well-considered strategic reasons, the ecomodernists failed to put the acid rain issue into the context of the structural failure of industrial society to address environmental degradation on a large scale. Ecological modernization would, above all, call for energy conservation. However, when put to the test, ecomodernists fell for the immediacy and the symbolic appeal of scrubbers and delegated the more fundamental solution to second place.

Moreover, ecomodernists could have taken a more offensive approach by arguing that unambiguous scientific proof should not be seen as an essential precondition for policy-making, and that, in face of the implied risks, prudence was just as valid a basis for decision making as knowledge. The realization that air pollutants acted in combination gave extra weight to this claim. Instead, ecomodernists tried to beat the traditional pragmatists at their own game by employing utilitarian and scientific arguments. The reason for this apparent failure is that all the actors tried to show they were "the right kind of people." The Friends of the Earth did not want to be portrayed as dreamers, the Royal Commission did not want to lose its image of respectability and thoughtfulness in a confrontation with the Royal Society, and the Select Committee wished to prove that it kept its distance from interest-based politics and that its arguments were based on "proper" science. However, in so doing the ecomodernists conformed to the old standards of credibility and failed to introduce the new concepts, even though these arguments were already being employed by government officials in the parallel debate on the abstract principles of environmental policy-making at that time. Furthermore, new standards, such as precaution, had also already been accepted in the international forums, for instance in the EC Environment Action Programs.

The second element that explains the convergence of the ecomodernists and the traditional pragmatists is the institutional context of the three practices in which this behavior is to be understood. These practices—the urban-health bias and urban monitoring system, the politics of consultation and best practicable means, and the science-based policy approach—reflected the institutionalized patterns of domination of the past. In the acid rain controversy these practices were a medium through which power was exercised. The practices of the traditional pragmatist discourse coalition dominated the actual experience of pollution politics: actors who chose to play by the rules had the inherent discursive logic imposed upon them. Both the science-based policy approach and best practicable means were designed to depoliticize pollution control, and the urban-health bias in monitoring reflected long-standing political priorities. Although each worked in a different discursive realm and had its own institutional logic, they shared a discursive affinity in promoting a pragmatic approach to environmental problems. This engendered a discursive bias that militated against an anticipatory response to the acid rain problem, which would have been characteristic of an ecomodernist approach.

In this context the role of the actors who occupied these positions and "operated" these practices is especially significant. They successfully tried to accommodate the challenging rhetorical principles without giving up the institutional commitments of their positions. The practical solutions, some of the labels, and many of the ecomodernist formulations were taken over while the traditional pragmatist practice continued. Acid rain simply was not recognized as an anomaly to this discourse: decision makers still approached acid rain as essentially an administrative issue to which, for instance, the rules of the reductionist science-based policy discourse applied. Normative arguments and politics were kept out of the decision making. The actors' arguments do not indicate any fundamental change from an ad hoc reactive strategy toward an offensive precautionary approach.

A third element can be derived from the strength of the symbolic order that was reproduced by the ad hoc technocratic discourse coalition. In the argumentative game the policy practices formed an essential reference. The normative appeal of the long-standing practices, with their proud record of success, made it difficult to argue for change. In many cases the traditional pragmatists sought to legitimize their inaction by *reifying* their discourse coalition: they presented the pragmatic practice as a permanent, natural state of affairs. These references to past success suggested that the traditional pragmatist way of dealing with pollution problems was not a historically specific, transitory state of affairs that, if circumstances changed, might have to make way for another approach. Furthermore, the discussion of the science-based policy approach illuminated the ideological strength of reductionist epistemology and the symbolic significance of the Royal Society. This was so well embedded that actors such as the Royal Commission refrained from calling for immediate action, in anticipation of a certain rebuff.

Moreover, the fact that FGD equipment was finally installed also illustrates the symbolic nature of politics. Placing scrubbers on a chimney was a clear act which could be interpreted as a sign of success by both coalitions. The critics could point to change,[62] and traditional pragmatists could claim that the legitimacy of their discourse still held.[63] Moreover, it accorded with the popular perception of the problem and avoided a direct conflict with the larger part of the community. The small rise in electricity prices was assumed to be more acceptable than interference with the symbol of liberty: the freedom to drive one's car.

A fourth element in the explanation comes from a reflection on the position of environmental politics in the overall order of governmental activity. First, ecological modernization would, if put into practice, affect the institutional practices of more than just the Department of the Environment. It would affect the Departments of Industry, Transport,

Agriculture, and, above all, Energy. All the actors knew from the very beginning that the introduction of a new discourse would succeed only if it was supported at the highest level, that is, by the prime minister. Although government ministers might have appreciated the value of the *idea* of ecological modernization, they would certainly resist the institutional repercussions; that is, the repositioning of their departments according to this discourse. In this respect acid rain was the first test case for the ecomodernist policy discourse. Clearly, the prime minister's support was not available at the time. Second, the acceptance of ecological modernization would not only jeopardize the institutional autonomy of many departments, it would also imply a major reorientation in the overall ordering of government priorities. Environmental politics in Britain, as, indeed, in most other countries, has always been subordinate to general industrial and economic politics.

In the post–World War II period the traditional pragmatist discourse in environmental politics worked in the context of Keynesian welfare state politics. The Keynesian hard-core values concerned the management of a "positive sum" growth-oriented economy based on a social contract between capital and labor with all kinds of welfare policies in a supportive role. With the coming of the neoliberalist era under Prime Minister Margaret Thatcher in 1979, environmental politics was even more unlikely to shake off its ad hoc status. Thatcher's priority was the restructuring and restoration of British industry's competitiveness. Ecological modernization assumed that the environmental dimension would be taken into consideration in this restructuring, but the Thatcher government preferred a policy of noninterference with regard to imposing ecologically sound innovations on industry. Subsidies, if given at all, came with no strings attached; and neither large public expenditure on FGD equipment nor the higher prices in electricity that would result from it were in accordance with the core policies of Thatcherism.

The net effect of this course of affairs was the reproduction of the predominant "single problem–single answer" construction of environmental problems. The acid rain controversy was resolved by implementing another end-of-pipe solution. However, although the case study of acid rain does not produce evidence to suggest that ecological modernization has a firm grip on pollution politics in Britain, it is too early to suggest that the practices of ecological modernization will never become institutionalized. It might well be that concepts like the precautionary principle, which was accepted by the British government at the 1987 North Sea Conference, will prove to be a Trojan horse. After all, various actors, including the European Community, will protest if Britain fails to comply to the new principle, and the European Court at Strasbourg could force Britain to comply. In that respect ecological modernization is a story with an open end.

Notes

1. *Acid Rain* is in fact a rather imprecise label. It is more appropriate to speak of *acid deposition* if one is referring to the biological phenomenon. In this essay I use *acid rain* to refer to the political problem, which, as I will show, addresses only a part of the problem of acid deposition.

2. For the British case see S. Boehmer-Christiansen, "Black Mist and the Acid Rain: Science as a Figleaf of Policy," *Political Quarterly* 59, no. 2 (1988): 145–60; Boehmer-Christiansen and J. Skea, *Acid Politics: Environmental and Energy Politics in Britain and Germany* (London and New York: Belhaven Press, 1991); C. C. Park, *Acid Rain: Rhetoric and Reality* (London: Methuen, 1987); as well as the more popular N. Dudley et al., *The Acid Rain Controversy* (London: Earth Resources Research, 1985); F. Pearce, *Acid Rain* (Harmondsworth: Penguin, 1987); S. Elsworth, *Acid Rain* (London: Pluto Press, 1984).

3. The most authoritative statement of the sustainable development approach is undoubtedly the report *Our Common Future*, by the Brundtland Commission of the United Nations (Oxford: Oxford University Press, 1987). For a critical analysis of the concept of sustainable development, cf. M. A. Hajer, "The Politics of Environmental Performance Review: Choices in Design," in E. Lykke, ed., *Achieving Environmental Goals: The Concept and Practice of Environmental Performance Review* (London: Belhaven, 1992).

4. In political analysis the concept of bias should be interpreted more as a predisposition and not so much as a distortion. The latter meaning would logically assume an undistorted position, which, in politics, does not exist.

5. The origin of much social constructivism lies in the work of Peter L. Berger and Thomas Luckmann; see, e.g., Berger and Luckmann, *The Social Construction of Reality* (Harmondsworth: Penguin, 1971).

6. See, for instance, J. Gusfield, *The Culture of Public Problems: Drinking-driving and the Social Order* (Chicago: University of Chicago Press, 1981).

7. Cf. R. J. Bernstein, *The Restructuring of Social and Political Theory* (Oxford: Basil Blackwell, 1976); F. Fischer, *Politics, Values, and Public Policy: The Problem of Methodology* (Boulder: Westview Press, 1980).

8. Cf. P. Bachrach and M. S. Baratz, *Power and Poverty: Theory and Practice* (New York: Oxford University Press, 1970).

9. In many cases, however, the discovery of discourse as an object of study led to the study of politics as the interaction of quasi-autonomous language games disconnected from the social practices in which they emerge; see, for instance,

E. Laclau and C. Mouffe, *Hegemony and Socialist Strategy* (London: Verso, 1985). For a critique, J. B. Thompson, "Language and Ideology: A Framework for Analysis," *Sociological Review* 35, no. 3 (1987): 516–36; B. Jessop, *State Theory—Putting Capitalist States in Their Place* (Cambridge: Polity Press, 1990), chap. 10. For an excellent analysis of pragmatic linguistic constructions in politics, see G. Lakoff and M. Johnson, *Metaphors We Live By* (Chicago: University of Chicago Press, 1980).

10. M. Billig, *Arguing and Thinking: A Rhetorical Approach to Social Psychology* (Cambridge: Cambridge University Press, 1987), 91.

11. The concept of discourse coalition was introduced by Peter Wagner and Bjorn Wittrock in their study of the influence of social science discourse on politics, but I use it here in a somewhat different sense. See Wagner and Wittrock, *Transformations in the Societal Position of the Social Sciences: Epistemic Drift or Discourse Structuration?* (Berlin: Wissenschafts Zentrum Berlin, 1989); P. Wagner, "Social Sciences and Political Projects: Reform Coalitions Between Social Scientists and Policy-makers in France, Italy, and West Germany," *Sociology of the Sciences Yearbook* 11 (1987): 277–306. My own contribution to the development of the concept has its origin in neo-Marxist theory of the state; see M. A. Hajer, *City Politics: Hegemonic Projects and Discourse* (Aldershot and Brookfield, Ill.: Avebury, 1989).

12. This is a temporary definition meant to build up the argument. Later in this section I will present a more complex one.

13. An obvious example of a successful discourse is Keynesianism. In the postwar period it dominated the way developments in society were conceptualized (discourse structuration) and materialized in the various institutions of the social welfare state (discourse institutionalization).

14. The disciplinary division in academia is a good example of discourse formation producing economists, physicists, or lawyers. Yet it can also be argued that academia uses one single discourse characterized by reason. The question is, of course, at which level one, given one's specific object of study, can usefully distinguish discourse or generate differences.

15. See M. A. Hajer, "The Discursive Paradox of the New Environmentalism," *Industrial Crisis Quarterly* 4, no. 4 (1990): 307–10.

16. See E. Ashby and M. Anderson, *The Politics of Clean Air* (Oxford: Clarendon Press, 1981).

17. Lord Derby, quoted in ibid., 21.

18. E. F. Schumacher, *Small Is Beautiful* (London: Abacus, 1974). Another protagonist of this modernization element in the environmental movement was Amory Lovins with his concept of "soft energy paths." For a detailed discussion see R. Paehlke, *Environmentalism and the Future of Progressive Politics* (New Haven: Yale University Press, 1989).

19. Anonymous, *The World Conservation Strategy—Living Resource Conser-*

vation for Sustainable Development (Geneva: International Union for the Conservation of Nature and Natural Resources, 1980); anonymous, *The Conservation and Development Programme for the UK: A Response to the World Conservation Strategy* (London: Kogan Page, 1983); Royal Commission on Environmental Pollution, *Tenth Report, Tackling Pollution—Experience and Prospects* (London: HMSO, 1984). The most influential international statement in this tradition is undoubtedly the United Nations report *Our Common Future* (Oxford: Oxford University Press, 1987). One of the best collections of essays on the subject of ecological modernization (in German and English) is probably U. E. Simonis, ed., *Präventive Umweltpolitik* (Frankfurt: Campus, 1988).

20. Royal Commission, *Tenth Report*, 179.

21. Quoted in ibid., 178.

22. W. Waldegrave, "Economic Development and Environmental Care—The Role of Government," in *Environmentalism Today—The Challenge for Business* (Proceedings of a conference organized by the United Kingdom Centre for Economic and Environmental Development and by National Economic Research Associates, April 1986).

23. Great Britain, Department of Environment (hereinafter DOE), *Our Common Future—A Perspective by the United Kingdom on the Report of the World Commission on Environment and Development* (London: DOE, 1968).

24. The best accounts of the history of acid rain are B. E. Cowling, "Acid Precipitation in Historical Perspective," *Environmental Science and Technology* 16, no. 2 (1982): 110A–123A; and G. S. Wedstone, "A History of the Acid Rain Issue," in H. Brooks and C. L. Cooper, eds., *Science for Public Policy* (Oxford: Pergamon Press, 1987).

25. M. Ducros, "Observation d'une plui acide," *Journal de Pharmacie et de Chimie* 3 (1845): 273–77. He concluded that rain contained nitric acid but regarded the source as natural. For this reference I am indebted to Peter Brimblecombe.

26. R. A. Smith, "On the Air and Rain of Manchester," in *Memoirs and Proceedings of the Manchester Literary and Philosophical Society*, series 2, no. 10 (1852): 207–17; he elaborated on the subject in R. A. Smith, *Air and Rain: The Beginning of a Chemical Climatology* (London: Longmans Green, 1872). Smith was the first to suggest that the symptoms of decay in vegetation, materials, and buildings in Manchester were caused by acid precipitation.

27. As it happened, this immediately followed the publication of a paper on rainfall acidity in northern Britain in *Nature* which revealed that the acidity of rain there was comparable with the areas of Scandinavia and North America where fish populations had been depleted. See D. Fowler et al., "Rainfall Acidity in Northern Britain," *Nature* 297 (1982): 383–86.

28. L. Kramme, "National and International Pressures in Environmental Policy Override Neo-Classical Prescriptions: The Case of the EC's Large Combustion

Plant Directive" (Paper presented at the European Consortium for Political Research Joint Sessions, Paris, 1989).

29. Because of differing geographical, economic, and fuel supply circumstances some countries were allowed different percentages. Britain, as a large coal-burning country, would have to reduce its emissions only by 20, 40, and 60 percent (by 1993, 1998, and 2003, respectively), as opposed to West Germany and the Netherlands, for instance, which were committed to a 30, 60, and 70 percent reduction by the same dates.

30. The discrepancy was bigger than immediately meets the eye since at that time it was believed that this percentage would be achieved by the then apparent tendency of SO_2 emissions to fall.

31. There is only a marginal role for a third, more radical and ethically inspired, ecological discourse in Britain. This is therefore left undiscussed.

32. Lord Marshall, *New Scientist*, September 25, 1986, 23.

33. Quotation from Lord Marshall, in House of Commons Select Committee on the Environment, *Fourth Report: Acid Rain*, vol. 2, *Minutes of Evidence* (London: HMSO, 1984), 20.

34. Lord Marshall, in ibid., 36.

35. DOE at the Ministerial Conference on Acid Rain held in Munich, June 1984.

36. DOE, *Government Reply to the Fourth Report of the Environment Select Committee* (London: HMSO, 1984), 3.

37. This was first officially acknowledged in a statement by L. E. Reed at the presentation of the DOE report "Effects of Airborne Sulphur Compounds on Forests and Freshwaters," *Pollution Paper* no. 7 (London: HMSO, 1976), before the 1976 Telemark conference (Norway).

38. DOE, "The United Kingdom Environment 1979: Progress of Pollution Control," *Pollution Paper* no. 16 (1979): 3.

39. Select Committee, *Fourth Report*, vol. 2, *Minutes of Evidence*, 18.

40. See, for instance, T. O'Riordan, "Culture and the Environment in Britain," *Environmental Management* 9, no. 2 (1985): 113–20.

41. Speech to closing session of the Munich Conference on Acid Rain, 27 June 1984.

42. DOE, "Environmental Standards: A Description of United Kingdom Practice," *Pollution Paper* no. 11 (1977): 7–8.

43. On the relationship of risk and trust, see A. Giddens, *The Consequences of Modernity* (Cambridge: Polity Press, 1990).

44. Quoted in Park, *Acid Rain*, 222.

45. National Environment Research Council, in Select Committee, *Fourth Report*, vol. 2, *Minutes of Evidence*, 228. This view was confirmed in many interviews that I conducted with scientists who had been involved in acid rain-related research.

46. The best account of the early years of the Alkali Inspectorate is undoubtedly R. M. MacLeod, "The Alkali Acts Administration, 1863–84: The Emergence of the Civil Scientist," *Victorian Studies* 9, no. 2 (1965): 85–112. For a good case study on recent abatement practice see K. Hawkins, *Environment and Enforcement: Regulation and the Social Definition of Pollution* (Oxford: Oxford University Press, 1984).

47. Quoted in the Royal Commission's *Tenth Report*, 45.

48. DOE, "Controlling Pollution: Principles and Prospects—The Government's Reply to the Tenth Report of the Royal Commission on Environmental Pollution," *Pollution Paper* no. 22 (1984): 2.

49. Select Committee, *Fourth Report*, 1; Royal Commission, *Tenth Report*, 147; evidence given by Friends of the Earth, in Select Committee, *Fourth Report*, vol. 2, *Minutes of Evidence*, 39.

50. Royal Commission, *Tenth Report*, 144; Friends of the Earth, in Select Committee, *Fourth Report*, vol. 2, *Minutes of Evidence*, 37, 40; Select Committee, *Fourth Report*, xi, xiii.

51. Select Committee, *Fourth Report*, lviii.

52. Ibid., xx.

53. Ibid., lii.

54. Ibid., lxvi.

55. Royal Commission, *Tenth Report*, 147. Subsequently the CEGB rightly argued that it was making the research effort that the Royal Commission had suggested (*Minutes of Evidence*, 6). The recommendations were also criticized in a joint statement by Nordic ministers of the environment (Statement to the British Ambassador in Stockholm, March 1, 1984), who described the recommendations of the *Tenth Report* as a "serious setback." The commission's apparent failure to apply its own criteria is explained in the discussion below.

56. Select Committee, *Fourth Report*, vol. 2, *Minutes of Evidence*, 8, 42, 51.

57. Cf. Fowler et al., "Rainfall Acidity in Northern Britain." The bias in the monitoring network was corrected in 1984 following recommendations by the Royal Commission and the House of Commons Select Committee.

58. This was even less surprising because the chairman of the commission at that time, Professor Sir Richard Southwood, was also chairing the SWAP project.

59. Cf. David Vogel, *National Styles of Regulation: Environmental Policy in Great Britain and the United States* (Ithaca: Cornell University Press, 1986), 80, 83.

60. Evidence presented by L. E. Reed, then chief inspector, in House of Lords Select Committee on the European Communities, *Sixteenth Report* (London: HMSO, 1982), 40, 41.

61. J. R. Ravetz, "Usable Knowledge, Usable Ignorance; Incomplete Science

with Policy Implications," in W. Clark and R. Munn, eds., *Sustainable Development of the Biosphere* (Cambridge: Cambridge University Press, 1986).

62. As indeed they did; see House of Commons Select Committee on the European Communities, *First Report: Air Pollution,* 2 vols. (London: HMSO, 1988).

63. As indeed they did; see DOE evidence to Select Committee, 1988.

Political Judgment and the

Policy Cycle: The Case of Ethnicity Policy

Arguments in the Netherlands

Robert Hoppe

The Politics of Meaning and Policy Analysis

Anticipating the linguistic and constructivist turns in the social sciences, Bertrand de Jouvenel formulated his first axiom of *The Pure Theory of Politics* (1963:99) as follows: "The working of words upon action is the basic political action." Pursuing this theme, other authors have developed a theory of the politics of meaning in which politics is viewed as an attempt to control a community's collective response to the adversities and opportunities of the human condition. Defined as an attempt to control shared meaning, politics thus becomes an arena for conflict over the concepts used in framing political judgments on social problems, public policies, and political leaders and enemies (Unger 1987:10; Edelman 1988). In the case of democracies, this conflict is managed by a public debate on and a negotiated definition of shared meanings (Sederberg 1984:5–11). Policy-making becomes the capacity to define the nature of shared meaning (Sederberg 1984:67); it is a never-ending series of communications and strategic moves by which various policy actors in loosely coupled forums of public deliberation construct intersubjective meanings. These meanings are continually translated into collective projects, plans, actions, and artifacts, which become the issues in the next cycle of political judgment and meaning constructions, and so on.

From this perspective, policy analysts and planning theorists have questioned the instrumental or technocratic conception of public policy analysis (Van Gunsteren 1976; Torgerson 1985; Forester 1989; Majone 1989; Fischer 1990b). Rejecting the role of the policy analyst as an adjudicator of the best means to a given end, these authors have begun asking questions such as the following: What can analysis contribute to political judgment through the process of public and democratic deliberation? Rather than stifling it, can planning actually improve the quality of public discourse? Can policy analysts as public officials enhance public deliberation as well as learning about the public interest?

In this essay I address these questions by conceptualizing the practice of policy analysis and planning as *the production of political judgments*. My main thesis is that it is the whole process of arriving at political judgments that matters to the policy analyst, not just policy analysis per se or the logic of political judgment. Policy analysts don't just *analyze* issues and give counsel to direct clients or superiors. Their work affects the entire *policy process*, willy-nilly.

Policy Analysis and the Logic of Political Judgment

If politics is an attempt to control shared meaning, then policy-making can be viewed as political philosophy in action (Hodgkinson 1978:3), and thus policy analysis as applied political philosophy (Anderson 1987:22). In this section I will elaborate on the notion of policy analysis as a logic of political judgment. First, I describe, phenomenologically, a policy analyst's workaday world. Thereafter I introduce the concept of political judgment and explain the relationship between political judgment and policy belief systems.

The Policy Analyst's Workaday World

Ask a policy analyst about the nature of his or her job, and you will surely hear that it mostly consists of talking to and writing for other policy professionals and policymakers. Anyone practicing policy analysis in the real world of politics and public administration lives in the middle of a cacophony of opinions, beliefs, positions, convictions, rules, and claims. In a political scene constituted around well-established policy issues, the policy analyst is riding an argumentation carousel that existed long before and will exist long after he or she climbed aboard.

The metaphor of an "argumentation carousel" is meant to reflect the policy analyst's workday world, coming to grips with a whirlpool of arguments. Starting from vague and ambiguous preconceptions, the analyst initially gathers all kinds of arguments in a happy-go-lucky fashion. Every shred of argumentation, however tentative, seems important enough to merit attention. But competing claims require the force of well-rounded arguments. In debating issues, the policy analyst evokes arguments and counterarguments. Other policy professionals and policymakers respond in discussions, consultations, negotiations, deliberations, and public hearings. Of course, they do so from their own positions and perspectives and with their own interests and agendas in mind. In other words, the argumentation carousel is made up of hobbyhorses laden with pet interests. It is precisely this which contributes to the erratic course and quality of the argumentation process called policymaking.

But, gradually, as the analyst juggles and puzzles through the arguments this way and that, the fuzzy preconceptions give way to clearer conceptions of policy. A more or less coherent piece of policy discourse thus takes shape by way of argument and counterargument. Usually the process culminates in a hectic period of drafting and redrafting before the policy document is presented to the client or some decision-making body. While writing the text, the policy analyst may temporarily entertain the illusion of being in control of the argumentation carousel. Indeed, high-quality policy documents may actually succeed in halting the argumentation process. The force of the analyst's arguments may have been so compelling as to define the terms for further debate. Or, alternatively, everybody is so satisfied with the delicate formulation of tricky issues that further debate is postponed indefinitely. But there will be more public debate sooner or later, and, while preparing the final draft of the policy document, the analyst is usually fighting a losing battle against time. More often than not public debate is off on another track before the rewriting is finished. The argumentative merry-go-round whirls on.

Political Judgment and Policy Belief Systems

If this alternation between argumentation and writing is accepted as a phenomenologically plausible reconstruction of the policy analyst's everyday experience, it follows that analysts are constantly concerned with political judgment. I think it appropriate, therefore, to start with some basics and briefly review the formal properties of policy analysis that characterize its practice as *the production of political judgments.*

What counts as a well-reasoned argument supporting a policy decision is largely a matter of sound political judgment. All judgment is a mental operation in which particulars are subsumed under one or more relevant universal(s). Immanuel Kant distinguished between two kinds of judgment: in *determinant* judgment, the universal (law, principle, general rule) is given in advance of the subsumption; judgment is *reflective*, however, if only the particulars are given in advance and the relevant universal(s) must somehow be found or constructed from the particulars (Vollrath 1977:14; Beiner 1983:34).

Political judgment is rarely determining. It's hardly ever just a question of applying a rock-solid principle to a particular case and in turn knowing under which general principle the particular is to be subsumed. In fact, the concepts through which we express political values, principles, and ideas are essentially disputed. Ronald Beiner calls their epistemological status expressive rather than objective, appellate rather than logical (Beiner 1983:146): "They provide a 'reservoir of appeal,' or a pool of criteria from which we draw justification for our judgments, although the ultimate responsibility for application to a given set of particulars rests with the subject who judges." Considering the finiteness and fallibility of the human being who is called on to judge political matters, it's little wonder that valid universals are nonexistent in political judgment (Dauenhauer 1986).

Of course, not all reflective judgment is political. Whether a reflective judgment is, for example, aesthetic or political is determined by the adjudicator's range of responsibilities. There is a hierarchy of moral accountability, with political judgment at its apex. Hannah Arendt (1977:241) expresses this idea by calling political judgment "circumambulatory" or "representative." Frank Fischer (1980:206) aptly captures the same idea: "The validity of a political argument is determined by its ability to withstand *the widest possible range of objections and criticisms* in an open, clear and candid exchange between the relevant participants."

One of the tools a practicing policy analyst utilizes to find his or her bearings in the maze of claims and counterclaims on the argumentation carousel is a map, or rather a "compass," of comprehensive political judgment. Using such a compass, the analyst can systematically lay out the type and persuasion of the arguments being used. She or he also can judge the completeness of both her own and her adversaries' reasoning vis-à-vis a given policy course. The most promising effort to provide the policy analyst with this kind of tool that I am aware of is Fischer's four-level model of political policy evaluation (Fischer 1980:205–14). Here I discuss the four levels as representing a comprehensive, well-reasoned policy belief system (Van de Graaf and Hoppe 1989:74; Hoppe et al. 1990).

A policy belief or appreciative system is a systematic "reservoir of appeal" for political judgment; it can be defined as the cluster of normative and causal assumptions adhered to by policymakers (Majone 1989; Sabatier 1987; Vickers 1968). Ideally, a policy belief covers all the stock issues that can be raised in public policy debate in an attempt to exhaustively justify some policy alternative (Edwards 1990).

Fischer's compass for comprehensive political judgment distinguishes between first-order and second-order policy discourse. In first-order discourse, the arguments revolve around the decision makers' given normative beliefs about a single policy program or project. At the level of *technical verification*, the arguments concern questions about meeting goals and using resources efficiently. At the level of *situational validation*, the arguments address the appropriateness of program goals, in view of both the decision makers' broader value orientations and their perception of opportunities and constraints in the decision-making situation.

In second-order policy discourse, arguments transcend the boundaries initially set by decision makers' normative beliefs. At the level of *systemic vindication*, policymakers' value systems are examined to determine their contribution to the dominant social order. At the level of *rational social choice*, dominant societal value systems and the social order are compared with alternatives in ways akin, for instance, to John Rawls's "original position" or Jürgen Habermas's "ideal speech situation."

Policy Cycles as Processes of Political Judgment

Comprehensive political judgment, then, is a type of reflective judgment in which the adjudicator's responsibility, in principle, extends all the way from technical verification particulars to Olympian abstractions of rational social choice. Constitutionally speaking, this impossible task is the unalienable right and duty of every citizen. In practice it has been subjected to a division of labor, knowledge specialization, and role differentiation. In reality, comprehensive political judgment is therefore a process of public deliberation, which develops sequentially and simultaneously on different levels of judgment and in separate but loosely coupled political forums among myriad policy actors. It is necessary, then, to examine the concept of policy cycles in terms of the realization or nonrealization of certain types of political judgments.

Political Judgment and the Policy Cycle

The notion of public deliberations as sequentially differentiated processes finds scholarly expression in policy cycle models (e.g., May and Wildavsky 1978). In these models *policy cycle* is defined as a dynamic and interdependent set of actions concerning ideology formation, agenda setting, and policy design/adoption, implementation, and evaluation. Each subprocess in the cycle reflects a particular level (or combination of levels) of political judgment. Laurence Lynn (1981:146–49) thus distinguishes between the policy cycle's high, middle, and low games.

The *high game* consists of interaction between ideology formation and agenda setting. This is the domain of political party elites, political think tanks, prestigious political commentators and ideologues, and some top-notch public managers. They debate issues on the levels of rational choice and systemic vindication. The *middle game* consists of interaction between policy design/adoption and (the initial stages of) policy implementation. Its players are the legislature, the upper and middle levels of the executive branch, interest groups, lobbies, journalists, and spokesmen of various social and political movements. Plenty of professional policy analysts make their living at the middle game. In terms of levels of political judgment, debate focuses on the borderlines and interdependencies between systemic vindication and situational validation—occasionally ascending to rational choice, but more frequently descending to technical verification. The *low game* is a continuous interaction between policy implementation and evaluation processes that results in the termination, adjustment, or maintenance of programs. Middle- and lower-level members of the executive branch, with its scores of professionals, technicians, and experts, make up this arena. The courts are also involved, because they arbitrate the many controversies over concrete policy decisions and actions brought to court by affected citizens, companies, trade union representatives, consumer organizations, and so on. Their debates focus on the interface between technical verification and situational validation. Figure 1 shows a conceptual map which projects the levels of political judgment and policy games into the policy cycle's five subprocesses.

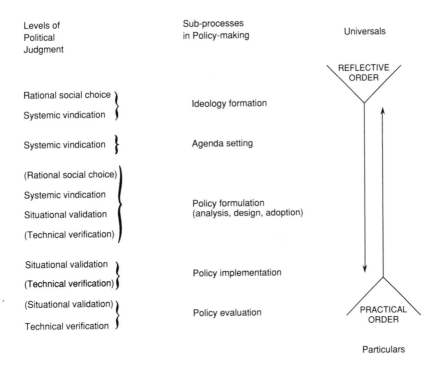

Levels of Political Judgment	Sub-processes in Policy-making	Universals

Rational social choice }
Systemic vindication }
    Ideology formation

Systemic vindication }
    Agenda setting

(Rational social choice)
Systemic vindication
Situational validation
(Technical verification)
    Policy formulation (analysis, design, adoption)

Situational validation }
(Technical verification) }
    Policy implementation

(Situational validation) }
Technical verification }
    Policy evaluation

REFLECTIVE ORDER

PRACTICAL ORDER

Particulars

Figure 1. Political Judgment in the Policy Process

Disorders in Public Debate and the Policy Cycle

Apart from capturing the gist of the argument thus far, the purpose of figure 1 is to distinguish between reflective and practical modes of policy-making. At the beginning of this essay politics and policy-making were viewed as the democratic control of collective response to the human condition. Debating and negotiating the definition of shared criteria to interpret reality are the means by which politics and policy-making are constructed. These criteria are internalized in political ideologies and policy belief systems at the same time that they are externalized in political projects, actions, and implements.

As internalized criteria are applied to reality, normative ambiguity and factual uncertainty arise. The process of social and political *reality construction*, where the aim is to cope with the twin problems of reducing ambiguity and uncertainty, may proceed in one of two ways. In the *reflective mode*, ambiguity or uncertainty is reduced by arguing on the levels of rational social choice and systemic vindication. These arguments are constructed in the processes of ideology formation and agenda building. In the *practical mode*, ambiguity or uncertainty is reduced by applying arguments that center on situational validation and technical verification. These are generated in processes of policy evaluation and implementation.

It is necessary to distinguish between reflective and practical modes of policy-making because, within policy science, the concept of a policy cycle is blind to the possibility of disintegration. The concept may even be misleading, for it suggests that postmodern, technologically advanced polyarchies, when subjected to extreme forms of policy discourse specialization, if not fragmentation, routinely (Lindblom 1965) achieve "a genuine articulation of the two-sided demand of political judgment—neither abstracting from the existing realities with which political man must contend, nor failing to distance [it]self from merely contingent institutional and existential givens" (Beiner 1983:150).

The wholeness and continuity implied in the concept of a policy cycle represent a telling example of the policy sciences' tendency to let logic drive the reality out of policy discourse. After all, the idea of comprehensive judgment, brought about step by step in a "rational" policy cycle, may be nothing but an artifact produced by the scholarly use of metaphors like *cycle* or *servomechanism*. But in reality we observe only spatially and temporally scattered people who may or may not *experience* their joint participation in policy discourse as a reality. Between political principles, their translation into policy, and their ultimate impact on the real world lies a long chain of political, administrative, and "sordid" managerial actions. The length of the chain facilitates psychological distancing, disconnected cognitive maps, and other kinds of discontinuities. Specialists concocting policies at the levels of rational social choice and systemic vindication are no longer "on speaking terms" with or "within earshot" of the experts who implement, evaluate, and experience programs at the situational validation and technical verification levels.

In those cases the policy process cannot function as the grapevine of the body politic. It fails to unite different sets of policy actors in a learning action and communication structure (Mayntz 1983:17) in which participants coordinate their acts. Because of structural disorders, access to the process of policy discourse produces a "garbage can" (March and Olsen 1976) instead of a "great political conversation" (Ricci 1984:300–301). By becoming a problem to itself, the policy cycle lacks political rationality in Paul Diesing's definition (1962:169–234): it no longer enables other problems to be attacked; it can no longer preserve or improve the capacity to make better policy decisions in the future.

Competing Policy Belief Systems and Shifting Discourse Coalitions in Dutch Ethnicity Policy

Let us now apply the concepts of policy belief systems and policy cycles to a specific case: the dynamics of policy-making on ethnicity in the Netherlands between the end of World War II and the end of the 1980s. I'll illustrate how a policy analyst, using Fischer's four-level model of a well-reasoned, complete policy belief system, may go about charting the political logic and the policy cycles in public policy discourse on this issue.

The historical dynamics of ethnicity policy-making in the Netherlands generated three politically viable policy belief systems: "economic mobility," "group identity," and "social integration." The period from 1947 until 1980 can be characterized as a cycle of muted policy evolution, during which two contrasting belief systems—economic mobility and group identity—were implicitly developed.

The second policy cycle started after 1980 with an explicit compromise between group identity and a third belief system, social integration, which together became official national policy. As one belief system was followed by and added to preceding ones, the discursive space for official policy doctrine acquired a layered, garbage can-like structure that contains elements of all three policy belief systems. This second cycle can be characterized as a period of shifting discourse coalitions (Hajer, in this volume) whereby official discourse on ethnicity derived from different mixes of policy belief systems.

Policy Cycle 1: Muted Policy Evolution (1947–1980)

By 1989 some 750,000 people of non-Dutch origin had settled in the Netherlands and made up more than 5 percent of the total population. This seemingly insignificant figure takes on more weight, however, when one considers that ethnic groups constitute a majority in some twenty neighborhoods in the medium and larger urban areas. These groups largely came to Holland in three successive migration waves.

The immigration was triggered in the late 1940s and early 1950s when more than 250,000 people fled Indonesia for the Netherlands. When Indonesia gained independence from the Netherlands, Dutch-

Indonesian political refugees turned into permanent repatriates, and Moluccan military officers and their families became political exiles. Supported by the group's willingness to assimilate as well as favorable economic conditions, government programs for Dutch Indonesians turned out to be successful. Once strong temporary measures concerning public housing, government loans, and special job-matching services had been set up, the policy problem went away in no time. These policy programs were coordinated and implemented by the newly established Ministry of Social Affairs, which later became the Ministry of Culture, Recreation, and Social Work.

The smooth and rapid integration of Dutch Indonesians appeared to vindicate an *economic mobility approach* to problems of migration and ethnicity. Implicit in this approach is a societal ideal consisting of ethnically random, ego-focused networks of freely contracting persons. The integration of aliens is defined mainly as an economic problem; the market functions as the big "integrator" and "equalizer." It imposes pragmatic, materialist criteria for success that are deemed color-blind and ethnically indifferent. State intervention should be based on revealed preference and confined to temporary crash programs that provide opportunities for upward mobility (see table 1).

Coping with the Moluccan issue, however, was to be almost traumatic. Because they considered themselves political exiles waiting to return to a liberated Moluccan Republic, the Moluccans resisted "assimilation." They demanded support from the Dutch government for their political cause as well as government sponsorship to preserve their group identity and culture. Of course, they were denied the former but largely got their way with respect to the latter. Ignoring the international and national political aspects, the government depoliticized the Moluccan issue by establishing the Department of Ambonese Care as a special unit with the Ministry of Social Affairs. Special treatment of Moluccans thus became institutionalized. Demands for group care and maintenance were honored mainly through the creation of "closed," but widely dispersed and relatively small, residential areas outside Dutch villages and cities for groups of Moluccans.

As Moluccan political aspirations became more and more unrealistic, a government committee hammered out policies between 1957 and 1959 which were implemented until well into the 1970s. The policy approach rested on the myth of temporary residence. This is a paradigmatic case of political compromise through willful confusion. To the Moluccan leadership, it embodied their raison d'être—to keep alive their political aspirations and to have them recognized by the Dutch govern-

Table 1. "Economic Mobility" Policy Belief System

Rational Social Choice	Systems Vindication	Situational Validation	Technical Verification
Society as sets of ego-focused, ethnically random networks	Minimal state; laissez-faire; revealed preference	Equal opportunity; upward mobility	Appropriate level of punishments/ rewards for individuals

ment. To the Dutch political elite, however, temporary residence for the Moluccans on Dutch territory was only an excuse to further depoliticize the issue.

Of course, the assumption of temporary residence generated ambiguous policies. This entailed a permanent neglect of Moluccan political aspirations, a pluralist policy on matters of culture and housing, and assimilationist educational policies. At the same time Moluccans kept emphasizing the political nature of their identity through flamboyant displays of paramilitary organization at Moluccan festivities and on Moluccan memorial days. But consultation at the national and local levels was strictly limited to a policy agenda defined by Dutch bureaucrats.

In a desperate effort to repoliticize their cause, Moluccan youths resorted to acts of terrorism in the mid-1970s. Ironically, the violence had a cathartic effect on Moluccan communities themselves, and their political isolationism became the object of fierce internal debate. Damaged relations between Moluccan representatives and the Dutch government were repaired in yet another government committee. But the Moluccan violence did have the effect of placing the ethnicity issue in general on the national agenda.

Here, too, the making of policy gradually gave rise to an implicit policy belief system, albeit a hypocritical one. At one level, this belief system was clearly premised on a *group identity* approach to problems of migration and ethnicity (the first order of the belief system; see table 2). Special programs for migrants aimed to grant group rights, preserve group identity, and create (proportional) equality of results between ethnic groups. Ideally, the group identity approach implies, at the next level, a multiethnic society in which every ethnicity maintains a quasi-autonomous status, while respecting basic constitutional constraints. Furthermore, ethnic political elites deal with each other through the accommodative practices of consociational democracy (Lijphart 1968). At this next level, then, the group identity approach was in fact tainted

Table 2. "Group Identity" Policy Belief System

Rational Social Choice	Systems Vindication	Situational Validation	Technical Verification
Society as institutionalized cultural plurifor- mity	Consociational democracy; group-partici- patory planning; expressed prefer- ence	Equal results and identity preservation	Group rights; group-directed social programs

by diverging motives. Although they formally endorsed a full-fledged group identity approach, the Moluccan leaders ultimately opposed the idea of a Dutch multiethnic state as inconsistent with their own political aspirations for a liberated Moluccan Republic. The Dutch political elite, behind clouds of stolen rhetoric, secretly hoped the Moluccan problem would just wither away.

The influx of "guest workers" from Mediterranean countries— Italians, Spaniards, Yugoslavians, and Greeks in one wave, with Turks and Moroccans following in a second, much larger, wave—was brought about by Dutch employers in the early 1960s. The government officially stepped in to regulate recruitment campaigns almost immediately by making bilateral agreements with several of the workers' home countries. This was meant to protect workers against overexploitative labor contracts and at the same time to control the number of migrant workers entering Holland. This policy on migrant workers was implemented by the Department of Social Affairs, which is in charge of regulating labor relations and the labor market. The policy operated on two core assumptions: first, guest workers fulfilled a temporary buffer function with the Dutch labor market; second, Holland was not be become an immigration country—a country of permanent residence for migrant workers. These assumptions determined the content of all the department's policy programs. Other aspects of migrant worker policies—housing, welfare, recreational facilities, and so on—were left to private initiative, especially to religious organizations and employers sponsoring special activities and programs.

The Ministry of Culture, Recreation, and Social Work gradually became involved in financing these initiatives. As the amount of governmental financing steadily grew, private organizations were able to employ more and better-trained personnel. By coordinating their efforts, these private concerns gradually rose to the status of semipublic organizations which provided the whole basket of noneconomic services to "their" special group of guest workers. Later on, Surinamese immigrants were quick to emulate these organizational forms. Backed by bureaucrats in a willing social-democratic government, professional "brokers" of ethnic interests thus succeeded in establishing an extensive, well-equipped, and well-financed ethnicity policy subsystem of public, semipublic, and private organizations. And all this was accomplished despite equivocal goals and improvised implementation. The field of education provides a telling example. In the 1970s initiatives for minority children included "early reception programs," "transition classes," additional training programs for teachers, and bicultural and bilingual programs in elementary schools. But these facilities were created with inconsistent goals in mind: preparing children both for repatriation and for permanent residence in the Netherlands.

In the late 1970s, the number of migrant workers continued to rise while cases of repatriation were few and far between. This fact, coupled with budgetary shortages and a growing bureaucracy, made it obvious that ambiguities in policy guidelines could no longer be tolerated. Gradually, contrary views emerged between the Departments of Social Affairs and Culture, Recreation, and Social Work. The former basically denied the existence of the problem by clinging to the "temporary residence" and "no immigration country" assumptions. The latter increasingly doubted the validity of these assumptions and (tacitly) shaped its organizational routines according to a full-fledged group identity approach.

At this stage there is once again not much evidence of second-order policy discourse. The myth of temporary residence—a bedrock policy assumption and recurrent thought reflex—fixated explicit, first-order public discourse. As long as this presupposition was unassailable, higher-level discourse was superfluous. At the levels of systemic vindication or rational social choice, the presence of ethnic groups posed no political problem: by definition, "guests"—be they Moluccans, Surinamese, or migrant workers—are problems that will go away!

But, hiding behind bureaucracy, the Dutch political parties also refused to discuss problems of ethnic policy publicly in the light of their avowed ideologies. Basically, ethnicity doesn't find a place in any party as a basis for political organization and mobilization or as a source of public policies. Social Democrats tend to subsume ethnicity under class interests; Conservatives are inclined to disregard ethnicity in favor of the self-actualization of (ethnic) individuals; and Christian Democrats tend to view ethnicity from the perspective of interreligious relations. Reasoning on the basis of traditional political and religious segmentation, the Dutch political parties deal with the ethnicity issue along lines of appeasement and depoliticization (Hoppe 1987b). Therefore, reconstructing the Dutch debate on ethnicity means reconstructing trends in scholarly and bureaucratic opinion (Entzinger 1984; Penninx 1988).

A window of opportunity opened only when the public was shocked by the Moluccans' acts of terrorism. This prompted some concerned members of Parliament in 1977 to demand a government initiative on *aggregate* ethnic policy. But even in this relatively favorable political climate, coherent second-order discourse on the ethnicity issue was achieved only by the Scientific Council for Government Policy (WRR 1979). The Council's attack on the temporary residence assumption and its outline for a more or less comprehensive policy on ethnic minorities finally paved the way for policy discourse on ethnicity on the levels of systemic vindication and rational social choice.

Policy Cycle 2: Divided We Stand; United We Fall (1980–1990)

In September 1983 the government's long overdue White Paper on (Ethnic) Minorities was accepted by Parliament. The delay was the result of several factors. The nature of the issue demanded time-consuming interdepartmental coordination as well as rounds of consultation with all interested parties, each voicing widely differing opinions and interests. Moreover, 1980–83 saw three government coalition changes, all of which had to do with expenditure cuts in the face of an economic crisis.

The major factor, however, was the cabinet's reluctance to address the ethnicity issue head-on. Secretary of Internal Affairs Ed van Thijn, who was responsible for producing the white paper during one of those three years, commented on ethnic policy-making in the Dutch Cabinet (van Thijn 1985:5): "When I was Secretary of Internal Affairs, questions about ethnic groups were always discussed *en marge* of cabinet council meetings. . . . These issues usually were about matters of procedure or turf. I cannot remember that in those days the cabinet ever seriously discussed substantive problems of ethnicity policy. Perhaps, in saying this, I wrong all those civil servants who were already deeply involved in these matters." Consider also the fact that Parliament was more or less forced to discuss the 1983 white paper. According to one authority (Ellemers 1985:2), "The Secretary of Internal Affairs proposed some politically hard choices. . . . Indeed, Parliament wants depoliticization: it refuses to make political decisions and merely votes for more money and research, while discussing relatively marginal business like the problem of repatriation."

Nevertheless, the white paper was finally written, and it paints a rosy picture of a multiethnic Dutch society of the future (Internal Affairs 1983:10): "Minority policy pursues effecting a society in which members of minority groups residing in the Netherlands will have an equal position and full-scale opportunities for development, both as individuals and as a group." The policy's target groups are exhaustively listed by name. The government thus limited aliens to two types of ethnic minorities: those connected to the Netherlands through its colonial past (Antilleans, Surinamese, and Moluccans), and those actively recruited as "guest workers" (mainly Turks and Moroccans).

Intermediate aims, such as the struggle against socioeconomic disadvantages and discriminatory practices, are deduced from this long-term goal. Equal access to general social welfare institutions and organizations is also called for—as opposed to the allocation of benefits through special treatment, as through semipublic organizations. The "emancipation" of ethnic groups is yet another goal. This is supposed to both strengthen the self-esteem and self-consciousness of minority group members and influence the public at large to accept minority members as permanent residents. During consultation, this dual interpretation was strongly advocated by ethnic group members and their professional brokers.

Ironically, the new-fangled emancipation goal, to a significant degree, represented sunk costs of the implementation structures for the existing group identity and special treatment policy programs. These sunk costs formed up to 55 percent of the total annual budget of about $400 million (Internal Affairs 1983:195–97). Thus, the new goals of emancipation and equal access were actually competing. The priority shift from emancipation programs to equal access programs—that is, the move away from group particularism, as advocated in the white paper—would entail a very substantial reallocation of public monies. Semipublic organizations, which exclusively served their own ethnic clientele and were often run by professional brokers, would suffer cutbacks. Organizations and programs that served the general public and provided special aid to a varied ethnic clientele would benefit.

If the policy shift was to be successful, changes in organizational design and policy formulation and implementation would be inevitable. Responsibility for coordinating the new policy at the national and subnational levels was vested in the Department of Internal Affairs, which received this mandate mainly because it was believed to occupy a strategic position to knit together the entire policy subsystem of public, semi-public, and private organizations. By sheer market forces, approximately three quarters of the immigrant population in the Netherlands dwells in disadvantaged urban areas of the four largest cities (Amsterdam, Rotterdam, The Hague, and Utrecht) and some twenty medium-sized cities. Internal Affairs established grants-in-aid to finance minority programs and their administration at the municipal level, thereby providing municipal governments with an incentive to duplicate the national coordination effort at the local level.

Examining the advice offered by the Scientific Council for Government Policy in 1979 as well as the deep structure in the policy argumentation of the 1983 white paper reveals a middle-of-the-road stance between two diverging policy belief systems. On the one hand, there are clear traces of the group identity approach. This appreciative system was advocated by a coalition of ethnic group representatives and implementors working in social and cultural policy areas. On the other hand, the white paper reflects influences from a third, *integrative* approach to ethnicity and migration, supported by the three main political parties and bureaucrats working within legal and economic professional traditions (see table 3). This approach's ideal is an integrated society made up of ethnically bounded but socially, culturally, and economically nested groups. The influx of newcomers inevitably threatens a society's stability, but permanent disruption may be averted by effecting a policy of gradual integration through state-supported participation in economic activities and vital sociopolitical institutions. Instrumentally, this requires controlled immigration, some (temporary) group rights, and strict enforcement of equality before the law. As integration is a process that lasts over two or three generations, ethnic issues are a very touchy subject, and some sacrifice on the part of established residents is essential. Therefore, majoritarian democracy should be balanced by (bureaucratic) expertise.

As a formula for political compromise, this dual-track approach (integration and group identity) was viable. The 1979 advice and the 1983 white paper fixed the concepts and the style of policy discourse for the 1980s. But the gain was merely symbolic. It exposed implementors repeatedly to the unresolved tensions between an integrationist belief system, implying adaptation to the dominant way of life, and a consociational model of ethnic emancipation, implying cultural pluralism.

For example, the white paper clearly departs from a historical policy of group particularism in favor of a shift toward programs, combating

Table 3. "Social Integration" Policy Belief System

Rational Social Choice	Systems Vindication	Situational Validation	Technical Verification
Integrated, multiethnic society of bounded but nested ethnic groups	Majoritarian democracy; state planning; expert standards	Gradual integration through participation	Controlled immigration; some group rights; procedural equality

"objective" legal and socioeconomic disadvantages. These programs obviously aim at eliminating gaps between disadvantaged Dutch groups and foreigners. "Minority problems" have largely been translated into "objectively measurable" disadvantages. A pseudoscientific "metric" that calculates disadvantages is used to reduce the ethnicity problem to a problem of "additional" disadvantages among ethnic groups relative to disadvantaged Dutch citizens. And the problem would be "solved" if these additional disadvantages—among which the continued reliance on native languages by members of ethnic groups figures prominently— were to disappear.

The best illustration of the implementation of this program is the equal access program, which aims to proportionally allocate the inputs and outputs of welfare organizations according to the number of ethnic and nonethnic clients they serve. In theory, this entails the temporary use of affirmative action. A system of conditional or absolute quotas is indispensable to implement and monitor such a program. But in practice such a system has not been developed. Rather, as with Britain's Urban Programmes and Inner Urban Areas policies (Young 1983), the Dutch government has resorted to indirect and covert policy instruments. The program for disadvantaged urban areas exemplifies this. Focusing on urban neighborhoods with large immigrant populations—which, administratively, were identified as areas of general social need—these programs typified the new turn in Dutch ethnic policy (Arends 1987).

In other respects, too, the effectiveness of the white paper's move away from group particularism and toward integrative strategies was doubtful. Insofar as respect for the (religious, cultural, artistic, and media) rights of ethnic minorities does not impede their upward socioeconomic mobility, the compromise between group emancipation and integration can be considered to embody a healthy dose of consociational wisdom. But the group emancipation goal also leads to an explicit defense of institutional pluralism with respect to (political) participation and consultation (Maas 1987), social case work, and even education. Especially in educational matters, special treatment of ethnic minority groups directly affects their economic opportunities.

In the late 1980s a general economic recovery occurred. Data revealed, however, that ethnic groups were not sharing in the benefits. In particular, unemployment among minorities had increased dramatically—to more than 40 percent for some groups. Youth unemployment rose, too. At the behest of the government, the Scientific Council for Government Policy drafted a new report in 1989 (WRR 1989). In response to the apparent "marginalization" of ethnic groups, the council proposed a new approach, which downplays group identity elements, strengthens the existing integration ingredients, and reintroduces important parts of the mobility approach.

The group identity approach was criticized for emphasizing group rights over individual responsibility and for creating dependence on special treatment as well as cultural isolationism. Instead, a mixed strategy of integration and mobility was advocated. "Integration" should be thought of as preparing ethnic persons for "self-determination" in Dutch society (Internal Affairs 1990:1), and ethnic minorities should be viewed as "human resources" worthy of investment. This is in their own interest as well as beneficial to the Dutch as a whole (WRR 1989:9–10). Investments should be concentrated in key areas such as the labor market and adult education so as to promote economic development and individual mobility. To a much larger extent, the paper proposes policy instruments based on individual rewards and penalties (WRR 1989:11–12). Labor exchanges and schools are to be financed through systems of output financing; entrepreneurs will have to adjust hiring practices to a new Employment Equity Act, with rewards or penalties for their (non-) cooperation through a system of contract compliance; compulsory education for ethnic youths will be more strictly enforced, and newly arrived immigrants will receive basic education.

Although the government is careful not to convey the impression that it is rashly dismantling its group identity policy (Internal Affairs 1990), the integration-cum-mobility mix is sure to become the new orthodoxy in Dutch ethnicity policy-making. Neoconservative trends in economic policy since the early 1980s have now also invaded ethnicity policy.

In sum, it can be observed that with respect to the political philosophy underlying its avowed ethnicity policy, the Dutch government is acting in the good old consociational tradition: divided we stand; united we fall. Yet, a shift in priority from an identity-integration compromise to an integration-mobility mix is easily recognizable.

Frustrated Policy Succession and Shifting Discourse

Analyzing forty years of policy-making on ethnicity in the Netherlands in terms of political judgment and belief systems shows a trend of increasingly shifting policy discourse derived from three different policy belief systems. Chronologically, Dutch governments have dealt with ethnicity problems on the basis of economic mobility, group identity, and social integration. Since the early 1980s, though, clear-cut reliance on one consistent (albeit largely implicit) set of beliefs—first, economic mobility, then group identity—has given way to mixed belief systems. Up until the mid-1980s group identity was married to social integration. More recently, as a belief system based on mobility has been revived, there has emerged a mixed strategy of integration and mobility (see figure 2).

Thus, as one policy belief system followed another and successive belief systems were molded together in a sort of political "marriage of convenience," the discursive space for official ethnicity policy doctrine acquired a layered, confusing structure which contains elements of all three systems. The remarkable phenomenon here is that at different levels of political judgment, different discourses and thus different policy belief systems appear to dominate. For example, at present, first-order political judgment on ethnicity issues is still dominated by an identity-cum-integration discourse, whereas second-order debate, at least since the mid-1980s, is dominated by an integration-cum-mobility discourse.

This seemingly inconsistent and garbage can-like pattern of beliefs among policymakers can be understood by considering the cycles in Dutch ethnicity policy. Up until the mid-1970s the first long-term policy cycle unfolded incrementally. Silently and implicitly, a policy evolved from immediate, small-scale responses to urgent problems of housing, unemployment, and recreation for different ethnic groups. This first policy cycle originated at the level of implementation and evaluation, and played itself out in the practical mode. As the case description shows, the policy belief systems behind this policy evolution—first, mobility, then assumptions of temporary residence and group particularism—were not discussed at the higher levels of political judgment. In a sense,

Levels of Political Judgment	Subprocesses in Policy-making	Cycle 1: Practical Order		Cycle 2: Reflexive Order	
		1947–48	1970	1979–83	Now
Rational social choice Systems vindication	Ideology formation	Mobility*	Identity and temporary stay*	Integration	Mobility*
Systems vindication	Agenda setting		Identity and permanent residence?*		
(Rational social choice) Systems vindication Situational validation (Technical verification)	Policy formulation			Identity and integration	Integration and mobility
Situational validation (Technical verification)	Policy implementation	Mobility	Identity Identity	Identity	Identity and integration
(Situational validation) Technical verification	Policy evaluation	Mobility	Identity Identity	Identity	Identity and integration

*Inferred beliefs.

Figure 2. Policy Belief Systems in the Dutch Ethnicity Policy Process.

this explains their "consistency." The moment the assumption of temporary residence was called into question and hypothetically replaced by that of permanent residence, the implicit political consensus broke down. This marked the beginning of a period of shifting, even gyrating, discourse coalitions.

The Scientific Council for Government Policy's 1979 paper and Parliament's acceptance of the 1983 White Paper on (Ethnic) Minorities represent the beginning of a second long-term policy cycle. This cycle clearly starts out in the reflective mode. The white paper's intention is to gradually adjust the historically understandable but "outdated" practice of group particularism in favor of a new integrationist vision. This second policy cycle now appears unable to move from the reflective or symbolic back to the practical mode. Because the newly designed programs have to replace or succeed their older counterparts still in operation, this can be characterized as *frustrated policy succession*. In the meantime, as illustrated by the council's 1989 report (WRR 1989), the debate continues at the levels of rational social choice and systemic vindication. Therefore the layered and confusing structure of ethnicity policy discourse is largely explained by political sluggishness and the time it takes for ideas to be implemented. More specifically, mobility and integration, ideas that are now fashionable at the level of second-order political judgment, are difficult to put into practice within entrenched organizational networks that were shaped by first-order notions of identity and identity-cum-integration in the earlier policy cycle.

Bringing Political Rationality back into Policy Analysis

This essay has explored the conditions under which political rationality can be brought back into policy analysis. After all, "the intent . . . is nothing less than to reduce the great imponderables of politics to rules of good practice." And "the modern policy sciences are perhaps no more than the lineal descendants of Aristotle and Machiavelli, who also sought to define doctrines of practical political reason" (Anderson 1987:22–23).

As practical political philosophers, policy analysts should take seriously Hannah Arendt's definition of politics as "organized remembrance" and the "sharing of words and deeds" (Arendt 1974:197–99). Given their prominent position in many policy-making processes, policy analysts have it in their power to guide the attention of substantial numbers of policy-making participants. Given the complexity and fragmentation of public policy discourse in technologically advanced polyarchies, policy analysts should see it as nothing less than their responsibility to discover "the means by which *all* who participate in policy-forming and policy-executing processes can live up to their potential for sound judgment" (Lasswell 1971:62–63). The practical tasks of the policy analyst can then be constructed as follows: (a) how to ascertain an argument's political plausibility for a certain audience, and (b) how to do this within the policy-making process so that it maintains and enhances the political community's character of authentic debate and collective action. This means that policy analysts must have tools and criteria to analyze and assess both the logic and the process of public policy discourse on a given topic, a problem to which this essay is a modest response.

Concentrating on the logic of political judgment underpinning policy discourse, I turned Fischer's four levels of judgment for evaluating policy into a practical tool, a "compass" for charting policy belief systems. This tool was used to reconstruct the three policy belief systems—economic mobility, group identity, and social integration—that dominate the political discourse on ethnicity policy issues in the Netherlands. But Fischer's model can be used in many other ways not illustrated in this essay. Essentially, the model provides the policy analyst with a normative standard for judging the completeness of political judgment in a given work (or a series of works) of policy analysis. A policy analyst can use the model, for example, to exploit omissions and weaknesses in opponents' positions; to advocate the neglected, underdeveloped, or downplayed strands in policy reasoning; or to design a more comprehensively argued, and therefore more defensible, policy position.

Finally, a framework for tracing both the structure and the historical process of public policy discourse was developed by linking levels of political judgment to a model of the policy-making process. The model proved helpful in explaining why Dutch ethnicity discourse has a layered structure involving all three policy belief systems. Two factors contribute to understanding the frustrated policy succession: (1) time lags and political sluggishness between policy cycles, and (2) divergent levels of political judgment dominating different subprocesses and various sets of actors and arenas in the policy process. Indeed, all this has brought progress in Dutch ethnicity policy-making to a halt.

References

Anderson, C. 1987. Political Philosophy, Practical Reason, and Policy Analysis. In F. Fischer and J. Forester, eds., *Confronting Values in Policy Analysis*, 22–44. Newbury Park, Calif.: Sage.

Arends, C. 1987. De mislukte invoering van het achterstandsgebiedenbeleid. In R. Hoppe, ed., *Etniciteit, Politiek, en Beleid in Nederland*, 135–62. Amsterdam: Free University Press.

Arendt, H. 1974. *The Human Condition*. Chicago and London: University of Chicago Press.

———. 1977. *Between Past and Future. 8 Exercises in Political Thought*. Enl. ed. Harmondsworth: Penguin Books.

———. 1978. *The Life of the Mind*. Vol. 2: *Willing*. New York and London: Harcourt Brace Jovanovich.

Beiner, R. 1983. *Political Judgment*. London: Methuen.

Brasz, H. A. 1986. *Kleine methodologie van de bestuurskunde*. Amsterdam: Free University Press.

Dauenhauer, B. P. 1986. *The Politics of Hope*. New York and London: Routledge and Kegan Paul.

Diesing, P. 1962. *Reason in Society*. Urbana: University of Illinois Press.

Edelman, M. 1988. *Constructing the Political Spectacle*. Chicago and London: University of Chicago Press.

Edwards, A. 1990. *Planning Betwist*. Amsterdam: Van Arkel.

Ellemers, J. E. 1985. Draagt een omvattend minderhedenbeleid bij tot goed bestuur? In Internal Affairs, Verkenningen van het openbaar bestuur, no. 12.

Entzinger, H. B. 1984. *Minderhedenbeleid*. Meppel: Boom.

Fischer, F. 1980. *Politics, Values, and Public Policy: The Problem of Methodology*. Boulder: Westview Press.

———. 1990a. The American Policy Agenda: Think Tanks and the Politicization of Expertise. Paper presented at the annual meeting of the American Political Science Association, San Francisco, August 1990.

———. 1990b. *Technocracy and the Politics of Expertise*. Newbury Park, Calif.: Sage.

Fischer, F., and J. Forester, eds. 1987. *Confronting Values in Policy Analysis*. Newbury Park, Calif.: Sage.

Forester, J., ed. 1985. *Critical Theory and Public Life*. Cambridge and London: MIT Press.

———. 1985. The Policy Analysis—Critical Theory Affair: Wildavsky and Habermas as Bedfellows? In J. Forester, ed., *Critical Theory and Public Life*, 258–80. Cambridge and London: MIT Press.

———. 1989. *Planning in the Face of Power*. Berkeley and Los Angeles: University of California Press.

Glazer, N., and K. Young, eds. 1983. *Ethnic Pluralism and Public Policy*. Lexington, Mass.: Lexington Books; London: Heinemann Educational Books.

Graaf, H. van de, and R. Hoppe. 1989. *Beleid en Politiek*. Muiderberg: Coutinho.

Gunsteren, H. van. 1976. *The Quest for Control*. London: Wiley and Sons.

Hodgkinson, C. 1978. *Towards a Philosophy of Administration*. Oxford: Basil Blackwell.

Hoppe, R., ed. 1987a. *Etniciteit, Politiek en Beleid in Nederland*. Amsterdam: Free University Press.

Hoppe, R. 1987b. Veertig jaar minderhedenbeleid. In R. Hoppe, ed., *Etniciteit, Politiek, en Beleid in Nederland*, 23–70. Amsterdam: Free University Press.

Hoppe, R., et al. 1990. Policy Belief Systems and Risky Technologies. The Dutch Debate on Regulating LPG-Related Activities. *Industrial Crisis Quarterly* 4:121–40.

Internal Affairs, Department of. 1983. *Nota Minderhedenbeleid*. The Hague: SDU.

———. 1990. Voorlopige Regeringsreactie op het WRR-rapport "Allochthonenbeleid."

Jouvenel, B. de. 1963. *The Pure Theory of Politics*. Cambridge: Cambridge University Press.

Lasswell, H. D. 1971. *A Pre-View of Policy Sciences*. Amsterdam and New York: American Elsevier.

Lijphart, A. 1968. *The Politics of Accommodation: Pluralism and Democracy in the Netherlands.* Berkeley: University of California Press.

Lindblom, C. E. 1965. *The Intelligence of Democracy.* New York: Free Press.

Lynn, L. 1981. *Managing the Public's Business.* New York: Free Press.

Maas, J. 1987. Lokaal participatiebeleid voor etnische minderheidsgroepen in vergelijkend perspectief. In R. Hoppe, ed., *Etniciteit, Politiek en Beleid in Nederland,* 105–34. Amsterdam: Free University Press.

Majone, G. 1989. *Evidence, Argument, and Persuasion in the Policy Process.* New Haven: Yale University Press.

March, J. G., and J. P. Olsen. 1976. *Ambiguity and Choice in Organizations.* Bergen: Universitetsforlaget.

May, J. V., and A. Wildavsky. 1978. *The Policy Cycle.* Beverly Hills: Sage.

Mayntz, R., ed. 1983. *Implementation Politischer Programme II. Ansätze zur Theoriebildung.* Opladen: Deutscher Verlag.

Nielsen, F. 1985. Toward a Theory of Ethnic Solidarity in Modern Societies. *American Sociological Review* 50:133–49.

Penninx, M. J. A. 1988. *Minderheidsvorming en emancipatie.* Alphen aan den Rijn: Samsom.

Ricci, D. M. 1984. *The Tragedy of Political Science.* New Haven and London: Yale University Press.

Sabatier, P. 1987. Knowledge, Policy-oriented Learning, and Policy Change. *Knowledge: Creation, Diffusion, Utilization* 8:649–92.

Sederberg, P. C. 1984. *The Politics of Meaning. Power and Explanation in the Construction of Social Reality.* Tucson: University of Arizona Press.

Thijn, E. van. 1985. Minderhedenbeleid in drievoud. In Internal Affairs, Verkenningen van het Openbaar Bestuur, no. 20.

Torgerson, D. 1985. Contextual Orientation in Policy Analysis: The Contribution of Harold D. Lasswell. *Policy Sciences* 18:241–61.

Unger, R. M. 1987. *Social Theory: Its Situation and Its Task.* Cambridge: Cambridge University Press.

Vickers, G. 1968. *The Art of Judgment.* London: Methuen.

Vollrath, E. 1977. *Die Rekonstruktion der Politischen Urteilskraft.* Stuttgart: Klett Verlag.

White Paper on Minorities (Minderhedennota). 1983. Tweede Kamer, 1982–83, 16 102, nos. 20–21.

WRR. 1979. *Etnische Minderheden.* The Hague: Staatsdrukkerij.

———. 1989. *Allochthonenbeleid.* The Hague: SDU.

Young, K. 1983. Postscript. Ethnic Pluralism and the Policy Agenda in Britain. In N. Glazer and K. Young, eds., *Ethnic Pluralism and Public Policy,* 287–301.

Counsel and Consensus:

Norms of Argument in Health Policy

Bruce Jennings

Writing in 1984, shortly after the Medicare Prospective Payment System inaugurated a very active decade of health policy reform, Carl Schramm posed the intriguing question of whether our democratic political system could, in fact, control health care expenditures and provide universal access at the same time. If not, we might remain frozen in the position of unjustly excluding people from the system in order to compensate for our inability to set social priorities among services offered by the system. "Can highly complex distributional problems," he asked, "be solved by democratic governments, which are, by design and tradition, responsive to individual *and* collective interests? . . . Only through government can we assert our collective best interest over our individual self-interest. . . . If we do not use our democratic institutions to stem this tide and to regulate ourselves and our medical system in the years to come, we will all be the poorer for it" (Schramm 1984:731–732).

The dilemma posed by health policy is typical of a broad spectrum of public policy problems endemic in the advanced welfare states of late capitalist societies. It is not merely coincidental, I think, that the argumentative turn in policy studies should occur at just the moment when the field of public policy analysis is forced to confront public policy problems that raise basic normative questions about the fundamental ends and purposes of our society—questions about how a viable political and social consensus can be formed around issues of economic and social welfare redistribution. The time when policy analysis could don the mantle of value neutrality and scientific objectivity and could merely oversee the instrumental administrative functioning of growth-oriented bureaucratic fine tuning, is now over.

For both conceptual and political reasons, policy analysis—understood both as a particular kind of political discourse and as a particular kind of political practice—must face a fundamental regrounding of its own authority and legitimacy. The danger, as I see it, is that a case for the authority and legitimacy of policy analysis will be made only by incorporating policy analysis as simply one more specialized discourse of advocacy within a pluralistic politics of interest group liberalism. This is a tempting and familiar move, but it comes at a significant price. For one thing, as many authors in this volume and others have shown, to see policy analysis merely as a discourse of advocacy is to overlook much of the richness, nuance, and texture that actually inform the real practice of policy analysis. Even more important than the descriptive poverty of the notion of policy analysis as advocacy is the fact that this conception of policy analysis deprives us of the normative expectations and demands a democratic society ought to place on the discourse of policy analysis within it. It is my contention that policy analysis ought to be held to a higher normative standard, one that attempts to capture a civic conception of participatory governance and policy debate leading to the emergence of a guiding consensus on the fundamental and common ends of public life.

My intent in this essay is to explore the prospects and possibilities of policy analysis as a discourse of counsel and consensus, both in theoretical terms and through the examination of Medicaid policy reform in the state of Oregon from 1989 to 1991. My discussion will proceed in two stages. First, I sketch a conceptual framework for policy analysis as a discourse of counsel, using the term *counsel* as a term of art. Next, I discuss in some detail the Oregon health policy reform experiment, giving special emphasis to the nodal points of argument that structured the debate about Medicaid policy in Oregon and drove the actual policy outcomes in certain directions.

The Oregon case illustrates in a particularly clear and telling way the importance of understanding public policy analysis in its normative, argumentative, and interpretive dimensions (Fox and Leichter 1991; Callahan 1992). Few areas of public policy today indicate the significance of interpretive policy analysis more clearly than the issues of access to health care, health care priorities, and health care rationing. These issues also underscore the importance of being able to mount a style of public policy analysis that can move beyond pluralistic advocacy and interest group liberalism. The lesson to be drawn from Oregon is not that advocacy and interest group liberalism can be entirely transcended (nor should they be), but that it is essential to supplement them with normative discourses of counsel and consensus in which the fundamental ends of public policy are critically reassessed, rearticulated, and refounded in a more public and accountable process of public policy choice.

In other articles I have discussed the model of policy analysis as counsel in reference to a sense of professional vocation and a professional ethic that could inform the practice of policy analysis and the moral conduct of individual policy analysts (Jennings 1987a; 1987b; 1988). Here the focus must shift somewhat from questions of professional ethics to questions of the underlying democratic and liberal values that we wish to embed in the policy-making process, of which the discourse of policy analysis is one component part. Counsel, therefore, can be a collective process as well as an individual practice. It is with the collective, policy process side of policy analysis as counsel that I am concerned here.

Advocacy and Counsel

The discourse of counsel and consensus within policy analysis can be understood as having three basic goals: (1) to grasp the meaning or significance of contemporary problems as they are experienced, adapted to, and struggled against by reasonable, purposive agents, who are members of the political community; (2) to clarify the meaning of those problems so that strategically located political agents (public officials or policymakers) will be able to devise a set of efficacious and just solutions to them; and (3) to guide the selection of one preferred policy from a range of possible options based on a general vision of the good of the community as a whole.

The counselor must construct an interpretation of present political and social reality that serves not only the intellectual goal of explaining or comprehending that reality, but also the practical goal of enabling constructive action to move the community from a flawed present toward an improved future. Counsel is attentive to the moral sensibilities, vocabularies, and forms of life that comprise the ethos of the political community it serves. It does not understand public policies as alien things imposed upon the malleable, manipulable desires and interests of the citizenry, but rather sees how the agency and moral imagination of citizens can construct both the need for public policies and the possible shapes public policies take. At the same time, counsel is attentive to concepts of justice and the common good that transcend the immediate self-understanding of a given community of political agents. It aims to inform public policy—always prone to considerations of expediency and compromise—with standards and ideals that ask the community to be better than it has been in the past.

From the perspective of discourses of advocacy, this notion of counsel seems idealized and utopian. Advocacy begins with skepticism about the possibility that any mode of policy analysis could either pay respectful attention to the mores and sensibilities of the community as a whole or provide the kind of critique that would realize higher moral ideals. In keeping with political theorists in the liberal pluralist tradition, such as James Madison, policy analysis as advocacy argues that natural human selfishness cannot be transcended; it can only be contained and channeled toward just ends. (It is nonetheless difficult in pluralist terms alone to define the nature of justice toward which those selfish interests should be channeled.) In a similar vein, policy analysis as advocacy maintains that policy advice will inevitably be informed by some particularistic interests that can be balanced but cannot be transformed into a more public-regarding *civitas*. One has either objective knowledge (as positivistic policy science claimed to provide) or subjective opinion; there is no middle ground.

Policy analysis as counsel searches for the middle ground between positivistic objectivity and subjectivism. Counsel can find this middle ground because the concepts and categories used in social inquiry and political argument are publicly available concepts—that is, they are drawn from a common intersubjectively meaningful set of cultural norms, traditional values, and commonsense understandings of what human beings need and how they react in various circumstances. The knowledge possessed by the counselor may be more systematic and reflective, but it is not qualitatively distinct from the everyday repertoire and cultural competency of the ordinary citizen. Neither counselors nor citizens can prescribe a definitive, regulative use of the concepts and categories of political argument, but alternative uses of them—alternative interpretations of public need, justice, and the common good—can be rationally debated and assessed. Analysis that survives an open and undistorted process of collective deliberation where the very meaning and applicability of key political and value terms is thrown open for public reassessment can legitimately be called a consensus that has authentic normative force (Benhabib and Dallmayr, eds. 1990). Sometimes counsel concerns how to set up a process leading toward such a public deliberation and consensus; sometimes counsel flows from the achievement of such instances of public consensus in the past.

Policy analysis as counsel strives to meet the objectives outlined above; in so doing, it seeks to fashion an interpretation of what the common good and justice require that can survive a collective process of rational assessment and deliberation. No individual analyst's specific policy advice will achieve this fully, and hence it will represent only one of several plausible perspectives. The same is true for arguments that ordinary citizens may make in various forums of public policy debate. But even though each individual analysis is limited and essentially contestable in this way, the discourse of counsel within this kind of public conversation continuously strives to offer a perspective on justice and the common good rather than (as with the notion of advocacy) a self-conscious articulation of some particularistic or group-specific interest. Policy analysis as counsel mitigates the adversarial ethos of the pluralistic public policy-making process. It recasts the relationship between policy analysts, policymakers, and citizens in the form of a conversation with many voices. Like policy analysis as advocacy, the discourse of counsel relies on a procedural mechanism to attain just policy choices. It does not supplant the liberal democratic representative political process, but it can help that process to function better than it ordinarily does. Counsel moves the normal political process in the direction of adjudicating among multiple perspectives on the common good and fashioning policy on the basis of a complementary "fit" among those perspectives.

Moral Argument and Medicaid Reform in Oregon

In 1987 a debate began in Oregon, and in other states, about how to contain the rapidly rising costs of health care and how to reform the public health insurance system to provide better access to those excluded from adequate medical care (Friedman 1991:2493). Oregon has gone further than any other state in attempting a comprehensive Medicaid reform. It provides an interesting case study of the prospects and possibilities of counsel and consensus, and a particularly telling example of the practical difference between policy-making in the mode of advocacy and interest group politics versus policy-making in the mode of counsel and civic consensus.

In 1989 Americans spent $604.1 billion (11.1 percent of the GDP) on health care (Friedman, 1991:2493). In 1992 that figure rose to $838.5 billion, and by 1994 health care costs may reach $1 trillion and over 16 percent of the GDP. Other Western nations with comparable or even better health indexes than the United States spend one-third to one-half less on their health care systems while providing nearly universal access to basic medical care (Pear 1993). America, by contrast, offers state-of-the-art medical technology and care to those well insured or supported by government benefits, but at the cost of denying access to basic, timely care to more than thirty-five million persons who lack any health care coverage and millions more who have inadequate coverage. These so-called medically indigent people are largely the working poor and their families, or those whose income is too high to qualify them for Medicaid in their state even though that income is well below the federal poverty line. One in four children under age eighteen lacks adequate insurance coverage, which hampers preventive and timely care. Nearly 30 percent of black Americans are uninsured, as are 41 percent of Hispanic Americans (Friedman 1991:2491). Persons without adequate health care coverage typically utilize medical services in a way that is not cost-effective, and they place a burden on hospitals for uncompensated care that reverberates throughout the entire health care financing system. For far too many Americans in urban areas the emergency room door may be their first and only portal into the health care system; in rural areas even that entry is sometimes lacking.

Limitations on access to health care in Oregon are fairly typical of the national scene. A 1988 survey estimated that 403,000 (14 percent) Oregonians were medically indigent, and in 1992 that figure was thought to be approximately 450,000, including 113,000 children and 68,000 people over the age of sixty-five (Campbell 1991:S551).

Against this background policy analysts and reformers in Oregon have worked to create public recognition of the fact that health policy-makers will soon have to determine—much more carefully, self-consciously, and systematically than ever before—what types of care will be available to whom, in what setting, at what cost, and who will pay for them. These are usually referred to as "rationing" decisions in health care. There is no purely scientific or value-neutral way to make them; ethical and value questions impinge on these decisions at every step. But what kind of public understanding and support will influence these decisions? What kind of public involvement and consensus will be needed if rational health policy initiatives in the future are to succeed? How can particular communities—and the country as a whole—forge an agreement about what is fair, what is beneficial and necessary, and what is affordable? How can we, in Schramm's words, construct a public policy setting health care priorities that asserts our collective best interests over individual self-interests? These are essentially the questions political leaders and public analysts in Oregon have sought to put explicitly on the agenda of policy debate (Kitzhaber 1988, 1989, 1990).

In 1989 the Oregon legislature passed an important package of legislation, the Oregon Basic Health Services Act (OBHSA), as the first part of a multifaceted approach to health policy reform designed to universalize basic health care coverage and to rationalize the ultilization of medical services. The various provisions of the act will take effect in several stages over a number of years and will attack the allocation problem on several fronts. (A Medicaid waiver from the federal government is necessary if the proposed changes in coverage and benefits are to be made. In 1992 the Bush administration denied Oregon's request for such a waiver, citing concerns about discrimination against persons with disabilities. The Clinton administration has recently granted the waiver.)

First, OBHSA extends Medicaid eligibility up to the federal poverty level, thereby adding some 116,000 people to the Medicaid program. Second, it creates an eleven-member Oregon Health Services Commission (HSC) charged with constructing a prioritized list of health services on the basis of which the legislature will establish and fund a basic benefits package for Medicaid. Third, it attacks the exclusion of the working poor from health insurance coverage by requiring that virtually all employers in the state provide their employees and their employees' dependents with coverage at least equivalent to the basic benefits package of the Medicaid program. This provision is expected to provide coverage to approximately 284,000 uninsured workers, and it follows a pattern set by other states, such as Hawaii and Massachusetts, in continuing to rely on the employer-based private health insurance system as a path to universal access. Finally, the OBHSA sets up a state fund to cover those who would otherwise be uninsurable because of preexisting medical conditions, a provision expected to affect approximately 10,000 people.

Medical services for the elderly and the disabled under Medicare and long-term care funded by Medicaid are not incorporated into the priority-setting process and basic benefits package. This feature of the program has drawn severe criticism nationally from groups such as the Children's Defense Fund (Rosenbaum, 1992). Once the elderly are excluded from the rationing scheme, mothers and children who receive funds under the Aid to Families with Dependent Children program (AFDC) are the main population that stands to lose benefits under Oregon's program. In the future Oregon planners hope to encompass Medicare and long-term care under the priority-setting scheme, and they also hope that private insurers will adopt the priority-setting results of the HSC and incorporate them into private plans (Dougherty 1991). In this way Medicaid, as it is presently constituted, would disappear as a separate—often vulnerable and stigmatized—program. These future developments would go a long way toward alleviating some of the ethical concerns that have been raised about the Oregon experiment (Daniels 1991). Whether they will come to pass, however, depends on some highly uncertain political calculations, which are very difficult at the moment to assess.

This discussion focuses on the Health Services Commission and the priority-setting process. In effect the HSC is the "policy analyst" in this case. The eleven-member commission, appointed by the governor, is made up of five physicians from various specialties, four consumer representatives, one nurse, and one social worker. Its task is to recommend a prioritized list of health services to the legislature and to recommend how many of those services should be funded over the next two years. An independent accounting firm projects the costs of all services on the list, and the legislature decides how much money to allocate to the Medicaid program. Once the appropriation is made, a line can be drawn on the prioritized list of services; services above the line will be covered by Medicaid, services below will not. The HSC does have substantial leverage and power in the process, however, because once the legislature accepts the prioritized list, legislators are not permitted to rearrange the order of services; they can only decide how far down the list to fund. Thus the medical expertise and value-laden social decisions that went into assessing the relative worth of health care services are not to be subject to a political process of legislative lobbying, bargaining, and compromise. If a lobbying group favors a service that the HSC has ranked low on the list (in vitro fertilization, for example), it cannot attempt to get that service moved higher. It can only try to get the line drawn below that service, a very costly move that is much more difficult to achieve politically.

In sum, the Oregon process shifts the center of argument away from the advocacy arena of the legislature and toward the environment of an appointed, representative (but professionally dominated) commission. The question is: Will the commission setting be more open and conducive to policy analysis as counsel than the state legislature traditionally has been, or will advocacy continue to dominate the discourse of priority setting?

The HSC is required by law to "actively solicit public involvement in a community meeting process to build a consensus on the values to be used to guide health resource allocation decisions." In fact, there has been substantial public involvement in the work of the HSC, and there is some evidence that the social values and attitudes expressed during this process have been factored into its final priority list and recommendations, which were sent to the legislature in June 1991 (Oregon Health Services Commission 1991). The initial priority list made public in May 1990 reflected a classical cost-benefit approach to setting priorities. According to cost-effectiveness theory, when developing a priority list of services, the cost of each service should be divided by some measure of the health benefit that is expected from treatment. Benefit is often defined in terms of "quality-adjusted life years," a notion that integrates the effect of the treatment on longevity with its effect on quality of life. The costs of the treatment were then factored in to give the treatment a priority rating. This procedure was based largely on reviews of the published literature, the work of expert professional panels, and public surveys inquiring about quality-of-life judgments. The HSC produced a list of more than 1600 condition and treatment pairs which had some very counterintuitive priorities and immediately caused considerable embarrassment to the commission. Dental crowns, for example, were ranked more highly than surgery for ectopic pregnancy or appendectomy.

Several months after the release of the preliminary priority list, the HSC completely revised its approach and effectively eliminated cost from the priority-setting equation (Hadorn 1991). It also decided to undertake the priority-setting exercise in two steps: (1) defining and rank-ordering general categories of treatment, and (2) assigning condition-treatment pairs to each category and rank-ordering them within the category. The result was a final list of seventeen categories into which 714 diagnosis-treatment pairs were placed.

The seventeen categories were rank-ordered according to three criteria: (1) the category's perceived value to the individual, (2) its value to society, and (3) the necessity of the category. In general, curative treatment of acute life-threatening conditions, maternal and child care, treatment of a fatal chronic condition with improvement in life span and quality of life, and preventive testing with proven effectiveness were most highly ranked. Treatment of self-limiting conditions, infertility services, and treatments that offer no benefit in terms of quality of life or duration of life were ranked lowest.

According to the commissioners themselves, the priority ranking of categories was guided to some extent by the findings of several public outreach activities sponsored by the commission—public hearings; specially commissioned public surveys designed to reach low income, minority, and disabled populations; and forty-seven town meetings held throughout the state by Oregon Health Decisions, a private community education group. Those attending these town meetings were asked to think about and articulate the basic values a health care system ought to serve. Their discussions revealed an emphasis on equity, quality of life, cost-effectiveness, functional independence, and community compassion (Hasnain and Garland 1990). The public did not rank-order medical services directly in these town hall meetings and opinion surveys, but the grass-roots process and its attendant publicity helped to produce a climate of public discussion and education on health policy questions in the state that is unusual for this or any other public policy issue. It was a first step in a process that should continue as the work of the HSC proceeds in the coming years.

The basic policy techniques of the Oregon experiment are neither original nor unique to Oregon. The employer mandate approach has been followed in Hawaii and Massachusetts, and the risk pool mechanism exists in some twenty states. Closing the Medicaid gap by raising eligibility to the federal poverty level is also an obvious, although as yet unusual, step. What is unique about Oregon is the systematic and visible approach that has been taken to priority setting.

Consider, above all, the ways in which policy discourse was framed in Oregon and the explicit value choices this framing reflects. First, ration services, not people. Policymakers succeeded in defining the issue as one of greater equity and justice in securing access to health care. They could then articulate their primary objective as creating universal health care coverage and access to basic care. This would put an end to the current practices of rationing and cost containment that function by excluding persons. Normally, the politics of Medicaid programs at the state level has been to deal with periodic fiscal crises by reducing eligibility levels or by lowering provider reimbursement rates, thereby making it difficult for Medicaid enrollees to locate health care providers who will serve them.

Coupled with an appeal to justice and equity, the Oregon policymakers appealed to efficiency and prudent stewardship of limited resources. They defined the problem not as one of cost containment or limiting taxpayer expenditures but as the need to reduce unnecessary or marginally beneficial services. This is to be done by standardizing health care utilization patterns in terms of the best available information concerning the efficacy of various treatments for various conditions and the overall impact of the treatment on the patient's well-being and quality of life. In this sense priority setting at the macrolevel becomes a prelude to the goal of reaching down to affect physician practice patterns at the bedside. The effect of this framing of the problem was to turn a liberal versus conservative debate about a social welfare program into a debate about how individual physicians' behavior could be guided by the most up-to-date technical knowledge.

In fact, the Oregon experiment will significantly increase health care costs in the state, if the federal government grants permission for the plan to go into effect. Accountants have estimated that the total cost of funding all 714 services on the priority list while expanding Medicaid enrollment would cost approximately $40 million. The HSC has recommended that the top 500 to 600 items on the list should be funded at an increased cost of $19 to $30 million. The legislature has agreed to fund approximately 575 items. When the HSC virtually eliminated cost as a weighting factor in its priority-setting methodology, the position of expensive curative and quality-of-life-enchancing treatments rose to a much higher position on the list, while less dramatic treatments that would give less benefit to a very large number of people at a low per-person cost dropped to a lower position.

Finally, and most important, the policy problem was defined so that priority setting, or rationing, appeared inevitable. The only question was how open, explicit, and accountable it would be. Indeed, most political leaders in Oregon believe that priority setting and rationing are already realities in the health care system but are invisible because public and private decisionmakers whose determinations allocate scarce resources are not publicly accountable. Aside from the value of openness per se, the Oregon approach is predicated on the belief that explicit priority-setting decisions will be subject to political forces that will, in the long run, be more democratically legitimate and more beneficial to the least advantaged. A closely related goal is to supplement the accountability of political representatives with the active participation of citizens at the grass-roots level. Interest group politics is viewed as having failed to meet the challenge endemic to health policy.

The Possible Community

From the perspective of policy analysis as a discourse of counsel and civic consensus, the important question to ask of the proposed Oregon Medicaid experiment is whether it moves beyond interest group pluralism and gives voice to different kinds of political and moral arguments, arguments genuinely based on a principled commitment to justice and a shared vision of the common good. This is not solely a question of the intentions, motives, and goodwill of individual leaders, analysts, and even citizens, although it is partly that. It is more fundamentally a question of creating an institutionalized space for a different kind of political discourse and policy argument. In the Oregon case, this space, if it exists, resides primarily in the Health Services Commission and in the public hearings, expert panels, and town hall meetings. These were the forums that gathered technical information and value judgments: information about what works in health care and judgments about what health care should be for and why it is a good that ought to be shared by all citizens as a matter of justice and right, and as a matter of community and social solidarity.

Thus far it appears that the Oregon experiment has been unusually successful in bracketing the normal, politics-as-usual approach to Medicaid funding and in creating a novel kind of self-consciousness about how decisions in this area should be understood and made. The rhetoric of openness and accountability won the day, and this policy experiment has been thematized as a communal and civic process. Of course, that does not mean that the outcome will in fact be just; nor does it mean that the actual process will be free from interest group politics. But at a time when any progressive extension of social welfare benefits has come to be portrayed as a special interest raid on the public treasury, it is no mean accomplishment to frame a policy question in a way that makes a significant extension of benefits (and a probable increase in government spending) seems like an ally rather than an enemy of the common good.

Still, counsel and civic consensus demand more than a newly framed rhetoric or a fresh idiom for policy debate. They demand a structure for public discourse that transforms, and does not simply transmit, moral reflection and civic deliberation. Here the domination by an elite group and the generally unrepresentative character of the participation that have marked the Oregon policy-making process are deeply troubling. Random telephone surveys elicited public judgments on quality of life and the worth of various states of health and disability, and these judgments were factored into the net benefit assessments that went into the rank-ordering of health services. But the special needs and perspectives of the disabled and the chronically ill were underrepresented in this process. Similarly, the town hall meetings, while open to all citizens and well advertised, were attended mainly by health professionals and affluent, well-educated citizens. Finally, it is not clear how genuinely representative the commission itself was, and how much it was swayed by technical expertise and professional opinion.

These shortcomings are not really so surprising, and they can most likely be corrected over time as the process gains more public visibility and as better outreach efforts are made to bolster participation in the town hall meetings. In and of themselves these faults do not destroy the legitimacy of the process. However short of the democratic ideal the

Oregon priority-setting process may have fallen, it was far more open and accountable than medicaid policy usually is or has been in the state legislatures.

What these issues of participation and representation really underscore is how demanding the counsel and civic consensus norms of policy analysis are. Policy analysis as counsel has—or should have—what philosophers call an "illocutionary" force as a speech act. That is, counsel not only says something, it also does something; it changes social reality and transforms the listener. Located in a public, participatory process like the Oregon priority-setting experiment, the purpose of counsel is to transform private perspectives into public vision, to move in the conversation from the voice of "I want" to the voice of "We, all of us, should have." If the broadly conceived form of policy analysis that is the Oregon priority-setting process cannot engage in this kind of argumentative transformation, there is a real danger that the discussion, mainly held among middle class citizens, will be about what "they [the poor] should be given" instead of being about what "we owe to and should provide for one another." If that happens, an important opportunity will be lost, and the discourse of counsel in policy analysis will, once again, not have been heard.

References

Benhabib, S., and Dallmayr, F., eds. 1990. *The Communicative Ethics Controversy.* Cambridge, Mass.: MIT Press.

Callahan, D. 1992. Symbols, Rationality, and Justice: Rationing Health Care. *American Journal of Law and Medicine* 18:1–13.

Campbell, C. 1991. Laboratory of Reform?: Setting Health Priorities in Oregon. *BioLaw* 2:S549–S563.

Daniels, N. 1991. Is the Oregon Rationing Plan Fair? *JAMA* 265:2232–35.

Dougherty, C. J. 1991. Setting Health Care Priorities: Oregon's Next Steps. *Hastings Center Report* (May–June): 1–10.

Fox, D. M., and Leichter, H. M. 1991. Rationing Care in Oregon, The New Accountability. *Health Affairs* (Summer): 7–27.

Friedman, E. 1991. The Uninsured: From Dilemma to Crisis. *JAMA* 265:2491–95.

Hadorn, D. 1991. Setting Health Care Priorities in Oregon: Cost-Effectiveness Meets The Rule of Rescue. *JAMA* 265:2218–25.

Hasnain, R., and Garland, M. 1990. *Health Care in Common: Report of the Oregon Health Decisions Community Meetings Process.* Salem: Oregon Health Decisions.

Jennings, B. 1987a. Interpretation and the Practice of Policy Analysis. In F. Fischer and J. Forester, eds., *Confronting Values in Policy Analysis: The Politics of Criteria*, 128–52. Newbury Park, Calif.: Sage Publications.

———. 1987b. Policy Analysis: Science, Advocacy, or Counsel? In S. S. Nagel, ed., *Research in Public Policy Analysis and Management*, 4:121–34. Greenwich: JAI Press.

———. 1988. Political Theory and Policy Analysis: Bridging the Gap. In E. B. Portis and M. B. Levy, eds., *Handbook of Political Theory and Policy Science*, 17–28. Westport: Greenwood Press.

Kitzhaber, J. A. 1988. Uncompensated Care—the Threat and the Challenge. *The Western Journal of Medicine* 148:711–16.

———. 1989. The Oregon Health Initiative. *Lancet* 8:106.

———. 1990. The Oregon Model. In *Improving Access to Affordable Health Care*, 69–80. Washington, DC: Institute of Medicine.

Oregon Health Services Commission. 1991. *Prioritization of Health Services: A Report to the Governor and the Legislature*. Salem: Health Services Commission.

Pear, R. 1993. Health Care Costs Up Sharply Again, Posing New Threat. *New York Times*, January 5, A-1, A-10.

Rosenbaum, S. 1992. Mothers and Children Last: The Oregon Medicaid Experiment. *American Journal of Law and Medicine* 18:97–126.

Schramm, C. J. 1984. Can We Solve the Hospital Cost Problem in Our Democracy? *New England Journal of Medicine* 311:729–32.

Analytical Concepts:

Frames, Tropes, and

Narratives

II

Survey Research as Rhetorical

Trope: Electric Power Planning

Arguments in Chicago

J. A. Throgmorton

Planning and policy analysis are rhetorical practices (Majone 1989; Throgmorton 1991).[1] At first glance, this notion might seem outlandish. Planners and analysts "know" that rhetoric is a matter of "mere words" that simply add gloss to the important stuff. In this view, planning and analysis are technical practices disciplined by objective methods: planners use survey research, computer modeling, forecasting, and other technical tools to discover the facts, then use language only to let those objective facts speak for themselves. Alternately, rhetoric might involve the use of seductive language to entice others into embracing a speaker's preferred values, beliefs, and behaviors. In this case technical tools can be used as political instruments to achieve political ends, like missiles that hostile forces let loose on one another (Myers 1990).

Facts or missiles? Mere words or seductive and manipulative language? There is a good way to bring together these two seemingly contradictory views of rhetoric in planning and analysis. Contrary to these common images, I want to suggest that *all planning and analysis is rhetorical*, and that tools such as survey research, computer modeling, and forecasting can be thought of as rhetorical *tropes*; that is, as figures of speech and argument that give persuasive power to the larger narratives of which they are a part. As rhetorical tropes used in practice, such tools also construct the planning analyst's character and the kinds of communities that can be formed between planning analysts and their audiences.

To consider this possibility more thoroughly, we need more details about such a rhetorical approach to planning and analysis. This essay will provide some of the needed details by outlining a rhetorical approach to planning and analysis and by relating that approach to other contemporary views of those practices. With this outline in mind, we will then examine one particular case to see how analyses work as rhetorical tropes in planning narratives. The case I have chosen involves the use of survey research in a five-year political conversation about whether the city of Chicago should "take over" part of Commonwealth Edison's electric power system. Probing deeper into that case, we will observe one survey researcher's effort to persuade a mayorally appointed citizens' task force that he had produced accurate estimates of how Chicago businesses would react to a city takeover. This lets us turn to how a rhetorical approach could improve the theory, pedagogy, and practice of planning and analysis.

A Rhetorical Approach to Planning and Policy Analysis

On December 14, 1987, the *Chicago Tribune* reported that a "random survey" of 454 Chicago businesses had found that a proposed "buyout" of Commonwealth Edison's electric power system by the city of Chicago could cost Chicago 250,000 jobs. Often quoting Samuel Mitchell, president of the Chicago Association of Commerce and Industry (CACI), which sponsored the survey, the article cited several specific "findings," including the following:

–Nearly 30 percent of the businesses surveyed indicated they would develop plans to relocate outside Chicago if the city became the sole provider of electricity.

–Some 250,000 jobs could be lost if the city of Chicago became the sole provider of electricity within its borders.

–Only one in four businesses surveyed favored the proposed takeover by the city; more than 63 percent opposed it.

The survey claimed a statistical validity for each finding of ± 3 percent.

The CACI's survey conveys a "just the facts" ideal that has long dominated policy-oriented professional planning and policy analysis in the United States. In this ideal view, planning is a technical process that compares the likely results of alternate courses of action systematically and before the fact. Surveys enable planning analysts to measure objectively how citizens and clients feel about diverse values; computer models enable them to represent reality; and forecasting methodologies enable them to project measurable consequences into the future. Together these tools allow planning analysts to identify the ends and define the means that perfectly represent "the public interest." Thus it is neither surprising nor inappropriate that planning analysts learn how to use tools (such as survey research) that enable them to account for the consequences of diverse public policies and government projects. According to this just the facts view, language is a bothersome necessity imposed by the need to transmit those facts to potential readers. What matters is not rhetoric (which in this view is merely a matter of style) but the logic of the argument and the rigor of the analysis. And the logic and rigor of planning arguments and analyses are independent of the contexts of application.

Despite the many attractions of the just the facts view, planning and analysis are highly politicized practices. So it is neither surprising nor inappropriate that students also hear (and practitioners always learn) that some planning analysts and their clients use language to seduce and manipulate others into embracing the client's preferred values, beliefs, and behaviors.[2] Oriented toward getting things done, this politicized view treats planning analysts and their research tools simply as political instruments to achieve political ends.[3] Analytical tools and rhetoric certainly can be used in such ways, and advice about how to speak persuasively in this strictly manipulative sense is easy to find (Gronbeck 1983).

Is it any wonder, then, that planners and analysts feel schizophrenic? They learn—and come to say—that planning and analysis are technical and disciplined by objective methods, but they also learn—and come to fear—that planning and analysis are political and subject to outrageous manipulations (Meltsner 1985; Baum 1983; Burchell 1988; Forester 1989). As practitioners, planners learn that they are immersed in a deeply politicized world where opponents do not hesitate to lie, distort, and deceive, and where they seemingly must do the same in order to survive. To modern planning analysts, trying to act in accord with the scientific ethics of the technician can appear naive at best and dangerous at worst (Wachs 1985). Thus we seem to face a tragic choice: to be right and do good or to get things done (Hoch 1984; Throgmorton 1990).

There is a good way to bring together these two seemingly contradictory views of survey research and other tools of modern planning and analysis. Rather than thinking of rhetoric as gloss or seduction, we can regard it as the study and practice of persuasion, and we can recognize that persuasion is constitutive.[4] And rather than divorcing analytical tools from their contexts of application or treating them simply as political ammunition, let us think of surveys, models, and forecasts as *rhetorical tropes*. Let us regard them as figures of speech and argument that give meaning and power to the larger narratives of which they are a part.[5]

How might we begin to characterize this rhetorical approach to analysis, this approach that is both persuasive and constitutive? Drawing on the recent work of Dick Leith and George Myerson (1989), I suggest that an adequately rhetorical approach to planning and analysis would be built on three principles:

-Plans, analyses, and other planning arguments and stories are always addressed to someone else. To persuade, those stories and arguments have to take that someone else into account. Therefore *audience* is an important concept.

-All planning-related utterances can be seen as replies to other utterances. Thus "to argue is not merely to put forward a view, but also to speak, or write, *in the awareness of a differing or opposing view*" (Leith and Myerson 1989:85).

-The meaning of the utterance will always go beyond the conscious control of the author. So rhetoric encourages us to think about the play of meaning and how audiences (or readers) construct the meaning of utterances.

A fully rhetorical approach to policy analysis and planning would therefore emphasize the importance of thinking of surveys and other analytical tools as partial efforts to persuade *specific audiences* in *specific contexts* to accept proposed explanations, embrace inspiring visions, undertake recommended actions, and so on. But it would also acknowledge that such persuasive efforts take place in the context of a flow of utterances, replies, and counterreplies (i.e., a narrative), and that each of those utterances and replies is likely to be interpreted in diverse and often antagonistic ways. Audiences can assign different meanings to key terms, fill gaps in the original analysis, and choose to read either with or against the analysis (Fish 1979; Tompkins 1980; Freund 1987).

At the heart of persuasion is the use of tropes, literary or rhetorical devices—such as metaphor, metonymy, synecdoche, and irony—that involve using words in other than their literal sense (Quinn 1982). As a word, *trope* implies a turn on or toward something, a turn induced by the device itself. When we say "the fifth floor of City Hall" to mean "the mayor," we are using *metonomy*, substituting the name of one object for that of a related object or part. When we use survey samples to represent entire populations, by contrast, we are speaking by *synecdoche*, substituting parts for wholes. When we tap computer models to simulate transportation patterns, we are using *metaphor* to compare or identify two different things. When we confidently forecast future conditions while knowing that our earlier forecasts proved far off the mark, we are being— whether we know it or not—*ironic*, conveying a meaning opposite to or otherwise undercutting the literal sense of our utterance. And when we weave such tropes together into a larger narrative, we are engaging in persuasive discourse.

Rhetoric is not, however, simply persuasive; it is also constitutive. To use James Boyd White's terms, the ways in which analysts write and talk shape both the analysts' character and the community that exists between planning analysts and their audiences (1984, 1985).

Consider community first. How we (authors) write and talk shapes who we (a community of authors and readers or speakers and listeners) are and can become. Each time we write or speak, we create ideal readers or listeners whom actual readers or listeners—as objects of our plans and analyses or even participants in them—may or may not be, may or may not choose to become.

To clarify this point, let us assume that planning analysts can occupy one of three pure roles (scientist, politician, or advocate) and that they can address three parallel types of audiences: scientists, politicians, and passionate lay advocates (Throgmorton 1989, 1991). They can write and talk like scientists—that is, they can rely on a formal technical language, cite the relevant literature, and express theoretical arguments and results in an impersonal and dispassionate way—and thereby call into being a scientific community. Or they can write and talk like politicians (or advocates) and create a political (or normative) community. These rhetorical approaches merely reproduce existing communities. But note what happens when analysts write or speak to audiences that are inconsistent with their chosen roles—when scientific analysts speak to lay advocates, for example. At that point we either experience a complete breakdown in communication or else open up the opportunity to constitute or invent new communities. Our language, our rhetoric, is constitutive: it can help to reproduce existing communities or create new ones.

Consider character (or what I just referred to as "role") as well. By our choice of how to write and speak, by our choice of tropes, we create images of the kinds of characters we are or want to become. When we speak metaphorically of the city as a machine, for example, we create a character for ourselves and for our audiences: we think of ourselves as akin to the scientists, engineers, and technicians who make machines run more efficiently; and of our audiences as passive and manipulable parts of the machine. When we construct econometric models of electric power demand—metaphorical ways of talking about who uses electric power, how much, and why—we imagine ourselves to be experts who can predict the consumption of electric power, and we imagine politicians and advocacy groups to be irrelevant agents; since they do not appear in the models, they cannot (and should not) influence electric power use behavior. Note, however, that our rhetoric has the potential to create new characters for ourselves and others as well. We could, for example, work with politicians and advocacy groups to construct models that explicitly account for their ability to influence electric power use behavior. Any trope, any rhetoric, is constitutive: it can recognize or transform the characters that populate our world.

Because rhetoric is constitutive, it connects intimately with narrative. Narratives are just stories, but they tie closely to tropes (as *figures* of speech and argument) because narratives *configure* the particulars evoked by our literal and figural talk. Stated differently, narratives establish the context within which tropes gain meaning and power. Thus a flow of utterances, replies, and counterreplies can be emplotted as a flow of action (as a narrative) which can be turned—through the use of particular tropes by particular characters at particular times and places—in a different direction.[6] Such narratives tell us how the details in our plans and analyses relate to one another. In that way they provide our policy discourse with the figures that connect characters with communities (MacIntyre 1984; McGee and Nelson 1985). They can help us see, for example, how a survey prepared for a Chicago business association in late 1987 fit into the public controversy about whether the city of Chicago should take over part of Commonwealth Edison's electric power system.

To acknowledge that our rhetoric can be both persuasive and constitutive should lead us to ask a crucially *ethical* question: What kinds of communities, characters, and cultures do we want to help create? Eventually I will argue that planning analysts should strive not to speak purely scientifically or purely politically but to find a rhetoric that helps to create and sustain a public, democratic discourse. This should be a persuasive discourse that permits analysts (and others) to talk coherently about contestable views of what is good, right, and feasible. And I will argue that analysts should strive to create arenas that facilitate and encourage just such a persuasive, public discourse.

What, then, does this kind of rhetorical approach have to do with survey research and with the *Chicago Tribune* article cited above? Briefly this: Surveys are rhetorical tropes that reply to prior utterances (hence are parts of larger narratives), seek to persuade specific audiences, create open meanings subject to diverse interpretations, and help to constitute characters and communities. Let us first place the CACI's survey of Chicago businesses into the flow of utterances, replies, and counterreplies concerning the city of Chicago's exploration of alternatives to staying in Commonwealth Edison's system. Doing so will enable us to

see that the attitudes, expectations, and intentions of Chicago businesspeople had, by the middle of 1989, become a potential turning point
in that flow. Commonwealth Edison (also Com Ed or Edison) and the
caci needed to persuade one crucial audience (a task force appointed by
the mayor of Chicago) that those businesspeople were averse to the idea
of the city "taking over" Com Ed. They needed a particular trope of
planning and analysis: a survey.

Electric Power Planning and Rate Making in the Chicago Area, 1985–1990

The Commonwealth Edison Company owns and operates the electric
power system that serves Chicago and the northern one-third of Illinois.
The company began the flow of utterances and replies in the early 1970s
by starting—with the approval of the Illinois Commerce Commission
(icc)—the nation's largest nuclear construction program. To the dismay
of many, however, that program proved to be far more expensive and
time-consuming than originally planned. Its last six nuclear units would
have been finished by 1982 at a cost of $2.51 billion if Edison's original
estimates had been correct. In the end, however, they were not completed until 1988, and they cost just under $14 billion.

Edison and its critics explained the delays and overruns with two
very different stories. Edison attributed the delays and overruns to infla-
tion and to other factors *beyond its control*. Accordingly, it sought and
obtained six substantial rate hikes during the first five years of the 1980s,
including an 11 percent rate hike for its Byron 1 unit in late 1985. Then, in
early 1986, Edison announced that it would need another 32 percent rate
increase to cover the cost of its last three nuclear units (Byron 2 and
Braidwood 1 and 2)—unless some nontraditional approach could be
found.

Consumer groups told a very different story. Attributing Edison's
delays and overruns to *managerial incompetence and profit seeking*, and
claiming that the utility was building plants that were not needed, consumer groups petitioned the icc to cancel the Braidwood units. These
groups appealed the Byron 1 rate hike to the Illinois Supreme Court and
strenuously opposed Edison's efforts to obtain a rate increase to pay for
its last three plants.

Consumer groups were not alone in their opposition to Edison's
rate increases. The mayor of Chicago, Harold Washington, opposed them
as well. The mayor worried about Edison's increases and their economic

effects on Chicago and its residents; especially he worried about the jobs and businesses lost due to Edison's high rates. So Mayor Washington supported the consumer groups in their opposition to the rate hikes. Perhaps more important, he took advantage of the fact that Edison served the city and its residents pursuant to a franchise agreement that was due to expire in December 1990 unless jointly renewed by Edison and the city. In October 1985, therefore, the mayor directed his planning staff to explore alternatives to remaining wholly dependent on Com Ed.

In August 1986, a city-sponsored report estimated that the Chicago area would lose 85,000 to 112,000 jobs over the next twenty years if Edison received a 32 percent rate increase to pay for the three nuclear power plants that were nearing completion (Ziemba 1986). A year later a second city-sponsored report estimated that Chicagoans could save $10 to $18 billion at a cost of $1 to $7 billion over a twenty-year period if the city bought and operated a portion of Com Ed's facilities (Beck et al. 1987).

Edison attacked the Beck report vigorously, in ways that I cannot fully recount here. One particularly interesting attack, though, was indirect. Roughly three weeks after the Beck report was released, and shortly before the Chicago City Council was to vote on whether to fund an additional $500,000 to study Beck's proposal, the CACI released the *results* of a survey of Chicago businesses that had been conducted by Michael McKeon and Associates. According to Sam Mitchell, president of the CACI, the survey showed that nearly 30 percent of the 454 firms surveyed would relocate outside Chicago if the city became the sole provider of electricity, *thereby costing the city 250,000 jobs.* "We think," Mitchell said, "it would be prudent for Mayor Sawyer and the City Council to think long and hard about whether it is worth spending an additional half-million dollars to study a proposal which sends a negative signal to the business community. . . . The government must realize that the moment a half-million dollars is authorized, they set in motion planning by the business community that could ultimately cost Chicago a quarter of a million jobs" (Rectenwald 1987).

Consumer and community groups such as the Chicago Electric Options Campaign (CEOC) condemned the CACI's survey as "sheer propaganda." A year later they placed referenda on the ballots in fifteen wards. The vote showed extremely strong support for the view that the city should seek lower electric rates by exploring alternatives to reliance on Edison.

In early 1989, Mayor Eugene Sawyer (who had replaced the recently deceased Mayor Washington) appointed an Energy Task Force to help him decide what to do about renewing Edison's franchise.[7] On April 13, 1989, the task force listened to a lengthy presentation by Edison officials and heard a vice president of Com Ed say that the CACI survey showed that the people of Chicago wanted Edison to be their electricity supplier. Three weeks later, representatives of consumer groups spoke to the task force. Sam Mitchell of the CACI was the second speaker that day, and he reiterated the results of McKeon's 1987 survey of businesses. A community group spokesman immediately criticized the task force for allowing Mitchell to speak at that time, claiming that Mitchell had merely reiterated Edison's position. He urged the task force to "consider whether or not you don't have a Trojan Horse in your midst" (Energy Task Force 1989).

The CACI's survey was thus part of a flow of utterances and replies pertaining to the city's exploration of options. Defining electric power as a commodity, Edison had attempted to portray planning as the ability to control the future, to make events conform to the company's desires. Consumer groups tried, however, to turn the conversation away from controlling the future and toward the character of Edison's officials. Mayor Washington, in turn, tried to make the others define electric power as a service, not a commodity. The city's reply to Edison's claim that it would need a 32 percent rate hike was based on a "service" definition. Edison counterreplied using the CACI's survey as a trope, a trope that gained rhetorical power from its claim to have produced scientific results. Likewise, Edison "constructed" a community in which it and other businesses were not part of "the city." Consumer groups counterreplied using another trope (the referenda) in response to the CACI's survey. By the middle of 1989, the survey had become a focal point for the Mayor's Task Force. Edison had to persuade the task force that McKeon's survey truthfully represented the attitudes, expectations, and intentions of Chicago businesspeople. Sam Mitchell and Michael McKeon met with the task force on August 16, 1989, to explain how the survey had been conducted. As we shall see, some members of the task force had interpreted the CACI's survey in a way quite different from McKeon and his clients.

The Energy Task Force's Response to a Survey of Chicago Businesses

As the meeting began, twenty or so people sat at the outer sides of a hexagonal grouping of tables.[8] On the left sat several task force members;

on the right, community and consumer group representatives. Another ten to twenty observers were scattered around the perimeter. Robert Wilcox—a conservatively dressed, graying, middle-aged businessman who cochaired the Mayor's Task Force—called the meeting to order, then asked the consumer representatives to comment on a written question from the task force. For the next hour or so they engaged in a calm and reasoned conversation—one well suited to the plain, unadorned, modernist room in which the meeting took place. The setting was rather typical for the conduct of modern planning.

Wilcox then interrupted the flow of the meeting to give Sam Mitchell of the CACI a chance to speak. Hunched forward, arms crossed, Mitchell read the following statement:

> Thank you, Mr. Chairman. We appreciate the courtesy. The task force in a directed question asked CACI, "Would you provide your survey instrument and the tabulation of results? What sources of information did you use to develop that instrument?" I believe that we have answered that question before both to this body and to others, and that answer is "no." Our rationale is that our research is proprietary and we do not release proprietary information. We release the results of our surveys and the questions concerning those results and the methodology used in conducting that research. That has been the policy of the association since 1904; it remains the same today. While many in this room will not find that answer to their satisfaction, that is the reality of the matter.
>
> Another reality is that our research appears to be the only document that has been brought to this body that has been impeached in this manner. To our knowledge no other group's work has been challenged. We believe that in . . . challenging the credibility of this research the association's credibility is placed in question. We can only draw the conclusion that some members of this task force did not like the results of our work and seek to discredit it in order to feature their own aims.
>
> As I said a moment ago, we have always been willing to answer questions concerning the results of our research and the methodology used in conducting that research. Toward that end we have asked Mr. Michael McKeon, of Michael McKeon Research, Incorporated, who conducted this research, to appear here to discuss the methodology and the results. Mr. McKeon is well known and highly regarded in the field of market research and is widely used by business in the region. I feel obliged to point out that Mike came back from vacation on the East Coast to meet with the task force and answer these questions and, if it pleases the Chair, I would like Mike to join us at the table.

The confrontation did not begin well. Mitchell indicated both that he felt the credibility of his organization (and the research it had sponsored) had been unfairly challenged and that he had no intention of giving the task force what it was asking for. But he did give them Michael McKeon.

McKeon began by indicating that he was unhappy about having to interrupt his vacation in order to speak to the task force. Then, interrupting a questioner, he said:

> Well, basically what the process was we were requested to do was do a survey of businesses in the Chicago area to see what their feelings was on a study that came out two years ago, the initial one, which called in some cases for—I'm not nearly an expert on the stuff which I'm not expected . . . I'm expected to test about the public opinions. Basically what we did was, is we had Dunn and Bradstreet generate in three divisions for us random names of companies located in the city of Chicago, based on 50 and under, 50 employees and under, 51 to 250 employees, and over 250 employees. We designed the survey to just basically test their mood on what they felt was the, the results have been released here, on what they felt the prospects of the city running the, having something to do with running, the taking over the electric service, providing electric service and things like that. The research was done under controlled means, statistical probabilities, and everything else like that. And, we just ran it. We designed the questionnaire so that we could, so that we got a free flow of information.

At that point McKeon shifted topics, angrily portraying himself as an expert whose work had been criticized by politically motivated know-nothings:

> I might point out that, just for the comments I've heard here, it's interesting, you know, it's the common problem I have with clients. I might point out that our firm was the first one in the country to track the LaRouche problem long before it ever it happened. . . . We were the first ones five years ago to release our findings nationwide on crime and drugs as a major problem in the country which everyone else ignored. . . . [I]n the governor's race of Stevenson versus Thompson we were the only one to hit it accurately. The last time around in the mayor's race we came out with the numbers far before anyone else in the public and was proved correct.
>
> Basically, what my business is, which is a lot different from most of the market research firms, is most of the time I have to back up my numbers with reality. The elections come, the elections go, the referendums happen and go down; [pounding his hand on the table] my numbers are in the

papers ahead of time so that they're checked and they're right. And quite frankly, from what I've heard questioned here, [voice rising] the only questions ever heard, the only ones that have questioned, the last three, four people have questioned my numbers. . . . Basically what happens is, is when people don't pay attention, they don't, they don't like the results, whether it's really reality or not. And my numbers have always been that way. Yeah.

So the issue according to McKeon was that he had had predictive success but his critics (his immediate audience) were too ignorant to know it. Furthermore, the quality of his work could be assessed by comparing his preelection surveys with actual election results. At that point one of the community representatives—Scott Bernstein, executive director of the Center for Neighborhood Technology—asked a question. Bernstein, a thin young man with short, wiry, black hair and beard, wondered whether there might be a significant difference between a survey of business intentions and a survey of voter intentions. "[I]f that's the case," he said, "you were widely quoted in the same newspaper, or your survey was by CACI, as having something to say about the likelihood of businesses' intent to leave should the city act to play some sort of municipal role. Would you comment for us on the nature of that question [here McKeon tried to interrupt] and what and how, and how you approached it and whether you feel as strongly about that as you feel about the likelihood of the outcome of the attorney general's race?"

By this time McKeon had become extremely hostile. His anger, coupled with the CACI's refusal to present the actual survey instrument, led to turmoil in the meeting. The confusion concerned the precise wording of the questionnaire and whether that wording had skewed the results in Com Ed's favor. Dodging Bernstein's question about comparability of surveys, McKeon focused on whether businesses would be likely to leave the city:

> Oh I think there would be significant shifts. I think there were two parts to that question. One . . . part of that proposed survey called for 50 percent cogeneration, if you recall[9] [pointing at Mitchell]. . . . Am I right or wrong? [Then, after hearing an affirmative answer from Bernstein:] Fifty percent cogeneration is . . . not what . . . we threw into the action, but what the report that your study and analysis [the Beck report] said was there. Fifty percent cogeneration for the businesses. . . . Are you familiar with that? It's in the study. It's in the Beck study [angrily jabbing his finger toward Bernstein]. True or false? Are you familiar with that?

At this point McKeon's barrage of hostile comments was interrupted by one of the task force members, Michael Bell of Certified Public Accountants for the Public Interest, who sought to bring the conversation back to the initial question. "I haven't made any comments pro or con," Bell said, "but I feel like you're getting in here and boxing with somebody. . . . Could we just talk about . . . what the issues are here, rather, because it just feels to me . . . that this is getting pretty loaded and kind of off the tangent. . . . What I am interested [in] right now is in process and in some of the questions the way they were asked. . . . We're not getting . . . the survey instrument so we're, we want to be able to rely on what you are saying."

After another brief flurry of heated exchanges, during which McKeon referred to the task force as a "hostile committee," the conversation returned to the 50 percent cogeneration issue. Martin Heckman, an informally dressed older man who represented the Labor Coalition on Public Utilities, asked thrice whether the survey instrument could be made available. Finally, Sam Mitchell of the CACI intervened, impatiently: "I'd like to answer that if I may. Mr. Heckman, at the last meeting I saw you in fact carrying a copy of an editorial from *Commerce* magazine which outlined in totality . . . the results of that survey. You have that material in your possession." McKeon then chimed in: "The questions that are on that survey are the questions we asked. Period. There was no other loading, there was no other bias or anything else like that. And so, what you see is what you got. The survey instrument is exactly what's on the poll."[10]

The task force then inquired about the actual phrasing of the questions. David Kraft of Nuclear Energy Information Services, a public interest organization that sought to inform the public about the risks associated with nuclear power, opened the inquiry: "What sort of reliability checks were done on the terms used and the questions—for example, the words *city*, *became*, and *sole provider*—to make sure that that was consistently interpreted from participant to participant in the survey?" McKeon had some difficulty answering Kraft's question: "There were . . . other questions of supply," he said. After McKeon rambled a bit about how the survey had been conducted shortly after Mayor Washington released the Beck report, Kraft responded, "Essentially what you're saying is, the only estimate of reliability was the context of what was going on at the time?" Though calmer now, McKeon still did not seem to understand. "All right," said Kraft,

> I'll explain more clearly if I can. If that question were given to me now, as opposed to then. . . . You see it's a different context first of all. And sec-

ondly . . . does the term *city* connote to those participants the aldermen as have been portrayed in the press, did it connote the Department of Planning, did it mean city hall? . . . I mean . . . there are different ways of interpreting it is what I'm . . . driving at. And the same with the word *sole provider;* did that mean that they were the ones who are actually going to produce the electrons or did it mean they would be the fiscal backers or the, see what I'm driving at, you see what I'm driving at?

McKeon finally seemed to understand.

First of all, what I think you have to look at . . . is . . . you're . . . an energy task force that's looking for this, looking for that. What we deal with is public perception. The public has a very limited perception of what's going on. You can talk about energy supplies. Mr. Bernstein talked about. . . . One of his top clients [Sears] moved out of Chicago now, moved to, moved right outside the city where the rates are still the same and everything else like that. . . . When they think of *city,* what do they think of? Any kind of municipalization. Now we could have been more negative, we could have said that the Chicago City Council is considering taking over the collection company. Right through the roof. My expertise, what I do best—I feel I do it better than anybody else—is, is we try and make the questions as neutral as possible so what we can get out of it is the people's interpretation of what's going on, not what the clients feel is there, or anyone else for that matter.

Kraft chose not to challenge the validity of McKeon's survey results. He did, however, repeat his worries about reliability: "What I'm driving at," he said, "is I needed a better clarification of the reliability of the particular instruments because you said, you say right now, what the name of the game is: it's public perception. . . . Depending on how these words were perceived, people will frame their answers." Undaunted, McKeon simply claimed that "they were highly neutral words."

The discussion then turned to another question that was, in the eyes of some task force members, "loaded." One of the consumer group representatives asked McKeon whether the survey asked a question that indicated the city would require businesses to reduce their electricity usage by 50 percent, either through reduction in demand or by replacing utility power with cogenerated power. McKeon's answer was difficult to follow: "We did the clear first, with 'the city of Chicago becomes a sole supplier of your electrical supply, how will this impact your business in your planning?' were the exact terms. OK? After that, we said well, what if they had to come up with cogeneration and things like that and conservation and things? And then the numbers went right off the chart. [Then he was asked again whether the question indicated that a 50 percent reduction would be required.] . . . What if you relied on 50 percent cogeneration? Yeah. . . . That type of thing." At last, something concrete. After scanning through some papers, Scott Bernstein zeroed in on the 50 percent figure:

> Just a point of clarification. The scenarios that were provided by the R.W. Beck Company for cogenerated power [thumbing through the Beck report] did look at the potential of 2,100 megawatts of cogeneration but the figures actually used in the various scenarios are [unintelligible] no, no way. We're talking about a base load of 4,500 megawatts at a range from 35 to 800 from cogeneration, a peak of 1,322 megawatts for conservation and cogeneration alone in the year 2005, when demand would have increased by almost 1,000 megawatts, also equaling roughly what we're projecting here, something like a 20 percent contribution from, in effect, improvements in technology. So if you ask the question, you know, would you, what would you do if you had to have 50 percent cogeneration, could you . . . [at this point both Bernstein and McKeon speak at once, and neither can be understood]. . . . Here's the study. You can read it yourself.

McKeon seemed surprised and a bit shaken. "Is there 50 percent?" McKeon asked. "Could that be 50 percent? No? Never could be interpreted so? With the cogeneration it never could be interpreted as 50 percent?" Sam Mitchell stepped in at this point and tried to shift responsibility for the erroneous question to the city. McKeon shifted his ground:

> But this is specious because of the fact that the question before that without even, without the cogeneration still had a ton of people moving out, and what were the numbers on that? It was still there, it was still a negative impact. . . . You can sit and shake your head. . . . If we had asked 20 percent [gesturing angrily again] . . . then they'd still have gone. Are you kidding me? You ask any company, do you own businesses around here, any of you own businesses? The city comes up and says, oh, by the way, you might have to do 20 percent cogeneration, what do you think the results are going to be? Do you think the results are going to be any different at 20 percent than 50 percent? [Jabbing his finger across the table at Bernstein:] Ask him. You are the one who thought of it? Do you think it's going to be any different at 20 percent than 50 percent?

Unpersuaded, Bernstein tossed his papers onto the table. Shrugging, he simply said, "I don't think that's the question. You've answered the question that's on the table, how you conducted the study and what your assumptions were. Thanks a lot. It's self-evident."

At that point the meeting appeared to be over. But then, after two or three minutes of side conversation, one other key issue returned: the credibility of the CACI and McKeon's research. Sam Mitchell stressed that he had asked McKeon to take part in the meeting because the survey research had been "impeached," and that offended Mitchell: "We know of no other document brought before this body that has been impeached. We consider that not only a question of the credibility of the research and the professionals we hire, we consider it a question of credibility of the organization. We . . ." At this point Michael Bell began objecting while Mitchell was still speaking. "The Beck report was impeached, Mr. Mitchell, too," Bell calmly insisted. "This is an open society. The Beck report was impeached on a number of different points. There is no reason why there should be any higher ground for a survey and the questioning of what the survey is." "Our point," Mitchell replied, "is there should be no lower ground." Bell found this response deeply irritating:

> Mr. Mitchell, I'm not going to let you get away with saying that no other report was impeached. That's incorrect. You are doing a disservice to a number of the members of this task force by . . . assuming that . . . a survey . . . that you conducted and so on is the only thing that is being impeached. That is not correct. . . . The body of the task force and a substantial number, I don't know if it's the majority, have a concern to try to be on an equal ground here, on a level ground. There may be people who have their biases, we come into life with biases, that's the way it is. But to say that a survey is the only instrument is misstating it. The Beck report was impeached; you've done it yourself. Let's get beyond that and see where we are. . . . I would very much appreciate having people in the arena to work some of this out rather than getting back into this, this business of them and us, with due respect. . . . It bothers me completely to have this gentleman come in [gesturing to McKeon], I respect your process I have no reason to doubt that process, to come in and box with everybody like we've all got the same maps. Let's stop it.

Sam Mitchell tried to indicate that the task force itself was biased and that its reaction to the survey reflected that bias. "I, in my exposure to this body," he said, "have heard this research impeached. I have heard no comments as to the Beck study, in front of this body when I have been here, and I have seen nothing of importance on the Beck study being impeached by others. I bring to you, to this body, then, my biases to what I understand, which is a severe question of the credibility of the product that we produced and the credibility of the organization. That's why I've gone to the process of bringing Mike in." Disturbed by use of "impeached," McKeon made one last comment, addressing Bell: "You said that this isn't the only instrument that's been impeached. I don't think my stuff has been impeached. You said the Beck study has been impeached; there is no reason to say why this study is. Do you think this study has been impeached? . . . The other thing is too, is that if the committee is going to operate on fair ground then the members of the committee shouldn't be taking shots in the papers about stuff that you don't even know.

McKeon then rose to leave the meeting. But before he left, Martin Heckman of the Labor Coalition made one last comment to co-chair Robert Wilcox. "Bob, I'd like to make one point. The point is the Beck report itself is impeached. The day that the Beck report was released, on that very day within a matter of an hour, Commonwealth Edison threw somebody in to raise the question about the city wants precinct captains to run Commonwealth. So they tried to impeach it within hours."

Planning and Analysis as Persuasive and Constitutive Discourse

Earlier I claimed that planning and analysis are rhetorical activities and that planning analysts should think of survey research and other tools as rhetorical tropes that reply to prior utterances (and give meaning and power to the larger narratives of which they are a part), seek to persuade specific audiences, create open meanings subject to diverse interpretations, and help to constitute planning characters and communities.

The case just recounted strongly supports such a rhetorical conception of planning and analysis. It shows, first, that the CACI's survey acted as a trope in a larger narrative about the desirability of the city taking over Edison's electric power system. The survey replied to two prior reports prepared for the city, reports that indicated Chicagoans would be better off if the city purchased all or part of the Com Ed system. How Chicago businesspeople felt about (and would react to) such a purchase was unknown. The survey, presented in the scientific terms of "results," supported a claim that the businesspeople would be deeply displeased. But the claim that the survey simply measured attitudes and intentions belied its tropal nature. Given the businesspersons' "limited perception," acknowledged by the survey researcher himself, the survey had to construct their understanding of the situation. Thus it had to prefigure their sense of how they would respond.

Here is one particularly revealing example. McKeon's survey read: "Part of the city's plan for the takeover of the electrical service would require a business to reduce electrical consumption by 50 percent or generate half the electrical power it uses. Under these conditions, what effect would this plan have on your company's future plans?" (Anonymous 1988). If we look at the wording of this question carefully, we can see that three particular aspects function as figures of language or argument.

First is *the city's plan*. In context, this phrase seems to refer to the Beck report, which was released a few weeks before the survey was conducted. Neither the city nor the Beck report, however, had referred to the report as the city's "plan." The city portrayed the report as a quantitative assessment of the likely economic consequences of alternative courses of action, not as a plan about what to do and how to do it. Indeed, the CACI's release of McKeon's survey occurred just a few days before the city council was to decide whether to fund the additional studies required to help the city decide what to do. Referring to the Beck report as "the city's plan" probably conveyed the misleading impression that the city already knew its intentions.

Second is the claim that the city's plan would *require* businesses to conserve or generate 50 percent of the power they use. As Bernstein's questions tried to demonstrate, nothing in the Beck report or in the city's actions up to December 1987 indicated that businesses would be "required" to do anything. The city was clearly inclined to encourage electricity conservation and cogeneration, and to do so by offering price and other institutional incentives, much as Commonwealth Edison was then offering numerous incentives for businesses *not* to conserve or cogenerate. But at no point had the city indicated an intention to require businesses to conserve.

And third is the survey's use of the term *takeover*. This word implied that the city was on the verge of seizing something that belonged to someone else, that it intended to expropriate property. This trope radically transformed the context and meaning of the city's actions. Though the survey never said so, the city's exploration of options was taking place in the context of an expiring franchise. In 1948 the citizens of Chicago had granted Edison the exclusive right to provide electric power and services to the city in return for payment of an annual franchise fee and other services provided to the city. That franchise agreement was due to expire in December 1990 unless jointly renewed by Com Ed and the city. Thus the city had every legal and moral right to explore options to remaining on Com Ed's system and continuing the exclusive franchise. Portraying this simply as a takeover twisted and impoverished the meaning of the city's actions in an objectionable way.

To be sure, the CACI and Mr. McKeon might want to defend the accuracy of such terms. But the issue here is more their figurality than their accuracy. Planning analysts and their instruments must use these kinds of words. Yet terms such as *the city's plan, require, takeover,* and *proprietary* can coalesce to make any survey into a powerful trope of argument—not just because such words might mislead readers but because they shape our understanding of the situation at issue. By using a particular language, the survey made *the city* into a synecdoche standing for the board of aldermen and the political machine in Chicago. By contrast, community groups used *the city* as a metaphor, meaning "the city is us." We can imagine a case for either construction, so my main point is not that one side is purely right and the other damnably wrong. Instead, the key lesson is that no instrument of policy-oriented planning can avoid persuasive, rhetorical construction of characters and communities. Scientific talk of survey "results" might obscure that crucial feature of planning and analysis, but it cannot eliminate it. The same tropality appears in the survey's division of *the business community* from *the city.* Surely this joined with *takeover* and other terms to help survey respondents think in terms of corrupt politicians expropriating private property and forcing private businesses to do what the politicians wanted. Would many businesses leave Chicago under such circumstances? What do you think? But remember, there can be no neutral words about contested issues: other survey phrasings would lead in other directions. The lesson is not to avoid or debunk surveys but to understand how they must work tropally. Then we can do them well and read them wisely.

The case also shows that the survey researcher and his client had to persuade a specific audience (the Mayor's Task Force) that the survey had been conducted competently and that its results were accurate and reliable. When the Mayor's Task Force began meeting in early 1989, it seemed as if that group would play a crucial role in determining what the city would do with regard to its franchise with Com Ed. The economic impact of alternate courses of action was a crucial factor for it to consider. The utility had to persuade this specific audience in this specific context that the economic effects of a city takeover would be disastrous for the city. The CACI's survey, and Mitchell and McKeon's subsequent meeting with the task force, were efforts to persuade the task force of the same things. Whether they would succeed in those efforts largely depended on the extent to which opposing or differing views were acknowledged in the survey.

Therefore, the case also shows the importance of speaking with awareness of differing or opposing views and how particular audiences can—due to the inherent plasticity of language—read meanings into surveys that differ from the one intended by the survey's client or researchers. The CACI's survey displayed no overt awareness of opposing views, and suppression of that awareness became quite evident during the task force's meeting. Intimately familiar with the flow of utterances, replies, and counterreplies of which the survey was a part, several members of the task force read the CACI's survey in ways different from the CACI. They challenged the CACI's motivation in producing the survey, and they convinced themselves that the survey was simply an effort to deceive and manipulate the business community. "You've answered the question that's on the table," said Scott Bernstein. "Thanks a lot. It's self-evident." Mr. McKeon's inarticulate but indignant response might make us wonder whether the situation was that simple. And it is interesting that the critics on the task force did not challenge the notion that surveys *could* produce objective results. Their implication was instead that the survey asked the wrong ("loaded") questions. They believed, perhaps with good reason, that other questions—possibly ones based on the views of community groups—would have yielded starkly different, and likely better, responses.

One might think, therefore, that good survey researchers could have obtained a true measure of the business community's response by testing the sensitivity of responses to language. That is the technical fix taught to modern planning analysts, and it is far from completely incorrect, though it typically forgets that any survey must figure as a trope of argument. At another pole of the postmodern arguments about planning and analysis we might postulate a survey conducted in the context of a Habermasian "ideal speech community." In that case the CACI and the community groups would gather happily together with a planning analyst to choose questions that would test the sensitivity of business responses to diverse phrasings (Habermas 1987). We can imagine that such a revised survey could have gone a long way toward reducing conflict between Com Ed and consumer groups, and we can hope that creating such a policy forum based on principles of honesty and trust would have led to a better understanding of what Chicago residents think of a potential takeover. But we must not forget that we have task forces and surveys precisely because they sometimes seem the closest we can get to such undistorted, democratic dialogue. Both the technical and the communitarian utopias are pleasant dreams, but they are dreams and figures nonetheless. Planning and analysis are deeply politicized practices, and no technical fix or ideal speech community is going to overcome that.

Last, the case also draws our attention to the ways in which planning rhetoric (in this case Michael McKeon's) constitutes character and community. The story reveals important differences between how to *do* survey research and how to *be* a survey researcher.[11] The tale encourages us to ask the following questions: What characters did McKeon's rhetoric create for himself and presume for his audience? How did task force members characterize McKeon, the CACI, and themselves? What kinds of community did McKeon create (or re-create) through his survey and his testimony? How might the meeting have gone had McKeon adopted a different character for himself?

We notice first that McKeon portrayed himself as an expert, a scientist who used neutral questions to generate results. He behaved, however, like a stereotypical combative Chicago political hack. His dress (unkempt), his gestures (jabbing his finger toward questioners), his vocal intonation (loud, angry), and his frequent lapses into grammatical incoherence all contradicted his claim to scientific character, leading many in the task force to conclude that he was deceitful and untrustworthy. By acting like a political hack, McKeon seemed to expect his audience to respond in a similar way: hostilely, aggressively, and evasively—and thus to reproduce a (Chicago) culture (of politics) based on deceit and manipulation. Was this strategy, stress, or something else? We cannot be sure. Contrary to McKeon's invitation, however, the task force members chose to be different characters. Bell, for example, appeared three times in the conversation: first, to ask a simple, straightforward question; then, to ask McKeon to "stop boxing"; and last, to protest Mitchell's claim that McKeon's survey was the only work to be "impeached." He did not allow McKeon to go unanswered, but he chose not to respond solely in McKeon's terms.

So McKeon posed (metaphorically, at least) as the "political hack." Why? Why did he come into the meeting reeking of intense hostility? Lacking the chance to ask McKeon directly, we can only consider some possibilities. Perhaps that is just the way he is, at least under pressure. Most of us have encountered—or have been—such characters at one time or another, so we cannot dismiss that possibility. A second alternative is that McKeon truly regarded the task force members as technically uninformed and politically motivated meddlers. We might infer this from McKeon's words and demeanor. But if he thought that when he entered the meeting, did he retain the opinion by the time he left? Bernstein and Kraft asked him too many technically sound questions to seem ignorant, and Bell was much too evenhanded to sound politically craven. A third, strategic, possibility is that McKeon and Mitchell jointly agreed that the best defense was a good offense, and hence attacked their opponents on grounds of ignorance and politics rather than directly answering questions and objections from the task force. My suspicion is that this is a better characterization. Looming behind McKeon's research firm, and behind Mitchell's association, was the pervasive shadow of Commonwealth Edison. As a power behind the scenes, it had nothing to gain and much to lose by revealing the extent to which survey research could have shaped the attitudes and intentions of Chicago businesses and residents. If McKeon had responded openly to Kraft's plea to design a survey that tested the respondents' sensitivity to terms like *city* and *sole provider*, he might have placed Edison's monopoly at risk. But a final possibility, one that also rings with truth, is that Mitchell simply threw McKeon to the lions. After all, the key question became whether the task force would be allowed to see the survey instrument, and Mitchell left McKeon in no position to allow that.

How, then, might McKeon have responded differently to his audience? Rather than appearing to be a cartoon of how to fail at persuasion using the mask of science, might he not have portrayed himself as a neutral professional, a polished deflector of uninformed questions from outside his realms of expertise? Presuming rhetoric to be mere words, might he not have spoken in a more polished and dignified way—while remaining just as uncommunicative—and thereby have been more likely to persuade his opponents? A more polished researcher could have obscured the central issue—the tropal (and perhaps loaded) nature of the survey's questions—by saying something like, "The majority of our respondents would not fully grasp a technical explanation of the complexity of the Beck report" or "We've learned that trying to fully capture subtle distinctions among options in survey responses diminishes the validity of the response." The polished planning analyst could then have argued that the survey might have contained some unavoidable, but minor, distortion. By obscuring the central issue, such a polished researcher would have appeared to be less of a hack but still would not have persuaded many in the audience. To persuade them, he would have to have been willing to discuss details about how the survey questions were selected and how the survey was administered, and he would have to have been open to the possibility of modifying his questions to account for his opponents' views. This he was unwilling or unable to do.

Alternately, McKeon might have remained true to his self-portrait as a neutral technician, a forthcoming expert. Had he done that, however, he might have been compelled by the ethics of his science to reveal much more about his survey instrument.[12] In that case his scientific ethos might conflict with the political nature of his commitment to the client, be it the CACI or Com Ed. McKeon, like planning analysts in general, would have faced the tragic choice of liberal politics: to be right and do good (in his own view) or to get things done (in his client's view).

A third alternative was probably unavailable to McKeon but is one that we should strive to make possible: he might have adopted the character of a thoroughly rhetorical planning analyst. Such an analyst would have learned more about the task force members—about how they thought and what kinds of questions they would be likely to ask. Having discovered the grounds for their opposing views—by learning about the prior flow of utterances, replies, and counterreplies—the analyst would have sought a different mix of tropes to persuade this particular audience. And, most important, the analyst would have adopted a rhetoric that could sustain public, democratic, persuasive discourse about contestable claims on what is good, right, or feasible—in this particular context. The difficult challenge now facing planning analysts, in Chicago and elsewhere, is to find better ways of listening and speaking and to conceive how we can begin to talk in those ways.

In the end, this story about the uses of survey research in Chicago teaches that planning analysts are engaged in a thoroughly rhetorical practice. Accordingly, they should surrender any further pretense to neutrality, objectivity, and universal truth, such as the "true" measure of business response to a city "takeover." Surrendering the pretense to objectivity does not, however, mean that analysts should flee to the extreme of defining planning and analysis as just more forms of politics gone amok. They should instead embrace persuasive discourse and political conflict and realize that survey results are, like all alleged "facts" of planning and analysis, inherently tropal and contestable. Surveys must be scientific *and* rhetorical, professional *and* political, because they—like all other planning and analytical tools—configure policy-oriented arguments.

Notes

I gratefully acknowledge the advice rendered by various people who have read this essay, including Ernest Alexander, John Friedmann, Helen Liggett, Dowell Myers, Charles Williams, several anonymous reviewers, and numerous participants in the Association of Collegiate Schools of Planning/Association of European Schools of Planning Joint International Planning Congress of 1991. I also thank John Nelson, Fred Antzack, Ira Stauber, Bob Boynton, Ed Arrington, Kathleen Farrell, and other participants in the University of Iowa's spring 1991

Scholars' Workshop on the Rhetoric of Political Argumentation and acknowledge the support services provided by the University of Iowa Center for Advanced Study. This material is based in part on work supported by the National Science Foundation's Ethics and Values branch under grant DIR-8911870. The government has certain rights in this material.

This chapter presents a revised version of an earlier publication: "Planning as a Rhetorical Activity: Survey Research as a Trope in Arguments about Electric Power Planning in Chicago," *Journal of the American Planning Association 59,* no. 3 (1993).

1. Planning and policy analysis are not identical practices. Many professional planners, particularly those who practice at the city or county level, define their activity primarily in physical terms: they seek to guide the physical development of their communities. But many other professional planners define their activity in more policy-oriented terms and seek to bring their professional expertise to deliberations about alternate courses of action at all levels of government and in both the public and private spheres. This latter set of planners (and some of the former) have much in common with policy analysts. Following Forester (1989), I will refer to policy analysts and policy-oriented planners collectively as planning analysts, and I will use the terms *planning* and *analysis, planners* and *analysts,* interchangeably. For a detailed comparison of policy analysis and policy-oriented planning, see Alterman and MacRae (1983).

2. Notice the similarity between the planning analyst's situation and the more general human situation as discussed in Martha Nussbaum's wonderful book *The Fragility of Goodness* (1986). As she explains, humans frequently have to choose between two or more valid ethical claims. Pained by this necessity, some analysts try, by defining planning and analysis narrowly as a purely technical activity, to structure their lives so as to escape such tragic choices. Nussbaum implies, however, that defining our practices in such a narrow way alters our characters, making us into something rather monstrous: technical automatons who, by seeking to simplify and control our world, choose not to risk our sense of openness. Fearing the vagaries of luck, happenstance, and politics, we imagine them away in crystalline plans of technical purity. Is it not, she would ask, ultimately better to plan in the face of contingency, uncertainty, and conflict?

3. John Locke (cited in Simons 1990:1) captures well the view of scientists who condemn this kind of manipulative rhetoric: "If we would speak of things as they are, we must allow that all the arts of rhetoric, besides order and clearness . . . are for nothing else but to insinuate wrong ideas, move the passions, and thereby mislead the judgement; and so indeed are perfect cheats; and therefore . . . they are certainly, in all discourses that pretend to inform or instruct, wholly to be avoided; and where truth and knowledge are concerned, cannot but be thought a great fault, either of the language or person that makes use of them."

4. For insight into current views of rhetoric in various professional and scientific activities see Bazerman (1988), Hunter (1990), Klamer et al. (1988), Majone (1989), McCloskey (1985), Nelson et al. (1987), Simons (1989, 1990), Throgmorton (1991), Wetlaufer (1990), and White (1984, 1985).

5. Characterizing planning as a rhetorical activity is part of a larger turn toward the importance of language, discourse, and argument in analysis and planning (e.g., Goldstein 1984; Forester 1989; Mandelbaum 1990, 1991; Throgmorton 1991). The rhetorical approach presented in this essay builds on that prior work by drawing attention to the importance of the speaker-audience or writer-reader relationship and to the constitutive role of planning and analytical discourse.

6. For further discussion of planning as persuasive storytelling about the future see Throgmorton (1992b). See also Cronon (1992) for a very interesting and compatible assessment of history as an endless struggle among competing narratives and values.

7. The task force consisted of thirty-six private citizens of varied backgrounds, including business, professional, labor, and community representatives (Mayor's Task Force on Energy, 1989).

8. A reader might wonder about the methods used to select and research this particular case. As the first portions of the essay should have made clear, the first step was to learn about the larger narratives of which the case is a part. Details about those narratives can be found in Throgmorton (1992a, 1992b). The flow of those narratives strongly suggested that the caci's survey marked a potentially critical turning point in the controversy. Subsequent conversations with ceoc representatives and Chicago Planning Department staff led me to learn that the department had videotaped a Mayor's Task Force meeting in which Michael McKeon discussed the caci's survey. (The meeting was also shown on the Chicago municipal information television channel, wctv). I obtained a copy of the videotape and watched it four times. Struck by its relevance to the rhetoric of planning, I asked a graduate student to prepare a verbatim transcript of the meeting, omitting such verbal ticks as "ah" and "uh." I added comments about physical gestures where appropriate. To save space, I shortened the transcript while trying to remain faithful to the original videotape. To check my own viewing for potential bias, I showed the tape to four colleagues and to graduate students in one of my courses. All their responses but one were consistent with mine. One major drawback to the tape is that it rarely shows members of the audience reacting to a speaker's comments and gestures. See Energy Task Force (1989).

9. Cogeneration is a technical process which involves the simultaneous generation of electric power and usable heat. A large-scale shift to cogeneration by businesses could have a dramatic effect on Edison's position as the sole provider of electric power in the Chicago area.

10. Mitchell's and McKeon's responses seemed to satisfy the task force members. But note that a *Commerce* magazine editorial (Anonymous 1988) leaves it

unclear whether there were additional questions, saying only that "selected questions and findings of the CACI survey include the following."

11. Some readers might argue that the story recounted in this essay is not really about professional planners and analysts except in the broadest sense. Michael McKeon surely does not fit the ideal conception of a professional planning analyst; but survey research is a vital part of policy analysis, and McKeon's survey acted as an important trope in arguments over the city's effort to explore options. We can learn a great deal by observing practitioners, regardless of whether they are formally trained as planners or analysts. My sense is that most schools of planning and analysis tend to teach their students how to do survey research, then have them read an article or two about how to be a survey researcher. That is not a good balance. Students cannot understand survey research (or any other analytical tool) without being aware of the diverse contexts in which it will be used and defended.

12. Babbie (1973:362) reflects this ethos when he insists that "each scientist operates under a normative obligation to share his findings with the scientific community, which means sharing them with nonscientists as well." For Babbie that means not just sharing findings but providing enough information on the survey to enable a reader to replicate the entire study independently.

References

Alterman, R., and D. MacRae, Jr. 1983. Planning and Policy Analysis. *Journal of the American Planning Association* 49:200–215.

Anonymous. 1988. Strong Opposition to Municipalized Electric Service. *Commerce* 84:15.

Babbie, E. R. 1973. *Survey Research Methods.* Beaumont, Calif.: Wadsworth.

Baum, H. 1983. *Planners and Public Expectations.* Cambridge: Schenkman.

Bazerman, C. 1988. *Shaping Written Knowledge.* Madison: University of Wisconsin Press.

Beck. R. W., and Associates. 1987. *Electric Supply Options Study.* Prepared for the city of Chicago Department of Planning. Indianapolis: R. W. Beck and Associates.

Burchell, R. W., ed. 1988. Symposium on Planning, Power, and Politics. *Society* 26:4–42.

Cronon, W. 1992. A Place for Stories: Nature, History, and Narrative. *Journal of American History* 78:1347–76.

Energy Task Force. 1989. Videotape of public meeting held on August 16. Chicago Department of Planning.

Fish, S. 1979. *Is There a Text in This Class?* Cambridge: Harvard University Press.

Forester, J. 1989. *Planning in the Face of Power.* Berkeley: University of California Press.

Freund, E. 1987. *The Return of the Reader.* New York: Methuen.

Goldstein, H. A. 1984. Planning as Argumentation. *Environment and Planning B* 2:297–312.

Gronbeck, B. 1983. *The Articulate Person.* 2d ed. Glenview, Ill.: Scott, Foresman.

Habermas, J. 1987. *The Philosophical Discourse of Modernity.* Trans. F. Lawrence. Cambridge: MIT Press.

Hoch, C. 1984. Doing Good and Being Right. *Journal of the American Planning Association* 50:335–45.

———. 1990. Power, Planning, and Conflict. *Journal of Architectural and Planning Research* 7:271–83.

Hunter, A., ed. 1990. *The Rhetoric of Social Research.* New Brunswick, N.J.: Rutgers University Press.

Klamer, A., D. N. McCloskey, and R. Solow, eds. 1988. *The Consequences of Economic Rhetoric.* Cambridge: Cambridge University Press.

Leith, D., and G. Myerson. 1989. *The Power of Address.* London: Routledge.

McCloskey, D. N. 1985. *The Rhetoric of Economics.* Madison: University of Wisconsin Press.

McGee, M. C., and J. S. Nelson. 1985. Narrative Reason in Public Argument. *Journal of Communication* 35:139–55.

MacIntyre, A. 1984. *After Virtue.* Notre Dame, Ind.: University of Notre Dame Press.

Majone, G. 1989. *Evidence, Argument, and Persuasion in the Policy Process.* New Haven: Yale University Press.

Mandelbaum, S. 1990. Reading Plans. *Journal of the American Planning Association* 56:350–56.

———. 1991. Telling Stories. *Journal of Planning Education and Research* 10:209–14.

Mayor's Task Force on Energy. 1989. Recommendations Concerning Electric Energy Policies for Chicago for the 1990s and Beyond. November.

Meltsner, A. J. 1985. *Policy Analysts in the Bureaucracy.* 1976. Reprint. Berkeley: University of California Press.

Myers, D. 1990. Interpreting Survey Data: The Stories Planners Tell. Paper presented at the Thirty-second Annual Meeting of the Association of Collegiate Schools of Planning. Austin, Texas, November 1–4.

Nelson, J. S., A. Megill, and D. N. McCloskey, eds. 1987. *The Rhetoric of the Human Sciences.* Madison: University of Wisconsin Press.

Nussbaum, M. 1986. *The Fragility of Goodness.* Cambridge: Cambridge University Press.

Quinn, A. 1982. *Figures of Speech*. Salt Lake City: Peregrine Smith.

Rectenwald, W. 1987. Edison Buyout Could Cut Jobs, Poll Says. *Chicago Tribune*, December 14.

Simons, H. W., ed. 1989. *Rhetoric in the Human Sciences*. London: Sage.

————, ed. 1990. *The Rhetorical Turn*. Chicago: University of Chicago Press.

Throgmorton, J. A. 1990. Passion, Reason, and Power: The Rhetorics of Electric Power Planning in Chicago. *Journal of Architectural and Planning Research* 7:330–50.

————. 1991. The Rhetorics of Policy Analysis. *Policy Sciences* 24:153–79.

————. 1992a. Planning as Persuasive and Constitutive Discourse: Exploring Electric Power Alternatives in Chicago, 1985–1990. In C. L. Oravec and J. G. Cantrill, eds., *The Conference on the Discourse of Environmental Advocacy*, 107–26. Salt Lake City: University of Utah Humanities Center.

————. 1992b. Planning as Persuasive Storytelling about the Future: Negotiating an Electric Power Rate Settlement in Illinois. *Journal of Planning Education and Research* 12:17–31.

Tompkins, J. P. 1980. *Reader-Response Criticism*. Baltimore: Johns Hopkins University Press.

Wachs, M. 1985. *Ethics of Planning*. New Brunswick, N.J.: Center for Urban Policy Research.

Wetlaufer, G. B. 1990. Rhetoric and Its Denial in Legal Discourse. *Virginia Law Review* 76:1545–97.

White, J. B. 1984. *When Words Lose Their Meaning*. Chicago: University of Chicago Press.

————. 1985. *Heracles' Bow*. Madison: University of Wisconsin Press.

Ziemba, S. 1986. Edison Rates May Cut Jobs: City Study Assails Proposed Increases. *Chicago Tribune*, August 5.

Reframing

Policy Discourse

Martin Rein and Donald Schön

Framing in Policy Discourse

Stubborn policy controversies tend to be enduring, relatively immune to resolution by reference to evidence, and seldom finally resolved. At best, they may be temporarily settled by electoral processes, power grabs, or bargaining; or, with shifts in a larger context, they may simply disappear for a time, only to reemerge later in some new form.

The careers of these controversies—for example, the disputes over nuclear arms, welfare, or the status of women—cannot be understood in terms of the familiar separation of questions of value from questions of fact, for the participants construct the problems of their problematic policy situations through *frames* in which facts, values, theories, and interests are integrated. Given the multiple social realities created by conflicting frames, the participants disagree both with one another and also about the nature of their disagreements.

Stubborn policy controversies pose the following epistemological predicament: What can possibly be the basis for resolving conflicts of frames when the frames themselves determine what counts as evidence and how evidence is interpreted? In response to this predicament, we shall propose an "empirical epistemology"—not a theory of knowledge in the philosophical sense but an inquiry into the knowing-in-practice by which, in our society, we deal with policy controversies in the absence of an agreed-upon basis for resolving them.

We use the term *policy discourse* to refer to the interactions of individuals, interest groups, social movements, and institutions through which problematic situations are converted to policy problems, agendas are set, decisions are made, and actions are taken. We recognize policy analysis as a form of intellectual activity that may function as cause or consequence of movements within the processes of a larger policy discourse. And we shall be particularly concerned with the conditions under which policy discourse may become frame reflective.

Framing

The idea of frames has recently come into good currency. Marvin Minsky (1978) introduced the term *frame* in the field of artificial intelligence, for example, to refer to a particular way of representing knowledge. Dan Kahneman and Amos Tversky (1974) have written about the frames that distort the interpretation and analysis of data, taking as their reference point a particular conception of rational decision making. The sociologist William Gamson (Gamson and Lasch 1983) has used the term *packaging* to refer to a particular type of framing—namely, the process by which a central organizing idea, or frame, is embodied in a policy position that is then expressed through such condensing symbols as metaphors or slogans. And Erving Goffman (1974) has developed a kind of "frame analysis" that serves primarily to explicate the structures that give form to processes of social interaction and communication.

Our use of the idea of framing bears a family resemblance to all of the above, but we wish to reserve the term for a more fundamental process in relation to which these other uses can be seen as specialized variations. In our use of the term, framing is a way of selecting, organizing, interpreting, and making sense of a complex reality to provide guideposts for knowing, analyzing, persuading, and acting. A frame is a perspective from which an amorphous, ill-defined, problematic situation can be made sense of and acted on.

Framing transpires at three levels: personal life, scientific or scholarly inquiry, and policy-making. Moreover, unless one wants to assume a world of policy uninhabited by people and lacking in knowledge, these three levels of framing must be related to each other.

Scholars from very different disciplines have independently discovered the importance of this more fundamental sense of framing. The anthropologist Clifford Geertz (1983:234) recognized the need for it when he observed that "the world is a various place and much is to be gained . . . by confronting that grand actuality rather than wishing it away in a haze of forceless generalities and false comforts." The social philosopher Geoffrey Vickers coined the term *appreciative system* to refer to the systems of values, preferences, norms, and ideas on the basis of which we frame the grand actuality of the world and thereby make it coherent to ourselves. An appreciative system must, in his view, meet three criteria: "First, it should correspond with reality sufficiently to guide action. Second, it should be sufficiently shared by our fellows to mediate communication. Third, it should be sufficiently acceptable to ourselves to make life bearable. It is thus a mental construct, partly subjective, largely intersubjective, that is, based on a shared subjective judgment, and constantly challenged and confirmed by experience" (1975). There must always be appreciative systems from which individuals, scholars, or policy activists construct their frames.

The philosopher Nelson Goodman (1978) introduced the term *worldmaking* to refer to the processes by which we frame and shape the realities of the worlds in which we live. And most significantly, perhaps, the sociologist Karl Mannheim (1936:265) long ago introduced the idea of a sociology of knowledge as the study of "the varying ways in which objects present themselves to the subject according to the differences in social settings (with the result that) mental structures are inevitably differently formed in different social and historical settings."

Mental structures, appreciations, worldmaking, and *framing* are terms that capture different features of the processes by which people construct interpretations of problematic situations, making them coherent from various perspectives and providing users with evaluative frameworks within which to judge how to act. No one is exempt from the need for framing. Personal, scholarly, and political practice all depend on it.

Policy Controversies

Framing is problematic because it leads to different views of the world and creates multiple social realities. Interest groups and policy constituencies, scholars working in different disciplines, and individuals in different contexts of everyday life have different frames that lead them to see different things, make different interpretations of the way things are, and support different courses of action concerning what is to be done, by whom, and how to do it.

If people see the world as different and act on their different views, then the world itself becomes different. Expectations, beliefs, and interpretations shape the worlds in which we live. Alfred Schutz's work on the structure of everyday life is a philosophical approach to the problem of multiple constructed realities mediated through signs, symbols, and languages and leading to different courses of social action (Schutz and Luckmann 1981). Wallace Stevens (1954:165) expressed a similar idea very aptly in a brief but incisive poem:

> They said, "You have a blue guitar."
> You do not play things as they are.
> The man replied, "Things as they are
> Are changed upon the blue guitar."[1]

Policy is always played upon a "blue guitar" because it defines, and to some extent creates, the way things are. When people disagree about a policy issue, they may be able to examine the facts of the situation and determine who is right; policy *disagreements* arise within a common frame and can be settled in principle by appeal to established rules. But policy *controversies* cannot be settled by recourse to facts alone, or indeed by recourse to evidence of any kind. Because they derive from conflicting frames, the same body of evidence can be used to support quite different policy positions.

Policy frames and their underlying appreciative systems are revealed through the *stories* participants are disposed to tell about policy situations. These problem-setting stories, frequently based on generative metaphors, link causal accounts of policy problems to particular proposals for action and facilitate the normative leap from "is" to "ought" (Rein and Schön 1977). Because the reality of any policy situation is always richer and more complex than can be grasped through any particular story, policy controversies are inherently subject to multiperspectival accounts. They always carry the potential for interpretation in terms of multiple, conflicting frames where there are no such commonly accepted frameworks for resolution. Hence, they raise the specter of epistemological relativism.

In the philosophy of science, Thomas Kuhn (1962) has distinguished periods of normal science, when scientists operate within a shared paradigm (frame, in our sense) and agree on rules of the game for settling disagreements, from periods of scientific revolution, in which scientific disagreement cuts across paradigms and there is no agreed-upon framework for settling disputes. In the latter, controversies may fade away because the holders of a competing paradigm suffer a conversion or because they simply die out and are not replaced.

In his *Philosophy and the Mirror of Nature* (1979) Richard Rorty gives a more general treatment of a similar theme. He distinguishes between "normal" and "abnormal" discourse in science as well as in other fields of inquiry. "Normal" refers, in his usage, to the discourse that proceeds under a shared set of rules, assumptions, conventions, criteria, and beliefs, all of which tell how, over time and in principle, a disagreement can be settled. Here, even though a conflict may in fact persist, there is a belief—perhaps illusory—based on the assumption that the ordinary rules of discourse "embody agreed-upon criteria for reaching agreement." "Abnormal" discourse occurs, by contrast, in those situations in which agreed-upon criteria for reaching agreement are not the essential elements upon which communication among contending actors is based. Such situations are not defined by the participants in terms of an objective framework within which disagreements can be arbitrated or managed. Yet even here, as Geertz (1983:223, commenting on Rorty's work) has observed: "Hope for agreement is not abandoned. People occasionally do change their minds or have their differences as to the result of intelligence concerning what individuals or groups of individuals whose minds run on other tracks believe." The task, for Rorty, is "how to study abnormal discourse from the point of view of some normal discourse." There is something very appealing about this formulation because it has a ring of truthfulness, although the terms *normal* and *abnormal* seem unnecessarily pejorative. Geertz proposes the use of *standard* and *nonstandard discourse;* but that terminology seems as unsatisfactory as Rorty's suggestion that we use *hermeneutics* to describe abnormal discourse and *epistemology* to describe normal discourse. None of these formulations seems right; none seems to offer a clear alternative to a relativist view of frame conflicts.

The extreme relativist interpretation of frames leads to the position that all frames are equally valid. But while it is difficult to refute the relativist logic to which a recognition of framing leads, that logic offends common sense and common understanding. Not all frames, and not all stories in which they are expressed, are equally acceptable or compelling. But there do seem to be implicit, perhaps even consensual, standards by which to judge the adequacy of different frames for interpretation, understanding, and action.

James March has suggested, for example, that we are guided in our judgment of different frames by the criteria of beauty, truth, and justice (March and Olson 1975). "Beauty" refers to eloquence in the formulation of an argument, especially to parsimony in its chains of inference. "Truth" has to do with the verifiability and reliability of the implications of the premises contained in the argument associated with a frame. "Justice" is guided by standards for the normative propositions contained in the framing of a situation, the resulting view of what it is right or wrong to do.

In many respects, these three criteria of frame evaluation may conflict with one another. Intuitively, however, we understand that not
all frames are of equal value. We can discern a terrain that lies some-
where between extreme positivism, according to which all meaningful
controversies are resolvable by reference to facts and logic, and extreme
relativism, according to which one framing of a situation is as good
as another. But March's proposed criteria of frame adequacy do not re-
move the specter of relativism or teach us "how to study abnormal discourse from the point of view of some normal discourse." Frame conflicts may resurface, for example, when the criteria of truth, beauty, and
justice are applied to evaluate frames operating in a specific policy controversy.

A study of frame discourse in social policy may reveal the ways in
which people actually deal, in society, with the epistemological predica-
ments posed by frame conflict. An empirical epistemology may help to
clarify the criteria that are actually employed in judgments of frame
adequacy and by what processes people actually approach frame conflicts in the absence of an agreed-upon framework for resolving them.
Such a study would address itself to the question of *frame shifts:* how the
problem-setting frames of social policy change over time. And it would
help to make clear the properties of a possible *frame-reflective discourse:*
a policy discourse in which participants would reflect on the frame
conflicts implicit in their controversies and explore the potentials for
their resolution.

An empirical epistemology would also focus on the possible functions of a particular kind of policy analysis. Conventional policy analysis
is concerned with choice; it asks how a decision maker can choose rationally among policy options in order to realize his or her values.
Frame-critical policy analysis seeks, on the contrary, to enhance frame-
reflective policy discourse by identifying the taken-for-granted assumptions that underlie people's apparently natural understandings and
actions in a problematic policy situation. It seeks to explicate the conflicting frames inherent in policy controversies so that we can reflect on
them and better grasp the relationships between hidden premises and
normative conclusions.

But the study of frames and frame conflicts is unfortunately hampered by conceptual and practical difficulties that are almost as hard to
identify as to overcome. If we are to make progress toward frame-
reflective policy discourse, we must first understand what makes it so
difficult.

Difficulties in Studying Frames

Although frames exert a powerful influence on what we see and neglect, and how we interpret what we see, they are, paradoxically, difficult to assess. Because they are part of the natural, taken-for-granted world, we are often unaware of their role in organizing our perceptions, thoughts, and actions.

In practice, it is difficult to distinguish between disagreements within a frame and conflict and controversy across frames. Partly, this is because frames are about action, and the desire to do something usually leads to a commitment to make the action we seek realizable. We often do so by "hitching on" to a dominant frame and its conventional metaphors, hoping to purchase legitimacy for a course of action actually inspired by different intentions. Hence the common discrepancy between what we say and what we truly mean. As a result, we are often unable to tell what frame really underlies a policy position. When participants in a policy discourse begin "gaming," they obscure their underlying frames.

Frame discourse is difficult to study for several other reasons. The same course of action may be consistent with quite different frames; in U.S. welfare policy, for example, there was a marked continuity of policy across the Ford and Carter administrations, even though their policy spokesmen espoused very different policy positions. And the same frame can lead to different courses of action; liberals who hold very similar policy positions nevertheless disagree among themselves about the proper treatment of ineligibles on the welfare rolls.

Frames are self-referential, but they are not self-interpretive. A discussion about our personal frames is almost always about some deep aspect of ourselves; hence a frame—the object we want to theorize about—cannot be separated from the person who holds it. But, as we have just observed, a frame does not determine a particular position on a substantive policy issue, and many policy positions may be consistent with a given frame. There is more than a logical connection between a frame and its practical consequences for action.

Policy, by and large, tends not to evolve through self-reflective, broadly encompassing shifts of frame of the sort Hugh Heclo (1985) has described as "changes in self-consciousness," which "imply the most comprehensive paradigm (frame) shifts: Where are we? Why are we here? Whither do we tend?" On the other hand, there are many examples of shifts of frame around specific policy issues. We need, therefore, to focus on the framing of policy issues that may or may not be related to broader shifts of frame. We need to ask what is problematic about these issues, in what policy terrains they lie, and what factors account for the ways in which they are framed. We know much less about these things than we like to believe—although, clearly, both material and symbolic interests come into play.

It is hard to distinguish between real and potential shifts of frame. In the field of welfare policy, for example, the introduction of supplementary security income could be interpreted as a reframing of U.S. policy toward the poor because it meant nationalizing the institutions and legislation associated with the Poor Law, integrating them into the framework of social insurance, at least for an important segment of the dependent welfare population. This event may have created a potential for a shift of frame at some later time; it might have led to a reframing of the problem of poverty in terms of a broader conception of social responsibility to aid the poor. But such a potential for reframing was not realized. No other reforms were introduced, so the potential for broader reframing lay dormant. Indeed, the aged are now seen as enjoying a privileged position at the expense of poor families and dependent children.

It is possible to have reframing without controversy and controversy without reframing. Policy can change without a frame choice, and we can debate frame choice without any political change resulting. For example, there was in the 1960s and early 1970s a debate in the United States over the introduction of a comprehensive negative income tax. Many social experiments were carried out to show that guaranteed income would not disrupt work effort and family stability, and legislative reforms were introduced. But the plan was aborted; no major change was forthcoming. In the meantime, U.S. public policy remained committed, ideologically, to the notion that individuals should have unrestricted cash income rather than in-kind benefits earmarked for such specific purposes as housing, medical care, or food. But in practice, despite the commitment to expansion of individual choice, what emerged was an increased rate of spending for in-kind benefits, which restricted individual choice to particular categories of expenditure such as fuel, food, and medical care. Thus, there was an important reframing of policy but no explicit public decision to move in the direction of the reframing.

Much policy change consists simply of adaptation to changing situations. Nevertheless, the cumulative effect of many such adaptations may *entrain* a reframing of the way we think about and act on the policy issue in question. We may be drawn into a change of frames by something other than the evolution of ideas or the experience of inquiry within a frame.

The several kinds of phenomena that hamper an empirical epistemology of policy discourse must become objects of study in themselves. A study of frame conflicts and frame shifts should focus on the framing of particular policy issues and attend to the interplay of such processes as "hitching on," framing at the level of espoused and enacted policy, and entrainment of reframing through multiple adaptations to changing circumstance.

A Preliminary Vocabulary for the Study of Frames

Naming and Framing

Once a policy terrain has been named, the name seems natural. But movement from an incoherent sense that something in a situation is wrong to a specification of what is wrong may be fraught with uncertainty that is intellectual and emotional in its manifestions.

In *The Feminine Mystique,* Betty Friedan (1964) describes the feeling she had in the 1960s when she was troubled about the position of women but did not know what to name her anxiety. "Female subserviency" both named the phenomenon she found so troubling and carried with it the remedy of "female liberation." And from the perspective of the resulting frame, specific policy issues—for example, the issues of day care and welfare payments to women—took on very different meanings.

The name assigned to a problematic terrain focuses attention on certain elements and leads to neglect of others. The organizing of the things named brings them together into a composite whole. The complementary process of naming and framing socially constructs the situation, defines what is problematic about it, and suggests what courses of action are appropriate to it. It provides conceptual coherence, a direction for action, a basis for persuasion, and a framework for the collection and analysis of data—order, action, rhetoric, and analysis.

When participants in a policy controversy name and frame the policy situation in different ways, it is often difficult to discover what they are fighting about. Someone cannot simply say, for example, "Let us compare different perspectives for dealing with poverty," because each framing of the issue of poverty is likely to select and name different features of the problematic situation. We are no longer able to say that we are comparing different perspectives on "the same problem," because the problem itself has changed. While we may be able to agree, for example, that poverty is lack of resources, the nature of what is lacking may be quite unclear. Income transfers aimed at responding to the lack of resources may create problems of dependency or an underclass that derives its income from government largess. When poverty is seen in terms of inequality, there is concern with the relative distribution of resources, so that in providing aid for the poor we are also compelled to consider the economic position of society's middle- and upper-income groups. In each case, the name given to the problematic situation of poverty selects different, at best overlapping, phenomena for attention and organizes them differently.

Context

The framing of a policy issue always takes place within a nested context. Policy issues tend to arise in connection with governmental programs, which exist in some policy environment, which is part of some broader political and economic setting, which is located, in turn, within a historical era. When some feature of the nested context shifts, participants may discover that the repetition of a successful formula no longer works. Then the perceived shift of context may set the climate within which adversarial networks try to reframe a policy issue by renaming the policy terrain, reconstructing interpretations of how things got to be as they are, and proposing what can be done about them.

It is useful to distinguish at least four nested contexts. First, a program may serve as its own, *internal* context, changing over time through replacement of its personnel, its sponsors, or its clients. Goals emerge from the possibilities of the internal situation and from the need to adapt to changes within it. Typically, the organization adjusts to its new situation rather than deliberately choosing to modify its frame. But new rules of doing business, adopted in the spirit of adjustment, may lay the grounds for a substantial frame change downstream.

Second, the *proximate* context is the policy environment in which a program operates. A program always exists in interaction with other programs, and reframing can take place as the proximate context changes. For example, public housing in the United States was redefined in the course of the development of an urban renewal program that dumped a different class of people into public housing, thereby changing the world of the program and forcing it to adjust to a new environment.

Third, the *macro* context includes changes in the directions of policy, changes in the institutions designed to carry out policy, realignment of party politics, and economic fluctuations. Shifts in the macro context do not necessarily set the conditions for policy reframing, at least in the short run, but they can lead to a symbolic reframing. Thus the rhetoric of disagreement may suggest a major reframing of policy while practice displays a remarkable continuity.

Fourth, *global* shifts of context are harder to specify, though they are extremely important. They involve changes at the broadest level of public context, including changes in the historical eras in which reframing of policy issues may occur. Little has been written about historical eras in a way that links them back to public policy, scientific understandings, and individual perceptions. Nevertheless, a change in historical era may have a striking impact on the framing of policy issues. We seem, for example, just to have left the era of the 1960s, with its apparent commitment to institutional innovation on behalf of the poor and the disadvantaged. The ramifications of the 1980s era are still unfolding, but such themes as reprivatization and the limits of governmental intervention appear evident, perhaps in reaction to the expansionist mood of the preceding era.

Long ago, Harold Innis (1951) reminded us of Hegel's famous aphorism that "Minerva's owl flies at dusk"—that is, wisdom about an era comes only at its end. This is a cynical observation because it is exactly at the point when an era has passed that we can no longer do anything about it. Maybe Hegel was only partly right, however. Perhaps a shift of context indicates that something in society has changed, though the change is not yet fully perceived. A shift of context might be seen as society's intuitive groping toward understanding in advance of the full development of societal change. Minerva's owl might therefore fly at dawn rather than at dusk. The ideas and symbols of the society's cultural system (in Talcott Parson's terms) may prefigure changes in its social system before those changes are fully understood (Parsons 1967).

So far, we have argued that the framing of policy issues is responsive to shifts in the larger contexts of policy, shifts that often entrain shifts of frame. But it is also true that the reframing of issues can shape the contexts on which that reframing is dependent. Some shifts of context occur as individuals and organizations adapt to their local situations, the cumulative effect of their adaptations producing a new social world that leads, in turn, to new forms of behavior. The reframing of policy issues grows out of shifts of context and also helps to produce them. Both adaptation and social learning are operative.

Frame Discourse

Interpersonal conversation is the root sense of the term *discourse*. The use of that term to refer to dialogue within and across institutions is a metaphoric extension. The prototypical case of interpersonal discourse may be construed in at least two different ways, however. Two individuals may be seen as talking with one another about an issue in which they are both directly involved. For example, each of them wants something only one of them can have; in this case the "policy controversy" is interpersonal in nature. Or two individuals may be seen as talking with one another about a larger policy issue in relation to which they function as agents of groups or institutions that are parties to the policy controversy. In this case the controversy is institutional in nature.

In either case, so long as discourse occurs in an interpersonal context, it is important to make reference to the *behavioral world* in which it takes place. As individuals talk with one another, their actions carry multiple meanings; they not only communicate messages whose meanings must be constructed by the other but also convey second-level attitudes toward the interaction itself. They also model modes of behavior that the other party may take up. They instantiate theories in use for interpersonal interaction (Argyris and Schön 1974). Thus, as Gregory Bateson (1972) has pointed out, interpersonal discourse may take on the property of schizmogenesis, or "the more, the more"—for example, the more one party advocates his or her position and tries to win, the more the other party does likewise. The patterns of interpersonal interaction may contribute to the creation of a behavioral world that is more or less open or closed, trusting or suspicious, authentic or deceptive, defensive or nondefensive, contentious or cooperative. Every move in an interpersonal interaction has meaning for the behavioral world as well as for the policy issue the participants treat as the subject of their discourse.

Interpersonal discourse must also have an institutional locus within some larger social system. There are no institutional vacuums. Even a chat between close friends occurs in the "institutional" setting of someone's house or a walk around the park. When scholars talk together about a policy controversy, it is within the institutional context of a university or research institute. This institutional embedding is important to the nature of discourse in several ways. The institutional context may carry its own characteristic perspectives and ways of framing issues, or it may offer particular roles, channels, and norms for discussion and debate. And discourse tends to conform to the norms of the institutions in which it is embedded. In a court of law, for example, where adversarial interaction is expected, each individual tends to suppress any doubts about his or her own position. At the bargaining table, each utterance tends to be construed as a move in a bargaining game. Even in such settings as these, however, individuals may use their discretionary freedom to act as deviants and violate institutional norms.

When discourse is *public,* it takes on the special properties of the institutions reserved in our society for public interactions about policy controversies of public concern: the *public forums* that serve as institutional vehicles for policy debate. These include legislative arenas, the courts, public commissions, the councils of government and political parties, the editorial pages of magazines and newspapers, radio and television programs, and the seminar rooms and lecture halls of academia.

Policy forums have their own rules. Here, individual utterances are likely to have meanings and consequences removed from the interpersonal context in which they occur. We may speak to one another, for example, but our words may be recorded and released to a larger public, detached from their initial, face-to-face interaction; and in that larger context, we may not know how others will interpret and respond to our words. Discourse may be framed within the arena of formal politics, interpreted as contributing to one side or another in an ongoing struggle among political parties. It may be shaped by the media of public communication—the press, scholarly publications, radio, television, and the like.

Among the rules of the game in policy forums are the criteria by which judgments are made about the legitimacy of participants—their *standing* as participants in the policy conversation. Disputes within a policy discourse may have to do with the struggle for standing. Those excluded from the conversation may strive to get in. As one aspect of this kind of struggle, social movements may take action to bring ideas into good currency and legitimize their own representatives as participants in a policy conversation, employing for this purpose the full repertoire of social action and protest. In this fashion, for example, the welfare rights movement of the 1960s sought to change the terms of reference of the welfare debate and introduce new participants as legitimate actors in the policy forums of the time.

In and around policy forums, a range of social roles occupy different positions in the process of policy discourse. There is a fundamental division of labor, for example, between those concerned with the mobilization of action and those concerned with the mobilization of intellectual consent. As in most situations, however, the boundary tends to be fuzzy. Mediating between thought and action leads some to emphasize the former, and others the latter, while still others seek to make a bridge between the two by combining research and practice.

Frames are never self-interpretive. The interpretation of particular policy issues in terms of various frames is always undertaken by someone—usually by groups of individuals or by formal and informal organizations. These entities act as *sponsors* of framing. The more natural and taken for granted the frames that shape our thinking, the less likely we are to be aware both of our frames and of the social carriers that interpret policy issues in terms of frames.

The sponsors of a frame seek to develop the frame, explicate its implications for action, and establish the grounds for arguments about it. They may also devise metaphors for communication about the frame— metaphors variously related to the metaphors that may have contributed to the generation of the frame itself.

Frame sponsorship may be assumed by research organizations within the social science community. Here, policy analysts may play a critical role in the development of frames as they work inside and outside governmental bureaucracies as entrepreneurs, middlemen, and idea brokers. They may name the policy terrain and specify how frames, policy designs, and policy actions are to be linked. They may function as technical specialists, debugging the problems that emerge in the framing of a policy issue and in the process of bringing it into good currency.[2] They may combine research and experience in the use of symbols, communicative metaphors, and simplifying assumptions. In all these ways, analysts help to develop frames; but these very processes may bring them to the limits of their frames, and thus to reframing.

Policy intellectuals play the special role of explicating the policy ideas and frames implicit in the social action of social movements. In this sense, for example, Francis Piven and Richard Cloward (1971) were among the intellectuals who helped to reveal and defend the ideas implicit in the actions of the welfare rights movement.

The three levels of policy discourse—individual, interpersonal, and public—are related to one another in complex ways. Each higher level of aggregation presumes the existence of those below it. In interpersonal discourse, individuals also conduct a parallel dialogue in their own minds, thinking to themselves as they talk to others. And in public discourse there are nodes of interpersonal dialogue; individual representatives of contending institutions may meet for informal discussion and talk with one another at the bargaining table, though their interactions there carry a larger institutional resonance.

Conversely, each lower level of discourse may mirror next the higher level. Individuals may talk together in a way that reflects their mindfulness of the political parties or divergent constituencies to which they belong. Even in the privacy of their own minds, they may use the language, obey the norms, and feel the feelings normal to the conduct of a public-policy controversy.

The interplay of the level of discourse and the manipulation of the institutional contexts of discourse may play important parts in the inquiry that shapes the career of a policy controversy. For example, the problem of achieving a satisfactory resolution of a policy dispute may be framed as one of enabling individuals to get *free* of the constraints of public policy debate. People say, for example, "Let's get the main actors together where they can interact as human beings!" Or the problem of resolving controversy may be framed as one of improving the functioning of the public institutions in question—for example, by improving the structure of a collective bargaining process. If two individuals have a special relationship that gives them a strong basis for mutual trust and cooperative inquiry, though they sit on "opposite sides of the aisle," their special relationship may be used as a vehicle for resolving the controversy. If one individual can find within himself a multiplicity of different and conflicting views of the issue in question, he may more readily enter into the views of the adversaries with whom he is locked in contention.

Frame-Reflective Discourse

We know of no well-described examples of frame-reflective policy discourse. But let us speculate here on what it might be like and what the conditions favorable to it might be. There seem to be two principal views of the participants in a policy controversy. We might think of them as *inquirers* who take the policy situation as an object of thought, experimentation, or analysis; from this vantage point, their self-interests are potential sources of distortion. Or we might think of the participants as *interested parties*—frame sponsors or advocates—who use inquiry to serve their interests. In the first view, we see politics as layered onto inquiry; in the second, inquiry emerges from a basically political process.

In the second view, frames give cognitive shape to interests that arise out of social roles, positions, memberships, and histories. The paradigmatic situation is that of two parties engaged in a struggle for control of something—a struggle that necessarily takes the form of a win or lose game. At stake in the struggle is the question of who claims to take priority. The function of reflection, in this view, is to mediate a settlement of the dispute or perhaps to transform the dispute so as make it more susceptible to satisfactory settlement. The attitude underlying appeal to reflection is something like, "Let's be rational about this!"

In the first view, the participants are seen as members of a cooperative social system. They face a common problematic situation that they have a shared interest in reframing and resolving, though they may initially view it in different ways. The paradigmatic situation is that of two individuals, engaged in the pursuit of a common task, who face an obstacle to their shared endeavor. The function of reflection is to facilitate their inquiry into the common problem. The underlying attitude is something like, "Let's think about what we are doing!"

Let us call these the "political" and "cooperative" views of policy controversy. Conflict and inquiry exist in both views, but they are conceived in very different ways. Given a view of policy controversy as basically cooperative, the appeal to reflection is an appeal to make shared inquiry more meaningful and effective. Given a view of policy controversy as political, the appeal to reflection is an appeal to the shared interest of the participants in minimizing, or at any rate reducing, the costs of the win or lose game: at most, transforming conflict into cooperation; at least, enabling the participants to achieve a satisfactory settlement of their dispute.

These general features of frame discourse can now be related to our earlier discussion of Rorty's search for some normal discourse in relation to which one can study, or influence, abnormal discourse.

One way of thinking about the relation of abnormal discourse to normal discourse involves translation across conflicting frames. We might focus, for example, on the work of those individuals whose special mission is the task of bridging normal and abnormal discourse not only in social policy but also in science. This point of view, based on the special role of the translator, seems to miss the essential point that policy controversies are substantive; they are about premises and axioms, as Herbert Simon (1983) points out, and not just about rules reaching agreement. Meaning precedes facts and makes sense only in relation to the purposes embedded in different frames. Indeed, frame conflict has contributed to the recent reformulation of the role of science in policy controversies. There is an increasing doubt about the neutrality of science as an agent in debates over the framing of policy issues. And if science can no longer be trusted to mediate frame conflicts, there is the risk of increasing the level of abnormal discourse.

On the other hand, we do live in a world that is both consensual and conflictual. Normal and abnormal discourse coexist. In some respects, we do seem to share metaframes—in science, the belief in reason and evidence; and in policy, the belief in democratic capitalism. The more abstract the principle, the higher the level of agreement. Disagreement arises when we become specific—that is, when meaning and purpose come alive in real situations. For example, although discussants may all agree on democracy, they may disagree about the level of government that should govern, what type of democracy should be emphasized, or how government should act on institutions to cope with economic fluctuations and protect individuals against uncertainty. It is in concrete situations, when politics and markets are joined, that frame conflicts are most evident. Even then, however, there is a symbolic home to which discussants can retreat for consensus at a higher level of abstraction, where vagueness is unifying and there is a common commitment to some normal discourse. Indeed, the very act of engaging with others in discourse presupposes some shared frame of reference, if only a shared knowledge of, and allegiance to, socially legitimated rules of the game. By their very controversy, actors declare themselves to be members of a social system in which tacit rules for this sort of fight are understood and obeyed.

Thus, there is a metalevel at which a kind of consensus congenial to social order exists. But this quasi consensuality can make the task of discourse even more difficult. At the higher level, people may talk past one another, unaware of their actual disagreement. It is only in the everyday business of making and analyzing policy that the clash between frames becomes clearly evident; it can be frustratingly elusive at other levels.

The debate about nuclear arms policy is a case in point. Normal discourse frames the debate in terms of a limited set of options. These are the thinkable and discussable alternatives that depend on a shared set of axioms and premises, the most important of which is the potential threat of other nuclear arms holders to the security of the United States. In this view, some defensive strategy is necessary, and unilateral disarmament is not a discussable option. An alternative frame sees the issue in terms of human aspiration and the annihilation that would follow a nuclear war. In that frame, strategic, military considerations are ruled out of order.

There is no serious attempt at communication across the two frames. The strategy of protest is cast in terms of personal drama, expressed in terms of appeal for the future well-being of the world's children. But, of course, some element of communication is not altogether ruled out. There is a hesitant discourse across these frames. Some hope of converting abnormal discourse to normal discourse remains, perhaps by converting controversy across frames to disagreement within a frame. But appeals to science, as in the recent debates over "nuclear winter," easily fall prey to a reembedding of normal into abnormal discourse; the two sides give predictably conflicting interpretations of the same data.

What would it mean for the participants in the debate over nuclear arms policy to engage in frame-reflective discourse? Policy disputes are sometimes settled through interactive processes that do *not* engage frame conflict. The participants may enter into a fight in any one of the institutional contexts for fighting that society provides, and one or another party to the dispute may win. Or, if a clear-cut winner fails to emerge, the parties to the dispute may bargain out a compromise to which they can agree in any of the institutional contexts for bargaining that society provides.

When discourse is in the political mode, and when the objects of reflection are the participants' positions or the conflicts among them, then the work of reflection may consist of adjudication, bargaining, "fogging," or management of conflict. But stubborn policy controversies such as the nuclear arms debate are not amenable to this sort of settlement. There are no real winners, and temporary victories leave the basic controversy unresolved. Bargains struck in a particular local context or around a particular issue, as in the case of the recent history of welfare policy, fail to achieve stable political consensus. Any process aimed at resolving stubborn policy controversies must engage their underlying frame conflicts, and policy analysts can play an important role in this process.

Frame-critical policy analysts would uncover the multiple, conflicting frames involved in a given policy dispute. They would inquire into the sources of conflicting frames in the histories, roles, institutional contexts, and interests of the participants. They would explore the ambiguities and inconsistencies contained in conflicting frames and the consequences to which their use may lead.

But such analysis, when undertaken from the detached perspective of a university-based scholar, would have limited potential for contributing to a mutually satisfactory resolution of policy controversies. At best, it could contribute to the participants' greater awareness of their ways of framing issues. It would not lead per se to the process Jürgen Habermas (1968) has described as "critical self-reflection that contributes to political consensus."

If one wishes to understand the potentials and limits of frame-reflective discourse in real-world contexts of political practice, then it is necessary to explore the space that lies between the political fights and bargains characteristic of ordinary policy debate and the frame-critical analysis of a protected and isolated university-based scholar. From this perspective, let us think of the participants in a policy controversy as agents (see Vickers 1975) in transaction (see Dewey and Bentley 1949) with the situations of which they are a part. They may succeed in changing their situations, which may also change as a result of changes in some larger social context; and they may be changed by changes in their situation, some of which they may have helped to produce. These transactional conditions are central to the unfolding history of a policy situation. In schematic terms, the following events take place:

> People find themselves in the presence of this situation, of which they take cognizance.
>
> Out of people's initial framing of the situation, they take action.
>
> Which contributes to change in the situation,
>
> By which they are affected.
>
> And people take cognizance of *this* change,
>
> On the basis of which they act again
>
> And are acted upon.

It is in the course of the participants' *conversation with their situation* that frame reflection and a resulting shift of frame may occur. It is important to notice that such a shift is unlikely to occur before one actually takes some action. It is more likely to occur over time, as one apprehends and responds to the changed situation in which one finds oneself—as we have already noted in connection with the reframings that occur as a consequence of individual and organizational adaptations to changed situations and shifts in the rules of the game for doing business.

A shift of frame may be thoughtless. One may simply *find* oneself having come to think about things in a different way. As Leon Festinger (1957) has pointed out, our abhorrence of "cognitive dissonance"—the mismatch of our beliefs to our actual behavior—may cause us, gradually and tacitly, to adjust our beliefs to accommodate changes in our situations. This means that cognitive work of a sort goes on, but without conscious criticism or control. Once having made such a change, however, one may consciously strive to justify it; or, if one finds that it cannot be justified, one may consciously strive to undo it.

A shift of frame may also be thoughtful. At one moment or another in the participants' conversation within a policy situation—typically, at a "joint" in the policy dialectic—they may, in discourse with one another, subject their conflicting frames to conscious thought and control and, in partial consequence, reframe the situation.

When discourse is frame reflective, the work of reflection consists, first, in recognizing conflicting frames, identifying their sources and consequences, and then in translating, restructuring, integrating, converting, or choosing.

The cognitive work of frame-reflective discourse depends on the *stance* of the participants: their relative distance from their materials and from the processes in which they are engaged, their attitudes toward the uncertainty that follows deframing, their willingness to engage in cognitive risk taking, their inclination to enter into one another's views, and their capacity for the double vision that can enable individuals to combine advocacy of one frame with inquiry into others. For all these reasons, the work of frame reflection is affective as well as cognitive; it involves both feelings and work on feelings.

Finally, reflection on frames is likely to be inseparable from reflection on context. As Thomas Kuhn (1977) has pointed out, scientists might possibly succeed at the cognitive task of translating from one paradigm to another, but how are they to be made to sit down together to do so? Reciprocal frame reflection depends on the creation of a behavioral world conducive to it.

All these factors merit exploration through further research on the conditions for frame-reflective policy discourse. Such research poses serious problems—most notably, that there are very few examples of such processes in the arenas of public policy. The study of frame-reflective discourse is, perforce, a study of rare events. Nevertheless, a somewhat extended definition of the boundaries of policy discourse would allow researchers to study framing, frame conflict, and frame reflection in the related arenas of institutional change, scholarly or scientific inquiry, and personal life. While the pursuit of such analogies to social policy discourse might be seriously misleading, a critical investigation of them holds the potential for illuminating the careers of stubborn policy controversies.

Notes

This essay will appear in a different form in Donald Schön and Martin Rein, *Reframing: Controversy and Design in Policy Practice* (New York: Basic Books, in press).

1. This reference was suggested by Lisa Peattie.

2. The description of policy discourse given here is a recasting of Schön's earlier description of the processes by which policy ideas come into good currency (Schön 1971).

References

Agyris, C., and D. A. Schön. 1974. *Theory in Practice*. San Francisco: Jossey-Bass.

Bateson, G. 1972. *Steps to an Ecology of Mind*. New York: Ballantine Books.

Dewey, J., and A. Bentley. 1949. *Knowing and the Known*. Boston: Beacon Press.

Festinger, L. 1957. *A Theory of Cognitive Dissonance*. Evanston: Row, Peterson.

Friedan, B. 1964. *The Feminine Mystique*. New York: Norton.

Gamson, W. A., and K. E. Lasch. 1983. The Political Culture of Social Welfare Policy. In S. E. Spiro and E. Yaar, eds., *Evaluating the Welfare State*, 397–415. New York: Academic Press.

Geertz, C. 1983. *Local Knowledge*. New York: Basic Books.

Goffman, E. 1974. *Frame Analysis: An Essay on the Organization of Experience*. Cambridge: Harvard University Press.

Goodman, N. 1978. *Ways of Worldmaking*. Indianapolis: Hackett.

Habermas, J. 1968. *Knowledge and Human Interests*. Boston: Beacon Press.

Heclo, H. 1985. Issue Networks and the Executive Establishment. Mimeo.

Innis, H. 1951. *Bias of Communication*. Toronto: University of Toronto Press.

Kahneman, D., and A. Tversky. 1974. Judgement under Uncertainty: Heuristics and Biases. *Science* 185:1124–31.

Kuhn, T. 1962. *The Structure of Scientific Revolutions*. Chicago: University of Chicago Press.

———. 1977. *The Essential Tension*. Chicago: University of Chicago Press.

Mannheim, K. 1936. *Ideology and Utopia*. New York: Harcourt, Brace.

March, J., and J. P. Olsen. 1975. The Uncertainty of the Past: Organizational Learning under Ambiguity. *European Journal of Political Research* 3:147–71.

Mead, L. 1985. *Beyond Entitlement*. New York: Free Press.

Minsky, M. 1978. Frames. Artificial Intelligence Laboratory Memorandum, MIT, Cambridge, Mass.

OECD. 1981. *The Welfare State Crisis*. Paris: Organization for Economic Cooperation and Development.

———. 1985. *Social Expenditures 1960–1990: Problems of Growth and Control.* Paris: Organization for Economic Cooperation and Development.

Parsons, T. 1967. *Social Systems and the Evolution of Action Theory.* New York: Free Press.

Piven, F., and R. Cloward. 1971. *Regulating the Poor: The Functions of Public Welfare.* New York: Pantheon Books.

Rein, M., and D. A. Schön. 1977. Problem Setting in Policy Research. In C. H. Weiss, ed., *Using Social Research in Public Policy Making,* 235–51. Lexington, Mass.: Lexington Books.

Rorty, R. 1979. *Philosophy and the Mirror of Nature.* Princeton: Princeton University Press.

Schön, D. A. 1971. *Beyond the Stable State.* New York: Random House.

Schutz, A., and T. Luckmann. 1981. *The Structures of the Life World.* 1973. Reprint. Evanston, Ill.: Northwestern University Press.

Simon, H. 1983. *Reason in Human Affairs.* London: Basil Blackwell.

Stevens, W. 1954. *The Collected Poems of Wallace Stevens.* New York: Alfred A. Knopf.

Vickers, G. 1975. Social and Institutional Reality. Mimeo. Cambridge, Mass.

Reading Policy Narratives:

Beginnings, Middles, and Ends

Thomas J. Kaplan

Stories can play an important role in argumentative policy analysis, and policy analysts and planners can frame and conduct their arguments through stories of a certain sort. In one sense, this contention is hardly surprising. All of us commonly use stories to make and support arguments, and the close relationship between stories and arguments is embedded in the English language. When the King in Shakespeare's *Hamlet* discusses the "argument" of the play presented by a traveling troupe of actors, modern readers have no trouble understanding that the King is referring both to the plot line of the play and to the play's implicit claim that Hamlet's uncle and mother killed his father to appropriate the throne.

Yet many policy analysts and planners with strong backgrounds in social science methodology seem to believe that an emphasis on storytelling oversimplifies their work. In part, this lack of appreciation for stories stems from a distrust among some policy professionals for the role of argument itself, a belief that professionals do not so much make arguments as state truths about the effect of past or proposed future actions. But the lack of appreciation for stories also stems from a failure—even among policy professionals with a less positivist notion of their work—to accept the usefulness of good stories in making claims about both the past and the future.

Positivist Conceptions of Policy Analysis

To positivists, scientific disciplines manifest three qualities: a rigorous methodology, empirical generalizations based on observed uniformities, and general laws that explain these empirical generalizations. A discipline lacking any of these qualities would not be a science as positivists use the term. The positivist distinction between empirical generalizations and the scientific laws that explain them is not always precise, but it derives largely from distinctions made in the natural sciences. It would not suffice in the natural sciences, as the philosopher N. R. Hanson has argued, to explain "a bevelled mirror's showing a spectrum in the sunlight by saying that all bevelled mirrors do this."[1] A physicist would want to explain why this happens using Newton's concepts of spectra and reflection.

Similarly, in the social sciences, positivist theorists such as Robert Merton argue the need for a "covering law" to explain observed uniformities. Consider, Merton proposes, the relatively lower suicide rates of Catholics in comparison to Protestants. Taking his lead from Emile Durkheim, Merton suggests that a satisfactory covering law to explain this observation would be the statement that "social cohesion provides psychic support to group members subject to acute stresses and anxieties," assuming that suicides result partly from unrelieved anxiety and stress and that Catholics exhibit greater social cohesion than Protestants. With such a covering law, a social scientist could both explain the different suicide rates and predict that if social cohesion among Catholics should ever decline, their rate of suicide would increase.[2]

Critics of positivism sometimes challenge this effort to attribute all events, including all human action, to covering laws. Such actions often defeat themselves, say some critics of positivism. For example, positivists such as B. F. Skinner run the risk of making claims that are logically self-defeating when they apply theories of classical and operant conditioning to all human action. If Skinnerian behaviorists' belief in the importance of classical and operant conditioning must itself stem from such conditioning, why give credence to the belief?

A second common challenge to positivism has come from philosophers and historians of the natural and social sciences. Even in the natural sciences, which provide the model for positivist development of the social sciences and policy analysis, practitioners lack ontologically valid covering laws. At least since Thomas Kuhn's publication of *The Structure of Scientific Revolutions* in 1962, some historians have held, in the words of Mary Hesse, that "every set of metaphysical or regulative principles that have been suggested as necessary for science in the past has either been violated by subsequent science, or the principles concerned are such that we can see how plausible developments in our science would in fact violate them in the future."[3]

It is possible, of course, to overstate the uncertainty of knowledge in the natural sciences. More than sixty years after the Einsteinian "revolution" against Newtonian physics, graduate students in physics still learn and apply Newtonian mechanics to practical questions of force and mass. The question is whether Newtonian mechanics merely predicts consequences from particular events or actually explains occurrences with an ontologically valid covering law. Philosophers of science now hold that natural sciences are predictive but not explanatory in the positivist sense. They view natural scientists as prisoners of their concepts of orderliness and proof, their language, and their instruments, and not as privileged spectators of ultimate reality. Indeed, even most physicists now hold that current theories of quantum mechanics describe only a statistically predictive world, one in which many phenomena occur predictably but with no apparent, or "local," cause that physicists can explain.[4]

Alternatives to Positivism

Because of these and other commonly discussed criticisms of positivism, at least two alternatives to it have emerged.[5] The most common alternative in the social sciences can be loosely labeled empiricism, which I define here as a focus on the rigorous methodology and the generalizations based on observed uniformities characteristic of positivism without its effort to establish covering laws.

Empiricist practice is certainly respected and useful within the social sciences, and publications in social science journals usually have a strong empiricist bent. Indeed, though writers such as Merton might complain that social scientists are not really being scientific when they fail to seek general laws, most people who call themselves social scientists are content to follow an empiricist approach, applying rigorous methodologies to show the presence or absence of phenomena or patterns of phenomena. By itself, however, empiricist work is often of little value to planners, policy analysts, or the policymakers who are their clients. Though rigorously grounded empiricist studies may be interesting and suggestive of policy hypotheses, the lack of a covering law makes it hard to obtain general principles and predictions from empiricist studies.

The limitations in the generalizing power of empiricism have led some practitioners wishing to give advice to policymakers to look elsewhere for a guiding epistemology. A few have turned to the study of "softer" forms of interpretation often practiced in the study of literature or legal precedent. The technical term for this interpretation is hermeneutics, which is derived from a Greek word usually translated as "interpretation." Hermeneutics as an organized field dates back to mid-nineteenth-century efforts to explain why one interpretation of a biblical text was superior to another interpretation of the same text. Since that time, hermeneutics practitioners have been at work delineating a methodology for their efforts. Recently, literary scholars such as E. D. Hirsch and philosophers such as Paul Ricoeur have tried to place hermeneutics into a modern context that both allows for different interpretive arguments and also guides the choice of the best argument in a particular situation.[6]

Critics of hermeneutic conceptions of planning and policy anlysis sometimes suggest that these efforts are necessarily fruitless, and that if hermeneutics practitioners become dominant in the field, policy analysis will become "merely" interpretive, with no hope of rational choice among contending interpretations. Actually, certain forms of interpretation can yield considerable certainty. It is possible, for example, to have studied an ancient text long enough to know not merely the author's stated meaning but also points in the text where the author omitted a critical word or otherwise did not say what a modern reader knows the author really intended to say.[7] At least in this sense of "getting inside the head" of other people (a process termed *verstehen* after the German word for *understanding*), hermeneutic interpretation can be quite precise.

This ability to get inside the head of other actors in the policy process is far from a trivial skill for planners and policy analysts. Whatever else one may think of Aaron Wildavsky's writings on the budgeting process, his description of the actual activity of federal budget officials is useful.[8] A central feature of that activity involves predicting how other actors in the budget process will respond to a particular budget proposal. Agency budget officials thus frequently ask themselves, "How will this Bureau of Budget (or OMB) official react to the proposal?" or "How will that committee chair react?" The ability to get inside the head of future reviewers and predict their reaction is thus a highly prized skill, and it is at its core an interpretive or hermeneutic act.

Of course, decision makers often want to know more about a particular proposal than about how future reviewers are likely to react to it. Among other things, they may want to know how a proposal will affect the real world if it is actually put into action. It is here, say some critics of hermeneutic analysis, that hermeneutics is most likely to be found lacking. Why should anyone believe one particular interpretation of future program effects rather than any other interpretation?

Critics especially question the predictive value of hermeneutics in the context of the "hermeneutic circle." According to the circle concept, a commonly acknowledged component of hermeneutics theory, the subject of the interpretation influences the interpreter, whose very interpretation then alters what is being interpreted, which is then reinterpreted and again influences the interpreter, and so on. For interpreters who start with approximately the same understandings and who can stay within the circle, interpretive discussions can be fruitful and meaningful. But, say many critics of hermeneutics, interpreters who do not start within the circle may find the interpretation barren or, at most, suggestive of the mind-set of a particular group of people at a particular moment in history, but certainly not likely to lead to anything useful.

Obviously, any community, including a community of scholars, is bound by a circle of conventions. Contemporary physicists, for example, share a view of what it means to make a strong or weak argument in their field. A portion of this view will doubtless seem quaint to scientists two hundred years from now, much as we view as quaint the belief in some societies that five miles across flat lands can be "equidistant" to one mile across a thick marsh. As the philosopher Stephen Toulmin has argued, a discipline is simply a core of techniques, procedures, and intellectual representations that are accepted as "giving explanations" within the scope of that discipline. Mastering these techniques and procedures is essential if one wants to attain membership in the discipline, but it also allows a person who becomes a member to change some of the core suppositions of the discipline while still staying within its basic structure.[9]

Viewed from this perspective, hermeneutics scholarship is no more or less subject to the viciousness of circularity than are more positivist or empiricist studies. A constant interplay exists among how we look at a problem, our tools for studying it, and our findings. Each of these elements can change the other elements and in turn be altered by those changes. What is needed in all forms of scholarship is some device for correcting and perfecting findings over time. I will argue next that the narrative structure helps provide that device for hermeneutic planning and policy analysis.

Narration and Hermeneutics

By *stories* or *narratives* I mean the Aristotelian conception of an organized form of discourse with a plot in three parts: beginning, middle, and end. Stories must contain, as Aristotle wrote in his *Poetics*, beginnings, middles, and ends so closely connected to each other that the "transposal or withdrawal of any of them will disjoin and dislocate the whole." The beginning must be "that which is not itself necessarily after any-thing else, and which has naturally something else after"; the end must be "that which is naturally after something else . . . and with nothing else after it"; and the middle must be "that which is by nature after one thing and also has another after it."[10]

Many commentators have noted the close relationship of narration to hermeneutics. Hans-Georg Gadamer, an important contemporary ex-ponent of hermeneutics, has argued that the central hermeneutic activity is the merging of the known into the unknown. "There is always a world," Gadamer writes, "already interpreted, already organized into basic relations, into which experience steps as somethimg new."[11] The hermeneutic experience consists of "appropriating" the unknown into the known through a process of constructive understanding. Ricoeur suggests that these appropriations are often accomplished through narra-tives. Narratives, like metaphors, says Ricoeur, have the ability to bring together what at first seem "distant" into something "close."[12] A per-son's thoughts about a problematic situation and the world it opens may thus become organized through narratives, without which the reader might fail to "comprehend or grasp as a whole the chain of meanings in one act of synthesis."[13]

The narrative form can offer a powerful tool to an analyst seeking a hermeneutic explanation. This is partly because the narrative structure, with its organized beginning, middle, and end, requires the establish-ment of a readable, coherent plot. A plot in such a form provides the policy analyst with a tool that can "'grasp together' and integrate into one whole and complete story multiple and scattered events."[14] A plot, says Ricoeur, "unifies into one whole and complete action the miscel-lany constituted by the circumstances, ends and means, initiatives and interactions, the reversals of fortune, and all the unintended conse-quences issuing from human action."[15] A plot is thus "more than just an enumeration of events in serial order. . . . Emplotment is the operation that draws a configuration out of simple succession."[16] As E. M. Forster put it, "'The king died and then the queen died' is a story. 'The king died, and then the queen died of grief' is a plot."[17]

Considerable analytic talent is needed to recognize an ordering plot in, or impose a plot upon, the differing values and events important to complex issues. Yet for the analyst who makes the effort, the reward can be a coherent plot that leads to insights and conclusions that might not otherwise have been attained.

To start to show why this is so, let me contrast the narrative approach with the "chronicle" approach, a style of policy analysis that is common within government agencies. A chronicle is usually terse and often takes the form of an outline or a list of pros and cons. The chronicle approach does not seek to tell a story, presents no plot, and exhibits no organized beginning, middle, or end. As an example of the difference between narrative and chronicle, consider the following narrative rendition of the choice between one proposal to provide a guaranteed child support level to single working parents to bring their income to the poverty level and a second proposal to offer free or reduced-price day care to these same parents. Then consider a more "chronicalized" assessment of the same issue.[18]

THE NARRATIVE APPROACH

A central part of this agency's approach to child support for the last eight years has been the creation of a guaranteed child support level. Under this concept, single parents whose children are eligible to receive child support from a noncustodial parent can choose either to enroll in the regular AFDC program or to participate in an assured child support benefit program. The assured benefit program guarantees each child a certain level of child support and provides government funds if the custodial and noncustodial parents cannot meet the support level through their own efforts.

Because the assured child support level will always be less than the AFDC benefit level, most program participants will do better than they would under AFDC only if they work. However, because benefits under the child support assurance program fall less quickly as earnings rise than is the case under AFDC, a recipient of the assured child support benefit program who is working at least half time at the minimum wage will do better than the same recipient on AFDC. The benefits in the assured child support program will increase in comparison to AFDC the more one works. More hours of work will always result in more take-home pay under the assured child support program, and participants can clearly see that this is the case.

Planning for the program has been under way for several years. Implementation has not yet occurred, largely because our agency has had to focus first on the collection side of child support in order to generate enough revenue to fund the assured benefit program. In the past legislative session, however, our agency received authorization to create pilot assured benefit programs in a few geographic areas.

Since the granting of the legislative authority to pilot some programs, another proposal that is in some sense complementary but in another sense competing has emerged. Under this proposal, participants would receive a subsidy for the child care costs they incur in order to work. The amount of the subsidy would decline with higher income, but it would decline very gradually and evenly and fit around the AFDC and food stamp benefit structures so that a recipient would always be better off working than not working.

Perhaps the most striking features of the day care supplement are its freshness and conceptual simplicity. Though both the child support assurance and the child care benefit are likely to be administratively complex, the child care program may be easier to explain to busy lawmakers. However, the freshness has its drawbacks. Our agency has been promoting the assured child support program for several years, whole political constituencies have grown comfortable with this concept of welfare reform, and several staff in the agency have invested much effort in the program.

The long history of the assured benefit program has allowed us to take the time necessary to obtain federal financial participation in it, something that will probably not be available for the child care subsidy. In addition, the child support assurance program has its own logic; single parents who are working are doing everything society can reasonably expect of them to achieve independence, yet many still cannot earn their way out of poverty. The child support assurance program recognizes this and supplements their income and their private child support payments so they can come closer to the poverty level.

It is true that the provision of free day care also acts as a form of income supplement, one which is not taxable to the recipient, does not affect eligibility for the Medicaid program, and does not lower food stamp benefits. Still, for any expenditure of our agency's funds, recipients will benefit more from the child support assurance program than from the day care program because of the federal financial participation in the child support program.

In addition, the funding of the day care on such a broad basis will likely lead to calls that our agency regulate the quality of child care more than it now does, and it is also likely that utilization of paid child care will increase dramatically while the provision of unpaid or less-than-market-rate day care by families and friends will decline. The increased regulation and professionalization of day care might be desirable but will certainly increase costs and complexity.

We should go forward with the assured child support program as it has been developed and forgo for now the child care payment program. Day care can still be an integral part of other welfare reform efforts, but we should focus first on providing a cash supplement to private child support for AFDC recipients and low-income single parents with earnings.

I. The Assured Child Support Benefit Program
   A. The assured child support level is set at $2,500 for one child. The levels for the second through sixth child rise in the same proportion as AFDC benefits.
   B. A wage subsidy of $1 per hour for one child and $1.75 per hour for two or more children is provided for those families with incomes below $8,000. The level of subsidy per hour is reduced on incomes above that point so that it disappears at $16,000 of annual family income.

II. The Day Care Subsidy Program
   A. Participants with earned income at a level that would qualify them for AFDC receive day care vouchers at a rate up to $1.25 per child per hour.
   B. The hourly benefit decreases as income rises. At all income levels, recipients would pay at least a small percentage of total costs to encourage them to use the least expensive day care possible, and the percentage would rise as income increases.

III. Advantages to the Child Support Assurance Program
   A. Families working 20 hours per week at minimum wage will do better under this proposal than under AFDC. Families would have to work 35 hours per week at the minimum wage to beat AFDC under the guaranteed day care program.
   B. The hours-based wage subsidy provides a very clear and direct work incentive and a strong disincentive against reducing the number of hours worked.
   C. Providing recipients with cash rather than day care vouchers allows recipients flexibility in how they spend the money.
   D. The child support assurance approach does not reward high-wage workers who work few hours (but presumably could work more).
   E. This program allows for federal financial participation.
   F. This proposal does not run the risk of "monetizing" a product now provided to a substantial degree by family members, and it does not implicate (through widespread funding) government in the quality of day care without simultaneously providing greater regulatory capacity.

IV. Advantages of the Day Care Payment Program
   A. It is easy to explain the basic concept of this program; everybody knows that single parents need day care if they have young children and are expected to work, and vouchers for day care will seem less like welfare than will an assured child support benefit.
   B. The guaranteed child support and wage subsidy combination will

           not cover the child care costs of two or more children in need of full-time professional child care.

   C. In-kind day care vouchers do not count as income for purposes of such federal programs as Medicaid, food stamps, and energy assistance. As a result, family benefits are not eroded through reductions in the benefits of other programs.

   D. Recipients may have a better understanding of this program from a "risk avoidance" perspective. If they know their child care costs will be covered up to a certain level, they may feel more secure in moving into the labor market than they would under the assured child support program.

Note the differences in the two analytic styles. The narrative approach has a plot with a beginning (the decision of several years ago to develop the child support assurance program), a middle (the legislative language of the last session and the subsequent development of the subsidized day care program), and a proposed end (go forward with one program and forgo the other). In the process, the narrative "grasps together," in Ricoeur's phrase, a variety of disparate information and thoughts and weaves them into a plot. The end flows naturally from the beginning and middle, so much so that it is possible to imagine our analyst not knowing or only loosely knowing at the beginning of the story how it will turn out and, as is often the case for novelists, being swept along to a particular conclusion by the force of beginning and middle.[19]

In contrast, the chronicle approach lacks a plot. After studying the characteristics, advantages, and disadvantages of each program, the reader is left hanging. What should the reader do next—count the advantages of each program and support the one with the greatest number? More important, this approach also leaves the writer hanging. It does not force a knitting together of a variety of qualitative and quantitative elements, and it fails to lead to what literary critic Frank Kermode has called a "sense of an ending."[20]

Narratives are thus useful to the actual process of planning and policy analysis, not just to the communication of the results of these efforts. By requiring beginnings, middles, and ends, policy analysis that uses a narrative approach forces an analyst to weave together a variety of factors and come to a conclusion that flows naturally out of these factors. There can, of course, be bad stories—stories that ignore some relevant factors and get others wrong—but the best stories create a tapestry that is both lovely and useful and that helps make sense of complex situations occurring within an environment of conflicting values.

But how does one know whether a narrative analysis is good or bad? If the ability to enhance a body of knowledge through the application of a set of accepted techniques represents the essence of a scholarly disipline, what narrative techniques and representations merit acceptance, and how does one know if a particular narrative has them?

One simple test of the quality of narrative analysis is whether it has a recognizable beginning, middle, and end. Many policy issues become muddled because analysts fail to think clearly about where the story they want to tell begins. Consider, for example, the culture-of-poverty issue. At least since the writings of Walter Miller and Oscar Lewis in the late 1950s and early 1960s the notion that the persistently poor live in a culture of poverty has engendered considerable controversy. Scholars have tried in many ways to shed light on the issue. Some have administered attitudinal surveys about work and future orientation to see if the poor respond differently from the nonpoor; others have conducted lengthy ethnographic observations; and still others have carried out complex efforts to establish and interpret longitudinal data sets that help assess the length of time in, and intergenerational transmission of, poverty.[21]

Despite many years of effort, the results have been ambivalent. The attitude surveys have generally not found a culture of poverty, the ethnographic studies often have, and the longitudinal data sets have proved to need increasingly refined techniques or more years of data. A clear sense of beginning would add coherence to some of these discussions. If there is a culture of poverty in which, say, many blacks are currently enmeshed, when and how did it begin? In slavery? But how, then, does one account for the apparently much more solid community structures of pre-1950 black ghettoes? In southern share-cropping? Then how does one account for the relative success of southern-born blacks who moved North?[22] If one cannot identify a beginning to the story, it is harder to argue the current existence of a culture of poverty or to suggest future actions likely to diminish it.

A sense of ending is similarly desirable. Reports of surveys of poor people, assessments of how long people stay poor, and ethnographic studies of low-income neighborhoods are all useful. Yet for all their value, they have no use to a planner or policy analyst trying to "speak truth to power" except as part of a story with a proposed end, or as a tool to help criticize someone else's story and create a better one with a more logical or happier ending. Public decisions and the dialogue that goes into them are inherently teleological. They suggest or point to desired ends, and policy analysis and planning that lacks this teleological focus is often—except in the sense that someone else may use it to a point to his own ending—irrelevant.

Besides the simple presence of a beginning, middle, and end, good narrative policy analysis must also be true. I have written elsewhere on the concept of narrative truth.[23] However, I want to say more in this essay about how to test for narrative truth, because I believe the narrative form itself provides an aid to truth testing in hermeneutic planning and policy analysis. One way to use the narrative form to assess truth is, as in the difference between realistic and nonrealistic fiction, to consider the degree to which the narrative describes actions that represent formal convention. This test is not an automatic indication of truth or falsehood. Stock characters—such as greedy politicians with no policy interests except those that lead to their own financial benefit and hopelessly lazy bureaucrats—doubtless do exist. But a policy narrative that rests entirely on stereotypical characters engaged in stereotypical action at least deserves extra scrutiny.

A better indication of narrative truth involves the internal connection among the five core elements of narrative: agent, act, scene, agency, and purpose (who, what, where, how, and why). According to basic rules of story telling, some underlying consistency must be presented among all five elements. Political scientists W. Lance Bennett and Martha S. Feldman have argued that the presence or absence of this narrative consistency serves as an important test of truth in a courtroom setting, and that jurors with little formal education can, with the help of attorneys, make sophisticated judgments about the internal consistency of most courtroom narratives.[24]

Bennett and Feldman suggest that the essential feature of courtroom argumentation is the effort by opposing attorneys to create and defend plots that present reality in a way most beneficial to their side. Bennett and Feldman cite a narcotics case in which the defendant was arrested for driving to the scene of a drug deal in a car containing narcotics. The defendant argued that he had been duped into driving the car, and he told a story to support his contention. He said his own car had broken down and that he had gone to a tavern looking for someone with the appropriate tools. While he was there, an acquaintance walked in and offered him the use of his car if the defendant would drop the acquaintance off at a nearby shopping center and pick him up an hour later. Only on the defendant's return to the shopping center, where the drug deal was to transpire and the police were waiting to arrest him, did the defendant realize that the car he was driving contained illegal drugs.

The core elements presented in this story (agent, act, agency, and purpose) are entirely consistent. The defendant's story explained why he was driving the drug dealer's car and why he happened to be carrying illegal drugs. However, in cross-examination, the opposing attorney introduced another core element into the story—scene—that created an important inconsistency. It happened that the defendant's house was just a few blocks from the tavern. Why, the attorney asked, had not the defendant simply walked home to get his tools instead of going to the tavern?[25]

Policy analysts and planners use stories in similar ways to represent reality and test their versions of the truth. As in a courtroom, the dialectic interplay between two competing stories is often a useful form for evaluating the consistency of internal story elements and the likely truth of the story. But even when an analyst is working without competition on a policy story, self-critical evaluation of the consistency of one's own story, or normal evaluation of narrative elements by a supervisor, can often provide a good indication of the story's consistency and likely truth. Tolstoy once wrote that "in a writer there must be two people—the writer and the critic."[26] The critic part of the writer-analyst has the special responsibility of rewriting the story to obtain the greatest possible internal consistency.

Two Objections to Policy Analysis as Narrative

Having argued that narratives are useful to policy analysis, I now address two theoretical barriers to narrative planning and policy analysis. The first is Aristotle's claim (supported by literary critics such as Northrup Frye) that the "emplotment" of a beginning, middle, and end applies only to fictional art, and not to descriptions of actual happenings. The second, which I must address to encompass planning about the future in my discussion, involves the claim of Arthur Danto and other analytical philosophers that narrative sentences apply only to the past.

Aristotle claimed that plot structures with true beginnings, middles, and ends could not apply to disciplines, such as history, that describe actual events. Unlike historians, writers of fiction can create an identifiable beginning, middle, and end only because they are the authors of their plots and can impose order on them.

Aristotle did not say why real human life must be judged to lack beginnings, middles, and ends. Certainly Greek historians like Thucydides and Herodotus wrote histories with clear plots and identifiable beginnings, middles, and ends. Just as certainly, however, mere listings of seemingly unrelated events constituted the only efforts during the Middle Ages to describe what happened in past generations. Such listings, called annals or chronicles, are distinct from narrative history, in which, in its tightest form, event A is described only because event B would not have happened as it did if event A had not happened as it did.

Literary and historical theorists such as Hayden White and Louis Mink agree with Aristotle on the nonnarrativity of human life.[27] White argues that history, as much as fiction, uses narratives that are the product of the author's imagination. Historians do precisely what fiction writers do: they employ the narrative structure of beginning, middle, and end to "endow what originally appears to be problematical and mysterious with the aspect of recognizable . . . form."[28] This does not detract, says White, from the status of knowledge that history offers, but it is the same kind of knowledge that literature offers—a knowledge of how human consciousness imparts meanings to events, and not a knowledge of the events themselves.[29]

Like Aristotle and Mink, White believes a story can provide no knowledge of events themselves because "we do not *live* stories, even if we give our lives meaning by retrospectively casting them in the form of stories."[30] Stories give to reality "the mask of a meaning, the completeness and fullness of which we can only *imagine*, never experience."[31] In historical writing, the plot of a narrative is presented as " 'found' in the events rather than put there by narrative techniques," but the opposite is actually the case.[32]

If White's and Aristotle's arguments were fully valid, of course, my own argument about the desirability of narratives to policy analysis and planning would be questionable. If we fictionalize our subject matter merely by telling stories, then stories should be of little use to policy analysts. Yet the argument that real life lacks beginnings, middles, and ends, and that we inevitably fictionalize life by imposing on it such forms of order, is in some ways puzzling, as philosophers David Carr and Alisdair MacIntyre have pointed out.[33]

The puzzlement arises because it is hard even to imagine experiencing something without at the same time conceptualizing it as something that follows one thing and is a preamble to something else. What would an experience of going to sleep be if we did not conceive it as a point on the way to full sleep? We are always in the midst of something— taking out the garbage so that the municipal workers will collect it or eating lunch so that our hunger sensations will stop—whose very existence as a prologue to something else is an essential part of the experience. At least in that sense we do experience life as a story, and beginnings, middles, and ends are integral parts of our lives, not something imposed on them from outside.

This is not to say that our lives always make for orderly or interesting stories. Our lives do often seem to lack an outside narrator telling only those small stories of our lives that seem necessary for interesting telling of the bigger stories. In the stories that are our own lives, Carr notes, "we are constantly having to revise the plot, scrambling to intercept the slings and arrows of fortune and the stupidity or stubbornness of our uncooperative fellows, who *will* insist on coming up with their own stories instead of docilely accommodating themselves to ours."[34] But to say that the stories are disorderly or boring or bad is far from denying the presence of beginnings, middles, and ends that are both intrinsic to the way we experience our lives and capturable in narrative form.

The second objection to the use of narrativity suggests that narrative statements can never apply to the future. Analytical philosophers such as Arthur Danto have shown convincingly that the narrative structure can explain why events occurred at the same time that they describe what has occurred. In the process, however, narratives apply logically only to the past.[35] This is because in order for a sentence to be truly part of a narrative, the narrator must know something that the character he describes did not know—namely, how the story comes out in the end. A sentence like "The author of the Emancipation Proclamation was born in 1809" is thus quintessentially narrative. Nancy Hanks Lincoln could not have known at the time she gave birth to Abraham what the author of this sentence knew.

Lincoln's mother could have told other stories about Abraham at this and later periods in her life. But the story that interests us is how Lincoln became president, what he did as president, and the implications of his actions for the future, and surely this story could not be told in other than the past tense. A narrating (as opposed to a chronicling) writer would try to describe only those events in Lincoln's life which, had they happened differently or not at all, might have made Lincoln a different president. We can tolerate, and even seek out, gossip about a president's personal life, but we know that the great biographers and historians emphasize material that is significant for something that happens later. To do that, of course, both the included event and the subsequent occurrence for which the event is significant must be past to the narrator.

How, then, does this argument about the essential "pastness" of narrative comport with my claim that narratives apply to future policy planning as well as to descriptions of how we got where we are? Without denying the force of Danto's arguments about the pastness of narratives, it is useful to recall that time can be multidimensional. As Seymour Mandelbaum has suggested, the now that we are in is really an extended, or "artificial," present.[36] When we say in policy discussions that the situation "right now" is such that day care is a great need for both single- and two-parent households, we do not mean that we know for sure that this is the case at the moment we say it. What we really mean is that we completed a study—say, last month—analyzing a survey conducted over a prior six-month period that showed the need for child care. When we say the need is "right now," we conflate the recent past and the moment in which we are talking into a more encompassing but artificial present.

The more distant past and future can often conflate into the present as well. There is not, Ricoeur has written, "a future time, a past time, but a threefold present, a present of future things, a present of past things, and a present of present things."[37] In this sense, a narrative proposing a future vision is simply a story of what we should try to do in the future because *now* we realize we have had a particular problem.

Conclusion

I have argued that narratives can be true and can describe a proposed future, that the narrative style forces a knitting together of multiple factors in a complex situation, and that the consistency of narrative elements in a plot provides an important test of narrative truth.

The fantasy novelist Ursula K. LeGuin wrote a narrative about the ability of stories to wrap a variety of factors into a cohesive whole that can support movement but also create problems. The narrative concerns the Western hoop snake, which can make rapid progress only if it forms itself into a circle. If it does not form a circle, it lies in the dust or moves only haltingly. To make real progress, it must "take its tail (which may or may not have rattles on it) into its mouth, thus forming itself into a hoop. . . . Rolling along, bowling along, is a lot quicker and more satisfying than crawling. But, for the hoop snake with rattles, there is a drawback. They are venomous snakes, and when they bite their own tail they die, in awful agony, of snakebite."[38]

As LeGuin notes, "very few things come nearer the real Hoop Trick than a good story."[39] Stories embrace the circularity of principled human thought and serve as powerful engines for moving us toward conclusions. They can also create problems, but the very nature of the narrative structure makes some of the problems—like the hoop snake's death—easy to discover. A good story with a true beginning and middle can send policy analysts and planners rolling along, bowling along, toward useful and defensible arguments.

Notes

1. N. R. Hanson, *Patterns of Discovery: An Inquiry into the Perceptual Foundations of Science* (Cambridge: Cambridge University Press, 1958), 71.

2. R. Merton, *Social Theory and Social Structure* (Glencoe, Ill.: Free Press, 1949), 92–94. See also the discussion in R. J. Bernstein, *The Restructuring of Social and Political Theory* (New York: Harcourt Brace Jovanovich, 1976), 11–14.

3. M. Hesse, *Revolution and Reconstruction in the Philosophy of Science* (Bloomington: Indiana University Press, 1980) x.

4. See N. Herbert, *Quantum Reality: Beyond the New Physics* (Garden City, N.Y.: Doubleday/Anchor, 1985), 221–32.

5. For a review of other criticisms of positivism, see D. Healy, "Interpretive Policy Inquiry," *Policy Sciences*, 19, no. 4 (December 1986): 381–96.

6. E. D. Hirsch, Jr., *Validity in Interpretation* (New Haven: Yale University Press, 1967); P. Ricoeur, *Interpretation Theory: Discourse and the Surplus of Meanings* (Fort Worth: Texas Christian University Press, 1976).

7. See D. D. Campbell, "Science's Social System of Validity-enhancing Collective Belief Change and the Problems of the Social Sciences," in D. W. Fiske and R. A. Shweder, eds., *Metatheory in Social Sciences: Pluralisms and Subjectivities* (Chicago: University of Chicago Press, 1986), 108–35.

8. See A. Wildavsky, *The Politics of the Budgetary Process*, 4th ed. (Boston: Little, Brown, 1984), 26–31.

9. S. Toulmin, *Human Understanding: The Collective Use and Evolution of Concepts* (Princeton: Princeton University Press, 1972), 158–68.

10. Aristotle, "De Poetica," in W. D. Ross, ed., and Ingrid Bywater, trans., *The Works of Aristotle* (Oxford: Oxford University Press, 1924), sect. 7, lines 26–34.

11. H. G. Gadamer, *Philosophical Hermeneutics*, ed. and trans., David E. Linge (Berkeley: University of California Press, 1976), 15.

12. P. Ricoeur, *Time and Narrative*, vol. 1 (Chicago: University of Chicago Press, 1984), x.

13. Ricoeur, *Interpretation Theory*, 72.

14. Ricoeur, *Time and Narrative*, x.

15. Ibid.

16. Ibid., 65.

17. Quoted in W. Martin, *Recent Theories of Narrative* (Ithaca: Cornell University Press, 1986), 81.

18. These examples, both assumed to have been written in the same state

social services agency, are for illustration only. Neither constitutes a fully satis-factory analysis, and I intend to advocate neither approach.

19. Martin, *Recent Theories of Narrative*, 65, describes how the beginning and middle of Tolstoy's *War and Peace* carried the author to different conclusions than he had originally intended.

20. F. Kermode, *The Sense of an Ending: Studies in the Theory of Fiction* (New York: Oxford University Press, 1967).

21. See, e.g., W. B. Miller, "Lower-Class Culture as a Generating Milieu of Delinquency," *Journal of Social Issues* 14 (July 1958): 5–19; O. Lewis, *La Vida: A Puerto Rican Family in the Culture of Poverty—San Juan and New York* (New York: Random House, 1966); C. A. Valentine, *Culture and Poverty* (Chicago: University of Chicago Press, 1968); L. Goodwin, *Do the Poor Want to Work? A Social-Psychological Study of Work Orientation* (Washington, D.C.: Brookings Institution, 1972); M. J. Bane and D. T. Ellwood, *The Dynamics of Dependence: The Routes to Self Sufficiency* (Washington, D.C.: Department of Health and Human Services, 1983); M. Corcoran, G. J. Duncan, G. Guria, and P. Guria, "Myth and Reality: The Causes and Persistence of Poverty," *Journal of Policy Analysis and Management* 4, no. 4 (Summer 1985): 516–36; L. M. Mead, *Beyond Entitlement: The Social Obligations of Citizenship* (New York: Free Press, 1986); and W. J. Wilson, *The Truly Disadvantaged: The Inner City, the Underclass, and Public Policy* (Chicago: University of Chicago Press, 1987).

22. See Wilson, *The Truly Disadvantaged*, 55.

23. J. Kaplan, "The Narrative Structure of Policy Analysis," *Journal of Policy Analysis and Management* 5, no. 4 (Summer 1986): 761–78.

24. W. L. Bennett and M. S. Feldman, *Reconstructing Reality in the Courtroom* (New Brunswick, N.J.: Rutgers University Press, 1984).

25. Ibid., 62–65.

26. Quoted in Martin, *Recent Theories of Narrative*, 170.

27. L. O. Mink, "History and Fiction as Modes of Comprehension," *New Literary History* 1 (1970): 541–58; H. White, *Tropics of Discourse: Essays in Cultural Criticism* (Baltimore: Johns Hopkins University Press, 1985); H. White, "The Value of Narrativity in the Representation of Reality," in W. J. T. Mitchell, ed., *On Narrative* (Chicago: University of Chicago Press, 1981), 1–23.

28. White, *Tropics of Discourse*, 90.

29. Ibid., 90.

30. Ibid.

31. White, "The Value of Narrativity," 20.

32. White, *Tropics of Discourse*, 90.

33. D. Carr, "Life and the Narrator's Art," in H. J. Silverman and D. Ihde, eds., *Hermeneutics and Deconstruction* (Albany: State University of New York Press, 1985); A. MacIntyre, *After Virtue* (Notre Dame, Ind.: University of Notre Dame Press, 1984), 211–18.

34. Carr, "Life and the Narrator's Art," 117.

35. A. Danto, *Analytical Philosophy of History* (Cambridge: Cambridge University Press, 1968).

36. S. J. Mandelbaum, "Temporal Conventions in Planning Discourse," *Planning and Design* 11 (1984): 8–10.

37. Ricoeur, *Time and Narrative*, 1:60.

38. U. K. LeGuin, "It Was a Dark and Stormy Night," in Mitchell, *On Narrative*, 189–90.

39. Ibid., 190.

Learning from

Practice Stories: The Priority of

Practical Judgment

John Forester

Ten years ago, Peter Szanton wrote an insightful book called *Not Well Advised* about the problems of linking the research capacities of universities to the needs of our cities. Making those linkages work had been very tough, and Szanton wanted to explain what had happened, what wasn't workable, and what might yet work. In the closing chapter, "What Have We Learned?" in a short section entitled, "'Generalizability' Is a Trap," a striking passage says simply, "F. Scott Fitzgerald commented—on the writing of fiction—that if he began with an individual, he soon had a type, but if he began with a type, he soon had nothing." A similar rule, Szanton was arguing, holds for applied social research.[1] In recent years, several other authors have been exploring closely related themes.

In a popular book on the uses of history in policy analysis, *Thinking in Time*, for example, Richard Neustadt and Ernest May recommend a practical maxim they call the Goldberg Rule. They tell planning and policy analysts, "Don't ask, 'What's the problem?' ask, 'What's the story?'—That way you'll find out what the problem really is."[2]

In planning, Martin Krieger's *Advice and Planning* begins to explore the importance of stories as elements of policy advice, and Seymour Mandelbaum has always argued that our stories define us in subtle political and social ways, expressing and reshaping who we are, individually and together.[3] And in political theory and philosophy, too, Peter Euben and Martha Nussbaum have argued that literature and drama, and tragedy most of all, can teach us about action, about ethics and politics, in ways that more traditional analytic writing cannot.[4]

In Nussbaum's view, for example, literature can give us a fine and responsive appreciation of the particulars that matter practically in our lives; literature, she suggests, can give us an astutely alert pragmatism, hope (with less false hope), a keener perception of what's really at stake in our practice; in effect, a realism with less presumptuousness about clean and painless technical or scientific solutions—be they the solutions of the hidden hand of the market or of the more visible fist of the class struggle.

The broader practical relevance of these writers' concerns is captured wonderfully by Robert Coles in *The Call of Stories*. The opening chapter, "Stories and Theories," provides a moving and resonant account of Coles's own early clinical training in psychiatry.

Coles introduces us to two of his supervisors: Dr. Binger, the brilliant theorist who sought out "the nature of phobias," "the psychodynamics at work here," and "therapeutic strategies"; and Dr. Lüdwig, who kept urging Coles to resist the "rush to interpretation"—the rush to interpretation—by listening closely to his patients' stories.

Coles writes that for thirty years he has heard the echo of Dr. Lüdwig's words: "The people who come to see us bring us their stories. They hope they tell them well enough so that we understand the truth of their lives. They hope we know how to interpret their stories correctly. We have to remember that what we hear is their story."[5]

The important point here is *not* that psychiatric patients have stories—we all do—but that Dr. Lüdwig was giving young Dr. Coles some practical advice about how to listen, about how much to listen for, and about the dangers of rushing in "theory-first" and missing lots of the action. Dr. Lüdwig was giving Coles, and Coles is passing along to us, practical advice about learning on the job, about the ways our current theories focus our attention very selectively—as a shorthand, perhaps— but if we're not very careful, too selectively.

Coles recalls his mentor, physician and poet William Carlos Williams, on this danger of theoretical oversimplification. Williams said, "Who's against shorthand? No one I know. Who wants to be short-changed? No one I know."[6] When we have practical bets to make about what to do and what might work, theory matters—but so do the particulars of the situations we're in, if we want those bets to be good ones, if we want not to shortchange others or ourselves.

But stories matter in the professional school classroom, too. In my undergraduate class "Planning, Power, and Decision Making" recently, my students read, as they typically do, a mix of planning case histories— historical and theoretical material about power and powerlessness. But in this particular class, the students also read thirty to forty pages of edited interviews with planners who were graduates of our program.[7] These interviews were produced in the format that Studs Terkel has used in his many books: the interviewer's questions were edited out, and what remained, in our case, were planners talking about their real work—its difficulties, surprises, rewards, and, of course, frustrations.

The result in the classroom was striking: "Now I can tell my mom what planners really do; it's not all one thing, but this is it; now I can tell her." Another student said, "This was the most practical thing I've read in three years in this program!"[8]

Several other students had similar reactions. Somehow, the profiles had "grabbed" them in eye-opening and obviously effective ways. But why had that happened? What was so striking, so catching and effective, about those stories told by planners about their own work?

Of course, the stories were concrete and descriptive, and not abstract, theoretical, and full of unfamiliar language, but that was no explanation. The same was true of the historical material I'd assigned. Something much more important than "concreteness" was at work here, with implications reaching far beyond the classroom, as this essay will argue.

Consider this classroom experience in the light of recent empirical and ethnographic work on policy analysts and planners. Typically, such work involves not only interviews with planners and analysts but also observations of and perhaps even participation in various formal and informal meetings in the "policy process," including, for example, planners' and analysts' own staff meetings.[9] Beginning to assess how much happens politically and practically when analysts and planners talk, and listen more or less well to others talk, this literature suggests that in actual practice, planners tell and listen to "practice stories" all the time.

Is it possible, then, that analysts and planners at work learn from each other's and other people's stories in ways subtly similar to the ways my students were listening to and learning from the practice stories they had read in class? Taking this question seriously can lead us to *watch* in planning and policy meetings in new ways, and to listen in new ways, too, to the stories that analysts tell at work, in their dealings with outsiders and with one another. Three questions about these practice stories quickly arise. First, what do planners and analysts accomplish in their telling of stories? Second, what kinds of learning from such story telling is possible and plausible? And third, what does such story telling have to do with the politics of planning and policy analysis?

These are the questions explored in the following sections. First, we examine an excerpt from a profile presented in the classroom. Second, we look closely at a segment of an actual city planning staff meeting—a segment in which the planning staff listen critically to, and reconstruct, a practice story told by the planning director. Third, we consider an essentially Aristotelian argument about the ways we learn from practice stories on the job (and more broadly as well).

Learning from Practice Profiles

How do we learn from the practice stories told by practitioners in their own voices? The following selection comes from an interview profile of "Kristin," a recent professional school graduate. Kristin had been describing a lengthy process of meetings she had held with residents and commercial interests in a neighborhood to discuss zoning issues—to allow concentrated, possibly mixed-use, commercial development and to prevent residential displacement, too. Out of the process came a proposal that went to the City Council, twice. Kristin put it this way:

> At the [second] meeting, there was movement toward an agreement, but a councilman made a motion to drop the height by thirty feet in all of the areas, and it undid the whole thing. It upset the balance we had worked out. The developers jumped to their feet and rushed to the microphones and said, "Look, we worked with the planning staff long and hard to determine these heights, and they're not just drawn out of thin air. They're related to densities and uses, and these are the numbers that work. You can't just go in and chop!"
>
> Fortunately, the council listened to the voice of reason and they agreed, but very hesitantly. They didn't want to, but they agreed, since it was only a land-use plan and wasn't the actual zoning itself. Since the zoning was to be decided later, the council figured, "If we want to change our minds, we'll do it then." And they let the plan go through.
>
> We'd built a consensus and it really was very fragile, because different groups had very different ideas from the start. When we went to City Council for the second time, we thought, "OK, now we have it, because now everyone's happy, and we're sure everyone's happy." Then the process breaks down a second time, because of this idea of heights. The people who were really affected were satisfied, but because of one voice, the process stopped. It was just a lot of delay, a lot of frustration, and a lot of uncertainty. I really thought the whole thing was going to just come apart.
>
> [And] I hate to say this, because it sounds terrible, but in the end it almost doesn't matter. When our office goes to the Planning Commission, we go with staff recommendations. Although we take into consideration a lot of what goes on, in the end we don't really need to have a consensus because we only present the staff position. It's up to the citizens and the developers and other interests to come and present their own perspectives

to the commission. In this city, our staff position doesn't carry the greatest weight. We can work on something for a very long time, but if someone comes into a Planning Commission meeting and makes a statement, they'll just undo what we've spent months working at. If we take long, hard months and go through the process of building consensus, in the end it almost doesn't matter. I don't think the Planning Department's work has a lot of clout.

I've been very disillusioned. Of course people are going to be self-interested, but I was surprised at the degree to which that's true, and at how people work very long and very hard simply to protect their own interests. The City Council is just an extremely political place. This is the first planning job I've had, and I often find myself wondering, "Is this how it is, or is this how it is here?" Most of the planners I talk to are fresh out of school and they say the same thing.

Still, there are little successes. We just relocated a government facility that the government provided and expanded, and it didn't really stand in the way of our plans for the area to try and transform it. We got in on time on that and helped to get them a place that was more appropriate, and everyone sort of won. It's those little things that make me feel that maybe in the long run I can make a difference. In the long run, it's the little day-to-day things that come up that give you a chance to make a neighborhood a more pleasant place to live in. The small things make up for other things. I say, "OK, I'll put up with certain things because that's the price I have to pay to be able to do the other small things that *do* have an effect."

It's also been a learning experience. This is my first job, and even though sometimes I'm not real happy with the way things go, I'm still learning a lot about politics.[10]

Now, how do we learn from such stories and what do we learn? Kristin's account tells us much more than the simple facts of a case. We learn, first of all, a good deal about her: her disillusionment, her sense of satisfaction with the "little successes." We learn about her expectations and her awakening to the politics of the planning process—and as readers we're obviously invited to compare our expectations of the process with hers, perhaps to be awakened in the same way.[11]

We learn about the vulnerability of planners' efforts: "We can work on something for a very long time" and "someone" can "just undo what we've spent months working at." We learn about a plausible, if uneasy, view of planners' roles ("Although we take into consideration a lot of what goes on, in the end we don't really need to have a consensus because we only present the staff position" to the Planning Commission); and we learn about what this view of her role implies about the encompassing politics of planning. So, she says, "It's up to the citizens and the developers and other interests to come and present their own perspectives," and having expressed this view, Kristin wonders if, and doubts that, the Planning Department's work "has a lot of clout."

And there's more, from insights about timing and politics ("Since the zoning was to be decided later, the council figured, 'If we want to change it, we'll do it then'") to Kristin's own sense of realism and hope ("This is my first job, and even though sometimes I'm not real happy with the way things go, I'm still learning a lot about politics"). What Kristin has learned can be a lesson to us, too.

Yet many people appear to believe that we learn nothing from practice stories that is not simply unique and idiosyncratic. For years it seemed, for example, that the distinguished practitioner turned academic Norman Krumholz doubted the value of writing up his ten years of experience, as the city of Cleveland's planning director, trying to make equity planning work. The urgings and encouragement of his many colleagues and friends notwithstanding, Krumholz suspected that his and his staff's experience would be too unique, too particular, too much "just about Cleveland" for others in other cities and towns to learn much from or to find really relevant.[12]

Krumholz's suspicions were fueled by an academic culture that often judges any work not conforming to canons of systematic social science as guilty before proven innocent. "Physics envy" in social research is alive and all too well. The point here is not to scapegoat positivism but to note that the imperial effects of social science narrowly construed have often terrorized both graduate studies and social inquiry more generally. We forget too easily that science is a cultural form of argument, not a valueless, passionless use of magical techniques.[13] Anthropology, for example, is a social science from which few would doubt we can learn, and it would be silly to dismiss anthropology, and perhaps history, too, because they're typically not "scientific" in the experimental, culturally conventional sense.[14] The point here is not to argue against hypothesis testing when it is possible, not even to argue for a desperately needed broader conception of social research, but to pursue the question of how practitioners learn and develop good judgment in practice—especially in applied and professional fields like the design and policy-related professions.

In practice, clearly enough, the real-time demands of work allow for little systematic experimentation. Just as clearly, practitioners at work engage in what we might call "practical storytelling" all the time—telling, for example, what happened last night at the meeting, what

Smith said and did when Jones said what she said, what the budget committee chair did when the citizen's action group protested the latest delay, what happened with that developer's architect's last project, and so on. In practice situations we find stories and more stories, told all the time and interpreted all the time, sometimes well, sometimes poorly; but we find relatively few controlled experiments.[15]

We're likely to find far more stories, too, in practice settings than we will find opportunities to "try things out," to test our bets, to move and reflect in action, as Donald Schön so powerfully describes it in *The Reflective Practitioner*. Faced with such stories and paying careful attention to them, planners and policy analysts do seem to learn in practice about the fluid and conflictual, complex, always surprising, and deeply political world they work in.

But how do they do it? What does it mean to pay careful attention to these stories and so to learn from them? How can we explain and dignify the ways planners and analysts can learn practically and politically as they listen to these stories?

Practice Stories Told and Listened to in Practice

To explore how practice stories might work in actual planning and policy settings, we can sit in, for example, on a city planning agency's staff meeting. Here we see not only that the professional planners tell one another practical, and practically significant, stories all the time, but also that they're creating common and deliberative stories together—stories about what's relevant to their purposes, about their shared responsibilities, about what they will and won't, can and can't, do, about what they have and haven't done.

To see how such common and deliberative stories can work, let us turn to a brief extract from a planners' staff meeting in a small city. We can think of listening in on a staff meeting as a way of getting inside the "organizational mind" of the planners, getting to know both how they perceive the situations they're in and how they begin to act on the problems they face.

In this case, the staff numbers roughly half a dozen professionals. The meeting followed a recent election in which the mayoral challenger, who lost narrowly, had run a campaign vigorously attacking the successful incumbent's planners—the planners holding this meeting. As the transcript suggests, the staff feel, to say the least, unappreciated and misunderstood by the public. This segment of their conversation follows:

> Vince (*director*): I think the Mayflower project [an apartment complex] was pivotal. That's the first time that we took a very high profile position on a very unpopular issue. We were outvoted on council seven to three; we were pushed right to the center of that controversy. We tried to hold what we thought was the right line, and we really lost a great deal of support in the general public because of our position.
>
> I think that was the first real bad one. And it gets blended in with the Northside. I think the Northside's the second one where we've been hurt, where those people who are afraid and concerned are really, really angry. And Lakeview Park's another one, although I don't think we're taking the heat for that one.
>
> George (*community development planner*): I think we are.
>
> Karen (*housing planner*): I think we are too.
>
> Pat (*assistant director*): I mean, I don't hear anybody saying, "The Board of Public Works really screwed up."
>
> Vince: It's interesting, because it wasn't our screwup.
>
> Karen: But *we never said* it wasn't our screwup. We never pointed the finger to the screwup.
>
> Vince: My perception is that people just think about any kind of change, and then they think about planning, and then they think about planners, and . . . somehow we're tied to everything.
>
> Bill (*senior planner*): It's guilt by association.
>
> Karen: If something goes wrong, the planners did it. If something goes right, the City Council members claim credit for it.
>
> Vince: *That's* the kind of problem I think we have to address. Ms. Smith here has been saying, "You've got to come out," and you have too, and many of you have been saying, "We've got to answer this, we've got to answer this." And I've always said, "No, we *don't*—because we don't want to get into a cursing war with a skunk; you know, you just get more heat that way."
>
> But now I think *we have to*. I think we have to set out a strategy over the next year or two of how we're going to sell the department and how we're going to position ourselves to get to those people whose minds aren't already made up. I mean, you'll never get Samuels [a local journalist] to think we're good guys, but there are a lot of people influenced by Samuels and the crap he's saying. If we could get to them with reason and explain to them what our job is and how we came to the conclusions that we've come to . . .
>
> George: What about the concept of developing something like a position paper for the individual projects, like the Mayflower project, that would

be very much a synopsis but at least it would state when it came to the department, what the developers' request was, what our recommendation was, what the council did, you know, a "who struck whom" sort of thing, and what the key issues were for the neighborhood, and how it turned out?

And the staff members here go on to discuss these issues.

Now, quite a bit is happening in this working conversation. The director tells a story about their efforts, what they have been up against, what they have tried to do. It has a time line; the Mayflower project was "pivotal"; "that was the first real bad one," he claims. And he connects that experience to others—the Northside and Lakeview projects. And he does more; he characterizes the people involved: they're "afraid," "concerned," and "really, really angry." He does not just describe behavior, he socially constructs selves, reputations: the kind of people—he is claiming—that the planners have to work with.

But the director is doing much more than that, too; he is telling a complex story, in just a few lines, about the allocation of responsibility and blame: "We tried to hold what we thought was the right line." "We took a very high profile position on a very unpopular issue." "We really lost a great deal of support." But, on Lakeview, "I don't think we're taking the heat." But then, when two of his staff think instead that they *are* taking the heat for it, the director says, "It's interesting, because it wasn't our screwup." So a story unfolds here about the courage of convictions, about the tension between commitment to a professional analysis and the desire for public support, about astute or poorly played politics, and also about "guilt by association," the vulnerability of the planning staff in a highly politicized environment.

This conversation begins with a working story of effective and vulnerable practice, practice that is strategic and "contingent" (as planning professors and consultants now say), and the conversation includes the retelling of this story, developing it so that a moral emerges: a lesson and a point, a clarification of the situation the planners are in and a clarification of what they can now do differently and better as a result.

The director speaks the most here, but he does not just tell a story to an audience; the planners together—with differences in their positions, power, and influence, to be sure—work to develop their own story, for it is, after all, the story they are willing and practically able to construct together.

So the housing planner echoes a pervasive problem in planning when she focuses on a particular irony of their practice: "If something goes wrong, the planners did it. If something goes right, the City Council members claim credit for it," and the director responds to her, affirming and building on her moral claim about the allocation of credit and blame: "That's the kind of problem . . . we have to address."

So he proceeds to reconstruct and present their working history again: "Ms. Smith here has been saying, 'You've got to come out' [more publicly]," and "Many of you have been saying, 'You've got to answer this,'" but "I've always said, 'No, . . . we don't want to get into a cursing war with a skunk.'"

And then he tells the staff he has changed his mind, so their collective story is changing: "But now I think we have to. We have to set out a strategy . . . to sell the department . . . to get to those people whose minds aren't already made up."

And the community development planner does not just take that as a personal tale of the director's change of heart. He takes it as a working story about where they are, practically speaking, as a staff, so he brings up a strategy to be considered: "What about . . . developing something like a position paper for the individual projects?" And he goes on to sketch his idea for the staff's consideration, for their deliberation.

What we see here, even in this short stretch of conversation from a staff meeting, is very rich, morally thick, politically engaged, and organizationally practical story telling. But the point here, of course, is not that planners tell stories, for everyone tells stories.

In planning practice, though, these stories do particular kinds of work: descriptive work of reportage; moral work of constructing character and reputation (of oneself and others); political work of identifying friends and foes, interests and needs, and the play of power in support and opposition; and, most important (here in the staff meeting, for example), deliberative work of considering means and ends, values and options, what is relevant and significant, what is possible and what matters, all together. Values and ends are not just presumed, and means and strategies alone assessed by the staff; what matters and what is doable are explored, formulated practically, together.

Most important, these stories are not just idle talk; they do work. They do work by organizing attention, practically and politically, not only to the facts at hand but to why the facts at hand matter. In any serious staff meeting, for example, these stories are ethically loaded through and through. They arguably ought to be relevant, realistic, and sensitive to the staff's political history, and respectful of important values at stake; and always alert, too, to the idiosyncratic wishes and strong feelings of community residents and public officials, planning board and city council members alike. So, carefully telling these practice stories and listening perceptively to them are both essential to the planners' work of astutely "getting a take" on the problems they face.

In their meetings, then, the planners do not simply tell individual tales, they work together (as they work with others in other meetings) to construct politically shaped, shared "working" accounts—commonly considered, deliberative stories of the tasks, situations, and opportunities at hand. In these stories the planners not only present facts and express opinions and emotions, they also reconstruct selectively what the problems at hand really are. And they characterize themselves (and others) as willing to act in certain ways or not, as concerned with these issues, if not so much with those, as having good or poor working relationships with particular others, and so on.[16] So not only do we tell stories at work, but our stories tell a good deal about us as well.

We began by exploring the ways we learn from planners' accounts of their own practice. But that problem of learning from practice stories appears to be widely shared among professionals of all kinds who must listen to and interpret the stories they hear from their patients and clients: the developer wanting to build, the neighbor wanting to protect his or her neighborhood, the politician wanting some action from the planning department, the planning board member asking why more hasn't been done (and done more quickly) on a given project. What professionals generally and planners particularly face in such cases are complex stories, and if they do not learn from them, and quickly, they are likely to find themselves in serious trouble.[17]

But we still have not answered the central question here: How do planning analysts learn from such practice stories, and how do they learn politically and practically from such story telling if they obviously do not do it through systematic experimentation? How do planners and policy analysts learn from other people's practice stories when they cannot do much hypothesis testing on the spot?[18] Or, better, perhaps, what image of practical and political learning can provide us with a fresh view of these questions if the imagery of learning through experimentation is not really apt in practice?

Learning and the Ethics of Friendship

When we ask how planners and professionals learn on the job, we want to know how they come to make practical judgments under conditions of limited time, data, and resources. We are not asking how scientific professionals can be; we are not asking how well they remember certain methods courses they took in school. We are after the ways they learn in the thick of things, in the face of conflict, having to respond quickly—not how they learn in the course of sustained research.

We should remember that when professionals learn on the job they have to make judgments of value all the time.[19] They have to find out not only how things are working but what is working well or poorly. They must learn not only about what someone has said but about what that means, why that is important, or why that is significant—all in the light of the inevitably ambiguous mandates they serve and the many, also ambiguous, hopes and needs of local residents.

With little time, and facing the multiple and conflicting goals, interests, and needs of the populace and their more formal clients, planners have to "pick targets"; they must set priorities, not only in their work programs but every time they listen to others as well. They cannot get all the facts, so they have to search for the facts they feel matter, the facts they judge significant, valuable. So whether they like it or not, they are practical ethicists; their work demands that they make ethical judgments—judgments of good and bad, more valued and less valued, more significant and less—again and again as they work. Ethical judgments, however embarrassingly little they may be discussed in planning schools, are nevertheless inescapable and ever present in practice. Really value-free professional work could well be literally what it says: value-free, worthless, without worth.

But what image, then, can help us make sense of the ways planners learn in practice as they listen to the stories they hear, and learn politically from them, too? Perhaps the simplest answer here is that we learn not just from scientific inquiry but also from friends.

We learn from friends—and we need to probe, here, our intuitions about friends and friendship to consider how we learn from planners' stories and how we learn, as planners (and practitioners more generally) on the job, when we work with others, when we listen carefully to others, paying careful attention to their stories.[20]

The point here is not, of course, that planners are, can be, or should be intimate friends with everyone they work with; the point is rather that if it is not clear how we learn from stories in practice settings, then we should think about the many ways we can and do learn from friends. Five related points deserve our attention here.

First, we learn from friends not because they report the results of controlled experiments to us but because they tell us appropriate stories, stories designed to matter to us. "Appropriate stories" are not appropriate in some ideal sense; they are appropriate to us and to the situations we are really in—insofar as our friends can bring their knowledge, empathy, thoughtfulness,[21] and insight to bear on our particular situation, needs, and possibilities. When we go to a friend with something important, we expect that friend not to respond with small talk and babble but with words and deeds, with little stories (sharing, confirming, reminding, consoling, perhaps encouraging) that can help us to understand practically and politically what is (and is not) in our *power* to do.[22] These stories are typically narrative and particularized, not formal, logical proofs, however argumentative our friends may be. So, for example, when the director quoted above tells the story not only of having wanted to avoid "a cursing war with a skunk" but of his change of mind, it is a story directly appropriate to, and responding to, the staff's problem of vulnerability.

Second, we learn from friends because we use their words to help us see our own interests, cares, and commitments in new ways.[23] They help us to understand not just how the world works but how *we* work, how we are, who we are—including what sorts of things matter to us.[24] They help us to understand not only how we feel but what we value, not only "where we're at" in the moment but how we are vulnerable, dependent, connected, haunted, attached, guilty, esteemed, or loved, and so in many ways how we are related to the world not simply physically but significantly, in ways that matter to us and to others.[25]

We look in part, too, to friends to be critical (in ways we can respond to), to think for themselves as well as for us, not simply to condone or agree with our every crazy or ill-considered idea.[26] So in the staff meeting the housing planner does not let the director off the hook about getting the "heat" for the Lakeview project, even though he thinks "it wasn't our screwup." She points to the staff's own responsibility: "But *we never said* it wasn't our screwup. We never pointed the finger to the screwup"—whether or not pointing a finger would have been effective.

Third, we learn from friends because they do not typically offer us simplistic cure-alls or technical fixes. They do not explain away, but rather try to do justice to, the complexities we face. They do not reduce complexities to trite formulas; they do not make false promises and sell us gimmicks, even though they might encourage us and might not tell us everything they think about what we are getting into if they are confident that we will do what needs to be done once we get going. Friends recognize complexity, but as pragmatists concerned with our lives, our practice; they neither paralyze us with detail nor hide details from us when they know details matter.[27]

But if they do not offer us technical fixes, what *do* friends offer us? Certainly not the detached advice of experts, for they do not typically invoke specialized knowledge to tell us what to do. Instead, they help us to see more clearly, to remember, to see in new ways, perhaps to appreciate aspects of others or ourselves or our political situations to which we have been blind.[28] So in the staff meeting, the housing director's moral tale is poignant and powerful, capturing part of the bind the staff is in (and setting up the director's response): "If something goes wrong, the planners did it. If something goes right, the City Council members claim credit for it."

Her insight teaches us about the complex rhetoric of democratic politics and participation, its ideals and its ironies. So listening here, we might be less wishful but more astute, less purist but more committed to doing what we can. We can gather from these stories, too, the differences between better and worse deliberation, between more and less inclusive participation, between a more or less "fragile consensus" (as Kristin put it).[29]

Listening here, we can understand more about how power and rationality interact, about how what seems well founded may never come to pass, and about how planners' and citizens' good ideas can be watered down, lost in a bureaucracy, held hostage to one politician's campaign. These stories might nurture a critical understanding by illuminating not only the dance of the rational and the idiosyncratic but also the particular values being suppressed through the euphemisms, rationalizations, political theories, and "truths" of the powerful.[30]

Fourth, we learn from friends because they help us to deliberate. When we are stuck, we turn to friends, if we can. When we need to sort out what really matters to us, we turn to friends—close at hand or, perhaps, in our imaginations. We look to friends to remind us of what matters, of commitments we have lost touch with, of things we are forgetting in the heat or the pain of the moment. We learn about our relevant history and our future possibilities of practice. We learn, too, about better and worse (and so, without calling it that, about ethics) as we consider our friends' judgments about how to act on our more general goals in the particular and often surprising situations we face. And enriching our capacity for deliberation is part of what the profiles of planners do, part of what practice stories on the job do.[31] If we listen closely, not to the portrayals of fact in these stories but to their claims of value and significance, we discover an infrastructure of ethics, an ethical substructure of practice, a finely woven tapestry of value being woven sentence by sentence; each sentence not simply adding, description by description, to a picture of the world, but adding, care by care, to a sensitivity to the practical world, to a richly prudent appreciation of that world.[32] So in the staff meeting, again, the community development planner does not let the director stew in his own juices; he suggests a strategy for the staff to discuss and consider: a position paper for projects.[33]

Fifth, and finally, we learn from these practice stories as we do from friends because they present us with a world of experience and passion, of affect and emotion, that previous accounts of planning practice have largely ignored.[34] These stories ask us to consider not only the consequential outcomes of planning or the general principles of planning practice, but the demands, the vulnerable and precarious virtues required of a politically attentive, participatory professional practice.[35] These stories enrich our critical understanding if they allow us to talk about the "political passions of planning"—the academic undiscussables of fear and courage, outrage and resolve, hope and cynicism, as planners (and other professionals, too, of course) must live with them, face them, and work with them.[36] If we cannot talk about these political passions, how could we ever talk about any critical practice at all? We would be left with passionless fictions of "correct politics," fantasies either of smooth incrementalist bargaining or "above it all" problem solving, which might inspire illusions of rational control but would hardly be true to anyone's experience. These politically passionless accounts of planning practice might be soothing and might promise a lot, but they would hardly inspire any confidence and hope about the challenges of planning, today and always, in the face of power.

How, then, can we learn from practice stories? We can learn practically from such stories in many of the ways we learn practically from friends. Both help us to see anew our practical situations and our possibilities, our interests and our values, our passions and our "working bets" about what we should do.

The argument here is hardly without precedent; the notion of friendship lay close to the heart of Aristotle's *Ethics*. Aristotle distinguished several types of friendship, ranging from forms in which friends simply provide one another with utility or pleasure to a form in which friends seek out not just the pleasures or benefits of association but far more: one another's virtues and excellence (their "real possibilities," some might say today).[37] The type of friendship from which we should consider learning is therefore not the friendship of long affection and intimacy but the friendship of mutual concern, of care and respect for the other's practice of citizenship and full participation in the political world. This is the friendship of appreciation of the hopes and political possibilities of the other, the friendship recognizing, too, the vulnerabilities of those hopes and possibilities.[38]

But, of course, neither friends typically, nor stories generally, promise—much less provide us with—decision rules for all situations. We get no gimmicks, no key to the inner workings of history, no all-purpose techniques for all cases. Instead, we seem to get detail, messiness, and particulars.

That messiness of practice stories is an important part of their power. To some degree, of course, the messiness is the message.[39] But that is far too simple a formulation. That messiness is important because it teaches us that before problems are solved, they have to be constructed or formulated in the first place. The rationality of problem solving, and the rationality of decision making more generally, depends on the prior practical rationality of attending to what the problem really is—the prior practical rationality of resisting the "rush to interpretation," of carefully listening to, or telling, the practice stories that give us the details that matter, the facts and values, the political and practical material with which we have to work.[40] If we get the story wrong, the many techniques we know may not help us much at all.

Consider, finally, a skeptical challenge: Is all this about practice stories, and by extension practical arguments, "just about words"?

No, certainly not. We have explored here what we do practically with words as we work together. In studying ordinary work we always face the danger that we will listen to what is said and hear words, not power; words, not judgment; words, not inclusion and exclusion; "mere words," and not problem framing and formulation, not strategies of practice. An Italian friend and colleague of mine put this worry beautifully recently when he wrote to a mutual friend and colleague, "No doubt, it is important to understand how [planners] behave in municipal offices. This is important for the sociology of organization and bureaucracy, for the analysis of policy, etc., and also for understanding a portion of planning implementation in practice. But for planning theory and practice it is less important than an apple [was] for Mr. Newton; in the end the apple is a metaphor, while what [planner] Brown says in his office—it is just what he says in his office!"[41]

But what planner (or policy analyst) Brown says in the office is not just what he or she says, though it is that, too: what Brown says also embodies and enacts the play of power, the selective focusing of attention, the expression of self, the presumptions of "us and them," and the creation of reputations—the shaping of expectations of what is and is not possible, the production of (more or less) politically rational strategies of action, the shaping of others' participation, and much more. What planner or architect Brown says involves power and strategy as much as it involves words.

So our ears hear sounds. A tape-recorder records what is said. Children might identify the words. But the challenge we face, as planners and policy analysts more broadly, is to do more: to listen carefully to practice stories and to understand who is attempting what, why, and how, in what situation, and what really matters in all that. That challenge is not just about words but about our cares and constraints, our real opportunities and our actions, our own practice, what we really can, and should, do now.

Notes

This essay benefited from comments of faculty and students who responded thoughtfully to its previous incarnation as an evolving lecture at the University of Illinois, Urbana-Champaign, the State University of New York at Buffalo, the University of Puerto Rico, and Cleveland State University. Thanks also to Pierre Clavel, Ann Forsyth, Davydd Greenwood, Jim Mayo, and John Nalbandian for critical comments.

1. He summarized results in this way:

   Third-party funders of [policy and program] advice (and especially federal agencies) tend to seek not merely useful truths, but useful truths of general applicability. They expect in this way to maximize return on their investment. Consultants suffer from the same temptation. . . . The intention is reasonable, but the results are poor. All communities believe themselves special, indeed unique. They want their advisors to address their *particular* concerns, not the problems of some category of communities to which a federal agency assigns them. The result is that where third-party funders insist on work whose results will be "generalizable," city agencies lose interest, fail to cooperate, or flatly resist. . . . And Fitzgerald's irony holds: solutions to the problem of a particular city do prove useful elsewhere. Many urban problems are widely shared. Good solutions, therefore, do have wide potential. And urban officials across the country are linked by a profusion of professional associations . . . most of which meet regularly on national, regional, and statewide bases, and which also publish journals. News of useful innovations is thus conveyed in the least threatening and most convincing way—by the reports of fellow professionals . . . . "Generalizability" will come, don't strain for it. (P. Szanton, *Not Well Advised* [New York: Russell Sage Foundation, 1981], 159–60)

2. R. Neustadt and E. May, *Thinking in Time* (New York: Free Press, 1986), 274, 106. Cf. related work of the other contributors to this volume.

3. M. Krieger, *Advice and Planning* (Philadelphia: Temple University Press, 1981); S. Mandelbaum, "Telling Stories" (Typescript, 1987); cf. P. Marris, "Witnesses, Engineers, or Story-tellers? The Influence of Social Research on Social Policy," in H. Gans, ed., *Sociology in America* (Beverly Hills: Sage, 1990).

4. See P. Euben, *The Tragedy of Political Theory* (Princeton: Princeton University Press, 1990); and M. Nussbaum, "Finely Aware and Richly Responsible: Literature and Moral Imagination," in her *Love's Knowledge* (Oxford: Oxford University Press, 1990); see also Nussbaum's *The Fragility of Goodness* (Cambridge: Cambridge University Press, 1986), especially chaps. 2 and 10 and Interlude 2.

5. R. Coles, *The Call of Stories* (Boston: Houghton Mifflin, 1989), 7.

6. Ibid., 29.

7. The interviews were done by Linda Chu, a master's student working with me, and Linda and I created a set of practice stories, loosely called "Profiles of Planners" (Ithaca: Cornell University Department of City and Regional Planning, 1990).

8. As the professor, frankly, I did not know whether to laugh or cry. I thought much of what I had assigned for the previous ten weeks had been quite practical!

9. See, e.g., H. Baum, *Organizational Membership* (Albany: State University of New York Press, 1990); M. Feldman, *Order Without Design: Information Production and Policy Making* (Palo Alto: Stanford University Press, 1989); J. Forester, *Planning in the Face of Power* (Berkeley: University of California Press, 1989).

10. From J. Forester and L. Chu, "Profiles of Planners," 63 (Typescript for classroom use, Cornell University, Department of City and Regional Planning, 1990).

11. Cf. M. Nussbaum's arguments regarding literature and moral imagination, especially "Finely Aware and Richly Responsible."

12. See N. Krumholz and J. Forester, *Making Equity Planning Work* (Philadelphia: Temple University Press, 1990).

13. An extensive literature discusses this point; see, e.g., D. McCloskey, *The Rhetoric of Economics* (Madison: University of Wisconsin Press, 1985); on applied social research see J. Gusfield, *The Culture of Public Problems* (Chicago: University of Chicago Press, 1981).

14. At some point every year at Cornell, I find myself attending one seminar on qualitative research in which a question arises from the audience: "Since you haven't tested any hypotheses in a systematic manner, how can you claim to have made any contribution to knowledge?" And I find myself then, barely restrained, asking the skeptic, "Are you really willing to say that the fields of history and anthropology—whose practitioners do not typically test hypotheses in a controlled manner—have made no contribution to knowledge? No contributions to

knowledge from ethnographic work? From historical research? Really?" "Oh no, no, no," comes the answer, "that's not what I meant . . ."

15. Don Schön shows us how practitioners "reflect in action" as they make moves, evaluate the results of those moves, and reconsider the working theories that guided those moves—as they consider what to do next. But the learning processes Schön focuses on presume a good deal of practical knowledge on the practitioner's part. Before moves can be refined—lay the school out this way or that way; expand the program this way or that way—the practitioner needs to have taken a role in an institutional and political world. Not only are the roles typically ambiguous, but the political world is fluid as well. We need to explore how planners learn as they listen and, significantly, learn far more than the facts. See D. Schön, *The Reflective Practitioner* (New York: Basic Books, 1983); and his edited, *The Reflective Turn: Case Studies in and on Educational Practice* (New York: Teacher's College Press, 1990).

16. Just how much is to be attended to, probed, not missed, responded to sensitively, and appreciated as significant in these stories is not typically obvious at all. Because these profiles and practice stories show us the vulnerability of planners' best-laid plans to much larger forces beyond their control, they echo the themes of the classical tragedies. If political theorists and ethicists can explore literature and theater as rich and vital sources of ethical and political teaching, surely we can turn to the richness of professional practice profiles and practice stories to teach us about the possibilities of ethically sensitive and politically astute planning practice. See especially here the work of Nussbaum and Euben, cited above.

17. For more general work on narrative and story, see R. Alter, *The Art of Biblical Narrative* (New York: Basic, 1981); B. Bettelheim, *The Uses of Enchantment: The Meaning and Importance of Fairy Tales* (New York: Vintage, 1976); R. Coles, *The Call of Stories* (Boston: Houghton Mifflin, 1989); S. Deetz, *Democracy in an Age of Corporate Colonization* (Albany, State University of New York Press, 1992); P. Euben, *The Tragedy of Political Theory* (Princeton: Princeton University Press, 1990); J. Gusfield, ed., *Kenneth Burke: On Symbols and Society* (Chicago: University of Chicago Press, 1989); S. Hauerwas, *Truthfulness and Tragedy* (Notre Dame: University of Notre Dame Press, 1977); A. MacIntyre, *After Virtue* (Notre Dame: University of Notre Dame Press, 1981); M. Nussbaum, *Love's Knowledge* (Oxford: Oxford University Press, 1990); S. Terkel, *Working* (New York: Avon, 1972); and S. Terkel, *Race: How Blacks and Whites Think and Feel about the American Obsession* (New York: W. W. Norton, 1992).

18. We can do some hypothesis testing on the spot, as Don Schön (*The Reflective Practitioner*) has shown with his analysis of the moves that enable reflection in action. We seem, though, to learn a good deal more, and to reflect upon a good deal more, than Schön's account encompasses.

19. The planners not only have to make value judgments "in their heads,"

they must make value allocations *as they speak* and make practical claims about what their listeners or readers are to take as important and noteworthy.

20. Cf. M. Sandel on the epistemology of friendship in his *Liberalism and the Limits of Justice* (Cambridge: Cambridge University Press, 1987), 181. See Iris Murdoch's fascinating discussion in *The Sovereignty of Good* (London: Ark/RKP, 1970) of attention to virtue and the Good; also Nussbaum's concern with Aristotelian practical judgment and deliberation in *Love's Knowledge*.

21. Cf. Hannah Arendt:

[Thinking] does not create values, it will not find out, once and for all, what "the" good is, and it does not confirm but rather dissolves accepted rules of conduct. . . . The purging element in thinking, Socrates' midwifery, that brings out the implications of the unexamined opinions and thereby destroys them—values, doctrines, theories, and even convictions—is political by implication. For this destruction has a liberating effect on another human faculty, the faculty of judgment, which one may call, with some justification, the most political of man's mental abilities. It is this faculty to judge *particulars* without subsuming them under those general rules which can be taught and learned until they grow into habits that can be replaced by other habits and rules.

The faculty of judging particulars (as Kant discovered it), the ability to say "this is wrong," "this is beautiful," etc., is not the same as the faculty of thinking. Thinking deals with invisibles, with representations of things that are absent; judging always concerns particulars and things close at hand. . . . If thinking, the two-in-one of the soundless dialogue, actualizes the difference within our identity as given in consciousness and thereby results in conscience as its product, then judging, the by-product of the liberating effect of thinking, realizes thinking, makes it manifest in the world of appearances, where I am never alone and always much too busy to be able to think. The manifestation of the wind of thought is not knowledge; it is the ability to tell right from wrong, beautiful from ugly. And this indeed may prevent catastrophes, at least for myself, in the rare moments when the chips are down. ("Thinking and Moral Considerations," *Social Research* 38 [1971]: 445–46)

22. Sandel (*Liberalism and the Limits of Justice*, 181) writes, "Where seeking my good is bound up with exploring my identity and interpreting life history, the knowledge I seek is less transparent to me and less opaque to others. Friendship becomes a way of knowing as well as liking. Uncertain which path to take, I consult a friend who knows me well, and together we deliberate, offering and assessing by turns competing descriptions of the person I am, and of the alternatives I face as they bear on my identity. To take seriously such deliberation is to allow that my friend may grasp something I have missed, may offer a more adequate account of the way my identity is engaged in the alternatives before me."

23. We may come to reconsider, for example, how we "rank" interests (to keep to a utilitarian language). Cf. F. Michelman, "Law's Republic," *Yale Law*

Review 97, no. 8 (1988): 1493–1537; and J. Forester, "Envisioning the Politics of Public Sector Dispute Resolution," in S. Silbey and A. Sarat, eds. *Studies in Law, Politics, and Society,* 12: 83–122 (Greenwich, Conn.: JAI Press, 1992).

24. Cf. C. Taylor on qualitative distinctions and our identities in *Sources of the Self* (Cambridge: Harvard University Press, 1989).

25. Cf., possibly, *Befindlichkeit*, "care and situatedness," in Heidegger and feminist notions of relationship.

26. It could be productive to generate further synonyms here: mapping the ways we know we can make judgments which we would want friends to help us reconsider. Cf. discussions of self-command in decision theory, e.g., T. Schelling, *Choice and Consequence* (Cambridge: Harvard University Press, 1984) and weakness of will, e.g., A. Rorty, *Mind in Action* (Boston: Beacon, 1988) and M. Nussbaum, *Fragility of Goodness* (Cambridge: Cambridge University Press, 1984). Can we read or listen to practice stories without sliding from "understanding" them to "accepting" them at face value, thus losing any ability to be critical of the practice they (re)present? Again, thinking about how we listen to friends might be helpful, for we seem no more to agree with or accept blindly whatever a friend says than we expect a friend blindly to agree with or accept whatever we (again blindly, rashly, mistakenly) say. Cf. "Can Phenomenology Be Critical?" in J. O'Neill, *Sociology as a Skin Trade* (New York: Harper and Row, 1972).

27. The lesson here is not that situations determine actions but that practical rationality depends on a keen grasp of the particulars seen in the light of more general principles and goals. By taking practice stories more seriously, we (ironically) make decision making less central to practice, making the prior acts of problem construction, agenda setting, and norm setting more important. Cf. Murdoch (*The Sovereignty of Good,* 37) here, undercutting decision-centered views.

28. Cf. Nussbaum, "Finely Aware," 160, on moral learning, seeing anew, and "getting the tip," where she cites L. Wittgenstein, *Investigations* (New York: Macmillan, 1968), 227e, on learning judgment.

29. Perhaps, too, we learn about the differences between dominated talk and "real talk," and all its contingencies, as Mary Belenchy et al. have described it in *Women's Ways of Knowing* (New York: Basic Books, 1986), 144–46.

30. Cf. here the work of M. Foucault, *Power/Knowledge: Selected Interviews and Other Writings, 1972–1977,* ed. C. Gordon (New York: Pantheon Books, 1980), and J. Habermas, *The Theory of Communicative Action* (Boston: Beacon, 1984), on discourse and power.

31. Roughly following Richard Bernstein's *Beyond Objectivism and Relativisim* (Philadelphia: University of Pennsylvania Press, 1983) and Seyla Ben Habib's "Judgment and Moral Foundations of Politics in Arendt's Thought," *Political Theory* 16, no. 1 (February 1988), this line of argument tries to bridge the work of Habermas (*The Theory of Communicative Action*) and Nussbaum (*Love's Knowledge*).

32. Iris Murdoch says, "If we consider what the work of attention is like, how continuously it goes on, and how imperceptibly it builds up structures of value round about us, we shall not be surprised that at crucial moments of choice most of the business of choosing is already over. This does not imply that we are not free, certainly not. But it implies that the exercise of our freedom is a small piecemeal business which goes on all the time and not a grandiose leaping about unimpeded at important moments. The moral life, on this view, is something that goes on continually, not something that is switched off in between the occurrence of explicit moral choices. What happens in between such choices is indeed what is crucial" (*The Sovereignty of Good*, 37).

33. In addition, such practice stories provide empathetic examples as well as abstract arguments about what ought to be done. They allow us to learn from performance as well as from propositions. Iris Murdoch puts this powerfully: "Where virtue is concerned, we often apprehend more than we understand and *we grow by looking*" (ibid., 31).

34. The works of Howell Baum and Charles Hoch are outstanding exceptions here. See, e.g., Baum's *Invisible Bureaucracy: The Unconscious in Organizational Problem Solving* (Oxford: Oxford University Press, 1987); and Hoch's "Conflict at Large: A National Survey of Planners and Political Conflict," *Journal of Planning Education and Research* 8, no. 1 (1988): 25–34.

35. We should consider applying the Foucauldian move of restoring or resurrecting or even reconstructing "subjugated" experience not only of suppressed and marginalized and dominated groups but of ordinary planners seeking to attend to issues of public welfare, inclusion, need, and suffering. Cf. Foucault, *Power/Knowledge: Selected Interviews and Other Writings, 1972–1977*, ed. C. Gordon (New York: Pantheon Books, 1980).

36. These stories—whether profiles of planners or practice stories actually told on the job—also engage our emotions and passions, allowing us to learn through them, to pay attention through them, too, to consider "how I might have felt in that situation," and help us recognize feelings we might not have recognized as relevant. These stories inform our repertoires of attentiveness and responsiveness; they teach us through empathy and identification; we learn about situations and selves—our selves—as we imagine being in the situations presented, as we ask, "Would or could I have done that? What should I have done?"

37. So commentators are careful to show that Aristotle's conception of friendship as an ethical ideal does not compromise broader claims of justice. And similarly, I claim that we can learn from the stories of planners in a way that speaks to the possibilities of justice, that does not compromise justice for the interests of a particular relationship.

38. The most helpful discussions of these issues—the relationship of story and literature to deliberation, ethics, and practice—are in the work of Martha

Nussbaum, whose essays on this subject have been most recently collected in her *Love's Knowledge*. In related work, Nussbaum writes, for example,

> [The Greek tragedies] show us . . . the men and women of [the] Choruses making themselves look, notice, respond, and remember, cultivating responsiveness by working through the memory of these events . . . and their patient work, even years later, on the story of that action reminds us that responsive attention to these complexities is a job that practical rationality can, and should, undertake to perform; and that this job of rationality claims more from the agent than the exercise of reason or intellect, narrowly conceived. We see thought and feeling working together . . . a two-way interchange of illumination and cultivation working between emotions and thoughts; we see feelings prepared by memory and deliberation, learning brought about through *pathos*. (At the same time we ourselves, if we are good spectators, will find this complex interaction in our responses.) When we notice the ethical fruitfulness of these exchanges, when we see the *rationality* of the passions as they lead thought towards human understanding, and help to constitute this understanding, then we may feel that the burden of proof is shifted to the defender of the view that only intellect and will are appropriate objects of ethical assessment. Such a conception may begin to look impoverished. The plays show us the practical wisdom and ethical accountability of a contingent mortal being in a world of natural happening. Such a being is neither a pure intellect nor a pure will; nor would he deliberate better in this world if he were. (*The Fragility of Goodness*, 46–47)

39. But is it silly to say that the messiness of case histories and profiles is an important part of their message? After all, planners face enormous social problems; what sense can it make to argue that they and we learn about practice, good practice, through messiness, complexity, and particular detail rather than through general rules, universal maxims, and all-purpose techniques? Nussbaum recognizes clearly the *suspicion* that meets the suggestion, and indeed the tradition "that defends the role of poetic or 'literary' texts in moral learning." Tackling this suspicion head-on, she writes, "Certain truths about human experience can best be learned by living them in their particularity. Nor can this particularity be grasped solely by thought "itself by itself." . . . [I]t frequently needs to be apprehended through the cognitive activity of imagination, emotions, even appetitive feelings; through putting oneself inside a problem and feeling it. But we cannot all live, in our own overt activities, through all that we ought to know in order to live well. Here literature, with its stories and images, enters in as an extension of our experience, encouraging us to develop and understand our cognitive/ emotional response" (*The Fragility of Goodness*, 186).

40. Cf. Murdoch's *Sovereignty of Good*. C. W. Churchman once described (in class) the pragmatist's theory of truth as follows: "A is B" (the car is red, the housing is substandard, it is raining) is to be read, "A ought to be taken as B"— thus taking descriptions to be pragmatic and selective actions, not corre-

spondence-like statements picturing a brute reality. Nussbaum's concern goes further—to the very identification of B—issues which can hardly be discussed here. See, e.g., C. W. Churchman's *Design of Inquiring Systems* (New York: Basic, 1971) and *Challenge to Reason* (New York: McGraw-Hill, 1968).

41. LM to PH, June 22, 1990.

Theoretical

Perspectives

III

Policy Analysis and

Planning: From Science

to Argument

John S. Dryzek

The argumentative turn in policy analysis and planning comes not at the expense of science—and still less, of rationality—but, rather, at the expense of unnecessarily constricted misconceptions of science and reason in human affairs. Science, on this mistaken account, consists of a single and universally applicable set of rules and procedures for the unambiguous establishment of causal relationships. Beyond the application of these rules and procedures and acceptance of their results, rationality consists of determining the best means to a given end.

These two constricted conceptions may be termed, respectively, *objectivism* and *instrumental rationality*. Both are central to the Enlightenment legacy, and both loom large in the history of policy analysis. Objectivism appears most prominently in the accounts of science developed by positivists, critical rationalists, and others who believe in a universal logic of scientific inquiry, which can be applied, with a few emendations, to the logic of public policy. But objectivism also underpins the moral philosophy of liberals from Kant to Rawls, who seek a transcendent logic for the establishment of moral principles rather than causal relationships. Recently, ethicists interested in philosophy and public affairs (the title of one of their journals) have sought to apply objectivist moral logic to public policy issues.

Instrumental rationality, for its part, is a widely held normative model for the behavior of individuals and for the conduct of public policy. Microeconomists and their fellow travelers believe, too, that instrumental rationality is an acceptable empirical model of individuals, if not collectivities. In conjunction, objectivism and instrumental rationality undergird one side of modernity—clean, calculating, and homogenizing.

The argumentative turn, in policy and planning no less than elsewhere, seeks to overturn objectivist and instrumental notions of judgment and action in the name of practical reasoning. The essence of judgment and decision becomes not the automatic application of rules or algorithms but a process of deliberation which weighs beliefs, principles, and actions under conditions of multiple frames for the interpretation and evaluation of the world. As such, the argumentative turn is part of the intellectual movement "beyond objectivism and relativism" celebrated by Richard Bernstein (1983).

My intent here is to locate the argumentative turn in such developments and to explain why it has happened in policy analysis and planning in particular. To this end, I begin by contemplating the different ways in which the turn can be explained and justified. I then pin down the identity of the aspects of, and approaches to, policy and planning which argument supercedes, explain their discrediting, and show why a turn to argument is the logical next move. Having established argument's centrality, I claim that argument itself is not enough. The defensibility of policy analysis, and planning depends on the conditions in which arguments are made, received, and acted upon. I therefore conclude with a discussion of the radicalization of the argumentative turn which involves a rational commitment to free democratic discourse.

Three Ways to Account for the Argumentative Turn

Justifications of the argumentative turn can emphasize intellectual history, political reality, or the logic of alternative analytical approaches. Let me begin with history.

Intellectual History

The history of policy analysis as practiced since the 1940s does not reveal a clear and clean switch away from approaches beholden to objectivism and instrumental rationality and toward more argumentative orientations. Indeed, whether based in public sector organizations, corporations, universities, foundations, or think tanks, most analyses (or at least those that are more than atheoretical mush) still cling to these traditional methodologies. However, history is useful in showing exactly why these methodologies became discredited, at least in the eyes of more reflective analysts and observers of policy and planning.

In this light, perhaps the most useful history is that of Peter deLeon (1988). In deLeon's view, the policy sciences in the United States have been shaped by several key events which have provided grist and funding for the efforts of analysts: World War II, the War on Poverty, the Vietnam war, and the energy crises of the 1970s. (Watergate is also mentioned, though only as a spur to incorporating the ethical dimension of policy into analysis.)

Of these events, only World War II represents anything other than a policy analysis disaster—and that is only because analysis in that conflict was mostly limited to mathematical modeling of the movement of persons and materials. The War on Poverty exposed the woeful inadequacy of sociologists' causal models of the determinants of poverty and the likely causal impact of policy measures that might alleviate poverty. The Vietnam war showed that sophisticated methodologies wielded by the best and brightest analysts could pave the way to disaster if the assumptions embedded in the models (for example, concerning the capacity of the North Vietnamese to absorb suffering) were erroneous, or if key factors were omitted, or if the data were fictions or falsifications. And the policy response to the energy crisis showed that elaborate models could provide, at best, symbolic substitutes for action, and, at worst, camouflage for ideological premises. In each case, technically sophisticated policy analysis was directly complicit in policy disaster. DeLeon concludes with an understatement: "If the Great Society programs, Vietnam, and the energy crises taught anything to policy scholars and practitioners, it should have been humility regarding both the power of their tools and their roles in actual political decisionmaking" (1988:96).

The policy field is indeed lucky that this disastrous history did not lead to its extinction, but it should come as no surprise that these failures led to major rethinking of the field's methodological and theoretical foundations. It should be noted, though, that this rethinking has not really affected the substance of the techniques taught in graduate schools of public policy, public affairs, public administration, and so forth. The discredited approaches are, if nothing else, easy to organize into a curriculum and, perhaps more important, help to secure respectability in the American university, where the trappings of science are all-important. So there were, and are, intellectually questionable but politically expedient reasons for resisting attacks on methods and techniques beholden to objectivism and instrumental rationality.

More justifiable resistance to the argumentative turn in particular would note that the way the field should turn in reaction to disaaster has remained a matter of some controversy. And intellectual history alone cannot be used to determine in which direction it should go, though such judgments can and should be informed by this history.

Political Reality

An emphasis on political reality as the cause for the demise of objectivist and instrumentally rationalistic policy analysis might also draw on the lessons of history, although those who have written in this vein generally believe that the policy process they portray has features inhospitable to technically sophisticated policy analysis which are invariant across time and space. Among these authors, the many works of Charles Lindblom (1959, 1965; Lindblom and Cohen 1979) and Aaron Wildavsky (1966, 1979) stand out. Both emphasize the role that political interaction plays in policy determination and the idea that such interaction can and should be a complete (Lindblom) or partial (Wildavsky) substitute for cogitation, be it policy analytic or otherwise.

Giandomenico Majone (1989) explicitly connects this idiom with the argumentative turn by recommending the latter as the appropriate analytic response to political reality. He takes the (United States) political status quo as given, in its constitutive principles if not in its institutional details. To Majone, liberal democracy is in large measure "government by discussion" (1989:1), though to reach determinate results that discussion must be constrained by rules—the familiar constitutional arrangements that involve (say) majority voting, parliamentary procedure, and executive authority.

Furthermore (Majone 1989:15), "decisionism" in policy analysis (instrumental rationality under a resource constraint) mistakenly assumes a unitary decision maker or benevolent policy dictator. Once one recognizes the existence of numerous, diverse, interacting players in the policy process, then it becomes more appropriate to think in terms of an audience for analysis rather than of a client who will implement the analyst's conclusions. And audiences need to be persuaded rather than simply informed of a conclusion. In short, the analyst must argue using "a complex blend of factual statements, interpretations, opinions, and evaluations" (Majone 1989:63). Majone believes that arguments so constructed and deployed do not necessarily supplant more established analytical endeavors and that there is nothing wrong with devising arguments to support conclusions reached on independent grounds; for example, using a mathematical model (1989:31–32). It is up to the audience to accept or reject such arguments on their own merits rather than through reference to any independent grounds.

History and political reality can and must be consulted in any attempt to account for the argumentative turn in policy analysis and planning. But the explanation I shall now develop is more spare in that it proceeds in terms of the logic of alternative kinds of inquiry. One should bear in mind, though, that postempiricist philosophy of science has demonstrated that the history and philosophy of science are inextricable (Burian 1977). Thus any plausible logic of inquiry or analysis must be able to account for, and must be subject to the judgment of, the history of the endeavor whose methodological essence it is trying to capture. Let me now discuss the models of inquiry that the argumentative turn rejects: positivism, critical rationalism, and the analycentric mode. This turn must also reject objectivist moral philosophy. But the latter has never claimed to provide a complete model for policy analysis and has made fewer inroads into policy and planning, so it merits less attention.

Alternative Logics of Inquiry

Positivism. I noted earlier that the argumentative turn involves rejection of objectivism and instrumental rationality in policy and its analysis. The word *positivism* is often used too loosely to capture such approaches. In fact, only a tiny proportion of policy analyses and methodological prescriptions could properly be described as positivist, unless the word is used as a generalized term of abuse. It is therefore unfortunate that metatheoretical debates in the field have often turned on positivism and its deficiencies, for such a focus alienates such debates from the history and reality that are properly their testing ground. This focus is as true for recent commentaries such as that of M. E. Hawkesworth (1988) as it is for classic critiques such as that of Brian Fay (1975).

Despite its long-established irrelevance in the philosophy of science, the ghost of positivism continues to haunt social science in general and, it seems, policy and planning in particular. My own justification for attending to positivism rather than simply ignoring it is that exposure of its contingent deficiencies enables one to do greater justice to nonpositivist, but still objectivist and instrumental, approaches to policy. These approaches are made of sterner stuff than positivism and so make a better foil for the argumentative turn.

So now I reluctantly join the crowd and discuss positivism. Positivism in policy analysis can be characterized in terms of a belief that policy interventions should be based on causal laws of society and verified by neutral empirical observation. Any practical import depends on policy-manipulable variables having a place in this causal scheme; if they did not, the result would be social science but hardly policy science. Assuming such variables can be located, policymakers can then manipulate policy in pursuit of any ends they see fit to pursue, for ends are treated as arbitrary and beyond the reach of scientific or rational determination.

Defined in this manner, it is hard to locate any contemporary advocates of a true positivist approach to policy and its analysis, though Thomas Dye (1976) and Heinz Eulau (1977) are among those who come close. Historical references to Comte, Saint-Simon, and perhaps even Weber are on more solid ground. If one more loosely characterizes as positivists all those who advocate or engage in hypothesis testing, data collection, statistical analysis, value neutrality, and an admiration of natural science (Hawkesworth 1988:40), then, of course, they are more easily found.

A true positivist program for policy and planning fails for the following reasons, which help explain why successful examples of positivistic policy analysis are almost impossible to locate. (My discussion here is brief; greater detail may be found in the works of Fay [1975:22–29, 49–64], Douglas Torgerson [1986a], Hawkesworth [1988: 37–40], and Bobrow and Dryzek [1987:128–34].)

First, general laws of society, let alone laws on which policy interventions might be based, have proven elusive. This is true even for well-studied areas such as violent crime (Wilson 1983) and macroeconomics.

Second, the goals of policy rarely constitute some clear and uncontroversial set which can be specified as the dependent variables for causal analysis. Values in policy and planning are generally multiple, fluid, and controversial; and different values will make different dependent variables pertinent. If analysts behave as if some uncontroversial goal set does exist, then they will typically adopt that set as given by the political or bureaucratic powers that be (Nachmias 1979:13–15) or impose one of their own choosing. In the former case, they are complicit in the instrumental or technocratic rationalization of society (as portrayed by Max Weber). In the latter, they risk irrelevance to the concerns of anyone in the potential audience of analysis. By ignoring or overriding the normative give-and-take of politics, analysts are complicit in what Hawkesworth (1988:25–27) calls "depoliticizing scientism." I should note in passing that moral philosophy applied to public policy is equally guilty of this kind of depoliticization.

Third, the intentional actions of human beings, including those involved in the formulation and implementation of policy, can subvert the purported causal generalizations of positivists. People can simply decide to behave differently, and that decision itself may be affected by knowledge of the purported causal laws in which they figure.

Fourth, causal statements about the effects of policy interventions cannot be empirically verified short of the intervention itself actually occurring. In other words, the idea of waiting for empirical verification before acting is incoherent.

Critical Rationalism. Critical rationalism is the school of thought spanning the philosophy of inquiry and political organization associated with Sir Karl Popper (1963, 1972). Popper (1959) believes that the positivists err in seeing verification and the accumulation of truth as essential to science. He avers that theories can never be verified, only falsified; their truth status is therefore always tentative. Repeated unsuccessful attempts at falsification increase our confidence in or corroborate a theory, but we should always be open to its future falsification. And that openness is secured only to the extent that the scientific community features free debate and does not defer to the authority of laws or their custodians.

This view of science has direct implications for politics, policy, and planning. According to Popper, policy should proceed through the tentative trial and error of "piecemeal social engineering." Policies are treated as analogous to hypotheses, and so their implementation becomes like a scientific experiment. Ideally, implementation should proceed in incremental fashion and should produce maximal information about the effects of a policy. Both before and after implementation, the policy should be open to criticism from all quarters, policy experts and ordinary citizens alike, in order to take into account the decentralization of relevant knowledge and the multiplicity of social values. Popper's (1963) political open society is modeled on his idealized view of the scientific community. This parallel is deployed by Popperians to justify the give-and-take of liberal democracy, though in these terms Popperians should have little time for the haphazard muddling through and the manipulative exercise of power which pervade real-world liberal democracies (Popperians tend to overlook such deficiencies).

A large literature in policy evaluation follows critical rationalist precepts, though not all evaluators care for Popperian limits on technical authority or the need for openness to criticism from a variety of directions. The connection between critical rationalist epistemology and policy evaluation is established most firmly by Donald Campbell (1969), the leading proponent of social experimentation (see also Dror 1984). Thus, unlike positivism, critical rationalism really does inform policy analysis and practice. Critical rationalism is not debilitated by positivism's incoherence. From an argumentative perspective, critical rationalism should be taken seriously because openness to criticism translates directly into openness to argument.

Unfortunately, the scope of such argument is unnecessarily constricted. Perhaps most seriously, only impoverished normative discourse is allowed. Now, critical rationalists do not share the positivists' view of the arbitrariness of values. Instead, normative schemes are to be evaluated in terms of their broad implications and subjected to criticism and gradual refinement with time. However, in any given policy dispute the pertinent set of values must be regarded as fixed and beyond contention rather than fluid and open to discussion, because a fixed normative grid is necessary for the conduct of critical rationalist policy experiments; standards must be set in advance in order to devise and calibrate the measuring instruments.

This fixity applies not just to normative standards but also to the conditions in which policy is implemented. If social experiments are to yield clear inferences, then conditions within the policy process and within the environment on which the policy is operating (inasmuch as these two can be separated) must remain fixed. Only the content of the policy intervention can change—and even this content, once chosen, must remain stable for the course of the experiment. The experience of real-world policy experiments, such as the notorious New Jersey negative income tax experiment, shows how difficult it is to achieve such invariance. But the whole idea of keeping constant the content of policy and potential contaminating influences recalls Weberian instrumental rationalization. Critical rationalism still operates under positivism's image of an elite of rational policy engineers; however, much lip service is paid to the possibility of open society pluralism and criticism. So no matter how hard it tries, critical rationalism cannot escape technocracy.

The critical rationalist conception of politics is, then, impoverished. Ordinary political actors are allowed to be rationalist critics of policy; but this participation cannot change their function as grist for causal generalizations of the sort that Popperians, no less than positivists, pursue. The idea of a self-guiding and self-transforming democratic polity is ruled out.

Finally, some things simply cannot be done piecemeal in the manner critical rationalism requires. Large-scale commitment of resources, a substantial waiting period, or both may be necessary before any results at all are generated (Schulman 1975; Goodin and Waldner 1979). In such cases one can argue about the merits of policy alternatives, but one cannot conduct experiments. (For further and more detailed criticisms of the approach see Phillips 1976; Bobrow and Dryzek 1987:144–47; and Hawkesworth 1988:43–48.)

The Analycentric Mode. Instrumentally rationalistic techniques such as cost-benefit analysis, decision analysis, multiattribute utility analysis, linear programming, systems modeling, and program budgeting are often grouped by their critics under the positivist umbrella. However, such techniques would not base policy on empirically verified (or even corroborated) causal relationships, let alone causal laws. Instead, the authority of the prescriptions is based on the method of their production. Data may be plugged in at the appropriate point, but no hypotheses are tested. The analyst knows in advance that a determinate conclusion will be reached. Conclusions take the form of "policy A will maximize the amount of value B produced" rather than "policy A will cause B to happen." William Dunn (1981:73–75) refers to these techniques as constituting the analycentric mode of policy analysis, and I follow his terminology here. Such techniques also fit well with the decisionism I noted earlier.

Much ink has been spilled about the inadequacies of analycentric techniques—especially those inspired by welfare economics. Perhaps the most devastating criticism of all such techniques is that they ride roughshod over political reality because they make sense only in terms of a policy process that has a benevolent dictator and automatic implementation. But even the conclusions of analyses are suspect, for they depend on the policy alternatives chosen for analysis. The techniques themselves are silent on the origins of such alternatives.

They are less silent, but no more defensible, when it comes to the source of values to be incorporated in the analysis. In the case of economistic techniques, these values are implicit in the technique itself. So in using cost-benefit analysis, the overriding value becomes economic efficiency, interpreted as the Kaldor-Hicks modification of the Pareto criterion. Other techniques are similar in that they assume constrained financial resources, but they are more flexible on the benefit side of the ledger. In decision analysis this will be the explicit utility functions of policymakers. Multiattribute utility analysis allows for the incorporation of the utility functions of a variety of stakeholders. But in either case, the treatment of values is no improvement over that in positivism or critical rationalism. Moral philosophers sensitive to the intrinsic rightness or wrongness of policy options will be additionally perturbed by the unremitting consequentialism involved; all that matters is how much of the target value is achieved. And political scientists who have criticized analycentric approaches (e.g., Wildavsky 1966) stress that politics is always much more than optimization within a resource constraint.

The analycentric mode often aspires to comprehensiveness in its analyses, but in practice both the policy alternatives and the normative judgments it incorporates are highly constrained and insensitive to the aspirations of ordinary policy actors. The models it uses are consequently never more than gross oversimplifications of a complex reality, rooted as they all are in a single analytical framework chosen from the many that could be employed within the analycentric mode.

Frames

In frames we encounter the major obstacle within social science that frustrates objectivist policy analysis and planning, be it positivist, critical rationalist, or analycentric. Numerous social science frames of reference can be applied to the analysis of policy. It is not just that these frames give different answers to policy questions. Rather, each frame treats some topics as more salient than others, defines social problems in a unique fashion, commits itself to particular value judgments, and generally interprets the world in its own particular and partial way. A frame of reference is akin to a language or even a culture shared by a tribe of experts. As we shall see, frames are not easily adjudicated, though I shall argue that conceiving of analysis and planning in terms of argument rather than technical authority goes a long way toward overcoming the partiality and apparent relativity of frames.

The major frames of reference available in the policy field as enumerated and assayed by Bobrow and Dryzek (1987) are welfare economics, public choice, social structure, information processing, and political philosophy. Welfare economics and public choice are internally consensual, but there are major internal divisions within the other frames. So social structure divides into subapproaches that respectively emphasize the endowments of individuals and groups. Information processing is home both to those who are highly (and naively) optimistic about the capabilities of decision aids such as cybernetics, computer modeling, and decision analysis and to those who regard such aids with extreme skepticism, emphasizing instead the limited information-processing capacities of individuals and the politicized nature of collective choice. Political philosophy features major disputes among utilitarians, deontologists, and others.

These frames really are very different in their policy applications. So public choice concerns itself with only the formal properties of political institutions and evaluates them in terms of their claims to Pareto optimality, employing deductive and methodologically individualist procedures. The group strand of social structure regards formal institutions of the sort that preoccupy public choice as thoroughly irrelevant, given that politics is no more than a reflection of the relative power of different social groups (one of which may be called "the state").

The existence of a multiplicity of apparently incommensurable analytical frames is devastating to the authoritative ambitions of positivist, critical rationalist, and analycentric policy analysis. Of these, perhaps positivism is more thoroughly confounded, for frames make nonsense of the idea of verification adding to a stockpile of accumulated theory. Our frames show that multiple theories can be brought to bear in any given situation. And each frame comes complete with both a lens for interpreting the world and procedures for testing its own hypotheses—but not necessarily for testing those generated in other frames.

Critical rationalism copes with a multiplicity of viewpoints more readily, but the kind of policy debate Popperians have in mind would proceed in narrow terms and concern only the likely causal effects of particular policy interventions. If different frames make different categories of intervention seem plausible and attractive, then this kind of constrained debate is undermined. Work in the analycentric mode begins to look arbitrary once one recognizes the variety of techniques that could be called upon, each based on very different premises.

The more complex a problem or situation, the greater the number of plausible interpretations of it, and so the greater the number of frames that can be brought to bear. If complex problems are most in need of good policy analysis, then it would seem to be the case that policy analysis, be it positivistic, critical rationalist, or analycentric in inspiration, is most helpless where it is most needed.

Adjudicating Frames Through Problem-solving Power

Despite the difficulties it causes, the existence of a variety of frames is not necessarily devastating to the policy field. Postempiricist philosophy of science has shown that such variety is, in fact, an ordinary condition of scientific disciplines, even though a single frame—what Kuhn (1970) calls a paradigm—might occasionally dominate. And since it has also been shown that rational choices across such frames are possible, might not the same be true for frames in policy analysis and planning?

The most important epistemological works in this regard are those of Imre Lakatos (1970), who discusses choice across research programs, and Larry Laudan (1977), whose concern is research traditions. Frames, research programs, and research traditions can be treated as equivalent without doing too much violence to these authors. Both Lakatos and Laudan believe that seemingly incommensurable frames can, in fact, be compared in terms of how well their problem solving is progressing. Of the two, Laudan's specification is more forgiving and more applicable to social science, so I rely on his account here.

To Laudan, problems confronting a tradition can be conceptual or empirical. Conceptual problems involve vague categories of analysis, internal incoherence, or conflict with well-founded beliefs from outside the tradition. An empirical problem is anything about the world that seems odd or in need of explanation. A research tradition is progressive to the extent that it succeeds in resolving conceptual and empirical problems. Rational practitioners of a discipline should choose the tradition that is solving problems at the fastest rate.

Though there is no space here to go into details, Laudan's account can be applied to choice across research traditions in explanatory social science, though any such choices will generally be contingent on a given set of social and political circumstances, and so a greater plurality of research traditions is rationally tolerated (see Dryzek 1986).

Such adjudication will not work in policy and planning, however, because these activities are concerned with resolving social or policy problems—undesirable states of affairs—not conceptual and empirical problems. So we are generally interested not in the relative power of an approach across the whole range of intellectual problems in which a discipline is interested, but rather in one particular social problem, which itself will not generally respect standard disciplinary boundaries. For example, public choice as a frame may be doing wonderfully well in explaining the committee system in the United States Congress, the structure of competitive party systems, the expansionist tendencies of bureaucracies, and so forth. But this success does not mean we should adopt public choice as our frame if we are confronted with a problem of unacceptably high rates of violence in urban neighborhoods. In addition, in policy and planning analysts should generally pay more attention to the normative judgments embedded in frames, an issue that is less serious (though far from negligible) in purely explanatory social science.

At this point it seems that the best that postempiricist philosophy of science can offer in terms of procedures for the rational comparison of frames is no help in policy and planning. So we now stand at the brink of a relativism in which, when it comes to the choice of frames, "anything goes," to use Paul Feyerabend's (1975) slogan.

Relativism has generally found little support in the fields of policy analysis and planning, except, perhaps, among skeptics such as Charles Lindblom and David Cohen (1979), who regard all "professional social inquiry" as little more than wasteful and distractive noise in policy processes which can get along perfectly well without it. Relativism is of little more comfort to critics of the field, who find it easier to portray and confront a repressive monolith rather than the extreme variety and obvious lack of orthodoxy and repression that relativism connotes.

The Forensic and Liberal Use of Frames

A withdrawal from the brink of relativism may commence with the recognition that frames in policy analysis and planning need not be conceptualized as entities to be weighed against one another and accepted or rejected in their totality. Instead, frames can be used as sources of arguments that make no claim to be authoritative. The task of analysis then becomes either to construct arguments that draw on one or more frames or to test and strengthen the frames from which arguments might originate.

Along these lines, forensic conceptions of policy analysis have been developed by, among others, Alice Rivlin (1973), Martin Rein (1976), Peter Brown (1976), Ralph Hambrick (1974), William Dunn (1981), David Paris and James Reynolds (1983), Frank Fischer (1980), and Charles Anderson (1988). Of these authors, Brown, Hambrick, Fischer, and Dunn are concerned with the logical structure of policy arguments, and Rivlin describes forensic strategies in one particular policy controversy over the determinants of educational achievement. The efforts of Rein, Paris and Reynolds, and Anderson are more explicitly sensitive to the multiplicity of available frames, and so merit more attention here.

Rein's suggested approach to policy analysis constitutes an early, if imprecise, intimation of the argumentative turn. Rein would have analysts engage in "story telling" about policy choices which mixes positive and normative statements, metaphors, and suggestions. Frames would be drawn on as sources of insight and inspiration. But Rein's approach is ultimately eclectic and implicitly relativist; there are no standards for distinguishing a good story from a bad one. Aside from his or her ability to cite widely, Rein's storyteller cannot be distinguished from a journalist, sage, or political partisan of any sort. And it is hard to point to any particular analyses that explicitly follow his prescriptions.

Paris and Reynolds (1983) present a more precise and applicable forensic program. They interpret all policy debate, including that entered and so partially constituted by analysts, as ultimately ideological, in that no position can be proven conclusively correct or incorrect. However, all ideologies are not equal. They vary in their internal coherence, their ability to provide cogent warrants for policy claims, and their congruence with empirical reality. In other words, some ideologies are more "rational" than others. Thus the goal of policy inquiry is not to test hypotheses or to develop policy evaluations or prescriptions but, rather, to enhance the rationality of particular ideologies. It is easy to interpret a good deal of social science, whether or not it has any explicit concern with policy or planning, in this light. Paris and Reynolds look forward to an undogmatic, liberal "polity of rational ideologies" in which policies would be determined by pluralist compromises following sustained argument (rather than the naked exercise of power).

However, there is no real escape from relativism and arbitrariness here. Paris and Reynolds themselves make no judgments as to which particular ideologies might be described as rational or irrational, or when. There are reasons to suppose such determination might be impossible, mainly because judgments about congruence with empirical evidence can often be made only through the lens provided by an ideology itself. Ideologies are quite capable of attending selectively to empirical evidence, interpreting it in line with preconceptions, and even making it up. Otherwise, they would hardly be ideologies, rational or irrational. (If we take Kuhn to heart, it seems scientific paradigms often do no more.) And if any ideology is as good as any other, then this version of the argumentative turn becomes just a turn backward into ordinary pluralistic political interaction, with all its well-known deficiencies.

Anderson (1988) more explicitly embraces such dissolution. He notes that policy analysis can be based on entrepreneurial judgment (instrumentally rationally resource allocation), trusteeship (the conservative exercise of accepted authority), rational criticism (the application of moral principles), or pragmatism (the incremental amelioration of problems), although none of these four modes of argument is decisive. Indeed, each represents an explicit, disciplined form of just one aspect of liberal democracy (Anderson 1988:197–98). Thus policy analysis does nothing more than sharpen existing arguments within a liberal context.

At this juncture the argumentative turn threatens to dissolve into, at worst, relativism, and, at best, liberalism. Those satisfied with liberalism might be content with this destination. Those more attuned to liberalism's deficiencies (among whom I number myself) might want to attend more closely to the conditions in which arguments rooted in different frames are made, accepted, modified, compromised, or rejected.

Radicalizing the Argumentative Turn

A liberal appropriation of the argumentative turn remains silent with regard to the grounds on which a policy argument persuades and the precise identity of the individuals who might be persuaded. Argumentation that informs action presumably does so through consensus, however rough or transitory, and so consensus becomes the primary device for the adjudication of arguments and frames. But consensus can be reached under all kinds of conditions, through reference to many kinds of standards, and on the part of all kinds of groups, not all of which are equally defensible.

The conditions of consensus formation might well be distorted by the influence of hierarchies based on prestige, professional status, or argumentative ability. Some participants may be less scrupulous than others in the kinds of arguments they advance and the way these are packaged. The public relations industry is at the disposal of the less scrupulous. The process may involve information overload, by accident or by design. Technical jargon, slanted rules of admissibility of evidence and argument, and the deliberate stigmatization of unconventional proposals can all affect the outcome of debate.

The standards through which consensus may be reached (or appealed to) can also vary. Commonly accepted value systems may embody unexamined normative constraints that systematically favor particular interests. So, for example, the possessive individualism of liberal societies is superficially neutral but in practical policy disputes may always favor the interests of the wealthy.

More superficial contexts in which consensus can be reached might involve the organizational culture of a bureaucracy or the taken-for-granted assumptions of a narrow policy-making community. There is, in fact, a literature which suggests that policy analysts seeking relevance should accommodate their efforts to the frames and standards of the political powers that be (see, for example, Palumbo and Nachmias 1983; for a review and critique see Bobrow and Dryzek 1987:161–68). Policy analysis of this sort would leave the world pretty much as it finds it.

Consensus translated into action may also be attained on the part of small and unrepresentative groups. At worst, these might be secretive assemblages of business officials and bureaucrats. The exclusionary bargaining of interest group liberalism as criticized by Theodore Lowi (1979) is only slightly more defensible. Marginal improvement is allowed by the symbolic representation of a wider range of interests in policy determination.

The factors I have enumerated, whether in isolation or in combination, can undermine the legitimacy of policy made on the basis of consensus following argumentation, and hence also of policy analysis that conceives of itself in argumentative terms. A vindication of the argumentative turn in policy and planning therefore requires its radicalization in the form of relentless efforts on the part of the analyst to counter these agents of distortion.

Guidelines are available to facilitate these efforts. John Forester (1981) recommends a set of communicative ethics for analysts and planners, which would involve exposing and counteracting manipulation of agendas, illegitimate exercises of power, skewed distribution of information, and attempts to distract attention. In a similar vein, Ray Kemp (1985) employs the precepts of the ideal speech situation as developed by Jürgen Habermas in order to criticize the conduct of planning deliberations. Dialogue in the ideal speech situation is free from deception, self-deception, domination, strategizing, and any exclusion of participants or arguments. The only power remaining is that of the better argument. Though impossible to achieve fully, the precepts of ideal speech can be used to expose unjustifiable practices. Kemp himself applies these precepts to a British public inquiry into the construction of a nuclear reprocessing plant and effectively exposes the systematic distortions involved in this purportedly open forum.

These kinds of considerations relate to the process of policy planning, not just to the content of analysts' arguments. Thus one cannot conduct defensible policy analysis without attending also to the political process with which analysis and policy are involved. Once again, the myth of neutrality is exploded. Analysts cannot avoid taking sides on very basic issues of political structure. They can choose to side with authoritarian technocracy or with liberal democracy. My own position is that defensible policy analysis must side with open communication and unrestricted participation; in other words, with participatory and discursive democracy (for further details see Dryzek 1989, 1990).

Argument, Science, and Democracy

At this point it might seem that science has been well and truly jettisoned in favor of argument, if not politics. But this would be an erroneous conclusion. For policy analysis as inspired by the argumentative turn is broadly consistent with the kind of scientific debate that occurs when different frames (research traditions, research programs, or paradigms) clash. It is less consistent with the paradigm working of Kuhn's (1970) normal scientists (who never question basic assumptions), or those who tinker with the interlinked theories that constitute "protective belts" in Lakatos's (1970) description of research programs. This similarity is unsurprising, given the multiframe character of all interesting planning and policy issues.

The argumentative turn in policy and planning, especially as it is extended into discursive democracy, involves not the abandonment of science but rather a selective radicalization of scientific principles. One image of science stresses the value-free investigation of causal relationships according to a fixed set of rules. But another face of science, however much it is observed in the breach, involves free debate and dispute in which the only legitimate force is a good argument. Popperians have long recognized this point and have extended this open society model into politics, policy, and planning. But their objectivist baggage leads them to impose all kinds of constraints on the kinds of arguments that can be made, by whom, and at what time, and on who can translate argument into action.

Thus even these vestigial constraints must be abandoned if the promise of the argumentative turn is to be fulfilled. In particular, there should be as few restrictions as possible on competent participation in policy discourse and the kinds of arguments that can be advanced, normative as well as empirical. Anything less would be untrue to analysts' and planners' claims to rationality, scientific or otherwise. As Torgerson (1986b) points out, a distorted, manipulated, and secretive policy process resists revealing itself to any community of inquirers, such as that comprising policy analysts and planners. That community can succeed in its inquiries only to the extent that the larger political system reveals its workings—in other words, to the extent that politics itself is governed by canons of free discourse.

The image of policy, planning, and politics that has emerged here combines argument, science, and participatory democracy. Of course, much remains to be done to make this combination a happy and workable one. In the meantime, the argumentative turn can strive to deliver on the promise made by Harold Lasswell (1951) four decades ago of a policy science of democracy.

References

Anderson, C. W. 1988. Political Judgment and Theory in Policy Analysis. In E. B. Portis and M. B. Levy, eds., *Handbook of Political Theory and Policy Science,* 183–98. New York: Greenwood.

Bernstein, R. J. 1983. *Beyond Objectivism and Relativism.* Philadelphia: University of Pennsylvania Press.

Bobrow, D. B., and J. S. Dryzek. 1987. *Policy Analysis by Design.* Pittsburgh: University of Pittsburgh Press.

Brown, P. 1976. Ethics and Policy Research. *Policy Analysis* 2:325–40.

Burian, R. 1977. More Than a Marriage of Convenience: On the Inextricability of History and the Philosophy of Science. *Philosophy of Science* 42:1–42.

Campbell, D. T. 1969. Reforms as Experiments. *American Psychologist* 24:409–29.

DeLeon, P. 1988. *Advice and Consent: The Development of the Policy Sciences.* New York: Russell Sage Foundation.

Dror, Y. 1984. On Becoming More of a Policy Scientist. *Policy Studies Review* 4:13–21.

Dryzek, J. S. 1986. The Progress of Political Science. *Journal of Politics* 48:301–20.

———. 1989. Policy Sciences of Democracy. *Polity* 22:97–118.

———. 1990. *Discursive Democracy: Politics, Policy, and Political Science.* Cambridge and New York: Cambridge University Press.

Dunn, W. N. 1981. *Public Policy Analysis: An Introduction.* Englewood Cliffs, N.J.: Prentice-Hall.

Dye, T. R. 1976. *Policy Analysis: What Governments Do, Why They Do It, and What Difference It Makes.* University: University of Alabama Press.

Eulau, H. 1977. The Interventionist Synthesis. *American Journal of Political Science* 21:419–23.

Fay, B. 1975. *Social Theory and Political Practice.* London: Allen and Unwin.

Feyerabend, P. K. 1975. *Against Method: Outline of an Anarchistic Theory of Knowledge.* London: New Left Books.

Fischer, F. 1980. *Politics, Values, and Public Policy: The Problem of Methodology.* Boulder: Westview Press.

Forester, J. 1981. Questioning and Organizing Attention: Toward a Critical Theory of Planning and Administrative Practice. *Administration and Society* 13:161–205.

Goodin, R., and I. Waldner. 1979. Thinking Big, Thinking Small, and Not Thinking at All. *Public Policy* 27:1–24.

Hambrick, R. S., Jr. 1974. A Guide for the Analysis of Policy Arguments. *Policy Sciences* 5:469–78.

Hawkesworth, M. E. 1988. *Theoretical Issues in Policy Analysis.* Albany: State University of New York Press.

Kemp, R. 1985. Planning, Public Hearings, and the Politics of Discourse. In J. Forester, ed., *Critical Theory and Public Life,* 177–201. Cambridge: MIT Press.

Kuhn, T. 1970. *The Structure of Scientific Revolutions.* 2d ed. Chicago: University of Chicago Press.

Lakatos, I. 1970. Falsification and the Methodology of Scientific Research Programs. In I. Lakatos and A. Musgrave, eds., *Criticism and the Growth of Knowledge,* 91–196. Cambridge: Cambridge University Press.

Lasswell, H. D. 1951. The Policy Orientation. In D. Lerner and H. D. Lasswell, eds., *The Policy Sciences: Recent Developments in Scope and Methods,* 3–15. Stanford: Stanford University Press.

Laudan, L. 1977. *Progress and Its Problems: Toward a Theory of Scientific Growth.* Berkeley: University of California Press.

Lindblom, C. E. 1959. The Science of Muddling Through. *Public Administration Review* 19:79–88.

———. 1965. *The Intelligence of Democracy: Decision Making Through Mutual Adjustment.* New York: Free Press.

Lindblom, C. E., and D. K. Cohen. 1979. *Usable Knowledge.* New Haven: Yale University Press.

Lowi, T. J. 1979. *The End of Liberalism.* 2d ed. New York: W. W. Norton.

Majone, G. 1989. *Evidence, Argument, and Persuasion in the Policy Process.* New Haven: Yale University Press.

Nachmias, D. 1979. *Public Policy Evaluation.* New York: St. Martin's Press.

Palumbo, D. J., and D. Nachmias. 1983. The Preconditions for Successful Evaluation: Is There an Ideal Paradigm? *Policy Sciences* 16:67–79.

Paris, D. C., and J. F. Reynolds. 1983. *The Logic of Policy Inquiry.* New York: Longman.

Phillips, D. C. 1976. Forty Years On: Anti-Naturalism and Problems of Social Experiment and Piecemeal Social Reform. *Inquiry* 19:403–25.

Popper, K. R. 1959.*The Logic of Scientific Discovery*. London: Heinemann.

———. 1963. *The Open Society and Its Enemies*. Princeton: Princeton University Press.

———. 1972. *The Poverty of Historicism*. Rev. ed. London: Routledge and Kegan Paul.

Rein, M. 1976. *Social Science and Public Policy*. Harmondsworth: Penguin.

Rivlin, A. 1973. Forensic Social Science. In *Perspectives on Inequality*. *Harvard Educational Review*, Reprint Series 8. Cambridge: Harvard University Press.

Schulman, P. R. 1975. Nonincremental Policy Making: Notes Toward an Alternative Paradigm. *American Political Science Review* 69:1534–70.

Torgerson, D. 1986a. Between Knowledge and Politics: Three Faces of Policy Analysis. *Policy Sciences* 19:33–59.

———. 1986b. Beyond Professional Ethics: The Normative Foundations of Policy Analysis. Paper presented at the annual research conference of the Association for Public Policy Analysis and Management, Austin, Texas.

Wildavsky, A. 1966. The Political Economy of Efficiency. *Public Administration Review* 26:292–310.

———. 1979. *Speaking Truth to Power: The Art and Craft of Policy Analysis*. Boston: Little, Brown.

Wilson, J. Q. 1983. *Thinking about Crime*. Rev. ed. New York: Basic Books.

Planning Through Debate:

The Communicative Turn in

Planning Theory

Patsy Healey

This essay is about what *planning* can be taken to mean in contemporary democratic societies. Its context is the dilemma faced by all those committed to planning as a democratic enterprise aimed at promoting social justice and environmental sustainability. The dilemma is that the technical and administrative machineries advocated and created to pursue these goals are based on a narrow and dominatory scientific rationalism. These machineries have further compromised the development of a democratic attitude and have failed to deliver the goals promoted. So how can we *now* support a renewal of the enterprise of planning? What must be its forms and principles?

During the 1980s and early 1990s, alternative conceptions of planning purposes and practices have been increasingly identified and debated in planning theory. One route to imagining alternatives has focused on substantive issues, moving from material analyses of options for local economies exposed to global capitalism to concerns with culture, consciousness, community, and "placeness."[1] Another focus has taken a "process" route, exploring the communicative dimensions of collectively debating and deciding on matters of collective concern.[2]

The problem with the substantive route is its a priori assumptions of what is good or bad, right or wrong. Local economic development is often presented as good, and national economic intervention as oppressive, or bad. By what knowledge and reasoning have we reached these conclusions? If such principles are embodied in our plans, will we not have fallen yet again into the trap of imposing the reasoning of one group of people on another? Does the process route offer a way out of this dilemma of relativism that treats every position as merely someone's opinion, and hence the dominance of a position pursued through planning strategies and their implementation as nothing more than the outcome of a power game? I believe that it can.

The Idea of Planning and Its Challenges

As with so much of Western culture, the contemporary idea of planning is rooted in the Enlightenment tradition of "modernity."[3] This tradition freed individuals from the intellectual tyranny of religious faith and from the political tyranny of despots. Such free individuals could then combine in democratic association to manage their collective affairs. The application of scientific knowledge and reason to human affairs made it possible to build a better world, in which the sum of human happiness and welfare would be increased. For all our consciousness of the errors of democratic management in the past two centuries, it is difficult not to recognize the vast achievements that this intellectual and political enlightenment has brought.

The modern idea of planning, as John Friedmann[4] has described in his authoritative account of its intellectual origins, is centrally linked to concepts of democracy and progress. It centers on the challenge of finding ways in which citizens acting together can manage their collective concerns with respect to the sharing of space and time.

In this century, Karl Mannheim's advocacy of a form of planning that harnessed systematized social scientific knowledge and techniques to the management of collective affairs in a democratic society proved inspirational for the influential Chicago school of rational decision making.[5] A procedural view evolved which presented planning as a progressive force for economic and social development in a world where democracy and capitalism were seen to coexist in comfortable consensus.[6] This modern view challenged populist "clientelism" (as in Chicago in the 1950s)[7] as much as idealist totalitarianism.

But as with any progressive force, procedures developed with a progressive democratic intention may be subverted for other purposes. In the early 1970s, this subversion was identified with the power of capitalist forces to dominate the public's life opportunities. Environmental planning, it was argued, put the needs of capital (through regional economic development and the implicit opportunities for land and property markets created by planning regimes) before citizens and the environment.[8]

However, a more fundamental challenge to the Mannheimian notion of planning was gathering force through the critique of scientific reason itself. German critical theorists and French deconstructionists elaborated ideas which challenged reason's dominance of human affairs. Reason, understood as logic coupled with scientifically constructed empirical knowledge, was unveiled as having achieved hegemonic power over other ways of being and knowing, crowding out moral and aesthetic discourses. Further, rationalizing power dominated the very institutions set up in the name of democratic action, the bureaucratic agencies of the state. Following Michel Foucault's analysis, planning could be associated with the dominatory power of systematic reason pursued through state bureaucracies.[9] Evidence for this seemed to be everywhere, from the disaster of high-rise towers for the poor to the dominance of economic criteria justifying road building and the functional categorization of activity zones, which worked for large industrial companies and those working in them, but not for women (with their necessarily complex lifestyles), the elderly and the disabled, and the many ethnic groups forced to discover ways of surviving on the edge of established economic practices.

This "challenge to systematized reason," and with it, to the planning enterprise, strikes at the heart of the project of modernity. The challenge is now labeled "postmodernist," drawing on a terminology first developed in art and architectural criticism. But whereas postmodernism in architecture is primarily a critique of a particular paradigm and style *within* Western art and architecture, philosophical postmodernism undermines the foundations of two hundred years of Western thought.

The postmodern challenge to Western thought is both progressive and regressive in its potential, as was the idea of systematized reason. It is also highly diverse, with different lines of development. Only some of these claim to *replace* the project of modernity with that of postmodernity. Others, following the position of the economic geographer David Harvey and the critical theorist Jürgen Habermas, seek new ways of reconstituting the "incomplete" project of modernity. Some of the strands of postmodernist debate leave space for a collective activity in planning. Others dismiss planning as, variously, impossible, irrelevant, or oppressive.

Beth Moore Milroy, reviewing the development of the postmodernist debate in planning thought, identifies four broad characteristics to the challenge postmodernism presents to modernism:

> It is *deconstructive* in the sense of questioning and establishing a sceptical distance from conventional beliefs and, more actively, trying both to ascer-

tain who derives value from upholding their authority and to displace them; *antifoundationalist* in the sense of dispensing with universals as bases of truth; *nondualistic* in the sense of refusing the separation between subjectivity and objectivity along with the array of dualisms it engenders including the splits between truth and opinion, fact and value; and *encouraging of plurality and difference.*[10]

This double challenge—to the tendency for progressive values to be destroyed by the very systems created to promote them and to the systems of technocratic rationalist thought that underpin so much of Western and Eastern bloc thinking about planning—seems so powerful as to be fatal to the idea of planning. However, as Harvey and Habermas both argue, some directions of the postmodern challenge to planning need to be actively resisted as regressive and undemocratic. Communicative forms of planning offer a progressive way forward.

Communicative Rationality

Communicative rationality is not the only direction new forms of planning are taking. Some argue for planning as a framework of rules within which collectively experienced impacts are addressed through pricing policies.[11] But this is merely to retreat still further into narrow rationalism. Others argue for the replacement of rationalism by some fundamental moral principle derived from religious principles, or environmental philosophy, or some other metaphysics, but it is hard to see how such an approach can advance the project of progressive democratic pluralism. A more centrally postmodern approach elevates experience and the aesthetic mode to the central dimension of human life. In this conception all experiences and individual interpretations are equally valid because there are no shared criteria for discrimination.

If planning has any role at all in this conception, it is to stake out and defend boundaries and at the same time to foster the celebration of difference. But what practices could constitute such planning in the absence of a discursive reasoning capacity? The progressive challenge is instead to find ways of acknowledging different ways of experiencing and understanding while seeking to "make sense together."

Another approach to inventing a "new" planning has been to develop the socialist project beyond a preoccupation with material conditions and economic classes. Traditionally, the socialist project was based on scientific materialism. The new socialism of the 1980s, in Britain at least, has been concerned with developing a pluralist understanding of people's needs, values, and ways of experiencing oppression.[12] Appreciating diversity and recognizing difference are key elements in this conception, requiring collective action to be informed by principles of tolerance and respect. There is not one route to progress but many, not one form of reasoning but many. The socialist project thus comes to focus on restructuring the control of economies and the flow of the fruits of material effort while at the same time discovering ways of "living together differently but respectfully."[13] Planning retains its traditional importance in socialist thought, but the planning enterprise is refocused to recognize diverse forms of disadvantage.

The focus of new socialism remains a struggle for opportunities for the disadvantaged against a systemically understood capitalist world order. This provides a frame of reasoning which interprets and selects among the various claims for attention that a pluralist socialism can generate. But the pluralist socialist project is still founded on systematized rationality and scientific understanding of social structure in its conceptions of "living together" and "difference."

Communicative rationality offers a way forward through a different conception of human reason, following the work of Habermas. Habermas argues that far from giving up on reason as an informing principle for contemporary societies, we should shift perspective from an individualized, subject-object conception of reason to reasoning formed within intersubjective communication. Such reasoning is required where "living together but differently" in shared space and time drives us to search for ways of finding agreement on how to address our collective concerns. Habermas's communicative rationality has parallels within conceptions of practical reasoning, implying an expansion from the notion of reason as pure logic and scientific empiricism to encompass all the ways we come to understand and know things and use that knowledge in acting. Habermas argues that without some concept of reasoning, we have no way out of fundamentalism and nihilism. For him, the notion of the self-conscious autonomous individual, refining his or her knowledge against principles of logic and science, can be replaced by a notion of reason as intersubjective mutual understanding arrived at by particular people in particular times and places; that is, reason is historically situated. Both subject and object are constituted through this process. Knowledge claims, upon which action possibilities are proposed, are validated, in this conception of reasoning, through discursively establishing principles of validity rather than through appeal to logic or science, although both may well be considered possibilities within the communicative context.[14]

In this way, knowledge for action, principles of action, and ways of acting are actively constituted by the members of an intercommunicating community situated in the particularities of time and place. Further, the reasoning employed can escape the confines of rational-scientific principles to include varying systems of morality and culturally specific traditions of expressive aesthetic experience. "Right" and "good" actions are those we can come to agree on, in particular times and places, across our diverse differences in material conditions and wants, moral perspectives, and expressive cultures and inclinations. We do not need recourse to common fundamental ideals or principles of "the good social organization" to guide us. In this conception, planning, and its contents, is a way of acting we can *choose*, after *debate*.

Habermas's conception of communicative action has been criticized in the context of the present discussion on two grounds. First, by holding on to reason, it retains the very source of modernity's dominatory potential. Second, Habermas would like to believe that consensual positions can be arrived at, whereas contemporary social relations reveal deep cleavages—of class, race, gender, and culture—which can only be resolved, some argue, through power struggle between conflicting forces.[15]

Habermas justifies his retention of reasoning as a legitimate guiding principle for collective affairs on the grounds that, where collective action is our concern, we need to engage in argumentation and debate. We need a reasoning capacity for these purposes. We cannot engage in aesthetic presentation or moral faith if at some point we are faced both with making sense together and working out how to act together. This does not mean that the language of morality or aesthetics is excluded from our reasoning. Habermas argues that our intersubjective practical reasoning draws on the store of knowledge and understanding of technique, morality, and aesthetics. In this way, our collective reasoning is informed by, and situated within, the various "lifeworlds" from which we come to engage in our collective enterprises.[16] Our intersubjective arguments may involve telling stories as well as analysis.[17] Thus the narrative mode should accompany and intersect with experiential expression and the analytical mode. But in the end, the purpose of our efforts is not analysis, telling stories, or rhetoric but *doing something;* that is, "acting in the world." For this, we need to discuss what we could and should do—why and how. There is an interesting parallel here with Michael Walzer's notion of principles of justice for different spheres of social activity.[18]

But does not the process of collective argument merely lead to a new and potentially dominatory consensus, as the agreement freely arrived at through argument in one period imposes itself on the different conclusions of the next? Habermas proposes to counteract this possibility through criteria to sustain a dynamic critique within the reasoning process. Claims should be judged by their comprehensibility, integrity, legitimacy, and truth.[19] John Forester has since developed these criteria as heuristic questions for planners to use in critiquing themselves and others as they search for a progressive, power-challenging planning.[20]

The mutual understandings and agreements reached for one purpose at one time are thus revisable as the flow of communicative action proceeds. Habermas himself would clearly like to see stable societies built around principles of mutual understanding. Several planning theorists have also proposed the development of a communicative "metalanguage" or a "metadiscourse" for planning discussion.[21] Such an enterprise parallels the search within the New Left in Britain for forms of a democratically pluralist participation.

But a metalanguage, however full of internal principles of critique, unavoidably contains dominatory potential. It could all too easily settle into assumptions of understanding and agreement detached from those whose ways of being, knowing, and valuing are supposed to be reflected in the agreement. To be liberating rather than dominating, intercommunicative reasoning for the purposes of acting in the world must accept that the "differences" between which we must communicate are not just differences in economic and social position, or in specific wants and needs, but in *systems of meaning*. We see things differently because words, phrases, expressions, and objects are interpreted differently according to our frame of reference. It is this point, long understood in anthropology[22] and emphasized in phenomenology, which underpins the strength of the relativist position. It is here that I would part company with Habermas and recognize the inherent localized specificity and untranslatability of systems of meaning. We may shift our ideas, learn from each other, adapt to each other, and act in the world together. Systems of meaning or frames of reference shift and evolve in response to such encounters. But it can never be possible to construct a stable, fully inclusionary consensus, and the agreements we reach should be recognized as merely temporary accommodations of different, and differently adapting, perceptions.

The critics of modernity argue that the system of meaning proposed by scientific rationalism has dominated and crowded out all other systems of meaning. If communicative action is to transcend this dominatory threat, its concern should rather be to develop understandings and practices of *interdiscursive* communication, of translation rather than superimposition. For, as Clifford Geertz argues, no system of meaning can ever fully understand another.[23] It can merely search for ways of opening windows on what it means to see things differently.

Developed in this way, communicative rationality offers a new form of planning through interdiscursive communication, a way of "living together differently through struggling to make sense together." Its openness, its exteriorizing quality, and its internal capacity for critique should counteract any potential to turn mutual understanding reached at one historical moment into a repressive cultural regime in the next. Communicative rationality offers the hope that progress, a "project of becoming," is still possible. This direction, in my view, holds an important promise and challenge for planning and for democracy generally, as Forester argues.[24]

Planning as a Communicative Enterprise

Planning, and specifically environmental planning, is a process for collectively, and interactively, addressing and working out how to act with respect to shared concerns about how far to go and how to "manage" environmental change. Mannheim argued that scientific rationalism provides the central resource for this enterprise,[25] but the collapse of the unidimensional domination of scientific rationalism has demolished this possibility. Any recourse to scientific knowledge or rational procedures must now be contained within some other conception of democratic acting in the world. Habermas offers an alternative which retains the notion of the liberating and democratic potential of reasoning but is broadened to encompass moral appreciation and aesthetic experience as well as rational-technical forms of reasoning. This wider understanding of what we know, and how we know it, rooted as much in "practical sense"[26] as in formalized knowledge, is brought into collective deciding and acting through intersubjective communication rather than through the self-reflective consciousness of autonomous individuals. The effort of constructing mutual understanding as the locus of reasoning activity replaces the subject-centered "philosophy of consciousness," which, Habermas argues, has dominated Western conceptions of reason since the Enlightenment.[27] Through it, the specificities of time and place, of culture, society, and personality, and of "habitus," as Pierre Bourdieu puts it,[28] are expressed and constituted. For Habermas, a conscious intersubjective understanding of collective communicative work is a force to sustain an internally critical democratic effort, resisting the potential domination of one-dimensional principles, be they scientific, moral, or aesthetic.

What can planning mean in this context of postrationalist, inter-communicative, reasoned, many-dimensional "thinking about and acting" in the world? What purposes and practices should it have?

A communicative approach to knowledge production—knowledge of conditions, cause and effect, moral values, and aesthetic worlds—maintains that knowledge is not merely a preformulated store of systematized understandings but is specifically created anew in our communications through exchanging perceptions and understandings and through drawing on the stock of life experience and previously consolidated cultural and moral knowledge available to participants. We cannot therefore predefine a set of tasks which planning must address, since these must be specifically discovered, learned about, and understood through intercommunicative processes.

Nevertheless, ongoing processes of debate about environmental matters have created a thought world, a contemporary "common sense," within which the elements of a substantive agenda are evident. The contemporary rediscovery of environmental planning is fueled by a widespread and interdiscursive concern with managing economic development, enriching cultural life, avoiding polarizing and segregating tendencies in life-styles and life opportunities, and undertaking all these within an attitude to the natural environment which is both respectful and sustaining of long-term ecological balances. The general purposes of environmental planning situated in this context are to balance these connecting but often contradictory aims. But what constitutes the "balance" in particular times and places cannot be known in advance.

If this is so, then attention to the substantive purposes of environmental planning needs to be complemented by consideration of the practices through which purposes are established and actions are identified and followed through. What does a communicative rationality suggest as appropriate when addressing environmental management issues in contemporary Western democracies? How can the recognition of appropriate practices avoid the trap of formulation as a "process" blueprint?

The outlines of appropriate practices for an intercommunicative planning began to emerge through the work of planning theorists during the 1980s. This work has been influenced not only by Habermas but by other, often conflicting, contributors to the postmodern and antirationalist debate, notably Foucault and Bourdieu, and by an increasing number of "ethnographic" studies of planning practice.[29] The following ten propositions summarize this "new" planning direction.

1. Planning is an interactive and interpretive process; it focuses on deciding and acting within a range of specialized allocative and authoritative systems but draws on the multidimensionality of "lifeworlds" or practical sense rather than a single formalized dimension (for example, urban morphology or scientific rationalism).[30] Formal techniques of analysis and design in planning processes are but one form of discourse. Planning processes should be enriched by discussion of moral dilemmas and aesthetic experience using a range of presentational forms, from telling stories to aesthetic illustrations of experiences. Statistical analysis coexists in such processes with poems and moral fables.[31] A prototype example here might be some of the new initiatives in Britain to help tenants and residents improve the quality of their living environments.

2. Such interaction assumes the preexistence of individuals engaged with others in diverse, fluid, and overlapping "discourse communities," each with its own meaning systems and hence knowledge forms and ways of reasoning and valuing. Such communities may be nearer or farther from each other in relation to access to each other's languages, but no common language or fully common understanding can be attained. Communicative action thus focuses on searching for achievable levels of mutual understanding for the purposes in hand while retaining awareness of that which is not understood (i.e., we may not understand why someone says no, but we should recognize the negation as valid; we know there is a reason but we cannot (yet) understand it).[32]

3. Intercommunicative planning involves respectful discussion within and between discursive communities, "respect" implying recognizing, valuing, listening to, and searching for translative possibilities between different discourse communities.[33] A prototype example here might be the public participation exercises undertaken by a few progressive local authorities in Britain when producing their development plans.[34]

4. Planning involves invention not only through programs of action but in the construction of the arenas within which these programs are formulated and conflicts are identified and mediated. Such a planning needs to be reflective about its own processes.[35] For example, organizing development plan preparation involves planners in considering not only whom to consult about what, but also the areas within which issues are identified, debated, and decided upon.

5. Within the argumentation of these communicative processes, all dimensions of knowing, understanding, appreciating, experiencing, and

judging may be brought into play. The struggle of engaging in inter-discursive communicative action is to grasp these diverse viewpoints and find ways of reasoning among the competing claims for action they generate, without dismissing or devaluing any one until it has been explored. Nothing is inadmissible except the claim that some things are off the agenda and cannot be discussed. All claims merit the reply: "We acknowledge you feel this is of value. Can you help us understand why? Can we work out how it affects what we thought we were trying to do? Are there any reasons why the claim cannot receive collective support?"[36]

6. A reflexive and critical capacity should be kept alive in the processes of argumentation, using the Habermasian criteria of comprehensibility, integrity, legitimacy, and truth. But the critical intent should be directed not at the discourses of the different participative communities (e.g., "We are right and you are wrong"; "We are good and you are bad") but at the discourse that surrounds specific actions being *invented* through the communicative process (e.g., "Watch out: this metaphor we are using blocks out the ideas our other colleagues are proposing"; or "This line of thinking will be dismissed as illegitimate by central government. Do we really think it is illegitimate? Are we really going to challenge their power? OK, so how?").[37] A sensitive illustration of this and the previous practice that was used in developing the women's agenda for the Greater London Development Plan is described by Judith Allen.[38]

7. This inbuilt critique, a morality for interaction, serves the project of democratic pluralism by according "voice," "ear," and "respect" to all those with an interest in the issues at stake. This is no easy matter; interests overlap and conflict, and the conflicts experienced within each one of us are magnified in the interdiscursive arena. The important point is that the morality and the dilemmas are addressed interdiscursively, forming thereby both the processes and the arenas of debate.

8. The literature on negotiation counsels us that apparently fixed preferences may be altered when individuals and groups are encouraged to articulate their interests together. Interaction is thus not simply a form of exchange or bargaining around predefined interests. It involves mutually reconstructing what constitutes the interests of the various participants—a process of mutual learning through mutually trying to understand.[39]

9. Communicative planning is not only innovative, it has the potential to change, to transform material conditions and established power relations through the continuous effort to "critique" and "demystify"; through increasing understanding among participants and

hence highlighting oppressions and "dominatory" forces; and through creating well-grounded arguments for alternative analyses and perceptions—through actively *constructing* new understandings. Ultimately, the transformative potential of communicative action lies in the power embodied in the "better argument,"[40] in the power of ideas, metaphors, images, and stories. This echoes Bourdieu's point that how we talk about things helps to bring them about.[41]

In this way, diverse people from different societal conditions and cultural communities are encouraged to recognize one another's presence and negotiate their shared concerns. Through such processes of argumentation we may come to agree, or accept a process of agreeing, on what should be done, without necessarily arriving at a unified view of our respective lifeworlds. The critical criteria built into such a process of argument encourages openness and transparency, but without simplification. If collective concerns are ambivalent or ambiguous, such a communicative process should allow acknowledgment that this is so, perhaps unavoidably so. So the dilemmas and creative potentials of ambiguity enrich the interdiscursive effort rather than being washed out in the attempt to construct a one-dimensional language.[42]

10. The purpose of intercommunicative planning is to help planners begin and proceed in mutually agreeable ways based on an effort at interdiscursive understanding, drawing on, critiquing, and reconstructing the understandings everyone brings to the discussion. The inbuilt criterion of critique, if kept alive, should prevent such starting agreements and "traveling pacts" from consolidating into a unified code and language which could then limit further invention. We may be able to agree on what to do next, on how to start out, and then travel along for a while. We cannot know where this will take us. But we can act with hope and ambition to achieve future possibilities. Neither the comprehensive plan nor goal-directed programs have more than a temporary existence in such a conception of communicative and potentially transformative environmental planning.[43]

Systems and Practices for Environmental Planning

How can this conception of communicative practices for constructing and critiquing understanding among diverse discursive communities assist in the development of systems for environmental planning, local realizations of these, and the specific contents of local planning systems? The very concept of a system immediately conjures up notions of dominatory practices which impose themselves on our actions. Yet, with respect to our mutual environmental concerns, a key purpose of communicative action is to work out what rules or codes of conduct we can agree we need, to allow us to live together but differently in shared environments.

Planning systems consist of formal rules to guide the conduct, resource allocation, and management activities of individuals and businesses. But they are more than a set of rules. The rules derive from conceptions of situations (contexts), problems experienced in these situations, and ways of addressing these problems and changing situations. It is where planning effort is deliberately focused on *changing* situations that we can speak of a planning with transformative intent.[44]

Urban design or physical blueprint approaches to environmental planning focused on transforming towns. Ideas of urban existence were consolidated into principles of urban structure and form, and from these into rules to govern proposals for development projects. Debates were confined to principles of urban form and conducted primarily within a narrow expert group (architects and engineers) legitimized by paternalist notions of "planning *for* people." The old approach was supported by a narrow architectural engineering discourse about the relative merits of different urban forms, drawing on aesthetic and moral principles. The dominatory consequences of this for our towns and cities are notorious. The urban design approach was essentially a continuation of a pre-Enlightenment tradition of city planning carried forward into the context of nineteenth- and twentieth-century industrialization and urbanization.

The Mannheimian conception of planning as the "rational mastery of the irrational"[45] provided a more appropriate realization of a modern conception of planning. Translated through the Chicago school, this became the rational-comprehensive process model of planning which has been so influential in planning practice. This model focused on the processes through which goals were formulated and strategies for achieving them were devised. Rule generation operated on two levels: the methodological rules for arriving at a plan or program and the criteria necessary for realizing that program. Both were designed to be recursive, with feedback loops via monitoring procedures intended to sustain an internal critique of planning principles. Planning effort was focused on comprehensive understanding of urban and environmental systems and the invention of sets of objectives and guidance principles for the comprehensive management of these systems. Rules to govern change in systems were expressed as performance criteria and linked back to objectives. In this rationalist conception, citizens contributed to the process, but only by "feeding in" their rationalized goals rather than by debating the understandings through which they had come to have their goals. The concerns of politicians and citizens were, in effect, "translated," converted into the technical scientific language of policy analysts and urban and regional science. The metaphors of this language focused on images of process forms, of strategy and programmatic action. The dominatory potential of the rational procedural model lies in the claims to comprehensiveness of what was primarily a narrow, economistic, and functionalist conception of the dimensions of lifeworlds. The critical capacity of the monitoring feedback loops merely shifted priorities within the discourse; it did not provide a mechanism for critiquing the discourse itself.

Pluralist conceptions of interest mediation, of the kind first proposed by Paul Davidoff[46] but later widely developed, seem to reflect more clearly the reality of environmental planning politics. The practice of environmental planning is now commonly described as one within which environmental perceptions and interests are asserted and mediated.[47] The strategies, rules, and the way rules are used are interpreted in this conception as the product of bargaining processes among conflicting interests. But, as Forester argues, this treats each interest as a source of power, bargaining with others to create a calculus which expresses the power relations among the participants. The language of environmental planning is that of the prevalent political power games. It is not underpinned by any effort at learning about the interests and perceptions of the participants, and with that knowledge revising what each participant thinks about the others' and his or her own interests. Only if this happened could a creative, inventive form of environmental planning develop to replace a merely power-brokering planning.[48]

The focus of an intersubjective communicative argumentation is exactly at this point. It starts by recognizing the potential diversity of ways in which concerned citizens (citizens with an interest in issues) come to be concerned. Citizens may share a concern but arrive at it through different cultural, societal, and personal experiences. Understanding each other must therefore be accepted as a challenging task which is unlikely to be more than partially achieved. The language of interdiscursive communication uses multiple modes, moving between analysis, moral fables, and poems.

The struggle within such interdiscursive communication is to maintain a capacity for critique. This requires the development of a critical, interactively reflexive habit. Of course, the dynamics of the ongoing flow of relations means that people cannot pause to reflect collectively at every instant, but taking a breath and sorting things out should become a normal part of the practical endeavor of planning work. The Habermasian criteria help here, but reflection is also required with regard to the arenas of the communicative effort itself. Are there other concerned people who should be involved? Are there other ways of understanding these issues or discursive practices which we should include? How should the position we have reached be expressed to maximize its relevance to all of us, allowing us to move on but still minimize the potential that what we have agreed will live on beyond our need for it and come to dominate us? Through these processes of active discursive critique, ideas for action may be invented, and necessary codes of conduct for the collective management of shared concerns may be identified and agreed upon.

This concept of a planning "invented" through reflective processes of intersubjective communication within which are absorbed internal criteria of critique is suggestive of ways in which existing processes of plan making, conflict resolution, and implementation programs might be transformed. Specifically, the active presence of a planning in this form will be reflected in the language and metaphor used within the various arenas constituted for environmental planning work. It would reflect efforts at honesty and openness without losing a recognition of the layers and range of meanings present among those concerned with the issue at hand. It would acknowledge with respect the limited scope for mutual understanding between diverse discourse communities while struggling to enlarge that understanding. It would accept other limits—to power, to empirical knowledge, to the resolvability of moral dilemmas—but yet seek to enable the world of action to begin and proceed toward something better, without having to specify a goal. Rather than Lindblomian marginal adjustments to the present,[49] its language would be *future seeking*, but not, like its physical blueprint and goal-directed predecessors, *future defining*. Its images and metaphors would draw on both the experiential and the abstract knowledge and understanding of those involved, recognizing the interweaving of rational-technical, moral, and aesthetic dimensions in our lives. It would seek to reason between conflicting claims and conflicting ways of validating claims. It would not force one dimension of knowledge to dominate another. It would be courageous, challenging power relations through criticism and the presentation of alternative arguments. It would reflect the internal critical monitoring practices of participants. It is thus by the *tone* of its practices that intercommunicative planning would be identified.

The Dialectics of a New Planning

To those seeking specific substantive solutions to particular problems, the planning outlined here may seem too leisurely. With environmental disasters so near at hand, can we afford to take the time to invent answers? To those seeking knowledgeable actions, this planning may seem too unfocused and diffuse. What happens if mystical perceptions or aesthetic reification crowd out the useful empirical and theoretical knowledge we have about cause and effect? To those conscious of the scale of inequalities in power relations, this concept of planning may seem idealistic and innocent. Does it not merely cocoon us within a naive belief in the power of democratic discussions while the forces of global capitalism ever more cleverly conceal the ways they oppress us?

To these doubts there are two replies. First, to engage in any other strategy is to regenerate forms of planning which have inherent within them an antidemocratic "dominatory" potential. Second, the practices involved are not really so far removed from our experience. Prefigurative examples can be found in Britain in some of the work of the New Left, for example, in the Greater London Council, particularly in dealing with women's issues,[50] and recently in a few of the new efforts in plan making in Britain resulting from requirements to prepare Unitary Development Plans and District Development Plans.[51] More generally, some branches of the environmental and feminist movements have been moving in this direction. Further prefigurative potentials can even be recognized in contemporary management theory's emphasis on group culture formation and empowerment rather than management through hierarchical authoritarian structures.[52] At a broader level, the "struggle for democracy" in eastern Europe and China has generated questions in Western societies regarding the real meaning of democracy.

"Inventing democracy" is thus an issue that is moving increasingly sharply into focus. This is a time for the invention of democratic processes. The field of environmental concerns is one of the critical arenas within which such invention is being demanded and tested.

However, there are many possible democracies. Learning and listening and respectful argumentation are not enough. We need to develop skills in translation, in constructive critique, and in collective invention and respectful action to be able to realize the potential of a planning understood as collectively and intersubjectively addressing how to act in respect of common concerns about urban and regional environments. We need to rework the store of techniques and practices evolved within the planning field to identify their potential *within* a new communicative, dialogue-based form of planning. This essay has drawn on the work of a number of planning academics who search within the lifeworld of planning practice for a better understanding of these skills. What is being invented, in planning practice and in planning theory, is a new form of planning, a respectful, argumentative form of *planning through debate* that is appropriate to our recognition of the failure of modernity's conception of "pure reason" yet is searching, as Habermas does, for a continuation of the Enlightenment project of democratic progress through reasoned intersubjective argument among free citizens.

As the planning community explores this hopeful new approach, it is important to remember the experience of past efforts at democracy making. Habermas offers the theory of communicative action as an intersubjective project of emancipation from fundamentalism, totalitarianism, and nihilism through deliberate efforts in mutual understanding through argument. But this can succeed for more than a historical moment only so long as the processes of internal critique are kept constantly alive, so long as what Habermas calls "the lifeworld" is constantly brought into the collective thinking about acting in the world in respect of common affairs, and so long as the communicative effort of mutual understanding is sustained as a critical as well as a creative process. Either we succeed in keeping a critical dialectics alive within communicative action or we remain caught within the dialectics of totalizing systems. As the opposition of capitalism versus communism collapses, perhaps there is a hope that, through dynamically critical communicative processes, the democratic project of "making sense together while living differently" can develop as a progressive force.

Notes

Debate is used in the title in preference to *argumentation*, as a more collaborative and positive word. Although others may see debate as involving opposition between two sides, it will become clear that this meaning is not what I associate with the word.

This essay is a very substantial development of ideas initially sketched in P. Healey, "Planning Through Debate," a paper presented at the Planning Theory Conference, Oxford, April 1990. My thanks to my sister Bridget, who allowed me to write this and read Habermas while on holiday. My thanks to Huw Thomas, John Forester, Seymour Mandelbaum, Jean Hillier, Jack Ellerby, Michael Benfield, Beth Moore Milroy, Gavin Kitching, Judith Allen, Michael Synnott, and Nilton Torres for their critical attention to an earlier draft.

1. This is evident particularly in discussions on locality, place, and local economic development. See, for example, P. N. Cooke, *Back to the Future* (London: Unwin Hayman, 1990); D. Massey, "The Political Place of Locality Studies," *Environment and Planning A* 23, no. 2 (1991): 267–81.

2. See J. Forester, *Planning in the Face of Power* (Berkeley: University of California Press, 1989); J. Throgmorton, "Planning and Analysis and Persuasive Storytelling: The Case of Electric Power Rate-making in the Chicago Area" (Paper presented to the Association of Collegiate Schools of Planning [ACSP] Congress, Austin, Texas, November 1990).

3. For discussions of the meaning of *modernity* and *post-modernity* in relation to planning, see J. Friedmann, *Planning in the Public Domain* (Princeton: Princeton University Press, 1987); B. Moore Milroy, "Into Postmodern Weightlessness," *Journal of Planning Education and Research* 10, no. 3 (1991): 181–87, and other papers in this issue of *JPER*; and B. Goodchild, "Planning and the Modern/Postmodern Debate," *Town Planning Review* 61, no. 2 (1990): 119–37. See also R. J. Bernstein, ed., *Habermas and Modernity* (Cambridge: Polity Press, 1981); M. Berman, *All That's Solid Melts to Air* (London: Verso, 1983); and D. Harvey, *The Condition of Postmodernity* (Oxford: Basil Blackwell, 1989).

4. See Freidmann, *Planning in the Public Domain*.

5. K. Mannheim, *Man and Society in an Age of Reason* (London: Routledge, 1960); J. Friedmann, *Retracking America* (New York: Anchor, 1973); Friedmann, *Planning in the Public Domain*; and A. Faludi, *Critical Rationalism and Planning Methodology* (London: Pion, 1986).

6. See the discussion in Friedmann, *Retracking America*.

7. See M. Meyerson and E. Banfield, *Politics, Planning and the Public Interest* (New York: Free Press, 1955).

8. This position was most forcefully articulated in M. Castells, *The Urban Question* (London: Edward Arnold, 1977). See also P. Ambrose and B. Colenutt, *The Property Machine* (Harmondsworth: Penguin, 1973); and A. Scott and S. T. Roweis, "Urban Planning in Theory and Practice," *Environment and Planning A* 9 (1977): 1097–1119.

9. See J. Habermas, *The Philosophical Discourse of Modernity* (Cambridge: Polity Press, 1987), for a helpful debate on the work of Adorno, Marcuse, Foucault, and Derrida.

10. Moore Milroy, "Postmodern Weightlessness."

11. For good critiques of this approach with respect to environmental issues see M. Hajer, in this volume; and R. Grove White, "Land, the Law, and Environment," *Journal of Law and Society* 18, no. 1 (1991): 32–47.

12. See for example, M. Rustin, *For a Pluralist Socialism* (London: Verso, 1985).

13. Interestingly, this thinking parallels ideas developed by Mel Webber on "persuasive planning" for pluralist, democratic societies in the 1970s, which

aimed to foster debate and encompass difference. See M. Webber, "A Difference Paradigm for Planning," in R. W. Burchell and G. Sternleib, eds., *Planning Theory in the 1980s* (New Brunswick, N.J.: Rutgers Center for Urban Policy Research, 1978).

14. See Habermas, *Philosophical Discourse.*

15. See B. Moore Milroy, "Critical Capacity and Planning Theory," *Planning Theory Newsletter* (Winter 1990): 12–18; and R. Sennet, *The Conscience of the Eye: The Design and Social Life of Cities* (London: Faber, 1991).

16. Habermas, *Philosophical Discourse.*

17. See J. Innes, *Knowledge and Public Policy: The Search for Meaningful Indicators* (New Brunswick, N.J.: Transaction Publishers, 1990); S. Mandelbaum, "Telling Stories," *Journal of Planning Education and Research* 10, no. 3 (1991): 209–14; and J. Forester, "The Politics of Storytelling in Planning Practice" (Paper presented to the ACSP Congress, Austin, Texas, November 1990), for an appreciation of the role of storytelling in policy analysis.

18. M. Walzer, *Spheres of Justice: A Defence of Pluralism and Equality* (Oxford: Basil Blackwell, 1983).

19. J. Habermas, *The Theory of Communicative Action,* vol. 1: *Reason and the Rationalisation of Society* (London: Heinemann Polity Press, 1984).

20. Forester, *Planning in the Face of Power.*

21. For example, J. Hillier, "Deconstructing the Discourse of Planning," and J. Throgmorton, "Impeaching Research: Planning as a Persuasive and Constitutive Discourse" (Papers presented to the Association of Collegiate Schools of Planning/Association of European Schools of Planning Congress, Oxford, July 1991).

22. See C. Geertz, *Local Knowledge: Further Essays in Interpretive Anthropology* (New York: Basic Books, 1983); and P. Bourdieu, *In Other Words: Essays Towards a Reflexive Sociology* (Oxford: Polity Press, 1990).

23. See Geertz, ibid.

24. J. Forester, "Envisioning the Politics of Public Sector Dispute Resolution," in S. Silbey and A. Sarat, eds., *Studies in Law, Politics and Society,* 12:83–122 (Greenwich, Conn.: JAI Press, 1992).

25. See a recent reassessment of Mannheim's thinking by D. van Houten, "Planning Rationality and Relativism," *Environment and Planning B: Planning and Design* 16, no. 2 (1989): 201–14.

26. See Bourdieu, *In Other Words.*

27. See Habermas, *Philosophical Discourse,* 296–97.

28. Bourdieu, *In Other Words.*

29. See Forester, *Planning in the Face of Power;* Throgmorton, "Persuasive Storytelling"; and also C. Hoch, "Conflict at Large: A National Survey of Planners and Political Conflict," *Journal of Planning Education and Research* 8, no. 1 (1988): 25–34; S. Hendler, "Spending Time with Planners: Their Conflicts and

Their Stress" (Paper presented to ACSP Congress, Austin, Texas, November 1990).

30. See Innes, *Knowledge and Public Policy;* and P. Healey, "A Day's Work," *Journal of the American Planning Association* 58, no. 1 (1992): 9–20.

31. See Mandelbaum, "Telling Stories"; and Forester, "Politics of Storytelling."

32. This goes beyond Habermas's argument into the ideas offered by "ethnographic" scholars such as Bourdieu and Geertz.

33. The emphasis on respect is powerfully expressed in John Forester's work. Geertz (*Local Knowledge*) highlights the challenge of translation.

34. R. Alty and R. Darke, "A City Centre for People: Involving the Community in Planning for Sheffield's Central Area," *Planning Practice and Research,* no. 3 (1987): 7–12.

35. See J. Forester, "Anticipating Implementation: Normative Practices in Planning and Policy Analysis," in F. Fischer and J. Forester, eds., *Confronting Values in Policy Analysis: The Politics of Criteria* (Beverly Hills: Sage, 1987); and, at a more organizational level, J. Bryson and B. Crosby, "The Design and Use of Strategic Planning Arenas," *Planning Outlook* 32, no. 1 (1989): 5–13.

36. The importance of this listening and learning attitude is emphasized in Forester, *Planning in the Face of Power.* See also Throgmorton, "Impeaching Research"; and Healey, "A Day's Work."

37. See Throgmorton, "Impeaching Research"; and A. Tait and J. Wolfe, "Discourse Analysis and City Plans," *Journal of Planning Education and Research* 10, no. 3 (1991): 195–200, for the critical deconstructive analysis of planning texts.

38. J. Allen, "Smoke over the Winter Palace: The Politics of Resistance and London's Community Areas" (Paper presented to the Second International Planning Theory in Practice Conference, Torino, Italy, September 1986).

39. See Forester, *Planning in the Face of Power;* "Envisioning Politics."

40. As Habermas (in *Philosophical Discourse*) claims.

41. Bourdieu (*In Other Words*) is referring to Marx's idea of class.

42. See Forester's discussion of Nussbaum's work in "Politics of Storytelling."

43. I am indebted to correspondence with John Forester about the qualities of a democratic plan for my thinking here, as well as to the ideas in R. Sennett, *The Conscience of the Eye: The Design and Social Life of Cities* (London: Faber and Faber, 1990), on designing with the grain of diversity.

44. Following the usage of Friedmann in *Planning in the Public Domain, transformative* here refers to changing the context deliberately as well as acting within the context.

45. K. Mannheim, *Man and Society in an Age of Reconstruction* (New York: Harcourt Brace, 1940).

46. P. Davidoff, "Advocacy and Pluralism in Planning," *Journal of the American Institute of Planning* 31 (November 1965): 33–38.

47. P. Healey, P. F. McNamara, M. J. Elson, and A. J. Doak, *Land Use Planning and the Mediation of Urban Change* (Cambridge: Cambridge University Press, 1988); T. Brindley, Y. Rydin, and G. Stoker, *Remaking Planning* (London: Hutchinson, 1989).

48. See Forester, "Public Sector Dispute Resolution."

49. C. E. Lindblom, *The Intelligence of Democracy* (New York: Free Press, 1965).

50. See Allen, "Smoke over the Winter Palace."

51. See P. Healey, "The Communicative Work of Development Plans" (Paper presented to the ACSP/AESOP Congress, Oxford, July 1991).

52. See C. Hardy, *Understanding Organisation*, 3d ed. (Harmondsworth: Penguin, 1985).

Policy

Reforms as

Arguments

William N. Dunn

The social sciences are an outgrowth of efforts to understand and alleviate practical problems through social reform. The development of social
science disciplines is therefore practice-driven, and not, as is mistakenly
assumed by those who squat in the shade of the natural sciences, a
product of "basic" research. This myth of the basic-to-applied research
cycle, together with derivative misconceptions about the role of "social
engineering," was challenged by Paul Lazarsfeld throughout his career
(Holzner et al. 1977). In his last published book he urged us to acknowledge the ordinary contexts of practical action which continue to drive
the social sciences:

> The argument goes that applied research is radically different from basic
> scientific work and therefore detracts talent and resources from true prog-
> ress in the discipline. This implies a false comparison with the natural
> sciences. It is true that technical engineers could not succeed without the
> knowledge provided by abstract research in mathematics and laboratory
> experiments of the "pure" sciences. But it is misleading to draw an analogy
> between the natural and social sciences. Nowhere in the social realm are
> there unconditional laws and basic theories already well established. Quite
> to the contrary, it is the study of concrete and circumscribed practical
> problem areas that has contributed a good part of the present-day general
> sociological knowledge. Adopting a famous dictum by Lewin, one could
> say that nothing is more conducive to innovation in social theory than
> collaboration on a complex practical problem. (Lazarsfeld and Reitz
> 1975:10)

While the social sciences are thus an outgrowth of attempts to
understand and alleviate practical problems, they nevertheless represent

more than "the growth of ordinary knowledge *writ large*" (Popper 1963:216). The social sciences have built upon but have also transformed ordinary knowledge, frequently in ways that produce unhappy results. For every *Authoritarian Personality* or *American Soldier* there is at least one Project Camelot, while countless apparently innocuous or incompetent applied research efforts have legitimized bureaucratic interests in the name of science. Indeed, the bulk of social science research appears to have made little if any contribution to improvements in social theory or social practice.

We are therefore confronted by a paradox: Those very sciences that owe their origins to practice rarely produce knowledge that enlarges our capacity to improve that practice. For many this paradox is resolved by elevating social scientists at the expense of practitioners, typically by urging that canons of scientific reasoning displace the routines of politics (Bernstein and Freeman 1975). For others the paradox dissolves under the weight of arguments that the social sciences simply yield less usable knowledge than do various forms of interactive problem solving based on common sense, casual empiricism, or thoughtful speculation and analysis (Lindblom and Cohen 1979). Here we are urged to displace the social sciences with ordinary knowledge that "is highly fallible, but we shall call it knowledge even if it is false. As in the case of scientific knowledge, whether it is true or false, knowledge is knowledge to anyone who takes it as a basis for some commitment to action" (Lindblom and Cohen 1979:12).

This radical juxtaposition of science and ordinary knowledge, while punctuating controversies surrounding the definition of *usable knowledge*, obscures important questions: According to what standards do policymakers, social scientists, and other stakeholders in social reform assess the "truth" and "utility" of knowledge (Weiss and Bucuvalas 1980a)? Are such standards properly confined to "threats to validity" or "plausible rival hypotheses" invoked to assess policy experiments (Cook and Campbell 1979)? Can social science theory and research themselves be used to investigate the social origins and practical uses of knowledge that has been certified on the basis of competing standards (Holzner and Marx 1979)? Can we raise these competing standards to an explicit level of consciousness where they may shape a genuinely critical public discourse (Habermas 1975)? Finally, are reforms best viewed as reasoned arguments or debates—that is, as "critical social transactions" aimed at improving knowledge and its social uses (Toulmin et al. 1984)?

In responding to these questions I offer five related claims. First, the metaphor of the "experimenting society" (Campbell 1969, in 1988), because it is still burdened with residues of a positivist philosophy of science, places unnecessarily strict constraints on the range of standards available to assess and certify claims about policy reform. Second, and in contrast, reforms are best viewed as arguments, a metaphor whose roots lie in the everyday social interaction of policymakers, scientists, and citizens at large. When we revisualize reforms as arguments it is no longer possible to make sharp distinctions between "science" and "ordinary knowledge"; nor are we likely to reach the patently false conclusion that knowledge derived from one or the other source is always superior. Third, a transactional model of argument adapted from Stephen Toulmin (1958) provides a conceptual framework which not only accommodates the experimental metaphor—including "threats to validity" and their philosophic justification—but also permits a radical enlargement of standards for assessing and challenging knowledge claims. The transactional model is therefore appropriate as a central organizing construct for a new social science of knowledge applications, because it clarifies the notion of "frames of reference" by providing specific "tests" for assessing the adequacy, relevance, and cogency of knowledge claims. Fourth, and relatedly, these tests may be transformed into threats to usable knowledge; that is, plausible rival hypotheses about the conditions under which knowledge claims should be accepted as a basis of action. Finally, the transactional model supplies the contours of a critical social science of knowledge applications; that is, a social science that uncovers and raises to a level of explicit consciousness those unexamined prior assumptions and implicit standards of assessment that shape and also distort the production and use of knowledge. By making such standards transparent and public, a critical social science of knowledge applications may contribute to an expansion of individual and collective learning capacities, and thus to emancipatory policy reforms.

The Experimenting Society

Among the many perspectives available for exploring the nature of social reforms, Donald Campbell's "experimenting society" (Campbell 1971, in 1988) has justifiably attracted great attention among applied social scientists in the United States. Drawing on analogies to physics, biology, psychology, and other laboratory sciences, this perspective is founded on an evolutionary epistemology which claims that the growth of individual and societal knowledge is a consequence of trial-and-error learning processes involving successive attempts to compare hypotheses with experimentally induced outcomes (Campbell 1959, 1974a). This evolutionary view, partly based on Sir Karl Popper's natural selection epistemology (Popper 1959, 1963), claims that the aim of experiments is to achieve objective knowledge by challenging conventional scientific wisdom and current opinion. While experimentation is "the only available route to cumulative progress" in education and other domains of social reform, it is not a panacea for social and scientific ills; nor is it an inherently superior substitute for well-tested ordinary knowledge that has evolved over many centuries of trial-and-error learning by practitioners (Campbell and Stanley 1963:3–4). Indeed, the growth of ordinary and scientific knowledge is a cumulative product of evolutionary changes in human cognitive capacities for causal reasoning (Campbell 1974; Cook and Campbell 1979). Causation, therefore, is an inherited property of human cognitive evolution and not a special prize reserved for academics.

The experimenting society, while conditioned by ineluctable changes in human cognitive capacities, is nevertheless an active and critical society (Campbell 1971, in 1988). The experimenting society requires a critical posture toward all knowledge, since there are neither essential nor necessary and sufficient causes in nature. This critical posture is embodied in the principle of falsification, where "not yet disproven" points to the impossibility of ruling out all relevant alternative hypotheses (Cook and Campbell 1979). While all data are seen as theory-dependent, thus punctuating subjective properties of all human inquiry, the experimenting society avoids epistemological relativism by positing an external reality, or "nature," against which hypotheses may be tested, notwithstanding the impossibility of fully testing causal claims against that nature. Moreover, causal theories are understood as passive instruments for identifying "nuisance factors" present in contexts of practice; the most valid causal inferences are those involving factors that may be actively manipulated by experimenters. Grounded in ordinary language and everyday interaction, this practical and active theory of causation does not presume full and complete causal explanations, as does basic research in scientific disciplines. Partial explanations suffice. Thus, for example, manipulable causes (e.g., a light switch) may be activated to produce a desired effect (illumination) without understanding theories of electronics or particle physics.

The metaphor of the experimenting society is therefore an extension of an evolutionary critical-realist epistemology, and not, as some critics would have it, a naive emulation of a natural science paradigm based on hypothetico-deductive methodology (Patton 1975, 1978). A critical epistemological posture is evident in the distinction between "trapped" and "experimental" administrators, the latter of whom are urged to advocate reforms "on the basis of the seriousness of the problem rather than the certainty of any one answer and combine this with an emphasis on the need to go on to other attempts at solution should the first one fail" (Campbell 1969, in 1975b:35). While it acknowledges the vicarious, distal, and socially embodied character of knowledge (Campbell 1959, 1988), the experimental metaphor is based on an ontologically realist posture that places primary reliance on experimentally induced outcomes that are independent of the desires of reform-minded social scientists and administrators.

The appropriateness of the experimental metaphor depends in part on our success in establishing that social systems in which reforms are carried out are analogous to the physical systems in which laboratory experiments are conducted. While a major aim of writings on quasi experimentation has been to show that laboratory experiments are not feasible in field settings—that "pure" experiments have been oversold and misrepresented—it is also true that the experimental metaphor retains an objectivist ontological platform appropriate to the study of physical systems. For example, in describing a nested hierarchy of evolutionary learning processes of which science is the most developed, Campbell observes that "what is characteristic of science is that the selective system which weeds out among the variety of conjectures involves deliberate contact with the environment through experiment and quantified prediction, designed so that outcomes quite independent of the preferences of the investigator are possible. It is preeminently this feature that gives science its greater objectivity and its claim to a cumulative increase in the accuracy with which it describes the world" (Campbell 1974a:434).

The characteristic feature of social systems, as distinguished from physical ones, is that they are created, maintained, and changed through symbolically mediated interaction (Holzner 1969). Whereas physical systems are *presumptively* characterized in terms of a stable external reality that *edits* experimental trials independently of the preferences of investigators (Campbell, 1974a:435), social systems are appropriately characterized (again presumptively) in terms of a dynamic external reality that *edits and interprets* experimental trials on the basis of outcomes that are independent of the preferences of some investigators but quite dependent on the preferences of others. Social systems, therefore, cannot be satisfactorily characterized as either objective or subjective entities, or even as both. Social systems, as dialectical entities, are *more than both:*

"Society is a human product. Society is an objective reality. Man is a social product" (Berger and Luckmann 1967:61).

This dialectical claim does not simply affirm that social systems are cultural entities whose symbolic and self-referential properties set them apart from physical ones; nor does it deny that social systems are perceived as objective entities by their members. Rather, it affirms that knowledge of social systems should be based on an understanding of the diverse meanings attributed to reforms by stakeholders who participate in the creation, maintenance, and transformation of humanly objectivated social structures. Policy reforms are therefore symbolically mediated change processes which can be understood only if we uncover the action-motivating reasons that guide efforts to alleviate practical problems.

Therefore, the case for social experimentation as the only "truly scientific" approach to reform (Campbell 1975b:72) stands or falls on the persuasiveness of the claim that experimental data are *not* symbolically mediated—that is, that experimental outcomes constitute the sole source of knowledge that is not determined by the purposes of the experimenter. Campbell asks us to imagine experiments as tribal rituals "meticulously designed to put questions to 'Nature itself' in such a way that neither questioners nor their colleagues nor their superiors can affect the answer. The supplicants set up the altar, pray reverently for the outcome they want, but do not control the outcome" (Campbell 1979b:198).

This tribal analogy, instructive because of its simplicity, raises several difficulties. First, it is unlikely that all tribal cohorts will accept the rule of empirical correspondence as an impartial standard for resolving the problems that originally created a need for experimentation. In fact, it is not the reasoned acceptance of this or any other scientific norm that alone lends authority to experimental data; also relevant are the diverse social sanctions, including disgrace and expulsion, that accompany the process of competitive experimental replication in scientific communities. "This competitive scrutiny is indeed the main source of objectivity in sciences . . . and epitomizes an ideal of democratic practice in both judicial and legislative procedures" (Campbell 1975b:80).

The social organization of inquiry implied by this ideal-typical community of experimenters, even if it did reflect the practice of physicists (cf. Kuhn 1971), fails to capture the behavior of policymakers, practitioners, social scientists, and other stakeholders in social reform. The key participants in social reforms share neither the standards of appraisal nor the incentive structure of this ideal-typical community. For this reason experimental outcomes are unavoidably mediated by diverse standards of appraisal which are unevenly distributed among stake-holders in policy reforms.

Thus, claims about the appropriateness of the experimental meta-phor are persuasive only if the nature of experimental results automat-ically forecloses options for symbolically mediated interpretation. While we might grant that experimental results "certainly are not speaking for one's hopes and wishes" (Campbell 1979b:198), neither do they speak for themselves. Thus, for example, experimenters might share norms of competitive replication and experience disappointment with outcomes that run counter to their preferences but nevertheless resist any inference that experimental results actually disconfirm a favored theory of reform. A principal reason for this resistance is that even well-socialized experi-menters cannot be expected to share the same theoretical framework that dictated the choice of the particular (disconfirmed) reform as a promis-ing experimental intervention. Social theories, unlike physical ones, are difficult to falsify with experimental data because the interpretation of such data is mediated by the assumptions, frames of reference, and ideol-ogies of social scientists and other stakeholders in reform.

The presence of symbolically mediated experimental outcomes is precisely what is at issue in policy reforms whose aim is to alleviate problems that have been described as ill structured (Mitroff 1974), squishy (Strauch 1976), or messy (Ackoff 1974). Ill-structured problems are those where the main difficulty lies in defining the nature of the problem rather than determining through selective experimental inter-ventions the most effective reform to alleviate it. Here the primary sources of invalidity are not those *first-order* threats to internal, external, construct and statistical conclusion validity detailed by Campbell and his colleagues (Campbell and Stanley 1963; Cook and Campbell 1979) but *second-order* threats that call into question the appropriateness of prob-lem definitions that create the need for experimental interventions and their assessment in terms of standard (first-order) threats to validity.

Second-order threats transcend or go beyond first-order threats (history, maturation, regression, instability, etc.) by providing meta-criteria against which the formulation of a problem—as distinguished from constituent causal inferences that represent a solution within the boundaries of that problem—may be assessed and challenged. Second-order threats are sometimes defined as conceptual errors by juxtaposing the formulation of the wrong problem (Type III error) to setting statistical confidence limits too high (Type I error) or too low (Type II error) in testing the null hypothesis (Kimball 1957; Raiffa 1968; Mitroff and Sagasti 1973). Since threats to validity have been explicitly invoked as a challenge to the error of misplaced statistical precision (Campbell and Stanley 1963:7), it is desirable to devise new terms that do not hinge on the dichotomy of errorful calibration (Type I and II errors) and errorful conceptualization (Type III error). Accordingly, first-order errors (E1) involve the choice of the less valid of two or more causal inferences, while second-order errors (E2) involve the selection of the less appropriate of two or more world views, ideologies, frames of reference, or problem definitions when the more appropriate one should have been selected (Mitroff and Sagasti 1973; Dunn 1988b, 1993:ch. 5).

Confronted by an ill-structured problem, the reform-minded administrator or social scientist might use "multiple measures of independent imperfection" (Campbell and Fiske 1959; see also Webb et al. 1966) to ensure that measures are responsive to the diverse aims of stakeholders. Further, "the loyal opposition should be allowed to add still other indicators, with the political process and adversary argument challenging both validity and relative importance, with social science methodologists testifying for both parties, and with the basic records kept public and under bipartisan audit." (Campbell 1975b:80). These adversary procedures are relevant only when stakeholders cannot arrive at a common definition of *reform*. Yet to justify a reform "on the basis of the seriousness of the problem rather than the certainty of any one answer" (Campbell 1975a:35) begs the question: On the basis of what standards are we to assess the appropriateness of the problem? First-order threats do not help to answer this question, since they are relevant and applicable only within a given problem frame. Required are second-order threats for critically challenging the appropriateness of the problem frame itself. To confuse these two levels is to violate a basic logical axiom: "Whatever involves *all* of a collection must not be one of the collection" (Whitehead and Russell 1910:101, cited in Watzlawick et al. 1974:6).

Thus, while threats to validity provide a critical mechanism for reducing the probability of first-order causal errors (E1), they do not deal satisfactorily with second-order conceptual errors (E2). The experimental metaphor acknowledges the priority of pattern identification over knowledge of details, but only at the level of first-order causal errors: "Qualitative, common-sense knowing of wholes and patterns provides the enveloping context necessary for the interpretation of particulate quantitative data" (Campbell 1974b:3). Thus, the experimental metaphor calls for the integration of qualitative and quantitative standards for assessing and challenging knowledge claims. Yet this general plea simply exhorts social scientists to recognize the dependence of quantitative on qualitative knowing; for example, to recognize that several threats to validity (e.g., history) are based on commonsense knowing (Campbell 1974b:15). Even here the loose translation of qualitative knowing into specific threats to validity excludes or ignores many varieties of qualitative knowing, including several forms of ethical and practical reasoning that are appropriate for understanding purposive social behavior (see von Wright 1971). In short, qualitative knowing is not explicitly, formally, and systematically incorporated into the critical methodological repertoire of social experimentation.

Jurisprudence as Metaphor

Any metaphor of policy reform should be assessed according to its capacity "to produce satisfactory explanations of the type of events which it investigates, rather than its success or lack of success in getting results by the methods of natural science" (Levinson 1966:144; Dunn and Fozouni 1976). Because reforms are symbolically mediated and purposive social processes aimed at changing the structure and functioning of some social system, they necessarily involve outcomes that are valuative as well as factual in nature. The success of reforms therefore depends on a rationally motivated consensus that some projected future social state is both possible and desirable. In turn, any applied social science that seeks to critically assess and improve the process of reform must address competing ethical as well as explanatory hypotheses (see MacRae 1976a; Fischer 1986; Alker 1988). For this reason reform is appropriately viewed as a process of reasoned argument and debate where competing standards for assessing the adequacy of knowledge claims include, but are not limited to, rules for making valid causal inferences. Here the appropriate metaphors are drawn from jurisprudence (Toulmin 1958), law (Levine and Rosenberg 1979), forensics (Brock et al. 1973; Brown 1976), and rhetoric (House 1980; Majone 1989), disciplines in which causal inferences play an important but nonexhaustive role.

The appropriateness of the jurisprudential metaphor becomes evident when we consider standards for appraising knowledge actually applied in the course of policy reforms. In the field of evaluation research Edward Suchman (1972) alerts us to the pervasiveness of experimental outcomes mediated by the worldviews, ideologies, and frames of reference of stakeholders in reform. Collectively described as "pseudoevaluation," these forms of symbolic mediation include the selective use of data to make a reform appear worthwhile ("eyewash"), the suppression of data that runs counter to the preferences of reformers ("whitewash"), the use of data to subvert a reform ("submarine"), the ritualistic collection of data on a reform for purposes unconnected with its consequences ("posture"), and the use of data to delay reform itself ("postponement"). Similarly, Martin Rein and Sheldon White (1977) call attention to several latent goals of government-sponsored policy research, including the containment, subversion, and policing of social reforms. Given the complexity of social problems, scientifically popular recommendations for improving the production and use of applied social research—including more rigorous research designs, better sampling procedures, and administrative centralization—are likely to be marginally effective, superfluous, or mystifying (Rein and White 1977:244–50).

These observations on the latent goals of applied social research suggest that we should begin with the *practice* of assessing knowledge claims made in the course of reforms, hoping to uncover concepts and standards of assessment which might later be used to develop theories of knowledge production and use. This aim can be facilitated by viewing reforms as reasoned arguments rather than as experiments that put questions to "Nature Itself." Arguments are like lawsuits, while conclusions are similar to claims put forth in court. Conflicts among stakeholders are analogous to cases in law where disputes are settled by invoking standards appropriate to different contexts; for example, criminal or civil disputes. Whereas the aim of jurisprudence is to study the variety of concepts and procedures used to resolve legal claims, the aim of the applied social sciences is to investigate concepts and procedures used to argue and settle practical claims. The applied social sciences may therefore be described as "generalized jurisprudence," or, alternatively, as "jurisprudence writ large" (cf. Toulmin 1958:7).

The jurisprudential metaphor is particularly appropriate for investigating policy reforms because the data or evidence introduced in a given case are only one of several elements necessary to make a successful claim. Equally important are the standards of appraisal employed to interpret data. Despite the belief that the applied social sciences produce conclusive fact and proof, "they are instead engaged in producing inconclusive evidence and argument. Problem complexity denies the possibility of proof and reduces the pursuit of fact to the pursuit of those selective facts which, if appropriately developed, constitute evidence in support of relevant argument" (Lindblom and Cohen 1979:81). Argumentation is therefore a social process in which all data or evidence are symbolically mediated. Whereas proof, demonstration, or validation hold that truth is directly and immediately attainable, argumentation sees truth as a social construction (Phillips 1973), a product of natural social comparison processes. "Put analogically, arguments are naturally occurring corollaries to research contexts. . . . It is rather as if we were to stand back and watch while our subjects framed their own hypotheses, selected methodological principles most appropriate to the hypotheses, utilized techniques appropriate to both, and conducted their own research act . . . [A]rguments give us more information than other kinds of research" (Willard 1980b:9–10).

The jurisprudential metaphor is closely tied to classical and modern philosophical traditions in which reason serves a practical and critical function in assessing knowledge claims. The jurisprudential metaphor "helps to keep in the centre of the picture the *critical* function of reason. The rules of logic may not be tips or generalizations; they none the less apply to men and their arguments—not in the way that laws of psychology or maxims of method apply, but rather as *standards of achievement*. . . . A sound argument, a well-grounded or firmly-backed claim, is one which will stand up to criticism, one for which a case can be presented coming up to the standard required *if* it is to deserve a favourable verdict" (Toulmin 1958:8). The jurisprudential metaphor thus emphasizes that argumentation is a process of rational advocacy in which stakeholders engage in the *competitive reconstruction* of knowledge claims. This competitive reconstruction, in contrast to the competitive replication of experiments, leads toward a pragmatic and dialectical conception of truth in which social discourse plays a reflective and critical role in producing new knowledge. Knowledge is no longer based on deductive certainty or empirical correspondence but on the relative adequacy of knowledge claims embedded in ongoing social processes.

A Transactional Model of Argument

Toulmin has operationalized the jurisprudential metaphor in the form of a structural model of argument (Toulmin 1958; Toulmin et al. 1984). Extensions of this model to issues of public policy have recognized that the growing complexity of social problems demands increased reliance on reasoned persuasion rather than on formal logical certainty and have called for systematic learning from practitioners as a major component of creative theory building in the applied social sciences (e.g., Brock et al. 1973; House 1977, 1980; Kelly 1980). In developing a reflective methodology for solving ill-structured problems Ian Mitroff and Richard Mason (1981) have linked the structural model to a dialectical conception of knowledge (also see Alker 1988) and have attempted to develop appropriate methodologies that may be employed by policymakers in concrete settings.

In his critique of positivistic ethical theories Jürgen Habermas (1975:107) employs Toulmin's distinction between analytic and substantial arguments to argue that the growth of knowledge takes place through the rationally motivating force of substantial arguments; that is, arguments that abandon criteria of conclusiveness, demonstrativeness, necessity, certainty, justification, or validity and rely instead on rational standards of achievement which enhance the persuasiveness of knowledge claims in particular social contexts (Toulmin 1958:234). Substantial arguments "are based on logical inferences, but they are not exhausted in deductive systems of statements. Substantial arguments serve to redeem or to criticize validity claims, whether the claims to truth implicit in assertions or the claims to correctness connected with norms (of action or evaluation) or implied in recommendations and warnings. They have the force to convince the participants in a discourse of a validity claim, that is, *to provide rational grounds for* the recognition of validity claims" (Habermas 1975:107; emphasis in original).

Toulmin's model of argument, since it accentuates the critical and socially transacted properties of knowledge production and use, is most appropriately described as a transactional model. The transactional model is important for the applied social sciences because, first, it provides a visual representation or structural schema which may be used to systematically map arguments offered by applied social scientists, policymakers, and other stakeholders in social reform. Second, the transactional model permits and even compels a reflective and critical examination of assumptions that constitute the worldview, ideology, or frame of reference of stakeholders who advance and contest knowledge claims. Third, the transactional model may be extended and elaborated to yield a typology of standards, rules, or tests for assessing and challenging the truth and utility of knowledge claims (see Weiss and Bucuvalas 1980b; Holzner and Marx 1979). This same typology also yields a classification of threats to usable knowledge; that is, rival hypotheses about the adequacy, appropriateness, and cogency of knowledge claims. Finally, the transactional model affirms that processes of knowledge production and use are symbolic or communicative actions involving two or more parties who reciprocally affect the acceptance and rejection of knowledge claims through argument and persuasion. Thus, knowledge is not exchanged, translated, or transferred; it is transacted by negotiating the truth, relevance, and cogency of knowledge claims.

The transactional model contains six elements: data (D), claim (C), warrant (W), backing (B), rebuttal (R), and qualifier (Q). Together these elements provide a visual representation or structural schema that may be used to map arguments. The first triad of elements parallel those of the classical syllogism: minor premise (D), major premise (W), and conclusion (C). The model is nevertheless designed as a challenge to the classical syllogism and other analytic arguments. For this reason Toulmin introduces a second triad of elements: backing (B), rebuttal (R), and qualifier (Q). The backing (B), which consists of additional data, claims, or entire arguments, certifies the assumption expressed in the warrant and is introduced only when the status of the warrant is in doubt. In analytic arguments the backings of warrants are tautological, since they include information conveyed in the claim itself. By contrast, the backings of warrants in substantial arguments do not contain information conveyed in the claim (Toulmin 1958:125). Practical arguments offered in the course of a social reform are seldon if ever analytic: "If the purpose of an argument is to establish conclusions about which we are not entirely confident by relating them back to other information about which we have greater assurance, it begins to be a little doubtful whether any genuine, practical argument could *ever* be properly analytical" (Toulmin 1958:127; emphasis in original).

The two remaining elements of the structural schema are the rebuttal and qualifier. The rebuttal (R) performs both a retrospective and anticipatory role by specifying conditions under which the adequacy or relevance of a knowledge claim may be challenged. Finally, the qualifier (Q) expresses the degree of cogency or force attached to the claim and is typically expressed with such terms as "definitely," "very probably," or "at the 1 percent level of significance (p = 0.01)."

The structural schema provides an explicit visual representation of these six elements and their role in making practical inferences, much in the same way that symbols used to depict different types of experimental, quasi-experimental, and pre-experimental designs provide a visual image of the role of independent and dependent variables in making causal inferences (Campbell and Stanley 1963). In contrast to experimental design notation, the structural schema surfaces and raises to a level of explicit consciousness the assumptions and presuppositions that provide rational backing for substantial arguments.

This critical function of the structural schema can be illustrated by borrowing from Campbell (1975b) a well-known example of quasi-experimental reform. Following record high traffic fatalities in 1955, the governor of Connecticut implemented a crackdown on speeding violators. After one year there were 284 traffic deaths, a 12.3 percent reduction from the record high of 324 deaths in 1955. On the bais of these data (D) the governor offered the following claim (C): "With the saving of 40 lives in 1956, a reduction of 12.3% from the 1955 motor vehicle death toll, we can say that the program is definitely worthwhile" (Campbell 1975b:75–76). Figure 1 illustrates the governor's argument, including suppressed warrants and backings and rebuttals based on threats to the validity of causal inferences (Campbell and Stanley 1963; Campbell 1975b).

The transactional model compels a reflective or critical posture toward the presuppositions of knowledge claims, whether practical or theoretical. For this reason it transcends overdrawn and facile distinctions between "professional social inquiry" and "ordinary knowledge" (Lindblom and Cohen 1979), viewing both as potentially ideological in the classic sense of beliefs that originate in unexamined assumptions. The transactional model can also assist in transforming the empirico-analytic and hermeneutic sciences into critical ones (see Habermas 1971) because the model forces the inspection of causal and ethical assumptions, as well as their underlying backings, as part of a social process of interpreting qualitative and quantitative data.

Thus, the claim that "the crackdown on speeding was definitely worthwhile" might withstand all threats to validity but lack persuasive force, and one or more stakeholders might question the adequacy of underlying causal assumptions ("strict enforcement of speeding laws caused traffic fatalities to fall") or moral principles ("Human life is always worth preserving"). If further support is required, certain axioms of economic theory ("The greater the cost of an alternative the less likely it will be pursued") might be introduced as backing for the warrant, as might ostensibly self-evident moral principles (human survival). The claim here is not that these particular axioms and principles are necessarily adequate, since they are likely to be challenged by stakeholders who hold competing theories, worldviews, ideologies, and frames of reference. The point, rather, is that adaptations of the empirico-analytic sciences (e.g., Cook and Campbell 1979) and extensions of hermeneutics (e.g., Patton 1975, 1978) do not address such questions in a systematic, critical, and self-reflective manner.

The transactional model thus accommodates all potentially relevant types of claims and forms of argument. Attention is not confined to descriptive and explanatory claims—the standard and exclusive focus of

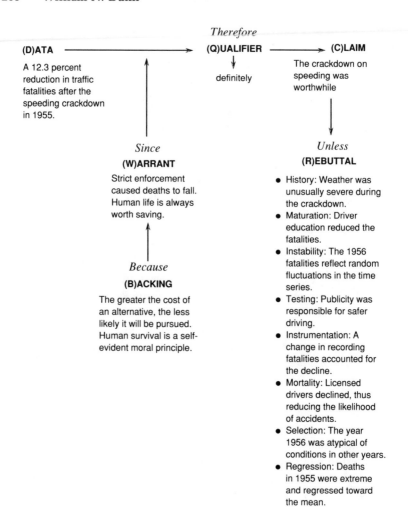

Figure 1. Structural Schema Applied to the Connecticut Crackdown on Speeding (adapted from Campbell [1975b] and Dunn [1993]).

the empirico-analytic and hermeneutic sciences—but extends to claims that have ethical content insofar as their aim is to evaluate or advocate action. Further, arguments are not limited to a particular causal form (for example, deductive-nomological explanation) but include other forms of causal reasoning such as those represented by quasi-naturalistic (historical), quasi-teleological (cybernetic), and teleological (practical) explanations (see von Wright 1971). This capacity to distinguish diverse forms of argument and types of claims clarifies a number of methodological inadequacies in the applied social sciences, including the pervasive misconception that "evaluation research" evaluates and the tendency among public policy scholars (e.g., Weiss 1991) to view claims that advocate or recommend courses of action as emotive, ideological, or political appeals that are devoid of rational content. As Laurence Tribe (1972), Martin Rein (1976), and Duncan MacRae, Jr. (1976a) recognize, this tendency reflects the implicit positivistic assumptions of policy analysis as an applied social science discipline that ignores or denigrates ethical discourse.

A related advantage of the model is its capacity to reveal and make explicit the processes of reasoning used to make knowledge claims. Whereas applied social scientists and practitioners frequently suppress steps in the process of reasoning from data to claim—for example, by claiming that coefficients of association or so-called predictive equations speak for themselves as a demonstration of causal patterns or sequences—the transactional model raises implicit causal and ethical hypotheses alike. This critical function is by no means limited to hypothesis testing, since the model may be used to reveal paradigms, worldviews, and frames of reference that unite epistemic communities (Holzner and Marx 1979), establish the boundaries of disciplinary matrices (Webber 1980), and distort the definition of social problems (Gregg et al. 1979).

By distinguishing analytic and substantial arguments, the transactional model provides the applied social sciences with a framework and methodology for transcending pseudoethical disputes whose resolution appears superficially to lie in greater logical consistency or better empirical data. In analytic arguments the major premise or warrant is taken for granted, and the main task is to demonstrate that conclusions or claims follow from the data with deductive certainty. Yet it is substantial arguments, and not analytic ones, that characterize the bulk of knowledge claims put forth in the course of policy reforms. For this reason disputes frequently turn on the presuppositions used to back warrants, and not on surface assumptions or data such as those found in authoritative moral principles or empirical observations that have been validated through intersubjective agreement.

It is therefore insufficient to treat ethical hypotheses solely in terms of standards appropriate for analytic arguments; for example, metacriteria of logical consistency, clarity, and generality (MacRae 1976a:90–98) or basic postulates of moral reasoning (L. Gewirth 1979). Much less is it proper to confine ethical discourse to standards of appraisal appropriate for the empirical study of social determinants of knowledge or its applications (Holzner and Marx 1979). The structural model, since it raises substantial arguments to a level of explicit consciousness, penetrates the rational content of ethical and nonethical assumptions which individually and jointly motivate the acceptance and rejection of knowledge claims.

Finally, the transactional model provides concepts and procedures of argument assessment that are reconstructable and public. The structural schema may be used retrospectively to describe and evaluate different types of claims and arguments, but it can also be used prospectively. While it is not possible "to list in advance the ingredients of a convincing argument" (Phillips 1973:178), the structural model can nevertheless be used prospectively to design arguments that withstand the diverse challenges or rebuttals that are commonplace in debates about reform. Mason, Mitroff, and Vincent Barabba (Mason and Mitroff 1981a; Mitroff et al. 1985), for example, report the use of the transactional model to conduct an interactive dialectical debate among stakeholders engaged in resolving problems of public statistics and corporate planning. Their interactive computer-assisted methodology not only permits stakeholders to attach ordinal plausibility values to each element of an argument and the argument as a whole but, more important, enables them to challenge and revise assumptions in the course of a reflective debate. A similar dialectical methodology, also based on the transactional model, has been used to select maximally usable performance measures in the domain of evaluation research (Dunn et al. 1981). The aim of these procedures is not to "scientize" the model of argument but to enhance prospects for its efficient use, recognizing that the capacity for reasoned debate and reflective understanding is a scarce resource.

Testing Knowledge Claims

Claims about policy reform are products of frames of reference; that is, they are sets of systemically related assumptions that provide standards for appraising knowledge claims. A central component of frames of reference is what Burkart Holzner and John Marx (1979:103–11) call reality or truth tests, and which Carol Weiss and Michael Bucuvalas (1980a) have investigated in the form of truth tests and utility tests. Truth tests, as Holzner and Evelyn Fisher write, are "decision points concerning evidence; the grounds for accepting or rejecting truth claims include . . . empirical as well as formal rational tests. Pragmatic tests rest on proof of workability . . . there are other tests of varying stringency and reliance on trust or authority" (Holzner and Fisher 1979:233). By contrast, utility or relevance tests are decision points concerning the delineation of an appropriate domain of inquiry or action. The basis for accepting or rejecting a relevance claim is the "potential significance of an item or line of inquiry . . . with regard to the inquirer's cognitive interests" (Holzner and Fisher 1979:233).

Concepts of truth and relevance tests pose practically and theoretically important distinctions. Nevertheless, it is now unclear how such tests are actually distributed among stakeholders in policy reforms and, indeed, whether the existence and functions of such tests can be investigated empirically. Available typologies of such tests contain ambiguities that impede directed empirical research. Pointing to the elusive nature of "relevance" and "utility," Holzner and Fisher (1979:235) observe that "questions remain about the exact manner in which some information comes to the attention of a person and how it is sifted." Weiss and Bucuvalas (1980a), while calling for a new sociology of knowledge applications, call attention the complexity of issues surrounding the concept of frame of reference and remind us of the many conceptual and methodological limitations facing those who wish to investigate the impact of truth tests and utility tests on individual and collective decisions.

The transactional model may be extended to generate a typology of knowledge claims and arguments which clarifies and specifies concepts of truth and relevance. Knowledge claims may be classified according to the explicit or implicit purposes of knowledge claimants or their challengers. Wayne Brockriede and Douglas Ehninger (1960), drawing from the fields of forensics and semiotics, classify claims into four types: definitive, designative, evaluative, and advocative. The purpose of definitive claims is to provide knowledge about the appropriate *definition* of some object (What is it?), whereas that of designative claims is to supply knowledge about *observed regularities* (Does it exist?). In turn, the aim of evaluative claims is to provide knowledge about the *value* of an event or object (Of what worth is it?), while the purpose of advocative claims is to supply knowledge about *policy* (What should be done?).

Relevance tests are closely related to these four types of claims. If relevance tests are decision points concerning the delineation of an appropriate domain of inquiry or action, policymakers and practitioners appear to be predisposed toward tests of relevance that reflect an interest in knowledge about what courses of action to pursue to resolve problems (advocative claims). Discipline-based social scientists, by contrast, are generally oriented toward tests of relevance that reflect an interest in definitions (e.g., definitive claims about poverty, health, or achievement) and in observed regularities in society and nature (e.g., designative claims about the sources of social inequality). These divergent purposes underlie contrasts between policy research and discipline-based research (Coleman 1972), distinctions between "macronegative" and "micropositive" research findings (Williams 1971), divisions within the "two-communities" theory of knowledge utilization (Caplan 1979), and the pattern of factor loadings reported by Weiss and Bucuvalas (1980a) in their study of the frames of reference of mental health policymakers. In turn, evaluative claims often reflect tests of relevance shared primarily by philosophers and social critics; for example, those who see in policy analysis an ideology in disguise (Tribe 1972). In each case the purposes of knowledge, as reflected in these four types of claims, affirm or diminish the relevance of that knowledge to different stakeholders.

The application of a relevance test does not guarantee that a knowledge claim will be regarded as sufficiently cogent or forceful. Tests of cogency are dependent on the relative force expected of a claim in particular circumstances. Hence, an advocative claim accepted as relevant to the aims of a particular stakeholder will not necessarily be viewed as cogent. Tests of cogency, which are an extension of Toulmin's qualifier, are evident in the practice of different professions. For example, members of the legal and medical professions use similar tests of relevance but different cogency tests (cf. Holzner and Fisher 1979:235–36). Members of the legal profession typically employ a conservative cogency test (qualifier) for knowledge claims offered in criminal cases: defendants are presumed innocent until proven guilty. By contrast, members of the medical profession often use a liberal test of cogency for claims surrounding the treatment of illness: patients are presumed to be ill, and are treated, until proven otherwise. In the first case the problem is to avoid "false positives," while in the second it is to avoid "false negatives." In other cases cogency and relevance interact—for example, when school officials set stringent reliability thresholds in validating the results of achievement batteries used to recommend students for jobs or further education but apply liberal tests of cogency when assessing the effects of existing curricula on student achievement scores.

The appraisal of knowledge claims is not exhausted by tests of relevance and cogency. Knowledge claims, apart from their relevance, derive force or cogency from truth tests. Truth tests may be represented in terms of different sets of assumptions and underlying presuppositions used to transform data into claims in a practical or theoretical argument. Truth tests are standards for appraising the *adequacy* of knowledge claims; for example, by challenging the causal assumptions that underlie a claim. By contrast, tests of cogency and relevance are standards for appraising the requisite *force* and contextual *appropriateness* of a claim, respectively. Typically, tests of adequacy and relevance are discrete assumptions, standards, or rules, while tests of cogency are best represented in terms of the varying levels of force required of a claim. Knowledge claims that are adequate and cogent may be irrelevant, while claims that are relevant may lack adequacy and cogency alike. For example, government-sponsored program evaluations may be regarded as relevant to the aims of reform-minded social scientists but nevertheless lack adequacy and cogency when assessed according to standards of research quality generally accepted by social scientists (Bernstein and Freeman 1975).

Whereas tests of relevance and cogency appear to be comparatively simple, truth tests are complex. Many options for classifying truth tests are available in the writings of philosophers, anthropologists, sociologists, and other social observers and critics. For example, Charles Sanders Peirce's contrasts among alternative methods of "fixing belief" (see Buchler 1955) and Bronislaw Malinowski's essays on science, magic, and religion (Malinowski 1948) point to a range of truth tests used to assess the adequacy of knowledge claims. Similarly, W. P. Montague (1925) and Walter Wallace (1971) distinguish alternative modes for generating and testing the truth of statements about the world, modes that differ along three dimensions: the status of knowledge producers, the use of approved methods to produce knowledge, and the reliance on observations as a check on knowledge claims.

The experimental metaphor, as we have seen, places primary reliance on the correspondence of claims to a presumed stable external reality and secondary reliance on procedures for determining the coherence of such claims among multiple experimenters (Cook and Campbell 1979). Authority is also important because claims are partly certified on the basis of their having been derived from a learning process (scientific experimentation) that is believed to be unique in its penetration of a stable and objective external reality (Campbell 1974a). The danger is that (necessarily) presumptive ontological claims about what is real or natural may improperly authenticate or certify epistemological claims about what is true (Michalos 1981). The ontology of objectivism, when used as a justification or warrant for science, may also result in the denigration of ethics on the grounds that only science produces corrigible knowledge claims (A. Gewirth, 1960).

The limitation of these schemata is that they do not incorporate a variety of potentially important truth tests that reflect alternative modes of explanation (von Wright 1971), different knowledge-constitutive interests (Habermas 1971), and competing standards for assessing ethical knowledge (MacRae 1976a). Any provisional classification of truth tests should therefore permit distinctions between naturalistic, quasi-naturalistic, and practical modes of explanation; enable distinctions among standards of knowledge adequacy appropriate for the empirico-analytic, hermeneutic, and critical social sciences; and foster an open consideration of possibilities for testing ethical hypotheses.

The classification of truth tests shown in Table 1 attempts to build on these diverse concerns with standards of knowledge adequacy. In contrast to Brockriede and Ehninger (1960), who employ Toulmin's model to classify artistic or rhetorical proofs, argument is used here as a unifying construct to classify standards of knowledge adequacy. This extension of the transactional model proceeds from a recognition that the decisive element of most contested knowledge claims is not evidence or data, but the underlying standards of appraisal which warrant the transformation of data into claims. Data themselves are rarely conclusive; most social theories are therefore radically underdetermined by data (see Mary Hesse 1980).

Equally important for our purposes, contexts of practical action appear to be radically underdetermined by generalizable standards or rules. As Karin Knorr (1981) argues, practical action is indexical and indeterminate insofar as "rules and decision criteria, and more generally definitions of the situation, are interpreted in context . . . it is the concrete, local translation of rules or decision criteria which determine the selections that are made, and which subsequently shape the outcomes of these selections." At the same time the underdetermination thesis, whether applied to theory or to practice, does not entail the conclusion that knowledge claims are properly explained solely in terms of externally imposed "sociological" factors (Larry Laudan 1981), since diverse standards or rules for certifying and challenging the adequacy of knowledge claims may hold as much or more explanatory import as do variables such as social structure (see Laudan 1977).

Truth tests may be classified according to the general and specific functions they perform in knowledge transactions. These general functions are (1) *empirico-analytic:* knowledge adequacy is certified by assumptions about the logical consistency of axioms, laws, propositions, hypotheses, or principles and/or their correspondence to empirically observed regularities; (2) *interpretive:* knowledge adequacy is certified by assumptions about the action motivating significance of purposes,

Table 1. Classification of Truth Tests

Type of warrant or backing	Function of truth test
Empirico-analytic	
Causal	A nomic connection (e.g., Boyle's Law) certifies that events described in data are causally related.
Quasi causal	A nomiclike connection (e.g., Toynbee's historical cycles) certifies that events described in data are causally related.
Typological	A typology (e.g., Jung's theory of psychological types) certifies that events, actions, or persons described in data are members of some class.
Representational	A representational rule (e.g., the Central Limit Theorem) certifies that events, objects, or persons described in data are typical or representative of some wider population.
Analogical	An analogy or metaphor (e.g., the servomechanisms of systems theory) certifies that relations among events, objects, or persons described in data are similar to those contained in the metaphor or analogy.
Interpretive	
Teleological	A statement about individual purposes, intentions, motivations, or reasons (e.g., goals of policymakers or social scientists) certifies that actions described in data are causally related to such purposes.
Quasi teleological	A nomic connection (e.g., Ashby's law of requisite variety) certifies that collective actions described in data are causally related to collective purposes.
Pragmatic	
Clinical	A symptomatology (e.g., the F scale of the Minnesota Multiphasic Personality Inventory) cer-

Table 1. *Cont.*

Type of warrant or backing	Function of truth test
	tifies that symptoms described in data are indicative of an abnormal or normal, deviant or healthy state.
Comparative	A parallel case or experience (e.g., socialized medicine in the United Kingdom or Planning, Program, and Budgeting Systems in the Defense Department) certifies that events or actions described in data are similar in their effects to those of the parallel case.
Authoritative	
Personal	The achieved or ascribed status of knowledge producers (e.g., gurus, scientists, or expert commissions) certifies that information described in data is accurate, precise, or reliable.
Ideological	An established belief or doctrine (e.g., scientism, capitalism, socialism) certifies that ideas described in data are orthodox.
Ethical	A norm, value, or principle (e.g., Rawls's principle of justice or the Pareto criterion) certifies that actions described in data are justified.
Methodological	The use of an approved method (e.g., path analysis or phenomenology) certifies that information described in data is accurate, precise, reliable, and valid.
Critical	
Ontological	A presumption about the nature or reality of valid knowledge (e.g., objectivism or subjectivism) certifies that ideas described in data are true or right.
Emancipatory	A presumption about the liberation of human potential (e.g., self-actualization, Theory Y, *Homo laborans*) certifies that ideas described in data are true or right.

intentions, reasons, or motivations; (3) *pragmatic:* knowledge adequacy is certified by assumptions about the effectiveness of past experiences in producing desired outcomes in parallel contexts; (4) *authoritative:* knowledge adequacy is certified by assumptions about the achieved or ascribed status of knowledge producers, the orthodoxy of knowledge, or the use of approved methods; and (5) *critical:* knowledge adequacy is certified by assumptions about the consequences of such knowledge in emancipating individuals and collectivities from unexamined or tacit beliefs that impede the realization of human potential.

Tests of truth, relevance, and cogency are distinct but interrelated standards for appraising knowledge claims. These three general classes of tests, together with specific variants, govern the adequacy, appropriateness, and requisite force of knowledge that offers solutions for practical problems. Truth, relevance, and cogency tests are potentially independent; the force of a knowledge claim (cogency test) depends on prior assessments of relevance and adequacy. The reverse is generally not true, because various tests of cogency (for example, tests of statistical significance) seldom establish the relevance or adequacy of knowledge claims. These generalizations and the typology on which they are based are merely hypotheses. With Weiss and Bucuvalas (1980a), this essay does not investigate these and other components of frames of reference in concrete settings of practice.

Threats to Usable Knowledge

In further extending the transactional model we may view threats to knowledge claims as rebuttals (R) to practical and theoretical arguments which affirm, explicitly or implicitly, the adequacy, cogency, or relevance of knowledge. In contrast to other approaches that encourage the separate exploration of rival hypotheses about causation (e.g., Cook and Campbell 1979), or those dealing with ethical norms (e.g., MacRae 1976a), the function of threats to knowledge adequacy, relevance, and cogency is to challenge both the substantial and the analytic bases of empirical and normative claims. Therefore, while threats to adequacy, relevance, and cogency provide alternative interpretations of the same data or evidence, they are not limited to assessments of the validity of causal inferences.

Table 2 summarizes three classes of threats to usable knowledge. The majority of these threats reflect methodological and practical issues not addressed by Donald Campbell and Julian Stanley (1963) and

Table 2. Threats to Usable Knowledge

Class or type	Representative threat
Threats to cogency	
Misjudged cogency	Setting statistical confidence limits too high (Type I error) or too low (Type II error) in testing the null hypothesis
Misplaced cogency	Correctly setting statistical confidence limits for the wrong problem (Type III error)
Threats to relevance	
Misplaced relevance	Production of cogent knowledge claims that are relevant to the wrong purpose
Untimely relevance	Production of cogent and relevant knowledge claims too late
Threats to adequacy	
Misplaced adequacy	Use of the less appropriate of two or more classes of truth tests when, instead, a more appropriate truth test should be employed
Subjectivity	Use of traditional causal test when explanation should be supplemented or replaced with a causal test based on subjectively meaningful action
Reflexivity	Use of quasi-causal test without recognition that social processes are subject to human reflection, initiative, and control
Misclassification	Use of typological test results to place events, actions, or persons into wrong class
Misrepresentation	Use of less appropriate of two or more representational tests, whether statistical or theoretical
Perspectivity	Use of analogical test as literal surrogate rather than perspective or metaphor
Objectivity	Use of teleological test when explanation should be supplemented or replaced by quasi-

Table 2 (*Cont.*)

Class or type	Representative threat
	causal test which identifies humanly objectivated but unreflected lawlike regularities
Clinical Spuriousness	Use of clinical test involving a set of symptoms which are less appropriate diagnostic or treatment indicators than another set of symptoms
Misplaced comparison	Use of comparative test when two or more cases are not similar
Counterauthentication	Use of personal, ideological, ethical, or methodological test when some other person, doctrine, norm, or procedure is more qualified, orthodox, fair, or scientifically sanctioned
Substantiality	Use of a (necessarily) presumptive ontological claim to certify epistemological or ethical claims when, instead, such claims are properly argued on substantial grounds
Misplaced reflexivity	Claims about the emancipatory role of self-reflection and reasoned discourse are treated as if they refer to concrete contexts of practice when, instead, they are unrelated to ongoing practices

Thomas Cook and Campbell (1979) in their list of classes of threats to the internal, external, construct, and statistical conclusion validity of causal inferences. Indeed, these validity threats are exclusively oriented toward standards of adequacy and relevance which are causal and designative, respectively. The one exception to this exclusive concentration on causal and designative standards is "irrelevant responsiveness of measures," a threat to external validity in which the imperfect validity of measures in adequately representing experimental outcomes *valued* according to conflicting standards held by diverse stakeholders is overcome by multiple operationism and triangulation (Campbell 1975b:79–80; Campbell and Fiske 1959; Webb et al. 1966). This threat to validity implies an interpretive test that is not easily reconciled with an experimentalist platform which contends that outcomes should be independent of the preferences of different stakeholders (Campbell 1979b).

Threats to the usability of knowledge may be divided into three classes: cogency, relevance, and adequacy (Table 2). Threats to the cogency of knowledge claims are of two main types: misjudged cogency and misplaced cogency. Misjudged cogency, a topic of standard statistical textbooks, is illustrated by errors of practical judgment which occur when one sets statistical confidence limits too high (Type I error) or too low (Type II error) in testing the null hypothesis. By contrast, misplaced cogency occurs when one correctly sets statistical confidence limits but addresses the wrong problem. The threat of misplaced cogency is evident in John Tukey's admonition to applied social researchers: "Far better an approximate answer to the right question, which is often vague, than an exact answer to the wrong question, which can always be made precise" (quoted in Rose 1977:23). This first-order threat has been generalized by Alan Kimball (1957), Howard Raiffa (1968), and Ian Mitroff (1974) as a Type III error and discussed by Campbell and Stanley (1963:6–7) under the heading "misplaced precision in one-shot case studies."

Threats to knowledge relevance are also of two main types: misplaced relevance and untimely relevance. Misplaced relevance involves the projection of cogent knowledge claims that are relevant to one kind of purpose when, instead, cogent knowledge claims relevant to another kind of purpose should have been produced. This second-order threat is frequently noted in published literature on policy research (e.g., Coleman 1972; Rein and White 1977). The threat of misplaced relevance is also noted by proponents of multiattribute utility analysis, who contend that experimental program evaluations offer designative claims but not evaluative and advocative ones (Edwards et al. 1975:140). By contrast, untimely relevance, a second-order threat that is more easily overcome, involves the production of relevant information too late to satisfy the needs of one or more stakeholders (see, for example, Weiss 1977).

Threats to knowledge adequacy are more diverse and complex than those pertaining to relevance and cogency. Twelve major threats to knowledge adequacy are listed below.

1. *Misplaced adequacy:* The use of the less appropriate of two or more classes of truth tests when, instead, the more appropriate truth test should be employed. This second-order threat is found in theoretical and practical disputes surrounding the appropriateness of contending

worldviews, paradigms, and frames of reference for policy research (e.g., Tribe 1972; Patton 1975; Rein 1976; MacRae 1976a).

2. *Subjectivity:* A classical causal test is used to explain human behavior when, instead, the explanation should be supplemented or replaced by one founded on subjectively meaningful action. Claims about the effectiveness of federally sponsored social experiments are frequently challenged on grounds of subjective inadequacy (e.g., Trend 1978), another second-order threat.

3. *Reflexivity:* A quasi-causal test is used to affirm the social or historical necessity of some process or event when, instead, such processes or events are subject to human reflection, initiative, and control. This second-order threat is sometimes applied to quasi-causal theories of revolutionary social change. Such theories are challenged on grounds that predictions of sociohistorical events hold true if and only if reflection by stakeholders does not lead them to change their values or behavior; or if unpredictable factors that arise through creative reformations of social problems do not intervene (MacIntyre 1973).

4. *Misclassification:* This second-order threat may be invoked to determine whether a typological test results in the placement of events, actions, or persons in the wrong class. The creation of social pseudoproblems by labeling healthy persons deviants reflects classificational inadequacies that derive from unexamined paradigms and social myths (see, e.g., Lowry 1974; Gregg et al. 1979).

5. *Misrepresentation:* The use of a particular representational test, whether statistical or theoretical, when another more representative rule should have been employed. The underenumeration of minorities in the 1970 U.S. census illustrates this second-order threat.

6. *Perspectivity:* The use of an analogical test as a literal surrogate for some social process when, instead, the analogy is no more than a perspective or metaphor of that process. Challenges to the adequacy of quantitative policy models illustrate this second-order threat to metaphorical adequacy (e.g., Strauch 1976).

7. *Objectivity:* The use of a teleological test to explain action when, instead, the explanation should be supplemented or replaced by a quasi-causal test which identifies the operation of humanly objectivated but unreflected lawlike regularities. The concept of unanticipated social consequences and the "self-fulfilling prophecy" illustrate this second-order threat (Merton 1976).

8. *Spuriousness:* Use of a clinical test involving one symptom or set of symptoms to diagnose or treat a social ill when, instead, some other

symptom or set of symptoms is a better indicator of the problem. Knowledge about the diagnosis and treatment of mental and physical illnesses is often subject to second-order threats of spurious symptomatology.

9. *Misplaced comparison*: Use of a comparative test to adopt a reform that has succeeded elsewhere when conditions surrounding that reform are not sufficiently similar to the case at hand. Misplaced comparison is a continuous second-order threat to knowledge claims about government-sponsored "exemplary" projects.

10. *Counterauthentication*: Use of a personal, ideological, ethical, or methodological test when some other person, doctrine, norm, or procedure is more qualified, orthodox, fair, or effective. Knowledge produced by mystics, seers, gurus, scientists, and expert panels and commissions is typically threatened by diverse forms of counterauthentication, as is knowledge that originates in ideological doctrines, ethical systems, and approved technical conventions of science.

11. *Substantiality*: A (necessarily) presumptive ontological claim about the nature of social reality, human nature, or knowledge certifies epistemological or ethical claims when, instead, such claims should be argued on substantial grounds. This second-order threat is countered by Campbell's criticisms of the naturalistic fallacy (i.e., deducing ethical from nonethical premises) in contemporary sociobiology (Campbell 1979a) and by efforts of critical social theorists (e.g., Habermas 1975) to challenge presumptive ontological claims of logical positivism on grounds that such claims, since they represent conclusions of substantial arguments, are corrigible and redeemable through social discourse.

12. *Misplaced reflexivity*: Claims about the emancipatory role of self-reflection and reasoned discourse are treated as if they refer to concrete contexts of practice when, instead, they are unrelated to ongoing practices. Misplaced reflexivity is a standing threat to much work carried out in ethnomethodology, phenomenology, and critical theory.

These classes of threats to knowledge adequacy may stand in a complementary relation, as when the threat of objective inadequacy induces the use of a combined teleological and quasi-causal truth test. In other cases threats to knowledge adequacy expose fundamentally irreconcilable standards of appraisal; for example, when subjective inadequacy reveals that nomic connections (laws) appropriate to knowledge claims in physics are inapplicable to sociocultural systems. Finally, threats to knowledge adequacy may be extended in the form of additional classes. The framework described above makes no claim to exhaustiveness or universality.

Conclusion

Problems of knowledge production and use cannot be satisfactorily clarified or alleviated by making exaggerated and facile distinctions between professional social inquiry and ordinary knowledge; nor should we accept the patently false conclusion that knowledge derived from one or the other source is inherently superior. The task is rather to distinguish between approaches to knowledge creation and use that recognize the critical function of reason in appraising knowledge claims and those that do not. The metaphor of the experimenting society, while it has introduced reasoned discourse into the examination of causal inferences, fails to recognize that reforms are symbolically mediated social processes aimed at changing the structure and functioning of some social system. Accordingly, experimental outcomes cannot be said to be independent of the preferences of stakeholders in social reforms.

The success of reforms depends on rationally motivated consensus that some future social state is possible and desirable. Reforms are processes of reasoned argument and debate in which competing standards for appraising knowledge claims include but are not limited to rules for making valid causal inferences. The jurisprudential metaphor not only captures these diverse standards for assessing knowledge claims, it also directs attention to processes of knowledge creation and use as critical social transactions involving issues of the comparative adequacy, relevance, and cogency of knowledge claims.

The jurisprudential metaphor has been extended and specified in the form of a transactional model of argument. The transactional model, since it distinguishes between analytic and substantial arguments, is well suited for critical inquiries into competing standards for assessing both theoretical and practical claims. The transactional model provides a visual schema for mapping arguments; compels a reflective and critical posture toward presuppositions of knowledge claims; yields a classification of truth, relevance, and cogency tests; and permits a provisional listing of classes of threats to usable knowledge. The role of the transactional model is not limited to retrospective inquiries into standards of knowledge assessment employed by contending stakeholders, because an awareness of threats to usable knowledge helps anticipate diverse challenges to knowledge claims. By supplying the contours of a critical social science of knowledge applications—that is, a social science that uncovers and raises to a level of explicit consciousness those unexamined prior assumptions and implicit standards of assessment that shape and distort the production and use of knowledge—the transactional model may contribute to individual and collective learning capacities, and thus to emancipatory policy reforms.

Note

An earlier version of this paper was presented in June 1980 at the International Conference on the Political Realization of Social Science Knowledge and Research: Toward New Scenarios, a meeting held in memoriam of Paul F. Lazarsfeld at the Institute for Advanced Studies, Vienna, Austria. I gratefully acknowledge helpful criticisms offered at that time by Thomas D. Cook, Burkart Holzner, Karin Knorr-Cetina, Niklas Luhmann, and Herman Strasser. This essay has since benefited from the comments and suggestions of Pittsburgh colleagues—Evelyn Fisher, Bahman Fozouni, Burkart Holzner, John Marx, Alex Weilenmann, Charles Willard, and Gerald Zaltman—and from the reactions of Andrew Gordon, Duncan MacRae, Jr., Ian Mitroff, and E. Samuel Overman. Finally, I am grateful to Thomas D. Cook and Donald T. Campbell, who, in a spirit of generous partisanship, supplied notes, materials, and references that challenged many initial assumptions and claims about philosophic and practical implications of quasi experimentation.

An earlier version of this essay was published in *Knowledge: Creation, Diffusion, Utilization* 3 (1982): 293–326. Although the present version includes updated references, including Campbell's response (Campbell 1982), I have not altered the original argument.

References

Ackoff, R. L. 1974. *Redesigning the Future: A Systems Approach to Societal Problems*. New York: Wiley.

Alker, H. R., Jr. 1984. Historical Argumentation and Statistical Inference: Towards More Appropriate Logics for Historical Research. *Historical Methods* 17:164–73.

———. 1988. The Dialectical Logic of Thucydides' Meliah Dialogue. *American Political Science Review* 82:805–20.

Anderson, C. W. 1987. Political Philosophy, Practical Reason, and Policy Analysis. In F. Fischer and J. Forester, eds., *Confronting-Values in Policy Analysis*, 22–42. Newbury Park, Calif.: Sage.

Berger, P. L., and T. Luckmann. 1967. *The Social Construction of Reality*. New York: Doubleday.

Bernstein, I. N., and H. Freeman. 1975. *Academic and Entrepreneurial Research.* New York: Russell Sage Foundation.

Brock, B. L., J. W. Chesebro, J. F. Cragan, and J. F. Klumpp. 1973. *Public Policy Decision Making: Systems Analysis and the Comparative Advantages Debate.* New York: Harper and Row.

Brockriede, W., and D. Ehninger. 1960. Toulmin on Argument: An Interpretation and Application. *Quarterly Journal of Speech* 46:44–53.

Brown, P. G. 1976. Ethics and Policy Research. *Policy Analysis* 2:325–40.

Buchler, J., ed. 1955. *Philosophical Writings of Peirce.* New York: Dover.

Campbell, D. T. 1959. Methodological Suggestions from a Comparative Psychology of Knowledge Processes. *Inquiry* 2:152–82.

———. 1971. Methods for the Experimenting Society. Paper presented to the American Psychological Association, Washington, D.C., September 5.

———. 1974a. Evolutionary Epistemology. In P. A. Schilpp, ed., *The Philosophy of Karl Popper,* 413–63. LaSalle, Ill.: Open Court Press.

———. 1974b. Qualitative Knowing in Action Research. Kurt Lewin Award Address, presented to the Society for the Psychological Study of Social Issues, American Psychological Association, New Orleans, September 1.

———. 1975a. Assessing the Impact of Planned Social Change. In G. M. Lyons, ed., *Social Research and Public Policies,* 3–45. Hanover, N.H.: Public Affairs Center, Dartmouth College.

———. 1975b. Reforms as Experiments. In E. L. Struening and M. Guttentag, eds., *Handbook of Evaluation Research,* 1:71–100. Beverly Hills: Sage.

———. 1979a. Comments on the Sociobiology of Ethics and Moralizing. *Behavioral Science* 24:37–45.

———. 1979b. A Tribal Model of the Social System Vehicle Carrying Scientific Knowledge. *Knowledge: Creation, Diffusion, Utilization* 1:181–202.

———. 1988. *Methodology and Epistemology for the Social Sciences: Selected Papers,* ed. E. S. Overman. Chicago: University of Chicago Press.

Campbell, D. T., and D. W. Fiske. 1959. Convergent and Discriminant Validation by the Multitrait-Multimethod Matrix. *Psychological Bulletin* 56:81–105.

Campbell, D. T., and J. C. Stanley. 1963. *Experimental and Quasi-Experimental Designs for Research.* Chicago: Rand McNally.

Caplan, N. 1979. The Two-Communities Theory and Knowledge Utilization. *American Behavioral Scientist* 22:459–70.

Coleman, J. S. 1972. *Policy Research in the Social Sciences.* Morristown, N.J.: General Learning Press.

Cook, T. D., and D. T. Campbell. 1979. *Quasi-Experimentation.* Chicago: Rand McNally.

Cox, J. R., and C. A. Willard. 1982. Introduction: The Field of Argumentation. In J. R. Cox and C. A. Willard, eds., *Advances in Argumentation Theory and Research,* iii–xx. Carbondale: Southern Illinois University Press.

Dunn, W. N. 1988a. Justifying Policy Arguments: Criteria for Practical Discourse. *Evaluation and Program Planning* 13:293–326.

———. 1988b. Methods of the Second Type: Coping with the Wilderness of Conventional Policy Analysis. *Policy Studies Review* 7:720–37.

———. 1993. *Public Policy Analysis: An Introduction.* 2d ed. Englewood Cliffs, N.J.: Prentice Hall.

Dunn, W. N., and B. Fozouni. 1976. *Toward a Critical Administrative Theory.* Sage Professional Paper, Administrative and Policy Studies Series. Beverly Hills: Sage.

Dunn, W. N., I. I. Mitroff, and S. J. Deutsch. 1981. The Obsolescence of Evaluation Research. *Evaluation and Program Planning* 6:141–59.

Edwards, W., M. Guttentag, and K. Snapper. 1975. A Decision-Theoretic Approach to Evaluation Research. In E. L. Struening and M. Guttentag, eds., *Handbook of Evaluation Research,* 139–82. Beverly Hills: Sage.

Fischer, D. H. 1970. *Historians' Fallacies: Toward a Logic of Historical Thought.* New York: Random House.

Fischer, F. 1986. Practical Discourse in Policy Argumentation. In W. N. Dunn, ed., *Policy Analysis: Perspectives, Concepts, and Methods,* 315–32. Greenwich, Conn.: JAI Press.

Gewirth, A. 1960. Positive Ethics and Normative Science. *Philosophical Review* 69:311–30.

Gewirth, L. 1979. *Reason in Morality.* Chicago: University of Chicago Press.

Gregg, G., T. Preston, A. Geist, and N. Caplan. 1979. The Caravan Rolls On: Forty Years of Social Problem Research. *Knowledge: Creation, Diffusion, Utilization* 1:31–61.

Habermas, J. 1971. *Knowledge and Human Interests.* Boston: Beacon Press.

———. 1975. *Legitimation Crisis.* Boston: Beacon Press.

Hesse, M. 1980. *Revolutions and Reconstructions in the Philosophy of Science.* Bloomington: Indiana University Press.

Holzner, B. 1969. *Reality Construction in Society.* Cambridge: Schenkman.

Holzner, B., and E. Fisher. 1979. Knowledge in Use: Considerations in the Sociology of Knowledge Application. *Knowledge: Creation, Diffusion, Utilization* 1:219–44.

Holzner, B., and J. Marx. 1979. *Knowledge Application: The Knowledge System in Society.* Boston: Allyn and Bacon.

Holzner, B., J. Marx, and E. Fisher. 1977. Paul Lazarsfeld and the Study of Knowledge Applications. *Sociological Focus* 10:97–116.

House, E. R. 1977. *The Logic of Evaluative Argument.* CSE Monograph Series in Evaluation, no. 7. Los Angeles: Center for the Study of Evaluation, University of California at Los Angeles.

———. 1980. *Evaluating with Validity.* Beverly Hills: Sage.

Karapin, R. S., and H. R. Alker, Jr. 1985. Argument Analysis: Student Introduction to a Post-Modern, Dialectical, Graphical Approach. Mimeo. Department of Political Science, Massachusetts Institute of Technology, Cambridge, Mass.

Kelly, E. F. 1980. Evaluation as Persuasion: A Practical Argument. *Educational Evaluation and Policy Analysis* 2:35–38.

Kimball, A. W. 1957. Errors of the Third Kind in Statistical Consulting. *Journal of the American Statistical Association* 52:133–42.

Knorr, K. D. 1981. Time and Context in Practical Action: On the Preconditions of Knowledge Use. Paper presented to the Conference on Knowledge Use, University Program for the Study of Knowledge Use, University of Pittsburgh, March 18–20.

Kuhn, T. S. 1971. *The Structure of Scientific Revolutions.* 2d ed. Chicago: University of Chicago Press.

Landsbergen, D., and B. Bozeman. 1987. Credibility Logic and Policy Analysis: Is There Rationality Without Science? *Knowledge: Creation, Diffusion, Utilization* 8:625–48.

Laudan, L. 1977. *Progress and Its Problems: Towards a Theory of Scientific Growth.* Berkeley and Los Angeles: University of California Press.

———. 1981. Overestimating Underdetermination: Caveats Concerning the Social Causes of Belief. MS. Center for History and Philosophy of Science, University of Pittsburgh.

Lazarsfeld, P. F., and J. Reitz. 1975. *An Introduction to Applied Sociology.* New York: Elsevier.

Levine, M., and N. S. Rosenberg. 1979. An Adversary Model of Fact Finding and Decision Making for Program Evaluation: Theoretical Considerations. In H. C. Schulberg and F. Baker, eds., *Program Evaluation in the Health Fields*, vol. 2, pp. 211–30. New York: Human Sciences Press.

Levinson, A. 1966. Knowledge and Society. *Inquiry* 9:132–46.

Lindblom, C. E., and D. K. Cohen. 1979. *Usable Knowledge: Social Science and Social Problem Solving.* New Haven: Yale University Press.

Lowry, R. P. 1974. *Social Problems: A Critical Analysis of Theories and Public Policy.* Lexington, Mass.: D. C. Heath.

McCloskey, D. N. 1985. *The Rhetoric of Economics.* Madison: University of Wisconsin Press.

MacIntyre, A. 1973. Ideology, Social Science, and Revolution. *Comparative Politics* 5:321–40.

MacRae, D., Jr. 1976a. *The Social Function of Social Science.* New Haven: Yale University Press.

———. 1976b. Technical Communities and Political Choice. *Minerva* 14:169–90.

———. 1988. Professional Knowledge for Policy Discourse: Argumentation versus Reasoned Selection of Proposals. *Knowledge in Society: The International Journal of Knowledge Transfer* 1:6–24.

Majone, G. 1989. *Evidence, Argument, and Persuasion in the Policy Process.* New Haven: Yale University Press.

Malinowski, B. 1948. *Magic, Science, and Religion and Other Essays.* Glencoe, Ill.: Free Press.

Marascuilo, L. A., and J. R. Levin. 1970. Appropriate post hoc Comparisons for Interaction and Nested Hypotheses in Analysis of Variance Designs: The Elimination of Type IV Errors. *American Educational Research Journal* 7:39–42.

Mason, R. O., and I. I. Mitroff. 1981. *Challenging Strategic Planning Assumptions.* New York: Wiley.

———. 1981b. Policy Analysis as Argument. In W. N. Dunn, ed., Symposium on Social Values and Public Policy. *Policy Studies Journal,* special issue, 2:579–84.

Merton, R. K. 1973. *The Sociology of Science.* Chicago: University of Chicago Press.

———. 1976. *Sociological Ambivalence and Other Essays.* New York: Free Press.

Michalos, A. D. 1981. Facts, Values, and Rational Decision Making. In W. N. Dunn, ed., Symposium on Social Values and Public Policy. *Policy Studies Journal,* special issue, 2:544–51.

Mitroff, I. I. 1974. *The Subjective Side of Science.* New York: Elsevier.

Mitroff I. I., and R. O. Mason. 1981. *Creating a Dialectical Social Science.* Dordrecht: D. Reidel.

Mitroff, I. I., R. O. Mason, and V. Barabba. 1985. *The 1980 Census: Policy Making amid Turbulence.* Lexington, Mass.: D. C. Heath.

Mitroff, I. I., and F. Sagasti. 1973. Epistemology as General Systems Theory: An Approach to the Design of Complex Decision-making Experiments. *Philosophy of Social Sciences* 3:117–34.

Montague, W. P. 1925. *The Ways of Knowing.* New York: Macmillan.

Paris, D. C., and J. F. Reynolds. 1983. *The Logic of Policy Inquiry.* New York: Longman.

Patton, M. Q. 1975. *Alternative Evaluation Research Paradigm.* North Dakota Study Group on Evaluation Monograph Series. Grand Forks: University of North Dakota Press.

———. 1978. *Utilization-focused Evaluation.* Beverly Hills: Sage.

Peach, H. C. 1985. Argumentation in Applied Research: Organizational Dances around a Circle of Freedom: The Hood River Consensus Experiment. Paper presented at the Eleventh Annual Meeting of the Society for Social Studies of Science, Rensselaer Polytechnic Institute, Troy, New York, October 24–27.

Perelman, C. 1984. The New Rhetoric and the Rhetoricians: Remembrances and Comments. *Quarterly Journal of Speech* 70:188–96.

Phillips, D. 1973. *Abandoning Method.* San Francisco: Jossey-Bass.

Polanyi, M. 1967. The Growth of Science in Society. *Minerva* 5:533–45.

Popper, K. R. 1959. *The Logic of Scientific Discovery.* New York: Basic Books.

————. 1963. *Conjectures and Refutations.* New York: Basic Books.

Raiffa, H. 1968. *Decision Analysis.* Reading, Mass.: Addison-Wesley.

Reich, R. B. 1988. Introduction to *The Power of Public Ideas,* ed. R. B. Reich. Cambridge, Mass.: Ballinger.

Rein, M. 1976. *Social Science and Public Policy.* Baltimore: Penguin.

Rein, M., and S. White. 1977. Policy Research: Belief and Doubt. *Policy Analysis* 3:239–72.

Rescher, N. 1977. *Dialectics: A Controversy-oriented Approach to the Theory of Knowledge.* Albany: State University of New York Press.

————. 1980. *Induction.* Pittsburgh: University of Pittsburgh Press.

Rivlin, A. M. 1973. Forensic Social Science. In *Perspectives on Inequality.* Harvard Educational Review Reprint Series, no. 8.

Rose, R. 1977. Disciplined Research and Undisciplined Problems. In C. H. Weiss, ed., *Using Social Research in Public Policy Making,* 25–35. Lexington, Mass.: D. C. Heath.

Strauch, R. E. 1976. A Critical Look at Quantitative Methodology. *Policy Analysis* 2:121–44.

Suchman, E. 1972. Action for What? A Critique of Evaluation Research. In C. H. Weiss, ed., *Evaluating Action Programs,* 42–84. Boston: Allyn and Bacon.

Toulmin, S. 1958. *The Uses of Argument.* Cambridge: Cambridge University Press.

Toulmin, S., R. Rieke, and A. Janik. 1984. *An Introduction to Reasoning.* 2d ed. New York: Macmillan.

Trend, M. G. 1978. On the Reconciliation of Qualitative and Quantitative Analysis: A Case Study. *Human Organization* 37:345–54.

Tribe, L. 1972. Policy Science: Analysis or Ideology. *Philosophy and Public Affairs* 2:66–110.

Von Wright, G. 1971. *Explanation and Understanding.* Ithaca: Cornell University Press.

Voss, J. F., T. R. Greene, T. A. Post, and B. C. Penner. 1984. Problem Solving Skill in the Social Sciences. In B. C. Bauer, ed., *The Psychology of Learning and Motivation: Advances in Research and Theory.* New York: Erlbaum.

Wallace, W. 1971. *The Logic of Science in Sociology.* Chicago: Aldine.

Watzlawick, P., J. Weakland, and R. Fisch. 1974. *Change: Principles of Problem Formation and Resolution.* New York: W. W. Norton.

Webb, E. J., D. T. Campbell, R. D. Schwartz, and L. B. Sechrest. 1966. *Unobtrusive Measures.* Chicago: Rand McNally.

Webber, D. J. 1980. Conflicting Worldviews, Competing Disciplinary Matrices, and the Utilization of Systematic Policy Analysis. Paper presented to the annual meeting of the American Political Science Association, Washington, D.C., August 28–31.

Weiss, C. H., ed. 1977. *Using Social Research in Public Policy Making*. Lexington, Mass.: D. C. Heath.

Weiss, C. H. 1991. Policy Research as Advocacy: Pro and Con. *Knowledge and Policy: The International Journal of Knowledge Transfer and Utilization* 4:37–55.

Weiss, C. H., with M. J. Bucuvalas. 1980a. *Social Science Research and Decision-Making*. New York: Columbia University Press.

———. 1980b. Truth Tests and Utility Tests: Decision Makers' Frames of Reference for Social Science. *American Sociological Review* 45:302–12.

Whitehead, A. N., and B. Russell. 1910. *Principia Mathematica*. Vol. 1, 2d ed. Cambridge: Cambridge University Press.

Willard, C. A. 1978. A Reformulation of the Concept of Argument: The Constructivist/Interactionist Foundations of a Sociology of Argument. *Journal of the American Forensic Association* 14:121–40.

———. 1980a. Some Questions about Toulmin's View of Argument Fields. MS. Department of Speech, University of Pittsburgh.

———. 1980b. A Theory of Argumentation. MS. Department of Speech, University of Pittsburgh.

Williams, W. 1971. *Social Policy Research and Analysis: The Experience in the Federal Social Agencies*. New York: Elsevier.

Zaltman, G. 1979. Knowledge Utilization as Planned Social Change. *Knowledge: Creation, Diffusion, Utilization* 1:82–105.

Guidelines for

Policy Discourse: Consensual

versus Adversarial

Duncan MacRae, Jr.

This volume concerns the discourse of policy analysts or planners with one another and with the public. The editors seek to synthesize two contrasting tendencies in public policy analysis (PPA) and planning related to this discourse so that students and practitioners can look beyond the two dominant models in the field—the rationalistic problem-solving model, which concerns the internal qualities of analysis, and the politicized context-determinant model, which deals more with external contingencies of analyses (see Editors' Introduction). Judging that either of these approaches alone would be incomplete, they seek to combine them. The combined field is to be neither methodological nor political alone, and it is to focus on argumentation, thus avoiding the separation of "epistemological concerns (the claims made 'within' the argument) from institutional and performance concerns (how in deed the argument is made)" (p. 5).

Policy analysts, claiming to give expert advice to political actors, must attend to both these approaches or concerns. The role of the analyst is, in fact, one type of synthesis of the two; the analyst must learn about both, using one or the other depending on circumstances, but separating rather than combining them. For the analyst, and for many citizens as well, I shall argue that there are distinct styles of discourse, one appropriate for like-minded discussants among themselves, and other styles suitable for participants in the world of adversarial politics (Burton 1990).

In this essay I propose not to stress the analysis of argument as it is, but to advance guidelines for desirable types of discourse, expecially within the analytic community. Rather than promoting a synthesis in a single style of discourse, I propose a clear distinction between two styles of discourse, to be used in different social situations. For one such situation, the consensual quest for "reasoned proposal selection," I propose detailed guidelines for a preferred style of discourse; for the other, "adversarial argumentation," only a more limited type of guidance is possible.

Errors and Guidelines

Let me first illustrate that there can be errors in the structuring of ordinary policy discourse and that using certain guidelines may correct them. Consider a citizen's argument: "The highway speed limit in this state should be lowered in order to reduce the number of accidents." In some circumstances this can lead to a reasonable conclusion; but an analyst might note that this argument, taken by itself and without qualification, implies the premise that whatever the speed limits being compared, a lower one would be better so as to reduce accidents. The analyst might point out that repeated application of this principle would lead to a zero speed limit and might ask the citizen to consider a more complete perspective on the problem. Other relevant criteria[1] might include travel time and the cost of operating vehicles (MacRae and Wilde 1979:133–52).[2]

This is an example of policy choice in the presence of multiple conflicting value criteria. Such conflict is widespread in policy assessment, as between efficiency and equity or effectiveness and cost. The public's discourse typically includes multiple criteria, often within the arguments of a single citizen, which the analyst must address. In dealing with multiple criteria, I shall be mainly concerned with criteria that can be balanced against one another, at least in verbal terms. "Peremptory" criteria, which cannot be traded off (Braybrooke and Lindblom 1963: 150–51), are important;[3] but I am assuming that all unacceptable (e.g., immoral or unconstitutional) alternatives have been ruled out, leaving alternatives for which the criteria can be traded off.

The analyst's counterargument about the speed limit is of a general type having the form, "Your particular argument can be misleading because it has not been placed properly within a broader structure of reasoning." My first task here is to define a domain of policy discourse in which analysts may properly make such claims. A second task will be to specify a corresponding set of guidelines (incorporating higher-order criteria, distinct from the substantive criteria involved in particular policy choices) for good policy reasoning, that can justifiably be taught to analysts and citizens. A third task will be to show that in another domain ("persuasion"), practices contrary to these guidelines are necessary.

The "Argumentation" Approach to Policy Discourse and Its Limits: Toulmin's Approach

A number of students of PPA (including those contributing to this volume) have recommended that public discourse be a major focus of this field. Some (Dunn 1981; Mason and Mitroff 1980–81; Goldstein 1984; Fischer 1985:240–41) have made use of a scheme proposed in a pioneering work by Stephen Toulmin (1958, chap. 3) for classification of the elements of an "argument." In this scheme, the central element is a *claim*—"some 'destination' we are invited to arrive at," such as supporting a policy proposal. Underlying the claim are *grounds*—information or data. The justifiable use of these grounds to support the claim depends on *warrants* such as "laws of nature, legal principles and statutes, rules of thumb, [or] engineering formulas." Warrants rest on *backing*, such as judgments that "legal statutes must have been validly legislated" or "scientific laws must have been thoroughly checked out." The overall argument can be expressed with a *qualifier* such as "usually," "possibly," or "barring accidents." Finally, unless the argument is logically certain, it can be accompanied by a *rebuttal*—a statement of the "circumstances in which the general authority of the warrant would have to be set aside."

Toulmin developed this scheme by moving away from the logic of syllogisms to a broader notion of the range of arguments that are actually used. Chaim Perelman and Lucie Olbrechts-Tyteca (1969) took similar steps away from "the absolute supremacy of formal logic" (Dearin 1982:80) in describing "the new rhetoric." But once we have recognized that good arguments can extend beyond formal logic, we must still ask how to judge them and how to teach others about their desirable qualities. Frans van Eemeren, Rob Grootendorst, and Tjark Kruiger (1987:258), criticizing Perelman and Olbrechts-Tyteca's approach, note that it involves "a thoroughgoing relativism, coupled with a norm-descriptive instead of norm-giving conception."

Several aspects of Toulmin's initial scheme need to be modified, or at least interpreted further, for our purposes. First, the scheme seems to suggest that policy discourse consists entirely of claims, each made by a presenter who seeks to bring others to a specified "destination." A discussion consisting only of such claims would seem to have no room for questions addressed to the speaker or for criticisms;[4] at least, the claims made or implied by questions or criticisms are not always claims for other policy proposals. Van Eemeren, Grootendorst, and Kruiger (1987:264) note that Toulmin's model "is concerned exclusively with pro-argumentation, while the 'adversary' remains completely passive." Rather than centering my discusseion on persuasive "claims" made by one presenter after another, I wish to include the possibility of a discussion that is a collective quest for best policies, in terms of general criteria shared by the participants. In such a discussion, one participant might be the citizen mentioned above, arguing for a lower speed limit; another could be the analyst asking the citizen to include more criteria. The analyst's reply would not center on a claim in support of another specified policy. It might resemble a rebuttal—"unless other values outweigh the reduction of accidents"—but this could be provided by a second participant in the discussion as well as by the initial proponent.[5]

Second, the approach of Toulmin and his colleagues implies a relativism that does not aid the development of better guidelines for policy discourse. They distinguish diverse "fields" of argument (Toulmin 1958:14–15) or forums of argumentation—"legal, scientific, financial, medical, political, or whatever" (Toulmin et al. 1979:15)—each with its own existing goals and criteria of relevance, sharing the general schema but differing in detail. Such an approach might seem to lead to a notion of "when in Rome, do as the Romans do" for each field. The critical procedures that they propose deal with the merits of arguments in support of claims within given fields. Participants in one field, such as policy analysis, however, receive little guidance from this approach in developing better guidelines for *that* field. Again, we need to go beyond the initial schema.

Third, Toulmin's scheme needs to be supplemented by consideration of more complex structures of argument and by recognition of diverse structures of social roles that allow participants to enter in different ways. When a set of criteria are agreed by the participants to be relevant to a policy choice, an argument centering on only one criterion contributes only a building block for such a structure. Even the consideration of a second criterion by way of rebuttal does not bring that second criterion to equal logical status with the first, as policy analysis requires. The participating group—or an analyst who tries to consider all the major value criteria of such a group—must discuss a complex structure of criteria and alternatives rather than simply favoring one value or alternative at a time by an isolated "argument."

Among the possible roles of participants in policy arguments are those of chairperson, mediator, and judge; proponent and responder;

speaker and audience; or unconstrained equality. Types of dialogue between a proponent and a responder have been described in formal terms by Nicholas Rescher (1977:2); Hayward Alker (1988), applying them to Thucydides' Melian dialogue, argues that such an approach is widely applicable to political discourse.

Types of Policy Discourse

Although Toulmin's 1958 schema seems to apply only to a single "argument" advanced by one participant, its applicability can be enlarged by introducing two distinctions made in Toulmin's later work with others. First, we may distinguish between *consensual* and *adversarial* discourse. In the former, participants have common goals (e.g., to deal collectively with a problem) and values (notions of what is good or desirable).[6] In the latter, they have opposing goals (e.g., individual ambition or group power) or values. Second, we may distinguish within each of these styles of discourse whether a profession (such as PPA) is attempting to provide guidelines for it. Discourse guided in this way may then be compared with discourse not so guided, or guided by preexisting standards independent of the profession in question. This contrast may aid us in our choice of new guidelines. Both consensual and adversarial discourse may be guided by teachable procedures.

In criticizing Toulmin's approach I have assumed that in at least *some* types of policy discourse the participants are collectively (consensually) seeking policy proposals rather than advancing them and asking support for them. If there is a central domain of expertise in policy analysis, it would seem to lie in the quest for policies that further *given* values more than in the reconciliation of *clashing* values in the political community. It would lie more in speed limit policy, for example, than in policies about prayer in public schools. This is a distinction not merely between types of issues, however, but also between types of discussion of a given issue. It concerns discussion within a political community as well as among analysts.

This domain of expertise corresponds to consensual discourse and, if this discourse is subject to guidelines such as those I propose here, to professionally guided discourse. It can occur among members of a policy-related profession such as PPA. Such professionals can also seek to guide citizens' discussion (as statisticians do) by education or by participating in public debate. Most of this essay concerns consensual policy discourse and guidelines for it. In my concluding remarks I will indicate possible guidelines for analysts in adversarial policy discourse, but they are much weaker than those I offer for consensual, professionally guided discourse.

Reasoned Proposal Selection versus Persuasion

Consensual discourse followed by adversarial: a special case. One important type of consensual, professionally guided policy discourse can occur when a subgroup in a larger political community selects policy proposals for presentation to the community. If the subgroup (either professionals or like-minded citizens) has some internal consensus on the ethical criteria to be used, it can engage in a consensual style of discourse for selecting one or more proposals. If, however, the larger community lacks this degree of consensus, its later discussion of these proposals may be more adversarial.

In this special (but prevalent) case we can thus distinguish two types of policy discourse: in the first, more consensual ("proposal selection") policy proposals are selected within a like-minded group in terms of shared values possibly related to the public interest; in the second ("argumentation"), the selected proposals are then advanced in more adversarial competition in the larger, less consensual, political community.

This distinction is analogous to that between the contexts of "discovery" and "justification" in the philosophy of science (e.g., Popper 1968:31, 315) or between "invention" and rhetorical persuasion in argumentation (Aristotle 1954:1355[b]). Toulmin, Rieke, and Janik (1979:9) make a similar distinction between "arriving at ideas" and "testing ideas critically."

Distinctions such as these often imply that the earlier stage of generating proposals—formulating and selecting them—is less systematic and more intuitive than the later stage of argumentation. This is not entirely true of policy discourse, however, because both the earlier stage and the later one are internally heterogeneous. The earlier stage includes not only the intuitive process of *formulating* proposals but can also include systematic procedures for *selecting* better policy proposals or eliminating worse ones.

The later stage of *argumentation*, centered on given claims rather than on a quest for better ones, can also take different forms depending on whether or not it is guided professionally. The arguments made for claims may be presented and justified either under the guidance of the procedures of an expert community, such as that of scientists or lawyers, or in a context where the acceptability of a style of argument is limited only by the tolerance of nonprofessional participants and audiences.

In either of these two stages, *justification* (governed by procedural rules or guidelines) can be mixed with strategic *persuasion*. An expert community is likely to involve relatively more justification, however, while strategic political discourse involves more persuasion. Thus, if we can propose appropriate guidelines, the systematic part of the initial stage (proposal *selection*) may be superior in reasoning to strategic argument—if we wish to seek a best policy.

The stage of generating proposals has two subprocesses: (1) the formulation of a larger set of alternative policy proposals for serving a set of general values, a relatively intuitive process[7] closely linked to the definition of the problem itself (Dery 1984); and (2) a possibly systematic process of proposal selection, from this larger set, in terms of these value criteria. The first of these subprocesses, even when it is not guided by rules, helps to bring up viable claims that happen not to have proponents. The second can help to ensure that the information used is more complete and is chosen with less selective bias.

At the stage of proposal selection we (a person or group) can begin with criteria that we wish to further by policy choice and compare a set of policy alternatives with respect to them. This quest is close to a process of "convincing oneself," or of persuading like-minded citizens who wish to discover how to further similar values. Let us call this winnowing process, guided as proposed, "reasoned proposal selection."

Our task, therefore, is not simply to distinguish an initial intuitive stage of analysis from a later rational stage of adversarial argumentation. Reason can be used in both proposal selection and argumentation, but it is applied differently in the two cases. I shall now contrast reasoned proposal selection with persuasion conducted through strategic, adversarial argumentation, referring to the latter simply as "persuasion."

Audiences, roles, and rules. The distinction between reasoned proposal selection and persuasion depends on the speaker's social role in relation to the audience; the degree of consensus between speaker and audience, and within the audience, on the basic premises of discussion;[8] and the rules of discourse by which speaker and audience are bound.

The narrowest audience is the speaker alone; that is, one is seeking to convince oneself or to discover a desired or desirable course of action. The values one brings to bear may then be personal interests, ethical principles, or both. The widest audience is the "universal audience," which "every philosopher addresses . . . as he conceives it." This audience "must necessarily include the orator himself, who is a principal judge of the value of his arguments. This is the reason why such a discourse must be sincere, honest, and cannot consist of a manipulation of the audience" (Perelman 1984:191, 194).

A similar situation of unconstrained rational discourse (in a narrower sense than the one I use here) has been proposed by Jürgen Habermas (1973:107–8):

> Discourse can be understood as that form of communication that is removed from contexts of experience and action and whose structure assures us: that the bracketed validity claims of assertions, recommendations, or warnings are the exclusive object of discussion; that participants, themes and contributions are not restricted except with reference to the goal of testing the validity claims in questions; that no force except that of the better argument is exercised; and that, as a result, all motives except that of the cooperative search for truth are excluded.

This condition of sincerity and honesty can also hold, however, for any audience with whom the speaker sufficiently shares basic premises of discussion—and therefore, presumably, trust. Thus Arnold Meltsner (1976:45) tells of a group of policy analysts on the staff of the Council of Economic Advisers who presented a united front in external arguments but had a different style for discussing policy choice with one another. They "shared a common liberal ideology [a notion of the public interest] and technical approach"; therefore, "if the problem was at the staff level, they could argue the merits among themselves, 'regardless of political feasibility.'"

Forums and styles of discourse. In discussions about public policy, various communicative situations differ from one another both in the degree of consensus and in the accepted rules of discourse. Such a situation may range from consensus and trust, on the one hand, to basic disagreement and manipulative argument, on the other. It may also be affected by procedural rules; different rules may lead to different results even when the participants have the same degree of consensus on substantive values. Even in adversarial argument, which lacks consensus or trust, audience and speaker may still participate in a "forum of argumentation" and collectively accept its rules, as in the courtroom (Toulmin et al. 1979:15–16). Similarly, in policy-related science an expert might be able to persuade laymen with specious or selective reasons that violate the norms of the expert group ("lying with statistics"); but the norms of a profession may forbid this.

We need not simply take such forums of argumentation (or discourse) as they are, as Toulmin (1958:14–15) seems to imply; we can construct and modify them. Toulmin, Rieke, and Janik (1979:199) suggest conditions under which consensual or adversarial procedures are preferable, but we need to extend such judgments and distinctions to the formulation of guidelines for policy discourse. PPA is not necessarily only a field of discourse; it may also self-consciously define and improve its rules. This self-definition can take the form of proposing shared rules or methodology (Fischer 1985; Anderson 1987b).

A consensual procedure involving a framework of such guidelines can encourage the quest for counterarguments, fostering reasoned proposal selection and decision. Thus Connie Ozawa and Lawrence Susskind (1985:32), proposing mediation instead of adversarial proceedings in science-related disputes, note that "while disputants in adjudicatory proceedings see every non-supportive piece of information as a threat to their claims, participants in a mediation process are encouraged to see information as a means of opening up new possibilities for dealing with differences." When legal disputes are subjected to alternative resolution procedures outside the courtroom, a similar change in rules of discourse is sought.

The relative importance of reasoned proposal selection and persuasion also depends on the subject at hand. Some topics involve greater valuative consensus in the group or community involved (e.g., speed limits versus school prayer). Some are better known by expert communities than others, and discussion of these is especially likely to be guided by rules. Even on these topics, however, there will remain burdens of proof, rebuttals, and qualifiers. Moreover, even when there is consensus, guidelines such as those I propose here are not the only ones possible. Austin Freeley (1981:7), for example, describes decision making by group discussion, presupposing consensus but not requiring special rules. Walter Fisher (1984) has proposed a "narrative" paradigm of communication that he believes more appropriate for broad public discussion; he hopes to involve citizens more broadly by *not* requiring them to have special training in particular styles of argument.

Education for more than one type of discourse. We must still ask, however, to what extent we should train policy analysts for narrative or adversarial argument, and to what extent for reasoned proposal selection. Narrative expository argument addressed to a sympathetic but un-trained audience can require skill in understanding the audience and in devising explanations. Adversarial argument requires additional skills. These skills must be accompanied, however, by skill in choosing best[9] policies; we do not wish to make successful persuasions for bad policies.

Consensual and adversarial argument, though different, may be appropriately used by the same analyst in different circumstances. Karl-Otto Apel (1979:333) points out that "*consensual* communication, i.e., striving for agreement about meaning claims, truth claims, and rightness claims, is a precondition of all types of communication, even of those that serve strategic purposes, e.g., negotiating and the like." He further notes (1979:339) that political communication in particular historical situations requires "a dialectical mediation of ethical rationality with strategic rationality." The first task in teaching policy analysis (to an-alysts or citizens) must still be to seek the general welfare; but an essen-tial supplementary task, often requiring much more work than the first, is to show how to do this effectively.

We may thus distinguish between reasoned proposal selection and persuasion (aimed at furthering desirable policies) as *stages* of anal-ysis—persuasion corresponding to political feasibility—and educate an-alysts for both, each in its proper context. Thus, "there is a time for advocacy and a time for holding to disciplinary values" (Meltsner 1976:45), and the student must learn to recognize *both* types of error that can be made by ignoring this distinction. We can also try to draw the two together by educating citizens in procedures of reasoned proposal selec-tion and by training a community of analysts whose members can enter public debate on more than one side, possibly differing with respect to criteria or to burdens of proof while using professional modes of reason-ing. Their professional norms may, however, lead them to stop short of "strategic use" of information that aims merely "to support positions already taken" (Whiteman 1985:302) on nonanalytic grounds and uses facts or values very selectively to do so.

Guiding Reasoned Proposal Selection

Policy analysts may advise citizens and public leaders not only about substantive policies, but also on ways to reason about them.[10] Among these ways of reasoning, rules for factual causal inference are better known than those for structuring policy problems. I pass over the former here but will return to them in treating adversarial argument. Guidelines for ways of reasoning, less often discussed, are equally important (Dunn 1988). Teachers of PPA may teach procedures of policy reasoning both to prospective analysts and to undergraduate students as citizens.

In reasoned proposal selection we (a deliberating group) wish to be guided by procedures of reasoning that will help us to further initially agreed-on general criterion values, often correcting our spontaneous impulses at justification and revising our initial intuitive policy choices. This calls for guidelines that will help us avoid certain common errors— errors, that is, from the point of view of discovering what policy we wish to support,[11] though not necessarily from the point of view of persuasion. The group, collectively assuming responsibility for these procedures, goes beyond Toulmin's initial unilateral notion of argument; together they encourage qualifiers and rebuttals.[12] Those who propose these guidelines also go beyond Toulmin's initial treatment of the style of discourse in fields of argument as given and established.

A Set of Guidelines

An especially important domain for professionally guided policy discourse is that of formulating the problem—listing criteria, alternatives, and the types of factual information that connect them. These are the initial steps in the process of proposal selection. The guidelines I propose are not altogether new, but they need to be combined and put forward clearly, for improvement through criticism as well as for use. After presenting them I shall discuss some of their possible shortcomings.

A. Completeness of the set of valuative criteria. A frequent error in the public's policy discourse is the use of only one criterion when others need to be added to allow a more balanced assessment of alternatives. This was shown in the speed limit example above. It also occurs, for example, when advocates of a program argue only in terms of its supposedly beneficial goal while opponents argue only in terms of costs. More generally, this error involves the selection for particular arguments of some, but not all, of the valuative criteria needed for choice—whether through lack of concern for consistency, emphasis on goals at the expense of side effects, or support for a predetermined conclusion. When committed, this error fails to ensure the completeness[13] of the structure of reasoning advanced (Toulmin et al. 1979:109; Weimer and Vining 1989:200; Dunn 1990).

One way for a group to seek completeness is to list the criteria to be used before they even discuss a policy choice. During discussion of the list, the group can encourage suggestion of further important criteria for inclusion. As in the speed limit example above, a critic can remind the speaker that a single criterion advanced is part of a larger set of criteria relevant to the problem, and that argument about one criterion at a time can be misleading. Similarly, the group can encourage scrutiny of the list for overlap or duplication. For example, an analysis of alternative water supply sources for Chapel Hill, North Carolina, provided information on the quality of untreated water from each source but also included estimates of the cost of purification—thus placing the lower-quality sources at a double disadvantage. Attention to this kind of problem may help to avoid errors of incompleteness or duplication of criteria.

A further way to seek completeness in the list of criteria is to take them from the community that is to decide, or from those affected if they are able to express their concerns. This is a somewhat democratic view, embodied in the notion that an analyst should begin with the "problem situation"—the diverse set of perspectives and key values linked to a policy problem by members of the community—and from it specify more precisely the "analyst's problem" (MacRae and Wilde 1979:17–21; Dunn et al. 1988). The analyst's task would then be to combine the competing values articulated by various groups in the community to synthesize new values.

Specialization among fields of knowledge can also leave a list of criteria incomplete. Specialists often produce partial analyses limited to a subset of the relevant criteria but interpreted as leading to policy recommendations. Thus an expert on highway safety might have approached speed limit policy from the narrow viewpoint of accident reduction alone, as in the argument cited above. As a remedy, an expert making such partial contributions should be encouraged to recognize their partial nature and should either call on others to contribute other parts to the discussion or contribute other ingredients of the decision without claiming expertise about them.

B. Ends rather than means. In proposal selection we are seeking to further certain values or to cope with a problem, not merely to advocate particular proposals. The corresponding "error" is elevation of means to the status of ends, thus excluding judgments as to whether the proposed means truly accomplish the ends sought (e.g., the discussion of health services instead of health, or police services instead of public safety). Such simplifications sometimes result from suboptimization due to division of tasks among parts of an organization; but serious errors can result from seeking such proxy goals unthinkingly (McKean 1967).

Consideration of ends rather than means can aid agreement on policies when parties enter a negotiation with sharply opposed proposals. Negotiation can help to bring the parties to agreement even when they have differences in interests; Roger Fisher and William Ury (1981, chap. 3) recommend that participants "focus on interests, not positions [proposals]," in order to escape from deadlock on conflicting positions. By doing so, the parties can then explore "shared and compatible interests, as well as conflicting ones" (Fisher and Ury 1981:43), and in this way "invent options for mutual gain" (Fisher and Ury 1981, chap. 4).

C. *Alternatives versus single proposals.* Participants can blind themselves to the real effects of their arguments if they commit the error of mere criticism or advocacy of single options (Weimer and Vining 1989:202). In contrast, I propose that policy arguments *compare alternative policies* (including doing nothing and allowing the status quo to continue). The type of arguments that I propose will not favor (by implication) jumping from the frying pan into the fire, nor imitating the judge of a singing contest who was said to have listened to only one singer before giving the prize to the other.[14]

D. *"Full" information versus biased selection.* Advocates of a particular policy can engage in ad hoc and selective choice of information to support that policy, omitting inconvenient facts that support the other side. We can recognize this as an error at the stage of proposal selection, even though critics of "rational" PPA have noted the difficulty of gathering all relevant information. One way to correct for this is through procedures of discussion: guarantees of free speech, provision of equal time on television for opponents of a proposal, design of adversarial procedures in the courts, or appointment of a devil's advocate or an ombudsman.

My approach here, however, deals more with forms of discourse than with regulating participation. For a group or an individual seeking good proposals, I propose a guideline ensuring that every alternative chosen for an analysis will be systematically linked to every criterion in the reasoning that follows. In these terms, a student must learn to ask, "What information do I need in order to deal with this policy choice?" and to give a structured answer. I show below that the criteria-alternatives matrix, which tablulates alternatives by criteria, provides a simple recipe for doing this; one of its uses is to "protect against or counter the biases of the analyst" (Weimer and Vining 1989:204; Quade 1975:101).

E. *Quantitative information where needed: the question of "how much?"* In the speed limit example, the criterion of accident reduction favors lower speeds, but that of time saving favors higher ones. Presumably these two (and other major criteria) must be balanced or traded off. Arguments that are mere statements of the direction of opposed effects do not help us tell which is more important or whether a secondary criterion can be disregarded. They risk either deadlock or the exaggeration of small effects, leading to wrong choices. We need to compare such effects quantitatively. Even if opposed effects are measured in logically distinct terms such as lives lost and hours saved, we can benefit from knowing their size.

A qualitative argument has often been advanced (without an effort to estimate its magnitude) in opposition to efforts to enforce child support payments, to regulate handgun sales or abortion, or to reduce transmission of AIDS by mandatory testing: "It would only drive them underground." An analogy often used to support this argument is the effect of Prohibition in producing conspicuous disregard for the law in the 1920s. Nevertheless, Clark Warburton (1932:260) estimates that Prohibition reduced the consumption of alcohol by nearly one-third and did not merely lead to evasion of the law. In other words, even if the analyst opposes such regulation on other grounds (such as freedom), he or she should be obliged to question unqualified qualitative arguments about "driving underground" the persons who are regulated; the magnitude of this effect needs to be estimated. By asking "How much?" instead of considering arguments about only the direction of effects, we can be led to seek information that is essential to policy choice.

Critiques and Limitations of These Guidelines

They require effort. All these proposed guidelines make discussion more difficult. Participants who take them seriously cannot just "let fly" with particular arguments that happen to support their positions. They must prepare a larger structure of reasoning, often in cooperation with others, and seek out information to make that structure less biased. These activities take time and effort. Discussions of public policies cannot, however, take place at a leisurely academic pace; they usually face deadlines, after which they can lose much of their relevance.[15]

They do not alone guarantee the correct choice. These guidelines are, of course, meant to be superimposed on rules for empirical inference, which affect the quality of information in the criteria-alternatives matrix. Beyond this, however, problems of values remain. For example, the procedure of listing criteria, while it limits arbitrary omission of certain criteria, does not guarantee that the criteria listed are good or even reasonably chosen. We need to inquire into the sources of the values chosen and the ways these values can achieve some acceptance or legitimacy. Similarly, the quest for completeness by ascertaining community values requires judgment of their relative importance and knowledge about errors, biases, and blindnesses of the community.

They are not appropriate for conflict in which experts are suspect. The approach I have proposed is based on a search for consensus, at least at the stage of proposal selection. The guideline that policy arguments consider alternatives, though axiomatic in PPA, can be questioned when consensus is not expected or desired. Some observers may feel that the political community is already biased toward certain options and simply needs dissent or criticism of the status quo. As in the case of guideline A, we must consider the larger system of argument and politics—possibly adversarial—into which the proposals will enter.

Some readers, moreover, will not necessarily value rule-guided consensus to this extent. These include proponents of debate who have more faith in "unguided" human choice, especially when we have no reason to believe there is a correct or "better" choice to be made (Rieke and Sillars 1975:27); political scientists who feel that consensus takes away some of the essential element of politics from public decisions; advocates of forensic conflict who feel that truth emerges from controversy or who fear that consensus can mask the dominance of powerful interests; and citizens who feel they have a right to support their own interests rather than the public interest. But I will leave these rebuttals to others, noting only that adversarial procedures themselves can risk protracted and unresolved arguments, when solutions or agreements might have been found by a rule-guided quest for them in an authoritative forum (Sabatier 1988:155–56).

Speed Limits and the Criteria-Alternatives Matrix: An Example

The guidelines proposed above can be illustrated and taught with the aid of a criteria-alternatives matrix (Quade 1982:218–21; Patton and Sawicki

1986:276–81) such as the one shown in table 1. This matrix, which summarizes arguments relevant to the choice of speed limits, tabulates policy alternatives by the valuative criteria used to compare them. We assume that not only the accident rate (here expressed for simplicity in terms of fatalities only) but also the time used and the operating cost of vehicles are relevant criteria.[16] The use of such matrices illustrates a more complex structure of policy discourse, going beyond Toulmin's initial notion of an "argument."

Entries in each row show estimated effects of the policies on the criterion value corresponding to that row. These assessments could also have been given in relative terms, as by setting the values of an existing situation (say, 55 mph) to zero and presenting only differences in the last three columns. Some readers may wish to translate the fatality figures into social costs measured in years of expected life so as to make them commensurable with the saving of driving time.

The matrix presentation requires the deliberating group to be explicit about alternatives and criteria; we assume that reasoned agreement has been reached as to which are to be listed. The error treated in guideline C above, limiting discussion to a single alternative, will then be eliminated. The matrix also directs attention to the task of listing criteria; this may reduce the chance of using an incomplete set of criteria (guideline A). Finally, the matrix directs the group to seek out systematically the information needed to link each alternative to each criterion rather than to choose only those cells that favor a predetermined alternative (guideline D).

The eventual decision made by the group usually requires balancing or trade-offs among the valued and disvalued effects of policies. This balancing, in turn, requires arguments that deal quantitatively with the magnitudes of various competing effects (guideline E). In the example shown, cost-benefit analysis could be used to compare the effects in the three rows in monetary terms (MacRae and Wilde 1979:133–52). If the deciding group does not accept this basis for comparing particular value criteria (Baram 1980), its members must either seek some other way to measure trade-offs or engage in less technical discussion about the relative importance of values such as human life, time spent, and costs of operating vehicles. Even then, the matrix will have made the discussion more complete. Edward Quade (1982:221) points out that "when there are multiple decision-makers, the scorecard [matrix] has the additional advantage of not requiring explicit agreement on weights by people with different social values. It is generally much easier for a group of decision-

Table 1. Criteria-Alternatives Matrix for Choice of Speed Limits (matrix entries are estimates on the basis of average speed, which is assumed to be equal to the speed limit; see MacRae and Wilde 1979:137–45)

	Alternate Speed Limits (mph)			
Criteria	55	60	65	70
Number of fatalities per 100 million vehicle miles	3.4	3.7	4.0	4.3
Time expended (years)per 100 million vehicle miles	354	323	299	279
Cost of operation (million $) per 100 million vehicle miles	5.9	6.2	6.6	7.0

makers to agree on a preferred alternative (perhaps for different reasons) than on weights to assign to the various impacts."

Analysts' Roles in Adversarial Argument

The guidelines I have recommended so far assume that participants in a discussion are collectively seeking policies to fulfill a set of ethical criteria that they have agreed on and are arguing only in terms of these ethical criteria, not personal interests or commitment to particular policies. In this case, a participant should be willing to admit that his or her initial proposal has shortcomings—that on some criteria it is inferior to other alternatives. Similarly, in the service of these criteria, a participant should be willing to tell others about self-damaging mistakes they have made.

I shall now contrast the previous guidelines with those of adversarial argument. This comparison deals with two polar types of argument and omits intermediate types of discourse that are only partially adversarial. For example, conflicting personal claims and interests can often be reconciled by bargaining and compromise. Lack of consensus does not automatically lead to adversarial argument of the sort I describe.

Thoroughly adversarial argument is a quite different game from reasoned proposal selection, because in it some participants are trying to *win* in terms of self-interest or of particular values that they do not share with the rest of the group. If enough participants are involved in this (in terms of numbers or power), others may have to imitate them. A different set of tacit guidelines must be imposed on the discussion because each participant will be trying to see that his or her own proposal prevails. One who survives contests of this sort will have recognized, with Leo Durocher, that "nice guys finish last." This resembles the response of a professor who, returning to campus after a year in Washington, was asked what he had learned there. His reply was, "Look both ways and keep your back to the wall."

This individual learning will have led experienced players to follow the "51–49 principle" of bureaucratic politics (Allison 1971:178), by which "the reasonable player is forced to argue much more confidently than he would if he were a detached judge." Whereas guidelines for reasoned proposal selection encourage a search for a better choice, in adversarial argument one is led (in the absence of guidelines) to choose arguments that persuade without encouraging this search. A persuasive line of argument may omit counterarguments that might have helped in discovering one's own best position, because they would undermine one's case relative to an adversary. The result, in this milieu, may be "strategic use" of information that aims merely "to support positions already taken" on nonanalytic grounds (Whiteman 1985:302) and uses facts or values very selectively to do so.

Guidelines for Adversarial Controversy

Participants (including analysts) in adversarial controversy must learn prudential (self-interested) guidelines. They must know how best to present the case, defend themselves from attack, and avoid aiding an opponent unintentionally. Such guidelines are for winning, not necessarily for producing a desirable result, unless this desirability can be shown independently. They are often opposed to those I have advanced for reasoned proposal selection; indeed, one can state the opposite of each of the five consensual guidelines above as a tactic for winning a controversy:

A. Introduce only those values that will favor your proposal, in the view of the audience.[17]

B. Center your argument on your proposal, and do not stress the possibility of more general ends that could be sought in various ways—a digression that might confuse and divide your supporters.

C. Do not compare your proposal with other similar and desirable alternatives; if alternatives are to be compared with your own (e.g., because the opposition has advanced them), choose your criteria so as to put competing alternatives at a disadvantage.[18]

D. Choose only those facts that the audience will believe to support your proposal.

E. To dramatize your argument and make it more forceful, center it on particular instances of persons who would be harmed or left in grave need by a rival proposal, including the existing situation. Do not try to present statistics on the prevalence of these conditions, as they might be less persuasive (Weimer and Vining 1989:304).

These guidelines, though I called them "errors" in reasoned proposal selection, are not logical fallacies. Neither, however, are they principles that teachers can advocate with pride; they are weapons usable by anyone, regardless of the merits of the case. We would not knowingly use these guidelines to convince ourselves reasonably. They cannot be said to advance truth or correctness of argument in the same way that the guidelines presented earlier do.

Some adversarial rules and procedures have, of course, been systematized and supported on the grounds that they lead to correct decisions. Courtroom procedures are perhaps best known in this regard; but there, at least, a judge or jury maintains a role above the struggle and can limit the abuse of the rules and ensure some degree of equality between contestants in their use. The rules of formal adversarial debate are similar. A rule-governed adversarial procedure can thus sometimes lead argument in more fruitful directions.

The Special Role of Analysts in Controversy

Policy analysts (and scientific experts more generally) who enter adversarial discourse to support a given policy and a sponsoring group thus face a conflict of values (Tong 1986). They are obligated by certain norms of their expert group and by commitment to a sponsor or employer, and they may have personal ambitions which, though not ethical obligations, are recognized as normal in such discussions (Halperin 1974).

Guidelines limiting tolerable tactics by analysts. The tactics listed above for winning a controversy are not guidelines for ethical professional practice. There are, however, professionally approved guidelines for proper factual inference in adversarial situations. These were assumed to hold, but were passed over, in my earlier discussion of consensual guidelines.

In the practice of policy analysis, it appears that demonstrable, deliberate falsehood is the greatest sin (Weimer and Vining 1989:305). What is demonstrable and intentional is sometimes hard to discover, however; several critical studies of benefit-cost analysis have revealed biases toward sponsoring agencies such as the U.S. Army Corps of Engineers (Hanke and Walker 1974) or the Tennessee Valley Authority (Gramlich 1982:146–54), without leading to the charge of "lying with statistics." Similarly, analyses in the executive branch that stress only the costs and not the benefits of regulation have not been castigated by the reviewers as deliberate errors, but rather have been treated as inevitable results of the lack of quality control (Whittington and Grubb 1984). Furthermore, the concealment of technical details inside complex presentations or in obscure endnotes has not been seen as a violation of the professional norm that says that critical readers should be told how a conclusion was reached.

There thus seems to be a range of tolerance by expert groups with regard to the use of expert information by their members in public debates that is limited only by the requirement that the information not be "false or grossly misleading" (Weimer and Vining 1989:305). Even this norm (in a scientific group) is not enforced as intensively for public debates as in the professional literature, because the expert group's central values are seemingly less at stake in arguments by a member about public policy.

The expert participating in politics is free to select and present information that supports only one side of a controversy. This can be done by timing and information control. David Weimer and Aidan Vining (1989:378–79) report that an analyst working in support of an EPA rule to reduce the amount of lead in gasoline learned of a plan by manufacturers to argue that such a rule would increase emissions of benzene, a carcinogen. He studied this issue quietly and found the manufacturers' argument to be untrue. Rather than telling the manufacturers of this finding, however, he waited, and "the day that the proposed rule was published, . . . put a memorandum on the docket covering the benzene issue, thus preempting the manufacturers' main attack." The analyst's finding was apparently true and met standards of analytic quality; but in this adversarial situation he did not treat the manufacturers as like-minded parties seeking means to common ends.

Professional constraints on analysts' adversarial arguments. Expert groups whose members are expected to enter public policy debates bear more responsibility for stating codes of ethics than do basic scientific groups; they thus sometimes impose limits on members' statements to nonmembers. For example, the "Guidelines for the Practice of Operations Research" (Operations Research Society of America 1971:1143) state that the analyst should not "use improper methods simply because they would sustain a line of argument."

Statisticians, another expert group often involved in public debate, have the reputation of conservative interpretation of results of analysis, including the judgment that professional standards allow no positive inference to be drawn. Thus "there is a strong inclination by statisticians to estimate only quantities for which there is a general professional consensus as to how the estimates should be made" (Roberts 1980:217–18). At an early stage in the debate on whether smoking caused cancer, leading statisticians defended tobacco on the ground that prospective studies of smoking and cancer incidence had not demonstrated the case sufficiently (Brown 1972:47).

Professional standards can thus be brought to bear on members engaged in public debate, but they are limited in their reach and are far from imposing the guidelines I have proposed for reasoned proposal selection.

Summary

Public policy analysts, although members of an expert group, must engage in discourse with public leaders and citizens. Some writers (e.g., Toulmin) have characterized this discourse as a form of argumentation, in which participants present claims and justifications that others review critically.

Prior to the assertion and justification of claims, however, there is often a more consensual process of proposal generation in which claims and arguments are fashioned. Part of this process involves the systematic winnowing of policy alternatives considered to deal with a given problem. This is a process of seeking the best proposals, for which claims can later be made, rather than simply of making claims; it involves systematically considering arguments and counterarguments. Within a group that agrees on a list of criteria to be considered, and whose members trust one another, this process can be carried out in a way that stresses the value criteria sought rather than particular claims that are the means to them—as a quest rather than a process of argumentation or justification. I have proposed some guidelines to govern the formal aspects of this process, suggesting that they can be taught to analysts and citizens. Such guidelines are a significant feature of PPA, but they have often been presented as though they were simply the result of economic analysis rather than more general provisions to improve the style of policy discourse.

PPA does involve argumentation. First, analysts may try to justify policy proposals to fellow analysts. When they discuss analysis with such a like-minded group, they may be governed by guidelines such as those proposed above for consensual, reasoned proposal selection; but the responsibility for following those guidelines lies on the discussing group as a whole rather than on the person presenting an argument. A speaker should then be bound to accept and encourage counterarguments and discussion of alternatives.

Second, PPA involves adversarial argumentation in strategic, political contexts with powerful participants who need not claim expertise.[19] These arguments are governed by "rules" of *persuasion*—of tactics and strategy—relatively more than are arguments among experts. The profession of policy analysis may propose rules of professional ethics for its members' adversarial arguments, but the scope of these rules is likely to be limited. Analysts must then learn to enter into adversarial discourse and distinguish it from consensual discourse such as that of reasoned proposal selection.

Notes

An earlier version of this paper was published in *Knowledge in Society* 1 (1988). I am indebted to Charles W. Anderson, V. William Balthrop, William T. Bluhm, J. Robert Cox, William N. Dunn, Frank Fischer, John Forester, Harvey Goldstein, E. Wood Kelley, Robert C. Kelner, Michael I. Luger, and John S. Nelson for helpful suggestions.

1. *Criteria* here are ethical principles associated with terms such as *ought, should,* or *right*. They include values such as the public's saving of time or money. They enter into any discussion of the general welfare or the public interest. Although persons and groups differ in their notions of the public interest, they can distinguish ethical arguments concerned with it from selfish goals.

2. These are not the only criteria that could be included; speed limits might

also affect air pollution or wear and tear on roads, involve enforcement costs, and discourage people from driving. I return to this example below.

3. Joseph Raz (1975:494–98) refers to nontradable norms, which take full precedence over others, as "mandatory norms." Norms of the opposite type have been called "defeasible" (Toulmin 1958:142); Albert Jonsen and Stephen Toulmin (1988) deal with rules that can be argued against because their boundaries of applicability are not clear. An intermediate type, in the law, is a "rebuttable presumption," which places a burden of proof on those who question it.

4. Toulmin, Rieke, and Janik (1979, pt. 3) follow their description of the above elements of an argument with a detailed treatment of processes of practical criticism—"critical procedures through which ideas are examined in competition with one another and judged by relevant [higher-order] criteria so as to make it possible for us to arrive at *reasonable* choices" (1979:16). Such critical procedures seem to go beyond the presentation of arguments centered on claims. One can also broaden the discussion of a proposal by introducing a counterproposal (Mitroff and Mason 1981).

5. An analogous rebuttal is illustrated by Toulmin, Rieke, and Janik (1979: 320–21), who point out that "difficulties and disagreements arise where . . . there are conflicting 'goods' or 'bads' between which a balance must be struck" (320). They also note that in ethical reasoning we are "balancing off the different *kinds* of consequences that will flow from one social decision or another" and that this may require "the help of some agreed standards for deciding on priorities" (322). But including these considerations would lead this discussion beyond a mere set of "arguments" that propose policies.

6. Toulmin, Rieke, and Janik (1979:119–20) discuss "adversary and consensus procedures" that characterize different argumentative enterprises. They note that in matters of public policy, where the goal is a practical decision, gains must be weighed against losses, and a mixture of adversary and consensus procedures is likely. In speaking of "given" values or criteria, I assume the deciding group can agree on a list of them, though not necessarily on their relative importance. Jonsen and Toulmin (1988), however, propose a procedure of argument that does not require such a list to be fixed at the start.

7. Sometimes it can be more systematic; Britton Harris (1981) notes that when a "policy space" can be characterized by a known set of parameters, this larger set of alternatives can be described mathematically.

8. By "basic premises" I mean basic understanding, shared criteria for valuation and for credibility of evidence, and the desire for a shared decision. Sharing of these premises precludes the introduction of competing interests or ambitions within the group as explicit bases of argument or of excluding arguments; and if implicit, such interests must be channeled into tenable rationalizations. The resulting trust involves the assumption that arguments are based on ethical prem-

ises and to be taken at face value, and that sanctions are not to be invoked against speakers for what is said in germane arguments.

9. Even though there can be disagreement as to what *best* means, we can identify many clearly wrong recommendations like the "zero speed limit" mentioned above.

10. Citizens and analysts may differ not simply in substantive judgments about policies but in styles and procedures of argument. From a relativistic perspective, the "argument fields" of analysts and citizens overlap in "interfield argument" (Willard 1982:62). If analysts wish to be more effective, they must either learn to speak citizens' language or educate citizens to speak theirs (Fisher 1984:4). Citizens often decline experts' advice; an example is the limited influence of statisticians on public debate (MacRae 1985:335).

11. These guidelines constitute a loose sort of rules. More general procedures of discussion can also be recommended, including attention to the justification of values in relation to larger value systems; Frank Fischer (1985:254) stresses the need to provide "alternative methodologies" that extend to these questions. Debate as to just what criteria should be used is also important (Fischer 1985:244–48; Taylor 1961, chaps. 3–6).

12. The rules of reasoned proposal selection may be used to derive rules of adversarial justification in science or policy analysis. That is, the most legitimate rebuttals for justification in an expert group may be those that a presenter would have had to consider in reasoned proposal selection.

13. Completeness may be sought even if it is never fully achieved. Charles Anderson (1987a:360) refers to a quest for a "larger, more reflective, balance."

14. Paul Taylor (1961:5–41) distinguishes between evaluation according to standards, which compares things with one another in a ranking, and according to rules, which typically evaluates action or thought as right or wrong in absolute rather than relative terms. If, however, our ethical system compares states of affairs, judging one alternative to be wrong will leave us with another possible state of affairs, perhaps more wrong, with which we are forced to compare it.

15. One way to cope with this scarcity of time and resources is to divide the stage of proposal selection into two parts: first, a generation of numerous alternatives by brainstorming (Mood 1983:31), followed by a rapid prescreening—an intuitive approximation of a careful analysis; and, second, a careful study of the smaller number of alternatives that remain—chosen for both merit and political relevance—in terms of a limited number of major criteria.

16. Three types of criteria that can enter into policy judgments do not appear in this matrix: (1) aspects of participants' self-interest, apart from general ethical criteria; (2) questions of political feasibility, which is more a multiplier or qualifier than a value of interest by itself; and (3) nonteleological rules, including questions of morality or constitutionality.

17. Psychological research has shown, however, that including counterargu-

ments in one's presentation, and the response to them, can make it more persuasive.

18. Another possible tactic is framing one's preferred alternative as a middle ground between two others that are presented as extremes, or comparing it with "straw man" alternatives (Weimer and Vining 1989:202).

19. The possible linkage of expertise with power can, however, be a significant problem. It is not undesirable as such unless we deem all power to be undesirable; rather, it requires examination of how that power might be used.

References

Alker, H. R. 1988. The Dialectical Logic of Thucydides' Melian Dialogue. *American Political Science Review* 82:805–20.

Allison, G. T. 1971. *Essence of Decision*. Boston: Little, Brown.

Anderson, C. W. 1987a. The Human Sciences and the Liberal Polity in Rhetorical Relationship. In J. S. Nelson, A. Megill, and D. N. McCloskey, eds., *The Rhetoric of the Human Sciences*, 341–62. Madison: University of Wisconsin Press.

———. 1987b. Political Philosophy, Practical Reason, and Policy Analysis. In F. Fischer and J. Forester, eds., *Confronting Values in Policy Analysis*, 22–44. Newbury Park, Calif.: Sage.

Apel, K.-O. 1979. Types of Rationality Today: The Continuum of Reason Between Science and Ethics. In T. F. Geraets, ed., *Rationality Today*, 307–40. Ottawa: University of Ottawa Press.

Aristotle. 1954. *The Rhetoric and Poetics of Aristotle*. Trans. W. R. Roberts and (*Poetics*) I. Bywater. New York: Modern Library.

Baram, M. S. 1980. Cost-Benefit Analysis: An Inadequate Basis for Health, Safety, and Environmental Regulatory Decisionmaking. *Ecology Law Quarterly* 8:473–531.

Braybrooke, D., and C. E. Lindblom. 1963. *A Strategy of Decision*. New York: Free Press.

Brown, B. W., Jr. 1972. Statistics, Scientific Method, and Smoking. In J. M. Tanur et al., eds., *Statistics: A Guide to the Unknown*, 40–51. San Francisco: Holden-Day.

Burton, L. 1990. Ethical Discontinuities in Public-Private Sector Negotiation. *Journal of Policy Analysis and Management* 9:23–40.

Dearin, R. D. 1982. Perelman's Concept of "Quasi-Logical" Argumentation: A Critical Elaboration. In J. R. Cox and C. A. Willard, eds., *Advances in Argumentation Research*, 78–94. Carbondale: Southern Illinois University Press.

Dery, D. 1984. *Problem Definition in Policy Analysis*. Lawrence: University Press of Kansas.

Dunn, W. N. 1981. *Public Policy Analysis: An Introduction*. Englewood Cliffs, N.J.: Prentice-Hall.

———. 1988. Methods of the Second Type: Coping with the Wilderness of Conventional Policy Analysis. *Policy Studies Review* 7:720–37.

———. 1990. Justifying Policy Arguments: Criteria for Practical Discourse. *Evaluation and Program Planning* 13:321–29.

Dunn, W. N., R. E. Basom, and C. D. Frantz. 1988. *Educational Policy Analysis: A Guide to Applications*. Andover, Mass.: The Network.

Fischer, F. 1985. Critical Evaluation of Public Policy: A Case Study. In J. Forester, ed., *Critical Theory and Public Life*, 231–57. Cambridge, Mass.: MIT Press.

Fisher, R., and W. Ury. 1981. *Getting to Yes: Negotiating Agreement Without Giving In*. Boston: Houghton Mifflin.

Fisher, W. R. 1978. Toward a Logic of Good Reasons. *Quarterly Journal of Speech* 64:376–84.

———. 1984. Narration as a Human Communication Paradigm: The Case of Public Moral Argument. *Communication Monographs* 51:1–22.

Freeley, A. J. 1981. *Argumentation and Debate*. 5th ed. Belmont, Calif.: Wadsworth.

Goldstein, H. A. 1984. Planning as Argumentation. *Environment and Planning B* 11:297–312.

Gramlich, E. M. 1981. *Benefit-Cost Analysis of Government Programs*. New York: McGraw-Hill.

Habermas, J. 1973. *Legitimation Crisis*. Trans. T. McCarthy. Boston: Beacon Press.

Halperin, M. H. 1974. *Bureaucratic Politics and Foreign Policy*. Washington, D.C.: Brookings Institution, 1974.

Hanke, S. H., and R. A. Walker. 1974. Benefit-Cost Analysis Reconsidered: An Evaluation of the Mid-State Project. *Water Resources Research* 10:898–908.

Harris, B. 1981. Policy-Making, Programming, and Design. In J. P. Crecine, ed., *Research in Public Policy and Management*. Vol. 1: *Basic Theory, Methods and Perspectives*, 279–88. Greenwich, Conn.: JAI Press.

Jonsen, A. R., and S. Toulmin. 1988. *The Abuse of Casuistry*. Berkeley: University of California Press.

McKean, R. N. 1967. Criteria. In E. S. Quade, ed., *Analysis for Military Decisions*, 81–102. Chicago: Rand McNally.

MacRae, D., Jr. 1985. *Policy Indicators: Links Between Social Science and Public Debate*. Chapel Hill: University of North Carolina Press.

———. 1987. Building Policy-related Technical Communities. *Knowledge* 8:431–62.

MacRae, D., Jr., and J. A. Wilde. 1979. *Policy Analysis for Public Decisions*. Monterey, Calif. Brooks/Cole.

Mason, R. O., and I. I. Mitroff. 1980–81. Policy Analysis as Argument. *Policy Studies Journal* 9:579–85.

Meltsner, A. J. 1976. *Policy Analysts in the Bureaucracy.* Berkeley: University of California Press.

Mitroff, I. I., and R. O. Mason. 1981. *Creating a Dialectical Social Science.* Dordrecht: D. Reidel.

Mood, A. M. 1983. *Introduction to Policy Analysis.* New York: North-Holland.

Operations Research Society of America. 1971. Guidelines for the Practice of Operations Research." *Operations Research* 19.

Ozawa, C. P., and L. Susskind. 1985. Mediating Science-intensive Policy Disputes. *Journal of Policy Analysis and Management* 5:23–39.

Patton, C. V., and D. S. Sawicki. 1986. *Basic Methods of Policy Analysis and Planning.* Englewood Cliffs, N.J.: Prentice-Hall.

Perelman, C. 1984. The New Rhetoric and the Rhetoricians: Remembrances and Comments. *Quarterly Journal of Speech* 70:188–96.

Perelman, C., and L. Olbrechts-Tyteca. 1969. *The New Rhetoric: A Treatise on Argumentation.* Trans. J. Wilkinson and P. Weaver. Notre Dame, Ind.: University of Notre Dame Press.

Popper, K. R. 1968. *The Logic of Scientific Discovery.* New York: Harper and Row.

Quade, E. S. 1975, 1982. *Analysis for Public Decisions.* 1st ed., 2d ed. New York: Elsevier.

Raz, J. 1975. Reasons for Action, Decisions and Norms. *Mind* 84:481–99.

Rescher, N. 1977. *Dialectics.* Albany: State University of New York Press.

Rieke, R. D., and M. R. Sillars. 1975. *Argumentation and the Decision Making Process.* New York: Wiley.

Roberts, H. V. 1980. Comments. *Proceedings of the Conference on the Census Undercount,* Arlington, Va., February 25–26. Washington, D.C.: Bureau of the Census.

Sabatier, P. A. 1988. An Advocacy Coalition Framework of Policy Change and the Role of Policy-oriented Learning Therein. *Policy Sciences* 21:129–68.

Taylor, P. W. 1961. *Normative Discourse.* Englewood Cliffs, N.J.: Prentice-Hall.

Tong, R. 1986. *Ethics in Policy Analysis.* Englewood Cliffs, N.J.: Prentice-Hall.

Toulmin, S. E. 1958. *The Uses of Argument.* Cambridge: Cambridge University Press.

Toulmin, S. E., R. Rieke, and A. Janik. 1979. *An Introduction to Reasoning.* New York: Macmillan.

Van Eemeren, F. H., R. Grootendorst, and T. Kruiger. 1987. *Handbook of Argumentation Theory.* Dordrecht: Foris.

Warburton, C. 1932. *The Economic Results of Prohibition.* New York: Columbia University Press.

Weimer, D. L., and A. Vining. 1989. *Policy Analysis: Concepts and Practice.* Englewood Cliffs, N.J.: Prentice-Hall.

Whiteman, D. 1985. The Fate of Policy Analysis in Congressional Decision Making: Three Types of Use in Committees. *Western Political Quarterly* 38:294–311.

Whittington, D., and W. N. Grubb. 1984. Economic Analysis in Regulatory Decisions: The Implications of Executive Order 12291. *Science, Technology and Human Values* 9:63–71.

Willard, C. A. 1982. Argument Fields. In J. R. Cox and C. A. Willard, eds., *Advances in Argumentation Theory and Research*, 24–77. Carbondale: Southern Illinois University Press.

Contributors

John S. Dryzek is Professor of Political Science at the University of Oregon. His books include *Policy Analysis by Design* (with Davis Bobrow, 1987), *Rational Ecology: Environment and Political Economy* (1987), and *Discursive Democracy: Politics, Policy, and Political Science* (1990).

William N. Dunn is Professor of Public Policy and Management at the Graduate School of Public and International Affairs, University of Pittsburgh. He publishes in areas of new policy research methodologies, political theory, and knowledge utilization. He is the founding editor of *Knowledge and Policy: The International Journal of Knowledge Transfer and Utilization*. His most recent books are *Advances in Policy Studies Since 1950* (contributor and coeditor, 1992) and *Public Policy Analysis*, 2d ed. (1993).

Frank Fischer is Professor of Political Science at Rutgers University in Newark and a member of the Bloustein Graduate School of Planning and Public Policy on the New Brunswick campus. His publications include *Politics, Values, and Public Policy* (1980), *Critical Studies in Organization and Bureaucracy* (coedited with Carmen Sirianni, 1984), *Confronting Values in Policy Analysis: The Politics of Criteria* (coedited with John Forester, 1987), *Technocracy and the Politics of Expertise* (1990), and *Evaluating Public Policy* (1994). A frequent guest of the Wissenschaftszentrum für Sozialforschung in Berlin, he is currently engaged in a comparative study of environmental policy in Germany and the United States. He also serves as book review editor for the *Industrial and Environmental Crisis Quarterly*.

John Forester is Professor of City and Regional Planning at Cornell University. His recent books on the politics and possibilities of planning and policy analytic practice include *Planning in the Face of Power* (1989) and *Making Equity Planning Work* (with Norman Krumholz, 1990). He is also the author of *Critical Theory, Public Policy, and Planning Practice: Toward a Critical Pragmatism* (1993).

Maarten A. Hajer is Assistant Professor of Sociology at the University of Munich, Germany. He is the author of *City Politics: Hegemonic Projects and Discourse* and is currently writing a book about discourse coalition formation in environmental politics in Britain and the Netherlands.

Patsy Healey is a specialist in planning theory and practice who studies planners' theories in use in practical contexts, the role and effects of land use development plans, and the impact of planning and related policy on local property markets and development activity. She has worked primarily in the United Kingdom but also in Latin America and continental Europe. Her books include *Professional Ideals and Planning Practice* (with Jackie Underwood, 1979), *Land Use Planning and the Mediation of Planning Theory: Prospects for the 1980s* (coeditor with Glen McDougall and Huw Thomas, 1982), *Land Use Planning and the Mediation of Urban Change* (with Paul McNamara, Martin Elson, and Joe Doak, 1988), *Dilemmas of Planning Practice* (with Huw Thomas, 1991), and *Rebuilding the City* (with Simin Davoudi, Mo O'Toole, Solmaz Tasvanoglu, and David Usher, 1992).

Robert Hoppe is Professor of Political Science and Public Administration at the University of Amsterdam and is currently a visiting professor and a Fulbright Fellow at Rutgers University. He is coeditor (with H. K. Asmerom and R. B. Jain) of *Bureaucracies and Developmental Policies in the Third World* (1992) and coauthor of a forthcoming book, *Handling Frozen Fire: Risk Management, Political Culture, and the Dutch LPG Controversy.*

Bruce Jennings is Executive Director of the Hastings Center, a prominent research and educational institute that studies ethical and social issues in medicine, the life sciences, and the professions. He has written and edited nine books and has published numerous articles on bioethics and public policy issues. He has also been a consultant to several governmental and private organizations, including the United States Senate Select Committee on Ethics and the American Society of Public Administration.

Thomas J. Kaplan is Associate Scientist at the University of Wisconsin-Madison's Institute for Research on Poverty, where he specializes in state government policy and administration. He has served as Director of the Bureau of Planning in the Wisconsin Department of Health and Social Services and as Associate Professor of Public Administration at Waynesburg College in Pennsylvania.

Duncan MacRae, Jr., is William Rand Kenan, Jr., Professor of Political Science at the University of North Carolina at Chapel Hill. He is the author of *Policy*

Indicators (1985) and coauthor (with James Wilde) of *Policy Analysis for Public Decisions* (1979).

Martin Rein is Professor of Social Policy at the Massachusetts Institute of Technology and a Co-Principal Investigator of the Social Service Labor Market for the Russell Sage Foundation. He previously held a Fulbright Fellowship at the London School of Economics and taught at Clark University and Bryn Mawr. Widely published, his books include *Dilemmas of Social Reform* (1982), coauthored with Peter Marris, and *From Policy to Practice* (1983).

Donald A. Schön is Ford Professor Emeritus and Senior Lecturer in the Department of Urban Studies and Planning at the Massachusetts Institute of Technology. As an educator and industrial consultant, a former government administrator, and a former president of a nonprofit social research consulting organization, Dr. Schön has worked as a researcher and practitioner on problems of technological innovation, organizational learning, and professional effectiveness and education. He was invited in 1970 to deliver the Reith Lectures on the BBC. His books include *The Displacement of Concepts* (1963); *Technology and Change* (1967); *Beyond the Stable State* (1971); *Theory in Practice: Increasing Professional Effectiveness* (1974) and *Organizational Learning: A Theory of Action Perspective* (1978), both with Chris Argyris; *The Reflective Practitioner* (1983); *The Design Studio* (1985); *Educating the Reflective Practitioner* (1987); and *The Reflective Turn* (editor, 1991). From 1972 to July 1990 he was Ford Professor of Urban Studies and Education at the Massachusetts Institute of Technology. He served as chair of MIT's Department of Urban Studies and Planning from 1990 to 1992.

James A. Throgmorton is Associate Professor in the University of Iowa's Graduate Program in Urban and Regional Planning. He has also worked as a planner for a local governmental agency, as an environmental scientist for three consulting firms, and as a policy analyst at Argonne National Laboratory. He has written numerous articles on the rhetorics of policy analysis and planning and is the author of a forthcoming book entitled *Passion and Power: The Rhetorics of Electric Power Planning in the Chicago Area.*

Index